Moving Homes

The Housing Corporation 1964–2008

Moving Homes

The Housing Corporation 1964–2008

Alan Murie

Professor of Urban and Regional Studies
Centre for Urban and Regional Studies
University of Birmingham

POLITICO'S

First published in Great Britain 2008 by
Politico's Publishing, an imprint of
Methuen Publishing Ltd
8 Artillery Row
London
SW1P 1RZ

10 9 8 7 6 5 4 3 2 1

A CIP catalogue record for this book is available from the British Library.

ISBN 978-1-84275-230-2

Set in Bembo by SX Composing DTP, Rayleigh, Essex
Printed and bound in Great Britain by Cromwell Press, Trowbridge

Contents

Acknowledgements

The Housing Corporation provided research funding for the work carried out in order to write this book.

Rick Groves carried out some of the interviews for this study and his thesis on voluntary housing in Denmark and Britain was a valuable source. I am grateful to him and to a long list of individuals who helped me by agreeing to be interviewed in connection with it: Pam Alexander, Eric Armitage, Sir John Baker, Ken Bartlett, Sir Christopher and Lady Benson, Lord Best, John Bright, Sheila Button, Richard Clarke, Tony Collinson, Helen Cope, Jim Coulter, Baroness Dean of Thornton-le-Fylde, Bob Dinwiddy, Peter Dixon, Steve Douglas, Rodney Dykes, David Edmonds, Mike Gahagan, Jenny Goodwin, Bill Hennessey, Roger Jarman, Derek King, Greg Lomax, Richard McCarthy, Mavis McDonald, Anthony Mayer, Adrian Moran, Atul Patel, Sir Brian Pearse, Norman Perry, Helen Pickering, Nick Raynsford, Brigadier Brian Ridley, Jon Rouse, Gavin Smart, Max Steinberg, James Tickell, Julia Unwin, Derek Waddington, Andrew Wiles, Peter Williams, Sir George Young, Raymond Young.

Adrian Moran, Peter Malpass, David Mullins and Bruce Walker made helpful comments on earlier drafts of this work. Steve Wilcox provided me with statistical material assembled for his annual housing review and this is referenced accordingly. I am also grateful to Carolyn Fox, Rebecca Murray, Lynne Beighton, Steve Forrest and Rob Rowlands, who helped by providing material or comments or in other important ways.

Any errors and shortcomings as well as the views expressed are solely the responsibility of the author.

Alan Murie
Centre for Urban and Regional Studies
University of Birmingham
July 2008

List of tables

1

Introduction: the direction of housing policy

This book provides a history of the Housing Corporation from its establishment in 1964 through to the end of its operations in 2008. It is a history which tells of the various transitions and phases through which the Corporation passed in this period. In 2008 the functions previously carried out by the Housing Corporation were split between two new agencies – the Homes and Communities Agency and the Tenant Services Authority. These new agencies are likely to maintain at least some of the traditions and practices which were successfully developed within the Housing Corporation. However, new agencies also have the opportunity to learn from others and to start again in many respects. In this context it is appropriate to reflect upon the experience of predecessor organisations.

This volume is not an evaluation of the Housing Corporation based on detailed analysis of costs and benefits. It presents an account of the development of what was the largest single non-departmental public body (in some terminology, 'quango') in the UK, and of the phases it has passed through. It offers judgements about successes and failures associated with the operation of the Housing Corporation at different stages and locates the account within the context of the wider development of housing and housing policy. While the focus of the book is upon England, similar changes have taken place in Scotland, Wales and Northern Ireland – indeed, Wales and Scotland were initially included within the Corporation's remit. The book is based on a wide range of published material including the Housing Corporation's annual reports (referenced as HCAR and by year), the minutes of Corporation board meetings (referenced as HCBM and by date) and the results of interviews with some of the key figures involved with the Corporation and housing policy over the period concerned. The results of these interviews are not apparent through direct attribution but have informed the account throughout. In some cases the phraseology used by those interviewed has been incorporated in the text and placed in quotation marks.

The book identifies lessons that can be usefully learned by the housing sector in particular but also by other agencies operating at arm's length from government. The Housing Corporation was one of the longest-lived major executive quangos in the UK, and reflections on its development, operation and successes form part of a wider reflection on changing patterns of government and governance within Britain.

Presenting the experience of the Housing Corporation involves an account of the shifting basis of welfare state provision in the UK since the 1950s. The post-1946 welfare state in Britain involved a dominant role not only for national but also for local government, and the subsequent reorientation and rolling back of the state has been a major feature of the restructuring of government and welfare since the 1970s. Housing has been described as the 'wobbly pillar' of the welfare state (see Malpass 2008) and it was not so radically reorganised in the 1940s as were health, education and social security. Nevertheless state intervention in housing and planning transformed post-war urban Britain, and direct state provision (through council housing) grew to become more extensive than anywhere outside Eastern and central Europe. While Britain chose local authorities to spearhead housing reconstruction, much of the rest of western and northern Europe used independent, not-for-profit bodies and co-operatives or a greater mix of different agencies. The advent of the Housing Corporation and its promotion and support of housing associations as well as (latterly) sales of council houses and transfer of council stock to housing associations came to transform the way the government in Britain has intervened in and directed housing. By 2008 the Housing Corporation was also of interest, both in Britain and elsewhere, as a key player in a regulated not-for-profit housing sector with development costs financed largely through private investment. Arguably this is a more replicable model than council housing ever was and one more in tune with the politics and economics of the 21st-century global economy.

While the central focus of this book is the Housing Corporation itself, any discussion of that organisation inevitably becomes a discussion of the housing associations that are registered with it and that were the main vehicles for the investment through it. However, there are a number of accounts of individual housing associations and Peter Malpass's authoritative history of the housing association movement provides a fuller discussion of this part of the story (Malpass 2000). There are also fuller accounts of housing policy throughout the period in which the Housing Corporation operated (Mullins and Murie 2006). While this book refers to key legislation and changes in policy, it does not attempt to do this in the detail available elsewhere. Finally this account makes reference to the economic, social, political and democratic context in which the Corporation operated, during a period of considerable change to which the Corporation itself contributed.

The remainder of this chapter sets out more fully the themes discussed in the book. These relate both to housing policy debates and to wider issues related to governance. There is a wide literature that has addressed the shifts in housing policy in Britain over the last century and referred to the modernisation of housing tenure and policy. This includes changes in the mode of state intervention and privatisation. While some of these works include significant reference to housing associations, the Housing Corporation is seen as a shadowy background organisation and does not come to the fore in any of them. This book adds to these accounts by specifically addressing the role of the Corporation in the modern development of housing in Britain. Through this it reopens some aspects of debates about the transformation of the rented sector and the modernisation of tenure. It also addresses issues of privatisation, demunicipalisation and centralisation of policy and considers the Housing Corporation and housing associations as key agencies in the changes affecting housing in the post-war period. These debates connect with a more general discussion of changing government and governance in Britain and elsewhere. There is a strong literature concerned with the withdrawal of the state from areas that it used to control – the hollowing out of the state and the development of an approach which involves working with other agencies, drawing on their resources and steering or sharing in governance rather than driving through government. While much of this debate relates to the more local governance and government of cities and towns, it connects with the central attention in this book – who directs policy and how far direction has come to be shared. The relationship between the Housing Corporation and ministers and departments in central government also connects with separate debates about central–local government relationships and the competence and control exercised by the central state.

These key themes recur throughout this book and are returned to in the final chapters following a more descriptive chronological account. The initial chapters set out the background to policy and the housing association sector at the time that the Housing Corporation was set up in 1964: Chapter 2 presents an overview of the development of housing policy in the period before the establishment of the Corporation, and Chapter 3 refers to the growth of the voluntary housing sector up to the 1960s. Chapters 4 to 8 present a chronological account of the key phases through which the Housing Corporation has passed. These chapters also refer to policy changes, key legislation and to economic and financial changes that have affected the development of housing. Chapter 9 refers to the immediate plans for the future, with new agencies taking over responsibilities previously held by the Housing Corporation, English Partnerships and Communities and Local Government. Finally, Chapters 10 to 12 reflect upon different dimensions of governance, draw conclusions and consider the lessons and achievements associated with the Housing Corporation and its work with partners.

Housing in Britain

British housing has undergone profound changes over the last century: in dwelling stock, in building rates, in the types of house built and in the sizes and types of household seeking housing. There have also been changes in the rights of occupiers, housing costs and ways of paying for housing. For this book, however, the focus is on housing tenure. The Housing Corporation operated in a period of dramatic tenure restructuring. It was set up in a period when council housing and owner occupation were both expanding at the expense of private renting and it was associated with a phase marked by the growth of housing associations and of home ownership and the decline of council housing. However, such dramatic restructuring was not a new feature associated with the Housing Corporation, for there had already been a dramatic change through the twentieth century as Britain changed from a nation of private tenants to one of home owners and council tenants.

Table 1.1 sets out statistics on housing tenure. There are no undisputed figures for housing tenure before the population census started collecting such data in 1961. Data for the years before 1919 show considerable local variation in tenure but all the research suggests that by 1914 less than 1 per cent of dwellings were owned by local authorities and some 10 per cent by owner-occupiers. Private landlords dominated the housing market, although their share was already dwindling by 1914 and was to fall steadily from then through to 1981. As private landlordism declined home ownership grew continuously, by 1971 becoming the majority tenure. Council housing also grew in this period – most rapidly in the 1940s and 1950s. Its growth was less steady and had come to an end by 1981 as an era of public sector investment was replaced by one of privatisation.

Table 1.1: Housing tenure in Great Britain until 1971

	Owner occupied (%)	Rented from local authority or new town (%)	Rented from private landlord (%)	Rented from housing association (%)	Total (thousands)
Late 19th century*	<10	<1	>90		n/a
1914*	10–15	1	84–89		n/a
1939	33.0	10.3	56.7		11,500
1953	34.5	18.8	46.6		12,745
1961	44.4	24.3	31.3		14,545
1971	52.1	28.2	18.8	0.9	17,024

*These are estimates for England and Wales.
Source: Pooley (1992: 84); Holmans (1987: 169–70).

The investment in council housing and home ownership over this period transformed housing conditions and changed the face of British housing in other ways. In 1947, 45 per cent of all households in Great Britain lived in terraced houses and about 12 per cent in flats or tenements. In 1977, only 28 per cent of households lived in terraced houses and 22 per cent were in flats or maisonettes. The proportions living in semi-detached (rising from 30 to 32 per cent) and detached houses (rising from 12 to 17 per cent) had remained relatively steady. By the 1970s the numbers of households living in over-crowded or unfit dwellings had been substantially reduced both as a result of housing investment and slum clearance and because of the decline in household size. There was a tendency within the policy community to see the housing problem as solved or at least restricted to a few local pockets. At the same time there were concerns about the older housing stock and problems of access to housing in all tenures, culminating in homelessness and continued occupation of sub-standard housing. The restructuring of tenure had been associated with improvements but also with new tensions and problems. One response to this pattern of change was the formation of new housing associations seeking to fill the gaps which had become evident.

Change and direction in housing policy

The Housing Corporation was established in 1964 and ceased its operations in 2008. In the intervening forty-four years it became a key agency of government in housing policy and a leading player in the transformation of housing provision in the United Kingdom. This book sets out the main elements in that transformation and describes the Corporation's changing role over that period. It is important, however, to set the story of the Housing Corporation in context. There had been some kind of British housing policy for more than a century before the Housing Corporation came on the scene and even during its years of operation it was not the sole or most important vehicle for housing policy.

Accounts of British housing policy emphasise failure and conflict: failure to anticipate or respond adequately to housing shortages and the new demands occasioned by demographic growth, migration, economic and social change and changing aspirations; and class, political and economic conflict about what to do to address failures. The policy response has not been some natural evolution where one event leads inevitably to another and the shared understandings of the needs of one era lead to the responses of the next. Rather policy developed as a reaction to demands and political ideology and actions and the policies ground out through this process have involved compromise and harsh dealing as well as enlightenment and insight. The responses included serious and sustained voluntary contributions and work by housing associations established in the nineteenth century and earlier. But the contributions by these agencies and philanthropic effort, which accepted low rates of return on investment in housing, repeatedly proved insufficient. There was also no agreement on how to deal with the housing problem. What are presented now as reforms had usually been resisted strongly by some and regarded as inadequate by others. Even among those committed to improving the housing situation there were disagreements – the resistance of Octavia Hill and the Charity Organisation Society to subsidised housing at the turn of the twentieth century was not because they were unconcerned about the effects of bad housing but because they thought the method of achieving change would have undesirable consequences. At the same time there have been both strong advocates for municipal housing and a consistent anti-municipal lobby that denigrated the achievements of council housing once it did expand.

The Housing Corporation was initially established to fill a gap in the market. It was a poorly defined gap, but there was an understanding that the institutional framework that had emerged after 1946 was not meeting the needs of all sections of the community. The clumsy attempts to change this by deregulating the private rented sector in the 1950s had speeded the decline of that sector rather than halted it and had generated a new crisis, with increased concern about homelessness and insecure housing. The failure to meet the housing needs of all sections of the community was not diminished and triggered a new policy experiment. In many ways, and in spite of the development of housing associations, that has continued to be the story of housing in Britain. There have continued to be market failures, inequalities, unevenness in the development of housing provision and arguments for initiatives and innovations to fill the gaps that have emerged. Rather than constantly invent new bodies to address these issues, the Housing Corporation was periodically transformed to spearhead different government programmes designed to deal with different gaps.

The transformations of the Housing Corporation over time were indicative of the changing preoccupations of the government and these can be set out in summary form as reflecting four phases of policy or four successive reinventions of the Corporation:

- The initial project was to establish an agency, well away from the main agendas dominating housing at the time, to promote cost rent and co-ownership housing for middle-income groups and to attract private finance to that activity.

- As policies towards slum clearance generated new concerns, including those related to the displacement of communities, so the need for a greater variety of organisations to promote rehabilitation and area renewal for existing communities was evident and generated new inner city housing associations. A new phase involved the Housing Corporation working with housing associations to address the problems of older inner city housing and develop new approaches to urban renewal through housing improvement areas, general improvement areas and housing action areas.

- A third distinctive role developed in relation to the need to build subsidised new rented housing for lower-income groups and to develop low-cost home ownership initiatives. The Corporation moved to the mainstream of policy with a dependence on public expenditure to improve older property and build new accommodation and special needs housing.

- A fourth phase involved developing and promoting a new mixed public/private-funded programme under which housing associations, regulated by the Housing Corporation, could draw on private finance. They became the principal agencies for the development of new social rented housing, for the progressive transfer of a significant part of the remaining council housing and for the development of affordable home ownership and shared ownership.

Each reinvention of the Housing Corporation was associated with a different phase of the wider housing policy agenda. Except for the period from 1974 to 1988, the Corporation was deeply involved in attracting investment from private lenders, which were reluctant to invest in private rented housing. In partnership with housing associations, it also became a key player in government attempts to develop regional and local programmes for specific groups (homeless people, elderly persons, ex-offenders, people with learning difficulties, black and minority ethnic groups).

The Housing Corporation was initially responsible for England, Scotland and Wales, but later moved to a narrower role in England alone. Alongside this it developed a more consistent and increasingly professional approach to the regulation of housing associations, monitoring and supervision, inspection and governance. The professionalisation of the housing association sector and the progressive adoption of modern managerialist approaches has to some extent become a substitute for the radicalism and innovative spirit of the 'movement' at earlier stages.

At this stage it is important to set out the different housing provision activities that the Housing Corporation and housing associations were involved in through this period. These are as follows:

- providing co-ownership housing; this is a form of co-operative housing developed through a co-ownership society whose assets the residents collectively own;
- providing cost rent housing; this is unsubsidised rented housing where rental and other payments cover all costs but do not generate a distributed profit;
- acquiring and improving older properties for long-term renting, with the rents and terms of tenancy reflecting different subsidy and legislative arrangements;
- acquiring and improving older properties for short-life use;
- supporting secondary co-operatives, which provide services to co-operative housing schemes;
- providing specially designed and adapted housing and supported tenancies for special groups including older people and people with disabilities;
- acquiring unsold newly built properties from the private sector in periods of market downturn;
- acquiring and improving older properties for sale under different arrangements;

- developing shared ownership (including community leasehold, do-it-yourself shared ownership and more recently various HomeBuy schemes);
- selling properties under the right to buy and the right to acquire;
- acquiring stocks of former municipal housing through stock transfer.

Directing policy

The question of who directs policy is usually presented, in the British context, as relating to two major interactions: between market and state and between central and local government. Nineteenth-century housing was provided by the market and, until the advent of public health measures, there was very little regulation. Undeniably the market failed to provide the housing needed by a modern competitive economy and those advocating direct state intervention to remedy this succeeded in building legislation that enabled local authorities to become major players in the provision of high-quality housing that appealed to the affluent working class as well as others. The implementation and operation of public policy involved an uneasy working relationship between different levels of government, motivated sometimes by a common concern about housing conditions but also at the same time by other, varying, factors. While central government's preoccupation with taxation and public expenditure issues affected how actively it applied powers, local government was more affected by the realities of implementation and delivery – with the where, what and when to build, and who for, and with the opposition associated with territorial defence (what became widely referred to as the 'not in my back yard' (NIMBY) attitude or 'build absolutely nothing anywhere near anyone' (BANANA)). Locally there has been a party and political culture difference towards how vigorously some policies should be pursued – leaving very different housing, especially council housing, legacies in different places, all operating within the same legislative framework.

The Housing Corporation was developed and operated as part of central government's response to housing problems from the 1960s. It was always an agency of central government; it was never a response to demands from local authorities and was not shaped by the pressures coming from housing associations. But to say that the Housing Corporation was an agency does not say very much. It begs important questions about how interaction through an agency role affected the part of government that was responsible for it, and how far the agency role left scope to influence or shape the development and delivery of policy at national and local level. The Housing Corporation formed a key component in a new area of housing policy charged with promoting, funding and regulating alternatives to both direct state providers and the market. This was explicitly presented as part of a strategy to develop a 'third arm', associated with different politicians and policy discourses. It has played a key role in the changing agendas and focus of housing policy throughout this period. Rather than the state versus the market and central versus local government being the only issues, a third agenda about the voluntary sector was added.

The government's view throughout the period was that it could only engage with and mobilise a third arm through a partly independent agency. And this adds a further set of issues: about relationships between the government and its agencies, about the degree of independence of the agency and about the relationship between the agency and the local third-arm organisations that have the will and capacity to deliver services on the ground. The issues concern partnership as well as agency and raise questions about the resources within central government departments to prepare, to consult and to consistently deliver and inform policy. They concern the relationships between the government and its regulator of housing associations, and between the regulator and the regulated. They also emphasise the degree of attention given to regions, sub-regions, neighbourhoods and consumers. The relationship between local authorities and housing associations has remained a continuing challenge throughout, within the predominant policy discourse related to tenure and to public and private sectors.

So the policy map has become much more complex – from a theoretical dualism of market and state with a command-and-control relationship between different levels of the state to an infinitely more complex reality of state, market and third sector with negotiated and constantly renegotiated relationships between all three and organisations operating with different roles within each. This reality of governance includes fragmentation, not just within the private sector, which plays key roles in the development, finance and exchange of housing, but within the central government network (the department with responsibility for housing and also the Treasury, the Department of Social Security and others), the local government team (planning, housing, other departments providing services that contribute to sustainable communities) and the third arm (competing housing associations as well as the Housing Corporation itself).

During its lifetime of more than forty years, the Housing Corporation's operation was marked by periodic changes in focus and this highlights the problems associated with British housing policy throughout the period. Chairs and chief executives occasionally left suddenly and in an environment of crisis, and there was often an atmosphere of uncertainty about the nature of the next phase or even whether there would be one at all. The continuities in policy were at a very general level. Home ownership was consistently privileged and the way in which housing policy was managed and directed generally involved a centralisation of controls. But debates about the intrinsic merits of public and private rented housing and home ownership were often conducted at a theoretical level or at least abstracted from any actual local context. The capacity to develop coherent or sustained local policy was damaged by repeated shifts in emphasis and direction, with stop and start, moratoriums and crash programmes.

It is appropriate to refer to some elements of how housing policy was directed in the 1960s. The important accounts by Griffith (1966) and Sharpe (1969) emphasised the extent to which central government operated in a laissez-faire manner in relation to housing. Central government did not pretend to know enough to be able to control policy at a local level. It saw itself as setting a framework and relied upon local authorities to operate effectively within this. It did not attempt to regulate or control even to the extent that it did, say, in the education service. It operated no inspectorate and did not set standards comparable with other services (although there were some important standards set in relation to dwelling size and design). There was no ambition to provide a universal housing service or indeed a housing service that fully catered for some identified sections of the population. Instead, the government adopted legislation that would enable local author-ities, as the best-informed local agencies, to respond to local needs as they thought fit. In debates about the withdrawal or the hollowing out of the state it is important to recognise that the government's ambition in housing policy before the 1970s fell far short the orchestration and control that applied in some areas.

The laissez-faire approach to housing policy had considerable merits. However, it also produced certain very clear outcomes. Some local authorities used their powers energetically and ambitiously and became major providers of housing but others sought to do very little. The geographical variation in council housing originates from political (not always simply party political) differences in the energy with which local authorities pursued their housing policies. It is apparent that the government was concerned about this in the 1950s and 1960s. There was debate about whether it should require some standards to be met and whether the most laggardly local authorities should be required to act more responsibly. At the same time some Conservative commentators expressed vigorous opposition to the 'waiting list society' and the development of 'a nation of council tenants' and the implication was that there should be a reduction in state housing in some districts.

Housing and the welfare state

The immediate background to the development of the third arm in housing policy relates to the post-war welfare state and the period immediately after 1945. While the most severe problems of housing shortage had largely been dealt with by 1939 (Cullingworth 1966), there were still major problems related to house condition, sharing and overcrowding. The cessation of building activity, war damage and the inability to adequately maintain properties in wartime generated new shortages and exacerbated other problems. The post-war period saw the greatest investment in high-quality council housing, associated mainly with Aneurin Bevan but also with Harold Macmillan, who, influenced by his experience in the inter-war period, shared the view that the government should be interventionist and should provide housing for ordinary families as part of post-war reconstruction and in response to a housing crisis. Macmillan's was a very different view from that of later Conservatives, who believed that housing was best left to the market. The decade after 1945 was one in which there was a managed market: most of the private rented sector was subject to rent control, the council housing sector was directly managed by the state, and only a minority of the rented sector was outside the managed system. It could be argued that even the owner-occupied sector was managed, although less directly by the state. The practices of building societies in rationing lending meant that there was a managed, bureaucratic process operating within the private sector and this partly reflected legislation and the regulation of the building societies and other financial institutions.

The managed market had certain characteristics associated with it. Tenants in the private rented sector benefited from low rents and security of tenure and this created a low-mobility segment to the market. While economists have represented this as highly inefficient, they have neglected the extent to which it created social stability and strong communities. Some of the images of working-class communities in the 1940s and 1950s are of stable neighbourhoods of private renting. Alongside this regulated, low-rent sector, new council estates and new towns were built for the affluent working classes and, where they could afford the higher rents of council housing, for new families with children. The council housing that was offered was very often significantly better than was available in the older Victorian private rented sector and in the least expensive owner-occupied housing – although not all of the private rented sector caught by rent control in 1939 was deficient.

There is considerable literature about the place of housing in the post-war welfare state settlement. Housing was not nationalised or reorganised in the way that education or health or some parts of the social services were. The mechanisms used before the war largely continued to be relied upon: rent control and local authorities as key players. However, the lasting effects of the extension of rent control, the reorganisation of the construction industry during the war, the increased subsidy for council housing, the introduction of a much stronger planning system and the powers in relation to new towns all mean that it may be unwise to simply represent housing as the wobbly pillar in the welfare state. In many ways it was one of the welfare state's underpinnings, with the low rents in the private rented sector a key element, along with the growth of a state-owned sector. Perhaps the importance of the underpinnings only became apparent as they were eroded in later periods and the welfare state as a whole was weakened. It is also relevant for those who stress the lack of commitment to housing in the post-war welfare state to puncture some myths about the commitment to other areas which are sometimes presented as much more central to the welfare state. Perhaps the best example here is pensions, where the government reduced its contributions to the National Insurance Fund as rapidly as it could, withdrawing from its commitments at an earlier stage than was the case with the housing programme.

It is also important to recognise that housing was part of the local, rather than national, welfare state. The images of the Beveridge-based welfare state are of universalism and uniformity and these principles at least nominally underpinned social security, education and health provision. Wherever you lived and whatever your circumstances you had the same rights to education, health and social security payments. The breaches to this fundamental arose in the detail – in the tripartite secondary education system, where class and place of residence as well as measured ability affected what schooling was received, in the different levels of health resources devoted to older people or to mental illness compared with acute illness. In social security the low rate of insurance benefit undermined the principle of universality and left many households dependent on means-tested assistance benefits and this arose because the treatment of rent in calculating the uniform benefit rate was critical. The underlying principles driving the welfare state were to provide uniform and universal benefits that would ensure that all households could afford the essentials for a healthy life. The approach was most severely tested by rents. In a period when there was no housing benefit system, no mandatory rent rebates for council tenants and not even powers for rent allowances in the private rented sector, rent levels varied substantially by region (more than was the case for food, clothes or fuel). The nationally uniform benefit rate that emerged was inadequate in some areas but it was sufficient in others. If the underlying approach struggled with the problem of rents it did not even attempt to address housing supply. In effect the planning of housing, and investment in housing, was a step beyond the Beveridge model and remained a local welfare state service: the local unevenness of demand, and of the legacy of supply, required different patterns of investment that were best understood locally. In the early post-war period this local welfare state provision operated within the managed housing system outlined above.

The highly managed system associated with early post-war housing had its own destruction built in and became progressively weaker. In particular, as the private rented sector continued to decline and became less attractive so this added to change in both the owner-occupied and council housing sectors. Deregulation of private renting, through explicit legislative action and through the turnover of properties, transfers of properties to owner-occupiers and the construction of new housing that was not subject to rent control, expanded the non-managed part of the housing system. At the same time governments increased the taxation and other privileges associated with home ownership. The local welfare state was operating in a less managed environment and the politics of housing tenure were becoming more prominent nationally and locally. By the late 1950s there were questions about the role of the state in providing housing, just as there were in relation to other state-provided services. The immediate post-war settlement associated with universal, uniform and redistributive social welfare provision had given way to a much more mixed economy of welfare, influenced by Conservative governments concerned about public expenditure but also buttressed by arguments reminiscent of previous debates about personal responsibility and choice. It is in this environment that the Housing Corporation came into existence.

Policy failure?

In housing the reaction against the managed system emerging in the immediate post-war years found a response in the increasing promotion of private sector solutions to problems. The role of local authorities in providing general housing needs gave way to a more targeted role related to slum clearance, redevelopment and rehousing. Home ownership was encouraged and rent controls relaxed after 1954 and particularly under the Rent Act 1957. But the consequences of these changes did not turn out as anticipated and severe problems became more apparent.

The slum clearance programmes of the 1960s and 1970s meant that households with more bargaining power (because they had been waiting for a long time as well as because of judgements about their housing need and merit) were more likely to obtain satisfactory rehousing, while a significant section of the population was effectively excluded from the rehousing benefits supposedly associated with slum clearance. In practice, because some households had moved into clearance districts at a relatively late stage, they had no rights to rehousing or, because they did not know what rights they had, they tended to move on before they were offered rehousing. The way housing was managed and directed and the practices of local authorities in letting and managing housing came under closer scrutiny. While some practices were not evidenced until the 1960s and 1970s it is apparent that they were long established. For instance, the Finer report, published in 1974, raised doubts about how allocation policies discriminated against one-parent families, and the same issues arose in relation to black and minority ethnic groups and other vulnerable sections of the community (see for example Rex and Moore 1967; Burney 1967; CHAC 1969). The pressure on council waiting lists created by the rehousing of households directly affected by slum clearance also made access for others in housing need more difficult and left them more dependent on a residual and often poorly managed and exploitative private rented sector.

The consequences of this were that a section of the community was missed by all of the key agencies and neglected in the housing process. The near-monopoly position of local authorities in providing (modern) rented housing became a matter for concern, as those who were excluded had diminishing alternatives in the declining private rented sector. Campaigns related to homelessness and bad housing increased. Awareness of the limitations of the post-war settlement in housing mirrored the wider challenge to the general complacency towards the effects of the welfare state, highlighted by the rediscovery of poverty. One outcome was a new array of pressure groups concerned with housing and poverty and, more locally, the establishment of a new generation of housing associations as bottom-up organisations dealing with the new housing crisis.

The modernisation of housing and changing tenure

The period of the parallel growth of home ownership and council housing and the continuing decline of private landlordism continued until the end of the 1970s. The focus of policy switched from house condition to housing tenure and the differential access to housing associated with tenure. The research literature became dominated by debates about rationing, gatekeepers and managers, choice and constraint and competition for housing (e.g. Rex and Moore 1967; Murie et al. 1976; Lambert et al. 1978; Henderson and Karn 1987). It was increasingly evident that the housing strategies of individual households were also directed at housing tenure. They were principally strategies to gain access to council housing or to home ownership. Whatever its limitations, public housing had grown to provide homes for almost one out of every three households and it mostly provided very high-quality houses with gardens, more modern, better built and better maintained than much of the housing in the owner-occupied and private rented sectors. It was a tenure that was most accessible to more affluent households but as it matured it developed a greater mix of age groups, household structures and occupational and income groups. Given the present-day view of the shortcomings of council housing it is important to recognise the strengths of the sector in the 1970s and earlier. Social housing in the period of reconstruction after 1945 was in its golden age (Harloe 1995) and a combination of circumstances sustained its attractiveness and its development alongside private housing. The urban sociologist Ray Pahl, writing towards the end of this era, stated:

> To a large extent, Britain has got a more humane and generous approach to housing than other, ostensibly richer, societies. This is largely due to the size and quality of its local authority housing, which, despite what its critics would say, is probably the best-managed publicly owned housing stock in the world. It is an asset to our society and should not lightly be allowed to diminish. (Quoted in Harloe et al. 1974: x)

Pahl went on to express regret at the lack of champions for council housing and the extent to which it was associated with 'problems', 'trouble' and 'poverty'.

There is a considerable literature charting these and subsequent changes in policy and the social roles of different tenures (Forrest and Murie 1990; Harloe 1995; Malpass and Murie 1999; Murie 2006). Public housing increasingly became social rented housing with a narrower social base affected by processes of residualisation. By 2008 the tenure structure and the meanings of tenures had dramatically changed.

The shifts in policy outlined above have been accompanied by a considerable debate about explanations. Differences in tenure in different countries and periods have been variously associated with different phases of economic development and different welfare regimes. The idea of modernisation of housing tenure as developed by Malpass and Murie (1987, 1999) is based on some of the outputs from the structures-of-provision thesis. Essentially this thesis argued that housing markets were modified and the government's approach to housing markets developed in connection with dominant economic problems. In the nineteenth century the preoccupation of government and capital was with a healthy population and interventions through public health legislation and, later, through measures to improve housing, were directly linked to ensuring that there was a good supply of labour in the right place and to the prevention of civil disturbance. The most dramatic elements referred to in the literature are the conscious government decisions to invest in housing, to avoid bolshevism and revolution and to improve the health of the labour force. The more theoretical literature argues that these basic considerations continued to operate through the twentieth century.

As housing conditions improved, or in periods when the influence of the labour movement declined, the government tended to reduce its ambitions in relation to housing; but with the interruptions occasioned by war, times of greater shortage and greater risk of civil disruption, and periods in which the labour movement was stronger, government concern increased. This basic thesis explains why the high points in the construction of council housing relate in particular to the periods immediately after both world wars. This political economy account can, at its crudest, involve a very simple economic determinism: that state intervention in housing and the development of the housing market itself were driven by the interests of business and investors. In a subtler version this would refer not just to the interests of these groups but also to working-class and other political pressures. It is also fair to argue that the account does not deny the importance of individual choices, aspirations and expectations although these are often given less prominence. Nevertheless there is a recognition that, for the mass of the population, the assumption that private rented housing was the norm gave way to one that council housing was the desirable tenure and latterly to one that owner occupation was the best long-term tenure. The affluent working class in particular changed its housing preferences and practices and these added to the pressures for modernisation of the housing market.

Malpass (2008) has discussed the contributions by Kemeny (1995, 2005) and Lowe (2004), which present a different explanation for the nature of tenure and tenure restructuring in Britain. Malpass argues that this perspective is less able to cope with the restructuring of housing in Britain. Kemeny and Lowe present English-speaking nations as culturally inclined towards home ownership in a way that does not apply to continental European countries and refer to an Anglo-Saxon model. For Malpass this thesis is less easy to reconcile with the evidence in relation to Britain before the 1960s, when owner occupation was the minority. It is also problematic once we come to the 2000s, when the levels of home ownership in Britain are lower than in many other European countries, which have undergone major privatisations.

The thesis advanced by Kemeny and Lowe links to attempts to connect the development of housing with the wider development of the welfare state. The Anglo-Saxon grouping fits loosely with the influential analysis of welfare regimes published by Esping-Andersen (1990). For example, Doling (1997) follows Kemeny and emphasises a distinctive Anglo-Saxon approach adopted by countries with liberal social welfare regimes as identified by Esping-Andersen. This presentation ignores Esping-Andersen's expressed difficulty in locating the UK within his framework and the cautions previously expressed by others (Harloe 1995; Cochrane and Clarke 1993). It also fails to recognise that housing has formed part of the local welfare state. In Britain a strong interventionist local welfare state has operated within what is presented as a less generous national system – traditions in relation to the local welfare state diverge from the national pattern. Nevertheless we have a framework that suggests that England (perhaps the whole of the UK, and Ireland too) will be exceptions within Europe, with higher rates of home ownership. If it followed an Anglo-Saxon path it would also have a smaller, more residual, social rented sector.

These different explanatory frameworks form part of the structure for this book. The Housing Corporation enabled a pattern of tenure change to take place that reflected shifting economic and political imperatives. This does not imply that it was the underlying driver of change or even the only mechanism for it, nor that all of the detail of decisions were determined by some underlying logic. The development of different tenures was linked to the changes in economy and society.

The renewed interest in housing associations can be understood in the context of a developing economy and society, rising affluence and expectations, shifting political pressures and the changing roles and limitations of individual tenures. Such a perspective highlights the weakness of examining the social rented sector or the activities of the Housing Corporation simply by looking at what was happening within the tenure that was its immediate sphere of influence. Its role was partly determined by what was happening to competitor tenures. As the private rented sector became less and less attractive in comparison with alternative tenures, so its role began to change. More affluent groups left, in many cases by purchasing the better properties as sitting tenants. Newly forming households which could afford to do so avoided the private rented sector or were only there for very short, transitional periods. The sector became increasingly residual – catering for a narrower social group unable to access or sustain owner occupation or a council tenancy. It became more and more associated with low-income, older householders and low-income newcomers, and also became increasingly the locus for exploitation. The weaknesses of the rent control system and the difficulties of enforcing rent regulation and tenants' rights meant that some private landlords began to operate at the margins of or outside the law. The most extreme cases were identified, for example, through the Milner Holland report of 1965 and were associated with Rachmanism and the practices of exploitative landlords, especially in high-turnover neighbourhoods of London but also in other cities.

By the mid-1950s the government stated that it believed it had succeeded in relieving the gross housing shortages that had existed at the end of the Second World War and it adopted new targets. Firstly it shifted its attention from the general needs of the population to more specific problems of overcrowding and slum clearance. Secondly it began more actively to seek the expansion of owner occupation – by increasing access to mortgage finance and using tax relief and other measures. These actions further affected the decline of private renting. The worst housing in the private rented sector did not transfer to owner occupation but became the subject of slum clearance activity. In turn this speeded the shift in the social base of council housing from a tenure for the affluent working class and a mixed-income community towards a more predominantly low-income community that had previously been in the private rented sector. This residualisation is associated with the decline of the private rented sector and expansion of home ownership, well before it was speeded up by the right to buy and other factors.

Table 1.2 sets out statistics on housing tenure in England, Scotland and Wales. Owner occupation was becoming the mass housing tenure by the 1960s and deregulation of housing finance in the 1980s, and the end of mortgage rationing, meant a final transition from a managed to a market system. In this environment the asset or wealth gap between owners and renters attracted more attention and began to be identified as an area requiring remedy (see for example Royal Commission 1977; Murie and Forrest 1980; Forrest and Murie 1989; Hamnett et al. 1991; Hamnett 1999; Hill et al. 2002). The private rented sector continued its dramatic decline, becoming a residual, often poorly managed sector but then beginning to recreate and reinvent itself under the influence of housing benefit and deregulation, with the development of niche markets and buy-to-let housing after 2000. As the post-war generation of controlled and regulated tenants declined, so the private rented sector shook off its earlier character and responsibilities and housed new sections of the population. State housing, unlike owner occupation, reached the point where it ceased to grow any further. This was a result of explicit policy choices at the end of the 1970s – the reduction of investment in new housing by local authorities and new towns, and the introduction of the right to buy and then of stock transfer.

The consequence of these changes was a decline in council housing, both as a proportion of the housing stock and in the number of council dwellings, and a change in the social role of council housing. The narrowing social base of the sector has been widely discussed as residualisation: a narrow social base is not an intrinsic feature of council housing but has become characteristic. While it is easy to identify the later stages of residualisation of council housing as associated with the right to buy and stock transfer, the expanding housing association sector has developed a similar social profile. It is normal to refer to residualisation affecting the social rented sector as a whole. The explanation for this trend across the sector principally relates to the development of alternative tenures and choices, but also to the actions taken internally within the sector (relating to supply, rationing and access). More affluent groups have chosen to move to owner occupation, leaving the continuing demand for social rented housing to come from older and poorer households and people in less skilled occupations. While these developments are associated with broader social, economic and demographic changes and with changes in the

Table 1.2: Dwellings by tenure in England, Wales and Scotland, thousands

	1971	%	1976	%	1981	%	1986	%	1991	%	1996	%	2001	%	2006	%
England																
Owner-occupiers	8,503	52.5	9,570	55.7	10,773	59.8	12,015	63.6	13,237	67.3	13,865	67.7	14,818	69.9	15,442	70.2
Privately rented	3,122	19.3	2,332	13.6	2,044	11.3	1,953	10.3	1,927	9.8	2,191	10.7	2,152	10.1	2,611	11.9
Housing association	0	0.0	281	1.6	410	2.3	475	2.5	608	3.1	942	4.6	1,424	6.7	1,850	8.4
Local authority	4,586	28.3	4,985	29.0	4,798	26.6	4,439	23.5	3,899	19.8	3,470	17.0	2,812	13.3	2,086	9.5
All dwellings	16,211	100.0	17,168	100.0	18,025	100.0	18,882	100.0	19,671	100.0	20,468	100.0	21,207	100.0	21,989	100.0
Wales																
Owner-occupiers	540	55.8	631	60.3	680	61.9	761	66.9	837	70.7	878	71.2	905	71.0	955	72.7
Privately rented	151	15.6	131	12.5	105	9.6	98	8.6	97	8.2	104	8.4	127	10.0	137	10.4
Housing association	0	0.0	0	0.0	24	2.2	25	2.2	28	2.4	45	3.6	55	4.3	66	5.0
Local authority	276	28.5	284	27.2	290	26.4	254	22.3	222	18.8	207	16.8	188	14.7	156	11.9
All dwellings	967	100.0	1,046	100.0	1,099	100.0	1,138	100.0	1,184	100.0	1,233	100.0	1,275	100.0	1,314	100.0
Scotland																
Owner-occupiers	569	31.2	645	33.6	718	36.4	884	43.1	n/a		1,293	58.0	1,474	63.4	1,614	67.1
Privately rented	305	16.7	234	12.2	191	9.7	154	7.5	n/a		155	7.0	156	6.7	178	7.4
Housing association	0	0.0	0	0.0	36	1.8	50	2.4	n/a		91	4.1	137	5.9	252	10.5
Local authority	948	52.0	1,042	54.2	1,027	52.1	962	46.9	n/a		691	31.0	558	24.0	363	15.1
All dwellings	1,822	100.0	1,921	100.0	1,970	100.0	2,050	100.0	n/a		2,230	100.0	2,324	100.0	2,407	100.0

Individual figures have been rounded to the nearest thousand. Totals are derived from unrounded numbers and may not equal the sum of the rounded numbers.

Source: Wilcox (annual).

housing market, they were also affected by conscious policy decisions. Perhaps there would have been some tendency towards residualisation anyhow, but the extent to which the social rented sector had by the twenty-first century become associated with very low-income and benefit-dependent households was much greater than would have occurred through the simple processes of market, demographic and economic change.

Building capacity

The growth of housing associations and the Housing Corporation has occurred in a period of retrenchment and weakening of local government. However, it has in some respects increased the alternatives to the market or to central government direction of policy and activity at a local level. The enormous growth in the activities of housing associations, a successful investment record and an effective regulation and supervision system have left a legacy at the beginning of the twenty-first century that was not there fifty years before. They have left a set of potential partners that have well-founded organisations and strong professional expertise and that can lead or be effective followers in important initiatives or in regeneration. While the capacity of local government has changed, the number of local agencies that are alternatives to the private sector has grown and their capacity to respond to different challenges has increased. It may be argued that there has been some fragmentation of local capacity, but at the same time there can be more diversity or plurality and if this can be effectively drawn on it may be an asset. There is greater complexity but also greater capacity than in the past to contribute to meeting housing needs and improving the quality and choice of housing both through the big national associations and through local organisations.

The development of private finance and the attraction of private funding to the housing sector can be represented as the most successful public–private partnership (PPP) in Britain and perhaps anywhere else. The organisational, financial and innovational capacities of these organisations are enormous and are astonishing because they have developed in an environment of declining public expenditure. This represents a challenging situation: challenging for anyone who denies that PPPs can work, that the voluntary sector can work or that PPPs can play only a marginal role in the provision of any particular service. However, if we look at it in a different way the overall housing situation and the situation of the social rented sector has become more fraught, there is greater segregation and concentration of deprivation and there are greater concerns about the impact of housing on life chances – or at least the concerns have been revived after a period in which there was some belief that progress had been made.

The maturation of housing and housing finance through the housing association sector is also an important dimension. As housing associations have grown, so they have developed an asset base which can be drawn upon to support future borrowing and they have become more capable of recreating themselves. This also enables them to operate counter-cyclically to embark upon investment in periods when the market is less likely to act. But they will only do this if the government encourages them to do so through both investment and regulatory regimes.

Conclusions

The Housing Corporation was set up in a very different environment than exists today and reinvented itself a number of times. It was shaped by other actors in the housing and policy world and by a changing economy and structure of housing tenures. At the same time it helped to change the housing provision system in Britain. It is possible to argue that the Corporation assisted the transition from a managed to a market system and contributed to the developing crisis within the housing sector, by being a pliable instrument of government: it was reactive and did too little to resist what the government was pressing upon it. It is equally possible to argue that without the presence of the Housing Corporation, a balancing factor in the agendas about demunicipalisation and the residualisation of council housing would have been missing. The continuing investment in social rented housing through the Housing Corporation offset some of the damaging effects associated with policies towards the rest of the housing sector. It may have been too little of a balancing or an enabling force, but it is important to recognise the two sides of the coin.

Although the Housing Corporation was undeniably an agency of government, its capacity and that of housing associations has made the relationship more complex than is represented simply by a master–servant or government–agency relationship. Government moved from a laissez-faire approach preoccupied with numbers of new housing units built to a much closer scrutiny of a wider variety of organisations. Government, and through it the Housing Corporation, adopted a cash-limited system rather than a system based on targets for the numbers of units built or rehabilitated. There was what has been referred to as the nationalisation of housing policy and this was followed by an increasing reliance on the planning system. But government has also been faced with new sources of ideas and innovation and has not been in a position to simply exercise control.

By 2008 the direction of housing policy was dramatically different from sixty years earlier. Unfortunately the crisis of housing shortage and affordability could be represented as having similarities at both stages. In 2008 there is not the same level of overcrowding, sharing of amenities, dilapidated housing or slum housing; but, unfortunately, there are still some areas of overcrowding and grossly deficient housing and there is evidence to say that these have begun to rise again after a period of sustained decline. These problems are especially apparent in London, and are also evident among vulnerable groups, among low-income black and minority ethnic communities and in the private rented sector. But by 2008 other examples had come to light of highly unsatisfactory living environments, sometimes associated with larger council estates: high concentrations of deprivation, people living in poorly maintained and managed dwellings, where not only are the individual dwellings deficient, but the neighbourhood and estate are also poorly maintained and managed, scarred with graffiti and rubbish and affected by other problems including crime and anti-social behaviour.

These problems are also evident in older, mixed-tenure areas (particularly in the Midlands and the north) with concentrations of deprivation and where the appreciation in property values was not always dramatic. These situations demonstrate that the poorest sections of the community and the problems of poor neighbourhood management are not tenure specific; they emerge in different environments, in different places.

At the end of the period it would also appear that some commentators had begun to see a crisis of residualisation. For example the work carried out by Feinstein et al. (2008) highlighted the concentration of deprivation in the social rented sector and the evidence that this concentration was linked with the reduced life chances of those living in the sector. Hills (2007) also highlights the associations between worklessness and the social rented sector. It is unfortunate that this crisis of residualisation was not accepted and acknowledged at an earlier stage. The evidence had been presented much earlier (e.g. Forrest and Murie 1983; Hamnett 1984; Bentham 1986) but ministers and civil servants turned a blind eye. Finally in 2008 the crisis associated with the credit crunch was about falling house prices and the fear of negative equity emerging as a result. But the long-term implications were of a change in lending patterns that halted the growth of the buy-to-let market and increased the difficulties of first-time buyers in accessing home ownership; and both of these factors had a dramatic impact on new building. The likelihood that once the credit crunch was over the market would not operate in the way that it had previously implied a continuing problem for access and the need for the government to find new ways of addressing housing problems.

By the time the Housing Corporation was being replaced by the new Homes and Communities Agency and the new Tenant Services Authority, there may have been more willingness to acknowledge the failures of previous policy, but it is not altogether clear that this is the case. There remain accounts which see housing problems as growing out of the security and rights of tenants, or suggest that the solution would be to do away with social housing or to weaken the rights of tenants. Just as in earlier phases, some commentators suggested that the problems in council housing were restricted to a few patches of poverty rather than being generic to the sector, thereby avoiding the interpretation that a more coherent and supportive policy towards social rented housing is needed and instead suggesting that the problem lies in the way it is managed internally or even in the very existence of the tenure.

2

Problems of housing policy

Introduction

There are a number of easily available accounts of the origins and development of housing policy in Britain (fuller discussions are available in Gauldie 1974; Merrett 1979; Holmans 1987; and briefer summaries in Malpass and Murie 1999; Mullins and Murie 2006). The focus in this chapter is on the development of a more interventionist housing policy after 1919 and the important but changing role developed by local authorities as providers of rented housing. Although the Housing Corporation itself was a relatively late entrant in the story of housing policy, housing associations are involved in the longer history of housing and this is more fully set out in Chapter 3.

The resistance to state intervention in housing

Most accounts of British housing policy start off by establishing the serious nature of housing problems in nineteenth-century Britain and explain the resistance to interventions in the market that would have been sufficient to address the problems. The default policy position was non-interventionist, reliance on the market or on self-help and the acceptance that intervention could have undesirable consequences. As the first industrial nation Britain experienced the economic, social and demographic changes associated with industrialisation and urbanisation earlier than any other country. Rural-to-urban migration packed a growing population into increasingly crowded cities and the housing market responded by sub-dividing properties, generating over-crowded and overused dwellings and neighbourhoods. In urban areas much privately rented housing, which catered for almost all households, was poorly designed and built to low standards with inadequate water and sewerage services. Dwellings in both urban and rural areas were small or were subdivided with shared amenities; they were poorly maintained, damp, badly ventilated, dark and sometimes structurally unstable. As landlords took advantage of high demand in expanding urban areas, rents increased and considerable overcrowding resulted as people sub-let rooms in order to pay the rent. The responses from government were inadequate, partly because the organisations providing both local and national government were ill equipped to respond to the problems arising from rapid urbanisation and partly because they lacked the inclination. Government was unwilling to fund interventions that would be sufficient to change the quality of housing in towns, and accepted arguments that such intervention would be undesirable because it would distort the free market in housing or encourage dependency and erode commitments to family and work (see for example Merrett 1979; Gauldie 1974).

The only real counter to this dominant view was the threat to the health of all classes and the 'health of the towns' problem. The universal threat occasioned by cholera and infectious disease did lead to effective interventions, but these were designed to safeguard public health rather than to provide more or more modern housing. The consequent public health legislation incorporated clear duties to be carried out by local authorities. A necessary part of this was the development of a more coherent and uniform structure of local government from the early 1870s. Central government was also reorganised and in 1872 the Public Health Act required the formation of sanitary authorities covering the whole country. This Act, along with the Public Health Act 1875 and the continued reorganisation of local government, provided a modern, comprehensive code of public health, including measures for intervention to affect housing conditions.

The Public Health Acts did not, however, remove the need for housing legislation. The 1875 Act, under which local authorities made their housing by-laws, and various local Acts, which individual authorities used to undertake particular schemes, provided housing powers. But these limited measures gave no permanent housing role. For example, powers related to individual dwellings and did not extend to encompass whole areas of slum housing or to combat shortages and overcrowding by building new dwellings.

Against this background there was a growing clamour through the last quarter of the nineteenth century for activity around the housing question. In some quarters, however, the instinct was still to deny the need for any widespread intervention in the market – and to oppose any attempt to alleviate the conditions of the poor by subsidising housing, because it was likely to undermine self-help and the responsibility of the citizen for himself (*sic*) and his family.

The story of housing policy then unfolds around measures, initially limited but becoming increasingly comprehensive, to provide local authorities first with powers and then with duties related to the provision of better housing. It is important to emphasise that while many of the accounts of housing policy take the development of national legislative responses as the connecting thread, the pressures behind these developments were mostly local (Rodger 1992). By the end of the nineteenth century there was a consciousness that adverse living conditions had an impact on physical health and on child development. Alarm about the impact of poor health on the imperial and defence capabilities of the nation increased towards the end of the century and became widely held. A series of commissions of enquiry and committees provided further evidence and reinforced the view that new action needed to be taken in relation to the housing question.

In this context it is relevant to note who was resistant to this view. The major interest group affected was the private landlord. The nineteenth-century housing market in Britain was dominated by private renting but was highly differentiated (Pooley 1992) with a series of sub-markets related to differences in quality, cost and location. Englander (1983) emphasises the political marginalisation of private landlords and their ineffectiveness in resisting demands for reform in the twentieth century. While the nineteenth-century interventions to improve the standards of public health did affect the private landlord and reduced opportunities for profit, it was not until the twentieth century that more severe interventions substantially eroded the position of landlord. The combination of interests antagonistic to landlords increased as awareness of housing problems developed and as working class organisations became increasingly effective.

It is important to recognise the resistance to state intervention in housing, but it is also important to recognise the contribution of the voluntary sector. From the 1830s onwards, housing investors willing to accept below-market rates of return developed housing schemes that have been collectively described as 'philanthropy and 5 per cent' (Ashworth 1954: 67). These schemes, however, failed to attract sufficient investment to make a real impact on the housing problem (particularly outside London). They were mainly targeted at better-off working-class households and were generally unpopular because of their design and density, and because of their management regime.

The failure of both the market and philanthropy added to arguments that direct state provision was unavoidable if problems were to be addressed. While the Housing of the Working Classes Act 1890 gave local authorities powers to build for general needs, it gave no subsidies to enable them to charge rents that would be affordable to working-class households. Gauldie (1974: 240) concluded: 'No real reform in housing was achieved by legislation during the nineteenth century.'

Table 2.1: Principal housing legislation 1851–1914

1851 Labouring Classes' Lodging Houses Act
Permitted local authorities to provide housing, but very widely ignored.

1851 Common Lodging Houses Act (amended in 1853)
Provided for control and monitoring of private common lodging houses.

1866 Labouring Classes' Dwelling Houses Act
Permitted local authorities and model dwellings companies to borrow at cheap rates from the Public Works Loans Commissioners.

1868 Artisans' and Labourers' Dwellings Act (Torrens Act)
Local authorities given powers to demolish individual unfit houses. No compensation for owners (until amended in 1879) and no municipal rebuilding.

1875 Artisans' and Labourers' Dwellings Improvement Act (Cross Act)
Permitted local authorities to purchase and clear areas of unfit housing. Local authorities permitted to build on cleared sites, but had to sell within ten years. (Amended in 1879 to limit compensation.)

1885 Housing of the Working Classes Act
Consolidating Act.

1890 Housing of the Working Classes Act
Consolidated and amended earlier legislation related to areas of unfit and insanitary housing and rebuilding powers, individual unfit houses, and local authority powers to build housing for general needs.

1900 Housing of the Working Classes Act
Amended 1890 Act to give London metropolitan boroughs as well as the London County Council powers to build housing for general needs.

1909 Housing, Town Planning &c. Act
Ended obligation for local authorities to sell houses in redevelopment areas, added powers to prepare town planning schemes.

Source: Adapted from Malpass and Murie (1999).

By 1915 councils had powers to build to replace slums and for general needs (see Table 2.1) and arrangements had been established to facilitate municipal borrowing at favourable rates of interest. Ways to compensate owners had been developed. But there was no duty to remove the slums or obligation to rehouse those displaced through policy action. Where municipal housing was provided, it was without subsidy from central government and rents were high. Local authorities may have had the power to address local housing problems but there were insufficient incentives or duties that would enable them to do so effectively even if they wished to. Merrett (1979: 26) indicates that by 1914 local authorities had built only 24,000 dwellings nationally and the impact on lower-income households had been limited.

The subsidy question and rent control

In the period up to the outbreak of the First World War in 1914, local government began to obtain powers to provide housing but those powers were relatively limited in their use and effect. They were not backed by resources that would enable them to build houses and let them at anywhere near affordable rents. They could clear slums or enable modern transport systems to develop by demolishing housing, but did not have sufficiently strong responsibilities or sufficient resources to rehouse those affected by such clearances. Against this background, proposals were increasingly being voiced to provide Exchequer subsidy for housing. Subsidy was seen as ever more necessary to enable new housing to be built at rents that would be affordable by ordinary households. The first report calling for Exchequer subsidy emerged in 1909, various Bills and proposals emerged in the period 1912–14 and the Liberal government in 1914 was preparing legislation to include grants to urban authorities in respect of housing (Wilding 1972). It is this evidence which suggests that the war delayed rather than promoted Exchequer subsidies and that the key factors leading to subsidy were not war and wartime pledges. Rather, they were the political pressures apparent before 1919 and the switch of investment, by those traditionally providing rented property, away from the housing sector. There is no doubt, however, that the introduction of rent control in 1915 and the difficulties of relaxing it immediately after the war, as well as the politics associated with the post-war promise of 'homes fit for heroes' and the fear of political unrest (see for example Rodger 1992), completed the pressure to introduce and maintain housing subsidies. These new subsidies would operate alongside the continuing control and regulation of private sector rents for the next sixty years, although the detail both of subsidy and rent control were to be repeatedly changed.

Accounts of housing policy in Britain identify a clear break associated with the First World War. Private landlords were already shifting their investments before 1914 but the introduction of rent control and the restrictions this placed on their ability to raise rents and maintain profits speeded the decline of the sector. The Increase of Rent and Mortgage Interest (War Restrictions) Act 1915 was only intended to continue until six months after the end of the war, but it was maintained by legislation in 1919 and 1920. In 1920, the range of properties subject to control was extended. In 1923, arrangements for decontrol on vacant possession were introduced. Legislation in 1933 and 1938 further relaxed rent control but dwellings with the lowest rateable values remained under control. Finally, with the outbreak of the Second World War in 1939, decontrol by vacant possession was abolished and controls were extended to virtually all privately rented housing.

The advent of council housing

The period 1919 to 1979 saw the expansion of two modern tenures – home ownership and council housing, at the expense of a declining, predominantly low-standard private rented sector. Council housing became established as a normal and permanent part of the housing system. Sixty years of the decline of private renting and the growth of these two alternative tenures transformed the structure of the housing market and the way that households occupied their housing in Britain. This journey was interrupted by war and marked by periods of greater public investment and greater policy emphasis on new building, slum clearance or reconditioning the slums.

Local authorities were the preferred vehicles for the drive to build new houses for the working classes throughout this period; housing associations were merely bystanders. Although Peter Malpass (2000; 2001) has demonstrated that it is inaccurate to argue that there was no investment by housing associations between the wars (see Chapter 3), there is, nevertheless, no doubt that they were the minor party in the modernisation of the housing sector over that period. The introduction of Exchequer subsidies triggered the era of the growth of municipal housing. The Housing, Town Planning &c. Act 1919 (the Addison Act) gave local authorities a duty to survey the needs of their

Table 2.2: Principal housing legislation 1915–39

1915 Increase of Rent and Mortgage Interest (War Restrictions) Act
Fixed rents and interest rates at their August 1914 levels.

1919 Housing, Town Planning &c. Act (Addison Act)
Introduced Exchequer subsidies for local authority housing. Withdrawn in 1921.

1919 Housing (Additional Powers) Act
Extended subsidy to private builders of working-class housing.

1920 Increase of Rent and Mortgage Interest (Restrictions) Act.
Continued the principle of rent controls but permitted certain increases.

1923 Housing &c. Act (Chamberlain Act)
Introduced a new Exchequer subsidy with fixed liability and no mandatory rate contribution.
Withdrawn in 1929.

1923 Increase of Rent and Mortgage Interest Restrictions (Continuance) Act
Introduced decontrol of rent at next change of tenancy.

1924 Housing (Financial Provisions) Act (Wheatley Act)
Introduced a new, higher subsidy with mandatory rate contribution. Withdrawn 1933.

1930 Housing Act (Greenwood Act)
New subsidy related to slum clearance areas calculated on the number of people rehoused.
Permitted local authorities to operate rent rebates.

1933 Housing (Financial Provisions) Act
Withdrew subsidy for all new housing, except slum clearance replacement.

1933 Rent and Mortgage Interest Restrictions (Amendments) Act
Extended decontrol of rent.

1935 Housing Act
New subsidies to help with the relief of overcrowding. Local authorities required to operate one
housing revenue account, and permitted to pool rent and subsidies.

1936 Housing Act
Consolidating Act.

1938 Housing (Financial Provisions) Act
Introduced a single subsidy for slum clearance and relief of overcrowding.

1939 Rent and Mortgage Interest Restrictions Act
Reintroduced rent control on all but the highest-value properties.

Source: Adapted from Malpass and Murie (1999).

areas, make plans for provision of houses, and, with the consent of the minister of health, to build dwellings. The ministry was to approve rents based on the controlled rents of pre-war housing, making allowances for the quality of houses and circumstances of tenants. Given these rents, Exchequer subsidy was intended to meet all the losses incurred by a local authority in excess of a specified local rate contribution. For the first time local authorities had both the powers and the resources to build houses and to keep rents at levels that were within the reach of some working-class households. The legislation provided for subsidies which enabled local authorities to build traditional houses with gardens and to construct them to very high standards. These were considerably better properties than those generally available in the privately rented sector.

Once the threat of civil disturbance was over, the government began to trim back on the subsidy regime. Subsidies for council house building were cut in 1921 and the Housing &c. Act 1923 (the Chamberlain Act) provided a less generous regime than in 1919. Nevertheless subsidies remained and local authorities in England, Wales and Scotland invested steadily in new high-quality housing. The subsequent history was of periodic revision of the subsidy scheme. The first Labour government, elected in 1924, provided a more generous regime through the Housing (Financial Provisions) Act 1924 (the Wheatley Act). This 'established the local authorities as part of the permanent machinery for providing working-class houses' (Bowley 1945: 40).

In 1930 there was a shift to slum clearance rather than general-needs building. The Housing Act 1930 (the Greenwood Act) reflected a view that the worst problems of housing shortage were over and the policy focus should shift to clearance of the slums. The abolition of the Wheatley Act subsidy in 1933 signalled the end of Exchequer support for general-needs building and the end of such building by local authorities except in exceptional circumstances (Gilbert 1970: 200). Larger local authorities (200,000 population or more) were required to produce five-yearly plans for slum clearance and replacement. Most significantly the Act redefined the criteria for declaring clearance areas and made it obligatory for councils to rehouse (or arrange rehousing for) all households displaced by slum clearance. The major innovation was that Exchequer subsidy was based on each person rehoused and paid for forty years. Additional subsidy was available where the costs of acquiring and clearing sites were excessive. A rate (local tax) contribution was required and local authorities could fix reasonable rents and provide rent rebates. The switch to slum clearance meant that councils built for lower-income tenants living in slum areas and unable to afford the rents associated with earlier legislation. The dwellings built under these slum clearance programmes were not as good as those built by local authorities earlier – they were smaller and included ill-designed flats and estates on the edge of cities with high travel costs and poor access to jobs, schools and community facilities. The formula kept construction costs and public expenditure down but meant that local authorities missed the opportunity to build when costs were at their lowest point between the wars.

Municipal rents had generally been set at levels that were beyond the reach of many households and not just the very poorest. The lack of any system of housing benefit or rent rebates affected this. In the present day, when the social rented sector is denigrated for having too little social mix, this may not appear to be a criticism. Municipalities chose to build to a higher standard rather than to reduce construction costs in order to keep rents low. This built a long-term social asset although it can be argued that there was also more concern to meet the needs of affluent sections of the working class rather than those on very low incomes. Organised labour represented on trades councils and through trades union membership and achieving elected positions through the Labour Party disproportionately reflected the interests of more affluent, employed working-class households. The marginalised worker, the less skilled and organised sections of the working class were not so strongly represented. The emerging solutions to housing problems paid limited attention to issues of major concern to the lowest paid, to the unemployed, to women and to non-family households. These issues have been apparent throughout the history of council housing, but have become more striking in recent years.

In 1935 the government changed the rules relating to council housing accounts (see Malpass 1990). Previously accounts related to dwellings built under each Act had to be kept separate, and each, separately, had to balance: so rents on higher-cost schemes were higher. The Housing Act 1935 required that, in future, authorities should consolidate all accounts into one housing revenue account, which must balance annually. This meant that rents and subsidies would be pooled and rents determined in some other way – related for example to the size of a property rather than the legislation under which it was built. Local reluctance to introduce rebate schemes persisted but one unanticipated effect – arising from inflation – was that the rents of new houses could be kept down by subsidising them from the surpluses made by charging higher rents than needed to meet scheme costs for cheaper, older houses. In spite of these changes council housing in the inter-war and post-war period still did not generally benefit the worst off. Exchequer subsidies were not large enough to bring rents within the reach of those with low or fluctuating incomes, with insecure jobs or in permanent or periodic unemployment. A gap continued to exist between the rents charged and the wages of the mass of tenants and prospective tenants. Central government preferred to reduce public expenditure than to respond to this. The only alternative was to make rate contributions above the statutory minimum and keep rents down. This did occur – especially in Scotland – but some local authorities considered any rate subsidy undesirable.

Cullingworth (1966) argued that in 1939 there was a rough balance between the numbers of houses and families. Between 1919 and 1939, 4.1 million houses had been built. The net increase of about 3.7 million dwellings was accompanied by an increase of probably 2.25 million households. Cullingworth concluded that 'the overall housing situation had improved very greatly' (1966: 26). Problems of housing shortage had been relieved and the condition of the dwelling stock had been improved by the addition of new council housing and private-enterprise building and the removal of unsatisfactory dwellings. Private renting had declined to some 58 per cent with 32 per cent of dwellings owner occupied and 10 per cent publicly owned. More than 50 per cent of the owner-occupied dwellings had been built before 1919 and some one million rented dwellings had been sold to owner-occupiers. (DoE 1977, TV 1, pp. 37–9).

By 1939, state intervention in the housing market in the UK was strongly established and council housing had begun to shape neighbourhoods. In spite of resistance to local authority housing, on economic, political and public expenditure grounds, no government had removed the Exchequer subsidy and local authorities had more than a temporary or emergency or sanitary role. But housing standards varied enormously and council housing had begun to highlight just what a poor-quality service private landlords provided. Changes to the details of subsidy available to local authorities under different legislation also impacted on the space and other standards of what councils built. The average floor areas achieved in 1919–20 were never bettered in the rest of the inter-war period and in later years increased densities, lower standards of layout and design, and cheaper finishes were all employed to save money. In 1927, 1929 and 1932 the government issued circulars calling on all authorities to build the cheapest type of house and after 1930 more blocks of flats were built. These were far inferior to the spacious, leafy cottage estates of the early 1920s. In contrast to housing built with full Wheatley subsidy, 'many of the estates built in the 1930s were to become the ghettos of the 1960s'(Merrett 1979: 57).

In contrast to the newly built council housing the older private sector stock was severely deficient (Titmuss 1950: 131–2, 177). Consider the proportion of homes without baths: 40 per cent in Hull (1943) and Bootle (1939); about 66 per cent in York's working class (1939); 90 per cent in Stepney (1939); 52 per cent in Salford (1943); about 50 per cent in Glasgow (1944). Also in Glasgow one-third had to share a lavatory with anything up to six families. In rural areas it was estimated that about 30 per cent of the population lived in houses not connected to or within easy access of a water-main (1939) and nearly one half of households were without a fixed bath (1947).

The welfare state

During the Second World War new house building ceased and some 3,745,000 houses in the United Kingdom were either damaged or destroyed by bombs. Repair work on damaged dwellings often involved temporary patching as labour and materials were shifted towards other construction more directly linked to the war effort. Almost one million more people were competing for a smaller housing stock (some 700,000 fewer than had existed in 1939) and the stock was in worse condition (Titmuss 1950).

In the plans for reconstruction after the war local authorities remained the key vehicle for the government's housing drive. The crucial decisions taken by the Labour government in response to the situation in 1945 were to maintain wartime controls over private building and to rely on local government to lead an expanded building programme. The continuity in approach can be seen as evidence of a belief that there was only a temporary need for an active housing policy and thereafter the private sector would be able to do what was needed. At least some parts of the policy community held this view (see Malpass 2004). However, important innovations in planning and new towns were introduced and rent controls were maintained. Aneurin Bevan as minister of health also articulated a positive rationale for using the tested vehicles for delivery: 'If we are to plan, we have to plan with plannable instruments, and the speculative builder, by his very nature, is not a plannable instrument … we rest the full weight of the housing programme upon the local authorities, because their programmes can be planned [quoted in Donnison 1967: 164].'

Table 2.3: Principal housing legislation 1945–64

1946 Housing (Financial and Miscellaneous Provisions) Act
Raised level of subsidies and rate fund contributions.

1949 Housing Act
Removed statutory restriction which limited public housing to 'the working classes'. Introduced improvement grants.

1952 Housing Act
Raised subsidies.

1954 Housing Repairs and Rents Act
Restarted slum clearance and encouraged private sector improvement.

1956 Housing Subsidies Act
Reduced subsidies for general-needs housing. Rate fund contributions made optional. Subsidy structure encouraged high-rise building.

1957 Housing Act
Major consolidating Act.

1957 Rent Act
A measure to begin decontrol of rents at next change of tenancy.

1958 Housing (Financial Provisions) Act
Consolidating Act for financial matters.

1959 House Purchase and Housing Act
Extended improvement grant system. Encouraged local authority mortgage lending.

1961 Housing Act
Reintroduced subsidy for general-needs housing, but at two rates.

1964 Housing Act
Extended improvement grants. Established the Housing Corporation.

Source: Adapted from Malpass and Murie (1999).

In the event local authority completions (excluding prefabricated and other temporary dwellings) rose from 3,364 in 1945 to 190,368 in 1948. This was a much more rapid recovery than after 1919 and exceeded the previous high point of 121,653 in 1939. However, it was not sustained and responses to economic crisis resulted in a reduction in the volume and quality of council house building. In 1951 the new Conservative government raised the subsidy to encourage higher levels of production. But once the target of 300,000 houses per year had been achieved, the subsidy was cut (April 1955). By the end of 1956 the subsidy had been switched to give effect to the slum clearance policy begun in 1954; subsidy on all general-needs housing other than one-bedroom flats for the elderly was removed.

Malpass (2004) argues that the 1954 Housing Repairs and Rents Act was a key turning point, marking a return to the pre-war role of local authorities within a 'market' approach to housing. However, rent control remained in place and the high continuing levels of both council house building and urban renewal activities highlight the extent to which local variation was the key feature of a 'laissez-faire' policy framework (Griffith 1966). Conservative governments took steps to deregulate and to move to realistic rents in public and private sectors but this was still a managed system – albeit in a weaker form. The Rent Act 1957 decontrolled all private rented dwellings with a rateable value of over £40 in London and over £30 in the rest of England and Wales. Other dwellings would be decontrolled only when let to a new tenant. In the public sector, the Housing Subsidies Act 1956 enabled rents to rise and there was the beginning of the shift from object (bricks and mortar) subsidies to subject (household needs and incomes) subsidies. By 1964 realistic rent policies had already drawn almost 40 per cent of housing authorities into operating means-tested rent rebate schemes – compared with 5 per cent in 1949 (Parker 1967: 42).

The housing legislation of this period did not have the effects intended and this calls into question the basis of the evidence on which policy was based. The 1957 Rent Act was designed to remedy underoccupation, immobility, underrepair and underinvestment, and an irrational rent structure but succeeded in exacerbating existing difficulties and producing new problems. The government was ill informed about who private landlords were and how they would respond, did not know how many properties would be decontrolled by the Act, did not appreciate the nature of regional housing shortages and did not take any account of demand or shortages in considering the likely impact of legislation. As a result 'the removal of rent controls which took place between 1957 and 1964 hastened the process of transfer to owner occupation and did little to improve the conditions of rented housing' (Donnison 1967: 237). This encouragement of owner occupation was aided by tax reliefs which increased in value with rising incomes, the abolition of Schedule A tax (tax on the imputed rent associated with home ownership) in 1962, the development of option mortgages (providing a mortgage subsidy for those not benefiting from tax relief on their mortgage payments), leasehold reform (enabling leasehold owners to purchase the freehold on their property), improvement grants and movements in house prices. At the same time, the whole episode was proof that central government lacked the knowledge and understanding to direct policy in a field where local market and other factors determined outcomes and the impact of national measures.

The question of government competence is illustrated in this same era by the debacle of high-rise council building. The media images of failed council housing at the beginning of the twenty-first century are not of the cottage estates and traditional houses with gardens that formed the majority of what local authorities built. Rather they are of multi-storey blocks – of degraded and poorly maintained mass housing estates. The reason why councils switched from building the estates that worked towards an untried alternative is not that the new-style multi-storey and high-rise estates were cheaper to build. Indeed the opposite was the case, with higher rates of subsidy paid by the government to encourage the new style. Why did the government promote a style of high-rise building when there were such strong reservations about it from the outset, and the model was so quickly tarnished and questioned? Dunleavy (1981) concludes that the explanation lay in the attractiveness of a technological short cut to social change. The government was concerned to replace the slums and build new modern housing but did not want to upset the social balance within different districts. It was concerned to keep low-income groups in the inner city, and to constrain the expansion of cities beyond their boundaries. The technological short cut represented by high-rise housing could be presented as in keeping with technical advances and representing the adoption of modern 'best practice'. It suited local government as well as central government, it suited the interests of the construction industry and the design professions, and it was actively promoted by the government, which not only increased subsidies to favour high-rise housing but also relaxed the regulations which previously restricted such development.

Prompted by higher rates of subsidy, the proportion of council dwellings in blocks of flats of five storeys or more increased. Flats represented 23 per cent of all completions of local authority and new town dwellings between 1945 and 1960, but rose rapidly to 52 per cent in 1965 and remained at over 50 per cent until 1973. Construction of very high blocks declined after 1970, while blocks of fewer than five storeys increased. The decline in building high flats was speeded by the technical failures exposed when the Ronan Point block in east London collapsed in May 1968. By then it was already apparent that there were problems with high-rise blocks, especially where families with children were housed in them (see Gittus 1976), that savings in land were negligible and costs excessive. The technological short cut promised by high rise produced developments which responded to the agendas of professionals and national government but left a problematic local legacy which subsequently contributed to the delegitimisation of council housing (Dunleavy 1981).

Between 1945 and 1951 council dwellings were built to a higher standard than recommended in the Dudley report, *Design of Dwellings*, and a three-bedroom house built in this period was on average 37 per cent larger than one built between 1934 and 1939. There were reductions in 'circulation space' in 1951 and reduced living space and equipment followed. Between 1949 and 1953 the average floor area of three-bedroom dwellings fell by 13 per cent. Smaller high-rise and multi-storey flats began to comprise a much higher proportion of all dwellings built. At the same time there was a 'rediscovery' of housing problems and homelessness. The discussion was more about speculation in land and housing, the ineffectiveness of protection for private tenants exposed to unscrupulous landlords, the inflexibility of local authority allocation policies and their treatment of the 'ordinary' households that became homeless in circumstances of continuing housing shortage where it was not easy to negotiate access to housing with the major public and private sector gatekeepers.

The Housing Act 1959 marked a shift towards urban renewal with the improvement of older housing at the heart of policy and this theme was further developed in 1964. The Housing Act 1961 acknowledged that all was not going to plan. It reintroduced a general-needs subsidy, and council house construction began to increase. Housing was a major issue in the 1964 general election, which brought Labour to power for the first time in thirteen years. The new government's objective was to increase local authority production and adopt the standards recommended in the Parker Morris report, *Homes for Today and Tomorrow* (MHLG 1961). At least for a period there was a more positive approach to council housing, although the commitment to home ownership was more strongly stated:

> The expansion of the public programme now proposed is to meet exceptional needs: it is born partly of a short-term necessity, partly of the conditions inherent in modern urban life. The expansion of building for owner-occupation on the other hand is normal: it reflects a long-term social advance which should gradually pervade every region. (MHLG 1965)

The publication of the Parker Morris report in 1961 provided a basis to improve average dwelling size and quality of council housing, but improving overall dwelling space standards had cost implications (an 11 per cent increase for a five-bedspace, two-storey dwelling). By 1964, only 14 per cent of new council dwellings included all Parker Morris standards while 39 per cent met its floorspace standards (Merrett 1979: 104). The wider policy agenda included action to modify the effects of the Rent Act 1957 and deal with the exploitation of private tenants by rogue landlords, personified by Perec Rachman in London and investigated by the Milner Holland committee, which reported in 1965. The Rent Act 1965 introduced 'regulated' and 'fair' rents, but held back from municipalisation of the sector. But it was evident that the death throes of private renting required continuing policy attention.

The rise of home ownership

Alongside the decline of the private landlord and the expansion of municipal landlordism, home ownership grew rapidly, to be the most substantial tenure by the 1960s. It had become the preferred route for investment by the private sector and by professional and financial institutions in the housing sector. It also became the preferred tenure for the mass of the population in Britain.

The origins of mass home ownership go back to working-class organisations in the eighteenth century. Mutual building societies were established to enable groups of people to pool their resources so that they could build their own houses and escape from the rented system, dominated by private landlords. The early examples of mutual building societies emphasised their working-class origins and the extent to which they were the product of demands for better housing from skilled artisans. The early building societies, known as terminating building societies, were organisations designed to assist members to build and buy houses, and they would cease to exist once they had achieved this on behalf of their members. These terminating societies were replaced by permanent societies, which provided loans for house purchase but also served as retail savings associations. They continued to be non-profit, mutual societies, with a strong identification with local communities. As retail banking concerns they enabled small savers to commit their savings to a local institution that was accessible to them and did not make large charges on their investment. These organisations operated within legislation which limited their activities and they concentrated their resources on lending for house purchase.

The expansion of new building in the private sector for purchase by home owners was facilitated, between the wars, by the growth in building society activity. In the post-1945 period, mutual building societies played an important role, supplemented by lending from banks and from local authorities, in enabling the expansion of home ownership. As a result the tenure changed from a relatively privileged, high-income tenure to one which penetrated a long way down the income scale.

Much of the growth of home ownership in this period was through transfer of properties from the privately rented sector and was therefore partly related to decisions by landlords to sell property. Through this process and through new building, the growth of home ownership has provided an important vehicle for the improvement of housing conditions among the mass of the population. Local authority activity to facilitate the expansion of home ownership and the privileged taxation and subsidy treatment afforded by central government to home owners, especially in the period since the mid-1960s, have been important ways of responding to demands for housing. The literature on home ownership emphasises its political perception as a mechanism to achieve political stability and electoral support (see for example Forrest et al. 1990). It was a bulwark against bolshevism. Tax reliefs were important for higher-income groups but began to affect a wider population from the 1960s onwards and specific grants also encouraged and enabled the growth of home ownership as the main parties competed to be seen as the strongest supporter of the owner-occupier. At the same time households which became home owners normally expressed high levels of satisfaction. Through most of the period they experienced an increase in the asset value of their homes and their wealth increased significantly.

The explanation for the growth of home ownership needs to incorporate a number of elements. The preference for home ownership emerging in the later part of the twentieth century was strongly encouraged by policy interventions and affected both demand and supply influences. The comparative advantage associated with that tenure when compared with others (Merrett 1982) was more important than some innate desire for ownership (Saunders 1990). Home ownership had comparative advantage over private renting in terms of property type and condition and arrangements for financing. Even without tax reliefs there were advantages in having housing costs that related to the historic cost of purchase, and the worth of increases in the asset value of the property also became more apparent over time. These elements in preference for home ownership are more compelling than some plausibly contrived 'innate' urge to own. They are likely to remain pertinent as long as family assets and intergenerational transfers continue to be increasingly important parts of the asset-based welfare state (Murie 2007) and provided that the long-term returns from investment in housing are better than from private pensions or other investments.

Conclusions

Political debates around the housing question in Britain have gone through a number of phases and collective action in relation to housing has changed. At least three major phases can be identified. In the first phase housing conditions were extraordinarily poor, and the landlord's interest was dominant. A coalition of interests built up against the private landlord and sought to achieve housing improvements through a different pattern of state intervention. While this demand was particularly associated with the labour movement and the Labour Party responding to the interests of tenants and residents, it is important to note that it also received widespread support from others concerned with the development of the economy and society, health and the threat of civil unrest. While the turning points in policy are associated with the First World War, they represent the combination of a longer process of collective action.

The second phase of policy, between 1919 and the mid-1970s but interrupted by the Second World War, represents one in which the private rented sector was largely abandoned politically and financially. Private sector interests increasingly identified with owner occupation, although it is important to recognise that the majority of council housing was also built by private developers. For a long period there was support for the parallel expansion of home ownership and municipal housing. At the beginning of the 1960s Britain had already changed from being a nation of private renters. The development of council housing marks the first dramatic reorganisation of rented housing provision in Britain. The generation that regarded renting from a private landlord as normal was followed by a generation that regarded renting from the council, or owning your own home, as normal. Council housing and owner occupation had grown alongside one another – both promoted by public policy and private interests. The success of these responses in dealing with the most obvious housing problems was apparent by the mid-1960s. The worst problems of overcrowding, slum housing and the absence of amenities had been removed. This was assisted by increased affluence and economic progress and by demographic changes which resulted in smaller households, contributing to the reduction of overcrowding.

By the early 1960s, however, the confidence generated by the volume of new high-quality housing built since 1945 and the improvement in housing conditions had been shaken. The confidence was tarnished by anxieties about the effects of slum clearance, the development of multi-storey flats and the reduction in standards of new building. It was also affected by the difficulties still being experienced by lower-income households. The decline of the private landlord had removed much of the potential exploitation faced by such households in the housing market but it was not apparent that the tenures that had expanded to replace private renting cared or catered for the households that had hitherto been dependent on it.

In the inter-war years local authorities were building for households which would not otherwise obtain modern dwellings of equivalent standard. But the ability of the poorest households to benefit from this was limited by rent levels and housing management practice involving eviction if rent arrears accumulated. In order to avoid this, minimum income requirements were not uncommon in tenant selection. The switch to slum clearance ended such exclusivity and increased the prospect of council housing reaching the poorest households. In order to keep rents down local authorities were encouraged to build smaller, cheaper houses or to set 'reasonable' rents and provide rent rebates or operate differential rent schemes. However, 'a very large proportion of local authorities ignored the Ministry of Health's advice on the rent problem' (Bowley 1945: 125). Local authorities regarded better-off households as better potential tenants and differential rents were unpopular among tenants because of antagonism to means testing and because they were achieved through increased rents for other tenants rather than passing the costs to society as a whole. In spite of the effects of rent pooling, council housing remained a tenure for the affluent working class and did not generally benefit the worst off, who remained in the private rented sector.

The Housing Corporation was established in this context in 1964. It was tasked with a niche role related to cost rent and co-ownership housing, but the new housing associations that developed in response to the failings of both market and public policy sought a more central role. In practice the Housing Corporation moved towards the housing associations as it acquired roles in relation to both renewal and rehabilitation of older housing and new building of housing let at fair rents.

3

Foundations for a new government agency

The true history of the Housing Corporation starts with its establishment in 1964. However, from the outset, it built on the foundations of the voluntary housing movement and, after 1974, it developed a wider role to promote and regulate this movement. In view of this, the present chapter briefly outlines the earlier development of housing associations and societies and refers to the initiatives that were taken in the period immediately before 1964 and that influenced the decision to establish a new government agency. This chapter draws heavily upon Peter Malpass's book *Housing Associations and Housing Policy: A Historical Perspective* (2000), which sets out the origins of the voluntary housing movement and traces its development in subsequent years. The term 'housing association' is used in current legislation and has come to be commonly used to refer to voluntary, non-profit-making organisations whose main purpose relates to providing housing. Until the 1960s they were more commonly referred to as housing societies, reflecting their legal registration as industrial and provident societies.

The early development of housing associations

Well before a modern housing policy developed, some kind of social housing was provided in Britain by almshouse charities. Almshouses continue to operate to the present day and many of them are registered housing associations, although they represent only a very small part of the not-for-profit housing sector. They have a long history stretching back at least to the twelfth century; Malpass gives the oldest member of the National Housing Federation as the St Lawrence's Hospital charity, based in Cirencester and originally endowed in 1235 for the benefit of two female lepers. He argues that the almshouse model was essentially a medieval solution to a medieval problem. The giving of alms was encouraged by the medieval church, for those who gave alms would benefit in the afterlife. Subsequently the Black Death, the Reformation and the Civil War would all have an impact on almshouse provision. There was a legacy of some very rich and some less well-endowed foundations but their capacity was very small when faced with the housing problems associated with urbanisation and industrialisation. Malpass states (2000: 31–2):

> What can be said with confidence is that by the middle of the nineteenth century social and economic change had reached a point where, although there was a continuing role for almshouses, there was also a need to devise new ways of tackling the problems of housing some sections of the poor in the emergent urban industrial society. Whereas almshouses provided for indigent and dependent elderly people, a group who have always been recognised to be deserving recipients of charitable assistance on account of their inability to work for their living, the problem posed by the growth of industrial capitalism and the creation of the urban working class was altogether different, centring on the question of how to provide for the housing needs of younger, able-bodied people, most of whom had some kind of earned income, or at least some earning capacity.

This book has already outlined government resistance in the nineteenth century to ways of providing for the urban poor other than through the market. The voluntary sector had an independent view and did respond. In effect a new generation of housing societies was set up after 1830 to provide housing for the industrial working class. Malpass (2000) argues that because much of the attention given to these societies has been associated with the evidence that they failed to provide an adequate response to the housing problems at the time, this has tended to obscure the contribution that they did actually make.

The new organisations from this period fall into two principal types: model dwelling companies and charitable trusts. The term 'model dwellings' captures the ambition to provide a model standard that was worthy of imitation and to demonstrate that the market mechanism could work and deliver adequate housing for the poor. Malpass (2000) indicates that the first model dwelling organisation was the Metropolitan Association for Improving the Dwellings of the Industrious Classes, founded in 1841, and goes on to refer to a considerable number of later entrants into the field. Charitable trusts were financed entirely by rich individuals and Malpass refers particularly to the donations by George Peabody that enabled the Peabody trustees to develop estates in London until the 1870s. While charitable trusts invested in endowments and were less interested in the rate of return, model dwelling societies generally depended on raising share capital and loan stock from private individual investors who did expect a return on their capital, albeit a lower one than might have been expected. Nevertheless, the trustees of charitable trusts did generally seek to achieve a positive rate of return, but less than that expected by private individual investors. Malpass (2000) notes that the Peabody Donation Fund sought 3 per cent while the Guinness Trust aimed at 3.5 per cent. The new housing societies of this period included those associated with 'philanthropy at 5 per cent'. Investors who agreed to limit their returns to 5 per cent on their investment were forgoing some of the profit that they would normally expect to receive but were still receiving a profit. However, by limiting it they would provide housing at more affordable rents than otherwise would be the case.

Outside London the activities of model dwelling providers were 'scarcely noticeable' (Ashworth 1954: 84, quoted in Malpass 2000: 37) and even in London the volume of provision by model housing companies was on a modest scale. The charitable trusts were more significant in this respect. The model dwelling companies were associated with small homes and there was severe criticism of the quality and appearance of some of the housing they provided. In order to make the sums add up the density of dwellings was very high, multi-storey buildings were normal and ornamentation was cut to a minimum, giving long, high facades a bleak and featureless appearance (Malpass 2000: 39). These developments were not highly regarded by working-class households and the mechanisms for management were also seen as unfriendly. In contrast, the housing built by the charitable foundations appears to have had much greater appeal and there were waiting lists for much of the housing in this sector. Even in these developments, however, landlords found it difficult to set rents that were really affordable to those on the lowest incomes. Although the Peabody Fund, for example, appears to have housed people on a broad spectrum of incomes, even it generally met the needs of the better-paid labouring class and artisans and clerks. It is this combination of criticisms that has left a largely negative view of the organisations from this era.

Malpass (2000) goes on from this to refer to a different approach to meeting housing problems, pioneered by Octavia Hill. This did seek to work with the poorest but concentrated on improving the management of existing houses rather than incurring the costs and facing the difficult financial dilemmas associated with new building. Rather than establishing a new generation of housing associations, Octavia Hill is associated with developing a different and systematic, albeit autocratic, housing management system which began to influence the way in which various providers of housing sought to provide good accommodation that would meet the needs of lower income groups.

Malpass (2000) is critical of the implicit view, taken by many historians of housing, that the model and even the charitable housing foundations that grew in the second half of the nineteenth century had failed by the 1890s. Whatever their limitations, third-sector provision continued to grow and remained important in the latter part of the nineteenth century and up to the outbreak of the First World War. Malpass argues that there is a case for presenting this period as the era of the charitable trusts because of three major endowments – the Guinness Trust, the Sutton Dwellings Trust and the Samuel Lewis Trust – and he sets out the very considerable contribution to housing made by these trusts, especially in London. Of the major organisations that he refers to only the Sutton Dwellings Trust had a brief to work outside London (Malpass 2000: 61), where the garden city movement was more important. While the academic treatment of the garden city movement tends to be dominated by the ideas of Ebenezer Howard, the practical development on the ground is associated with Port Sunlight on the Wirral peninsula in Cheshire, the Bournville estate in Birmingham and New Earswick outside York. These developments were each of significant size and of high-quality, mixed housing and preceded Letchworth in Hertfordshire, which is seen as the first genuine garden city.

Malpass (2000) goes on to refer to co-partnership societies, which flourished before the First World War, and garden suburbs, which were influenced by the ideas of the garden city movement. What was emerging was the diversity of voluntary organisations, affected by the locations within which they developed, influenced by different individuals and philosophies and adopting different strategies to develop housing for different target groups, although commonly seeking to reach the industrial working classes. This diversity has continued to be a feature in the subsequent periods.

Changing policy contexts

The next phase of development of housing associations occurred against the backdrop of an emerging housing policy. As outlined in the previous chapter, legislation providing powers and then duties began to appear on the statute book and to change the way the housing sector operated. The Housing, Town Planning &c. Act of 1909 referred for the first time to public utility societies, registered under the Industrial and Provident Societies Act 1893. The rules were to prohibit the payment of any interest or dividend at a rate exceeding 5 per cent per annum.

The introduction of rent control in 1915 and the development of housing subsidy in 1919 marked the clearest watershed in the development of housing policy in Britain. Following 1919 there was a marked shift from local authority housing as a small aspiring contributor to housing provision, through very rapid expansion to the acquisition of a permanent role in the provision of rented housing. Against this background the tendency is to imply that housing associations ground to a halt and the story of housing provision is taken over by local authorities and the private sector.

While local authorities emerged from this with the lead role, that should not be taken to mean that housing associations went into decline. They remained a significant, if small, player within the housing provision system. Housing societies in this period also became more visible in the inner city areas, which had been largely ignored by local housing policies. These policies were preoccupied with building new council estates in the growing suburbs rather than in addressing the problems of run-down inner city neighbourhoods. Malpass (2000) has highlighted the significant numbers of new associations established in the early decades of the twentieth century. These include the so-called 'front line' housing societies, such as the William Sutton Trust (Garside 2000) and the Birmingham Copec House Improvement Society (Gulliver 2000), set up by philanthropists to improve slum housing and more focused on the inner city.

Between 1919 and 1933, housing associations found themselves working in difficult economic circumstances and in a policy framework which, if not actually hostile, gave them little scope to expand their work on a large scale (Malpass 2000: 81). Consequently voluntary housing organisations made very little impact in terms of the numbers of houses built or acquired. Nevertheless, Malpass argues that there was a marked increase in the number of new organisations coming into existence and that the new societies, trusts and associations formed after the war amounted to a second wave of voluntary housing providers. By the early 1930s they had begun to generate significant impetus. Malpass gives examples of associations that were active and expanded in this period, including those that were associated with particular employers – especially mining and manufacturing.

While many of the longer-established organisations carried out little new development or acquisition of housing until the mid-1920s, they were still providers of housing and they did become more active in the later period when the difficulties facing any organisation seeking to build housing began to abate. At the same time there were a variety of different housing organisations developing in London and, increasingly, outside London. The sector was marked by growing diversity: as the old model dwelling companies and large charitable trusts became inactive, newer, more energetic organisations were set up (Malpass 2000: 88).

The Moyne committee and its legacy

Recent accounts of the development of housing associations have attached considerable importance to the Ministry of Health's departmental committee on housing under the chairmanship of Lord Moyne. This reported in 1933 and recommended measures that could have encouraged the development of housing associations to a much greater extent. The decision to appoint the Moyne committee was a response to criticisms of government housing policy (Malpass 2000: 94). The Moyne committee report precipitated a struggle that effectively marked the triumph of the local authorities as the main providers of new rented housing for the working class – with the result that the voluntary organisations remained on the margins of housing policy for the next forty years (Malpass 2000: 95).

In the inter-war period local authorities could use their powers to grant loans to public utility societies to achieve housing objectives. The Moyne committee described the difficulties facing public utility societies under existing legislation. Many local authorities were reluctant to use their powers of granting assistance and the period within which repayment must be made was too short to allow low rents to be charged. Advances from the Public Works Loan Board were restricted to two thirds of the estimated value of the properties and the method of valuation meant that in practice the societies usually obtained much less than anticipated. The consequence was that there was very limited development by housing associations through this route.

The Moyne committee proposed the establishment of a Central Public Utility Council (CPUC) to approve societies and their housing projects; it has been argued that this would have been an organisation very similar to the Housing Corporation, which emerged subsequently. The Moyne committee also proposed that local people should be encouraged to form housing societies but where they could not, local authorities would be expected to establish local housing management commissions. Local authorities were also to be encouraged to make use of the proposed powers of compulsory purchase for reconditioning and managing property. Where they declined to do so, public utilities could appeal to the minister of health to obtain similar purchase rights as local authorities.

The terms of reference of the committee ruled out consideration of slum clearance and it concentrated on the question of reconditioning or refurbishment and whether public utility societies could play a greater role in this work. The basis of the approach was that action was needed where private landlords neglected their responsibilities but that local authorities were not best suited nor interested in taking on the management of scattered properties in working-class areas. Consequently local authorities should have compulsory powers to acquire working-class houses in need of reconditioning and which could be given a life of at least twenty years, but they would generally acquire such houses and pass them on to public utility societies to carry out the necessary work and then manage them on Octavia Hill lines (Malpass 2000: 96–7). Where suitable societies did not already exist to do this, new organisations could be established.

Malpass (2000) suggests that the reception of the Moyne report, especially within the Ministry of Health, indicated a lack of support for or confidence in public utility societies. The committee's recommendations were largely rejected and it appears that the strong reservations from local authorities were important in this. There was also concern not to create unfair competition for private enterprise. The committee was very much influenced in its debates by the National Association of Building Societies (NABS), the National Federation of House Builders and the National Federation of Property Owners, which claimed that competition would effectively prevent private builders and investors from re-entering the field of working-class housing (Ministry of Health 1933: 47, quoted in Groves 1971). The consequence was a reluctance to provide subsidised loans or advantageous loans to public utility societies.

The period between the Moyne report and the emergence of the Housing Act 1935 was one in which the public utility societies failed to press home the arguments that they should have an expanded role. Instead the view taken was that local authorities should lead and be left in the position of managing as well as purchasing and reconditioning properties. The Ministry of Health retreated from the Moyne report and the focus on public utility societies faded (Malpass 2000: 101). Policies relating to refurbishment were given less attention than those concerned with overcrowding and the redevelopment of inner city areas, and the role of housing societies in these activities was relatively limited. The new subsidy introduced in 1935 reflected this shift and related to overcrowding.

The government's decision to disregard other Moyne committee recommendations was significant. The proposals to establish the CPUC and a central funding authority would have put housing associations' finances on a sounder basis. The failure to adopt either of these recommendations maintained the marginal position of the voluntary organisations and their dependence on the discretionary co-operation of the elected local authorities, with eligibility for subsidy made subject to associations entering into an agreement with the local authority.

The Housing Act 1935 consolidated the idea of authorised arrangements between housing societies and local authorities. This had been initiated in 1930. It extended the scope of these arrangements to rehousing persons displaced by the local authority from unfit houses, providing housing accommodation for the purpose of relieving overcrowding, carrying out the whole or a new part of the housing work involved in the redevelopment of a congested area and undertaking the alteration and reconditioning of property to serve as working-class housing, bought by the local authority for that purpose. The Act effectively confirmed the subordination of housing associations to the control of local authorities, even though this had been a principle that the Moyne committee had rejected. The legislation was also permissive and there was no requirement to co-operate or work with housing associations, although local authorities were encouraged to do this. The Act empowered local authorities to sponsor and assist housing associations and with the consent of the minister to provide them with loans and grants. An association which provided houses by arrangement with a local authority received the same government subsidy as the authority would itself have done if it had built the houses. However, the responsibility for ensuring that all the loans and subsidies received were properly used rested with the local authority. Thus associations were wholly dependent on local government if they wanted to look beyond charitable and other private sources of finance to fund their building (Lewis and Harden 1982).

Gulliver (2000) indicates how Copec in Birmingham (subsequently part of the Focus housing association and then Midland Heart) worked with Birmingham City Council to use the measures included in the Housing Act 1935. The city council and Copec agreed over types of house, rents chargeable and tenants in order to rehouse people displaced under slum clearance schemes. The first subsidies for new building were obtained in 1936. These were granted to rehouse people displaced from demolished property under the Act and enabled Copec to rehouse not only tenants from some of the city's clearance areas but a few from its own demolished houses. Further subsidy was later obtained under the Act for rehousing people from overcrowded accommodation; however, the absence of public subsidy for reconditioning, Copec's core business, remained a major constraint on its growth. The Act therefore enabled some limited development but was not a springboard to a new phase of growth.

The Housing Act 1935 also empowered the housing minister to recognise and extend a grant in aid of expenses to a central promotional body to advise and assist housing associations, to which some voluntary housing bodies responded, setting up their own trade association, the National Federation of Housing Societies (NFHS), in June 1935. It was recognised in this role and received an annual grant, although the bulk of its income came from membership subscriptions. Waddilove (1962: 128) has observed that, if the amount of the grant was an indication of the importance the minister attached to the work of the federation, then his expectations were clearly modest. The federation, although it succeeded in representing housing associations, was unable to provide what Waddilove describes as 'corporately organised services' such as legal and procedural advice, advice on the purchase of land or architectural services.

Malpass (2000) emphasises that the debate in this period relates to continuing issues of accountability and who should provide the lead role in the provision of housing promoted through public policy. The Moyne committee report was discussed in terms of whether it was possible to take housing out of politics. Would taking control away from directly elected bodies, including local authorities, and moving to voluntary organisations (public utility societies) mean a less politicised and more rational approach to housing provision? An alternative view was that the attempt to foist public utility societies on the policy community was a direct attack on the involvement of local authorities and local politicians and an attempt to demunicipalise the housing programme. A third interpretation is that the notion of taking housing out of politics was primarily about improving technical efficiency.

In addition Malpass (2000) draws attention to new and very large associations set up as part of a strategy to address problems in the regions most affected by economic decline and unemployment in the 1930s. The North Eastern Housing Association was supported under the Special Areas

(Development and Improvement) Act 1934, which enabled funding to be channelled to housing associations for housing purposes whereas it could not provide assistance to local authorities to build houses. A similar arrangement applied with the establishment of the Scottish Special Housing Association in 1937. Both of these associations were registered under the Companies Act 1929 and had no share capital or membership beyond the appointed members of their council of management. It is relevant also to note the failure of local authorities to use the powers provided under the Housing Act 1935 to buy run-down houses on behalf of associations and to transfer them at cost (Malpass 2000).

Associations could appeal to the minister against a local authority which refused to enter into an arrangement and thus entitle them to government subsidy, but this was little used, even though in many areas local government was indeed most reluctant to co-operate.

Diversity and distinctive roles

The reluctance to enter into real partnerships with housing associations is a continuing feature of the development of housing policy and does not appear to have been restricted to local authorities. In 1945, during the reconstruction period, the minister of health, Aneurin Bevan, emphasised a willingness to consider sympathetically, on their specific merits, all applications for financial assistance to be given by local authorities to housing associations, but he was not prepared to encourage housing authorities to farm out their housing powers (Malpass 2000: 119).

Against this background and the explosion of local authority house building in the early post-war period, housing associations remained at the margins of policy. In most cases local authorities were driving the agenda themselves and did not seek support from housing associations. There was no programme either centrally or locally which sought to use the diversity of organisations within the housing sector in an effective way, and the preoccupation of policy led to a concentration on local authority provision. The dominant view in this period was that the voluntary sector should supplement rather than duplicate public services and should focus on areas where the public sector was not able to do enough. In this environment the role of housing societies and associations in providing housing for elderly people began to receive more attention (Malpass 2000: 123). Specialist societies for older people began to become more prominent. Other kinds of specialist society included associations promoted by employers or groups of employers in particular industries, which were established as industrial societies, their main purpose being to provide for employees who needed to be housed within reach of their place of work but might not qualify for a council house. Malpass (2000) gives the example of the British Overseas Airways Corporation developing Airways Housing Trust Ltd and refers to numerous industrial housing societies set up in the period up to 1960, when the total stood at eighty-four. He also refers to the development of self-build societies, established by people banding together to build their own houses.

Different eras produced different types of housing society but the societies established in earlier periods continued to operate. The diversity that was identified as a characteristic of the housing association movement in the nineteenth century had become even greater by the 1960s. Malpass provides some indications of the growth of the housing association movement by referring to the overall membership of the NFHS. This rose steadily during the years after the war from 180 in 1944 to 679 in 1961 (Malpass 2000: 127). The NFHS at this stage, however, was not a strong trade organisation; the diversity of associations and slow growth in the number of units provided by housing associations were more characteristic than any strong lobbying position in relation to housing.

Nevertheless there had been important changes that affected the way the housing association sector developed. The Housing Act 1949 enabled housing associations to receive direct financial assistance to recondition properties they already owned (but not to purchase run-down housing) and provided grants for improvement and conversion, at the discretion of local authorities and where the property was judged to have a useful life of at least thirty years. Rent controls, which had applied to housing association properties, were removed by the Housing Repairs and Rents Act 1954. This enabled housing associations to ease their financial difficulties by raising rents and meant that they could consider greater involvement in grant-aided improvement work. While this was seen as a distinct boost to prospects, Malpass (2000: 129) argues that by 1956 optimism had given way to pessimism. As in previous periods, however, the diversity of the housing association movement increased again as new organisations were formed to meet newly identified needs. The example Malpass uses is housing provided for new arrivals, especially from Commonwealth countries, during the 1950s; and the specific example he gives is the Birmingham Friendship Housing Association. At the same time he identifies that many of the older housing trusts were reinvesting in their existing stock, which was now of some considerable age.

It is important, at this stage, to recognise the slowness with which the government had come to recognise the changing nature of housing problems: how much the housing situation had changed between the period of planning for reconstruction and the period 15 and 20 years later. This particularly applied to the slowness to recognise that the continued decline of private renting had left a gap that needed to be filled. Government did recognise the special needs element in this gap and housing associations were encouraged to move in to provision for older people and other groups. Malpass (2000) also refers to hostels for single young people and some homes for families.

New initiatives

By the early 1960s the changed dynamics of the housing sector could no longer be ignored. The political debate had moved on from the complacency of Macmillan's 'You've never had it so good' to criticisms of 'thirteen wasted years' of Conservative government. The evidence that the changing nature of the private rented sector was creating severe tensions and stresses experienced by particular groups was overwhelming. It was visible in relation to special needs groups and particular social groups but also in particular parts of the city, especially inner city areas where changes in occupiers enabled landlords to escape from the provisions of the Rent Acts. The problems associated with winkling out tenants (through the application of unreasonable pressure and small incentives) and exploiting those who were not aware of their rights or whose rights had been reduced because they had started out as unprotected tenants had become scandalous. It was in this climate that the Housing Corporation was set up. The government, seeking to respond to another perceived gap in the market, saw the need for a programme to provide cost rent and co-ownership housing for more affluent groups rather than the very poor. But existing housing associations did not appear to be interested and a new approach was needed to stimulate private landlords or other organisations to take this on.

The continuing decline of the private rented sector and the evidence of ordinary families' problems in accessing rented housing began to stimulate a debate about other forms of provision and in particular alternatives to the privately rented sector for households which could afford reasonable rents. The first experiment that broke the mould of a monopoly by local authorities was a very modest one. In 1961, £25 million of Exchequer funds were made available to promote two new types of housing society. These were promoted through the agency of the NFHS. The societies themselves were to find 5 per cent of the total costs of site and buildings, while the remainder would be borrowed from the NFHS at current rates of interest payable over a period of sixty years and funded through the Exchequer funds given to the NFHS. The experiment contributed to the formation of the Housing Corporation in 1964. Effectively, the Corporation was established to assume the role that the NFHS had taken in the experimental phase and there is some reason to believe that the government wanted an organisation that was more independent of housing associations rather than using the trade association to promote and develop housing societies.

At this stage, under Section 19 of the Housing Act 1957 local authorities had the power to 'promote', 'extend' or 'assist' housing associations. Most housing associations obtained their loans through the agency of the local authority, under this section or the provisions of the same Act. Leaving aside the financial considerations, the arrangements with local authorities remained problematic. Local authority powers were permissive and therefore the response towards associations tended to be patchy. In some areas there was a strong antagonism towards housing associations. This was sometimes related to the enthusiasm of Labour-controlled councils for municipal housing and an objection to philanthropic and middle-class housing providers, but in other cases it was Conservative-controlled councils that were opposed to housing associations – perhaps for the same reason.

There were also difficulties involved in negotiating with local authorities, and the variation in the ways that local authorities worked meant that things were not straightforward for housing associations that worked across administrative boundaries. Research published in 1970 highlighted a number of inadequacies, especially with regard to helping to find suitable land or property for conversion, delays in negotiations with local authorities and the lack of co-ordination between local authority departments (CURS 1970). This survey also revealed that a third of the authorities interviewed had had no dealings with housing associations whatever and several were clearly, and understandably, confused over the apparently idiosyncratic distinctions between housing associations and housing societies. The housing association sector increasingly referred to itself both as voluntary and as a movement at this stage; local authorities were not performing efficiently and enthusiastically as promotional agents for the voluntary housing movement.

Some of the fault no doubt rested with the housing associations themselves and the confusion about their titles remained something that would get in the way of effective working relationships. The biggest problems, however, arose in relation to finance. Again, the later research identified reluctance among local authorities to work with housing associations. The reasons suggested were various. Some collaborations were refused for technical reasons; in other cases local authorities seemed to distrust the abilities or the intentions of housing associations. Associations could, in theory, apply directly for a loan to the Public Works Loan Board under Section 47 of the Housing (Financial Provisions) Act 1958, but the research identified only two associations that had made successful applications in the previous ten years and an official of the board referred to this as an obsolescent statutory power (CURS 1970: 24).

Alternatively and for a similar variety of reasons, local authorities chose not to grant the full 100 per cent advance, or else the conditions required to establish an agreement proved unacceptable to housing associations. In this respect, nomination rights proved to be a bone of contention. One of the most recurring criticisms of local authorities, however, was that of delays, particularly with regard to approval from finance and planning committees. In view of these considerations it was highly unlikely that housing associations would make any significant contribution while local authorities remained their major source of finance. Whether by design or because of administrative failings, local authorities did not provide the supporting environment that enabled housing associations to use their expertise and energy to contribute significantly to the housing drive. Notwithstanding this there were some housing associations that developed successful links with individual local authorities: for example, Harloe et al. (1974) refers to successful working relationships between housing associations and some London boroughs.

In the London context, however, it is important to recognise that some of the antagonism to housing associations related to the politics of housing between inner and outer London; while the Greater London Council had facilitated the rehousing of inner London residents to outer London boroughs, there was a general resistance by outer London boroughs to importing needy households, and the housing association development in outer London would be likely to speed up that process. The resistance of development by outer London boroughs can then be seen partly as related to their attitude to the general movement of population and the management of their administrative area.

Accounts of the new phase in the development of housing associations that emerges in the 1960s emphasise the changing housing environment following the post-war development of council housing and the decline of private renting. A lack of choice of landlord or tenure began to become a feature of debates about housing. Private landlords were not providing good quality housing and slum clearance was beginning to reduce the quantity of housing that they offered. Better quality privately rented housing was increasingly being transferred to owner occupation. At the same time local authorities, which drove the slum clearance programme and whose contribution dramatically improved the standards and quality of housing, were monopoly landlords. They had very strong rules of allocation and access, and of management, and those who did not fit within the regime offered by council housing found that they had very little choice.

It is not the intention in this discussion to elaborate upon this story, although it should be mentioned that there are some key groups that evidently were finding it very difficult to access council housing. These included non-standard household types, lone parents, new migrant groups, people with disabilities, people who had not been long-term residents in areas, and people who had difficulties in maintaining a tenancy and who required support. The management style of local authorities in many cases meant that these groups were either excluded or offered a very limited choice.

The Milner Holland report of 1965 and research on homelessness (Greve 1964) as well as the more widely publicised television play *Cathy Come Home* (1966) drew attention to the problems faced by ordinary families as well as those who had particular needs and problems. Although there had been dramatic improvements in the quality and supply of housing, reductions in overcrowding and sharing and in slum housing conditions, there were groups for whom this had not generated successful housing outcomes. The system was not working well for households leaving the private rented sector, those with lower incomes, those dependent on benefits, larger families and those from minority ethnic groups.

Despite changes in the precise terms of subsidy introduced by successive statutes, the type of support obtained by associations did not fundamentally alter between the Housing Act 1935 and the Housing Act 1961. The background to the change in 1961 was the establishment by the Ministry of Housing and Local Government, in April 1960, of a working party on building to let, to which it invited the Building Societies Association, as the NABS was now called, and the National Federation of Building Trades Employers (but not the NFHS or the Co-operative Party) (Malpass 2001). The objective was to find a way to stimulate investment in private renting and it was considered that some kind of non-profit-making housing co-operative trust might be appropriate, along lines already established in Scandinavia (Malpass 2001: 239). As a result the Housing Act 1961 included provision for a scheme to encourage housing associations to build unsubsidised dwellings with the assistance of government loans (through the Public Works Loan Board) that would provide up to 100 per cent of the necessary capital finance for the project. The sum of £25 million was made available in England and Wales to provide 100 per cent advances to finance cost rent housing schemes and a few experimental schemes in co-ownership.

Practically all the £25 million was committed by May 1964. A similar pilot scheme had been undertaken in Scotland under the Housing (Scotland) Act 1962 and some £3 million had been committed there. Although the Act spoke of arrangements between the minister and housing associations, the NFHS undertook the examination of projects and the rejection of those thought unsuitable. Most of the funds went towards cost rent schemes, with eighty such schemes in England and Wales, involving 5,540 dwellings built by thirty-nine societies (CHAC 1971: 36). Malpass (2001) questions how far the experiment enabled by the 1961 Act was a success in view of the fact that the policies that emerged from it did not continue to give responsibility to the NFHS but set up the Housing Corporation to do the job. He quotes Emsley (1986: 232) to suggest that the NFHS had failed to impress the ministry with its capabilities (Malpass 2001: 240). On the other hand, the experiment did indicate that there was potential for a continuing scheme of that type. It generated an alternative to council renting and home ownership and drew in private finance. It was sufficiently successful to merit its development under the Housing Act 1964, but the NFHS was not the right vehicle to take it forward. Lewis and Harden comment (1982: 123):

> This remarkable example of extra-statutory 'delegation' of a key process in a novel policy departure to a private body meant that whilst the '£25m scheme' was the first government support for housing associations that was not confined to local authority channels, the government avoided direct responsibility for the initial scrutiny of potential schemes. The government had regarded their £25m as essentially a pump-priming sum to stimulate new investment in this type of rented housing by private landlords. Although in this respect the scheme failed completely, it was otherwise accounted highly successful since the money available was rapidly used to create new housing units and the government came to envisage the provision of rented housing by associations as a way of filling the gap left by the continuing decline of the privately rented sector.

If the experiment was a success it related to cost rent provision. Only 102 co-ownership dwellings were completed in five schemes under the 1961 Act. 'This initial experiment in co-ownership can therefore be regarded as a success on a very moderate scale [CHAC 1971: 55]'. Co-ownership had not been mentioned in the 1961 legislation and the analogy with owner occupation had not been recognised as a reason for allowing tax relief on mortgage repayments – the Finance Act 1963 extended such reliefs to co-ownership. There were other difficulties, associated with the length of leases, the amount of deposits and whether by making regular payments co-owners were really purchasing a share in the freehold. All of these factors would need to be resolved before co-ownership would take off.

Some of the published accounts emphasise the influence of co-operative ideas on the development of the £25 million scheme and later co-ownership schemes promoted by the Housing Corporation after 1964. This is logical because of the influence of investigations of European, particularly Swedish and Norwegian, experience in co-operative housing in the lead-up to the legislation of 1961. Interest in the potential of co-operative housing was initiated by individuals from the voluntary housing movement and the subject was taken up by the Ministry of Housing and Local Government, which supported the enquiry work. But the key enthusiasts for co-operative housing appear to have been excluded from the working parties and kept at arm's length from the policy discussion.

Clapham and Kintrea (1987) note that British policy makers and researchers had been visiting Scandinavia and reporting on the success of housing co-operatives for many years (see also Waddilove 1962). They refer to lobbying by Harold Campbell of the Co-operative Party and by Lewis Waddilove of the Joseph Rowntree Memorial Trust and note that the White Paper that preceded the legislation of 1961, *Housing in England and Wales*, stated: 'Schemes of co-operative ownership on lines already established in the Scandinavian countries and elsewhere will also qualify for approval, and the government hope that housing associations will take the opportunity to experiment in this field [quoted in CHAC 1971].' They also refer to the statement of Sir Keith Joseph in winding up the parliamentary debate: 'I am sure that we all hope that we shall soon have in this country examples of the co-operative housing that has served the people of Scandinavia so well [quoted in CHAC 1971].' While this makes the case that attention was paid to Scandinavian co-operative housing experience, it does not establish that it had considerable influence. In introducing the Bill, the minister for housing and local government, Henry Brooke, also referred to his hope that co-operative housing associations would spring up as a result of the Bill and to their value 'in developing mutual responsibility based upon home ownership' (quoted in CHAC 1971). This is not the language of the committed co-operator and elsewhere the reference to co-operative influence is more cautious. The co-operative movement did not mount any consistent campaign and its parliamentary representatives were mostly silent on housing co-operatives (Clapham and Kintrea 1987).

In discussing co-ownership societies, CHAC (1971) refers to co-ownership as a halfway house between renting and owner occupation and acknowledges links both with earlier British experiments in co-operative housing and with Scandinavian examples, but it states: 'The Scandinavian example prompted the British government to leave the way open for the development of co-ownership in this country, although the emphasis was placed upon the provision of cost rent housing [CHAC 1971: 53–4].' This picture of a reluctant endorsement rather than strong enthusiasm fits with what emerged. It helps to explain why there were such differences in practice between co-ownership as it developed in Britain and Scandinavian models – not least in terms of who developed the form of housing and how it was presented to potential residents. The subsequent history includes continuing evidence that there were enthusiasts for co-operative housing in positions of influence but it fails to demonstrate that either they or the ideas from Scandinavia had any wide influence on policy or practice.

Conclusions

Housing associations passed through a series of phases of development in the industrial era. While some of the big players in today's housing association movement, the Peabody and Guinness Trusts for example, were established in the nineteenth century, there are examples of distinctive associations from other eras. There were, however, a variety of reasons why local authorities rather than these organisations came to lead local housing policy and, in the period following 1919, became the principal alternative, as a source of rented housing, to the declining private landlord. Housing associations continued to exist but they were small organisations and in many parts of the country were largely irrelevant.

The Housing Corporation's establishment in 1964 following the experiment set up under the Housing Act 1961 marked a small step to encourage housing societies to respond to a particular perceived gap in the market. This was not the first time that this had happened and indeed the history of the voluntary sector had been one of responding to new needs and opportunities rather than maintaining a fixed and unchanging role. Because of this, the sector had started out diverse and had become more so over time – such that it was hardly a 'sector' at all. It had, however, never been the favoured vehicle for state housing policy. It had developed in specific contexts when the government was reluctant to intervene in housing and preferred to rely on the market, and it had adopted new and specialist roles while local authorities were the preferred vehicles for active (and more restricted) state intervention. The experiment under the 1961 Act was regarded by some as successful and there were various stakeholders in the private sector who could see opportunities in its extension. There were also some who saw the potential of co-ownership as a different form of tenure and as the vanguard in developing a distinctive co-operative sector in Britain. The decision to continue the experiment and set up the Housing Corporation to oversee it was announced in May 1963, well before the full impact of the experiment could be assessed. It reflected a continuing conviction that there was a need to stimulate new activity and organisations rather than evidence of the success of the experiment.

The role set out for the Housing Corporation in 1964 was wholly consistent with the government's practice of seeking to supplement the role of local authorities rather than to compete with them. The decision to set up a new body rather than use the NFHS can not reasonably be regarded as any more unusual than if the NFHS had taken on the continuing role in developing a new funding scheme. Setting up the Housing Corporation was an innovative step at this stage but it did not mean bringing housing associations in from the cold. Housing associations remained outside the main focus of policy but, as in previous eras, responded in their own ways to the gaps in provision, the problems left by the decline of the private rented sector and the deficiencies in its management. While the Housing Corporation was to stimulate the development of a new generation of co-ownership and cost rent housing associations, a separate generation of housing associations was emerging alongside, although not because of the Corporation.

4

First steps: cost rent and co-ownership 1964–74

Introduction

The White Paper *Housing*, published in May 1963, announced the intention to establish the Housing Corporation to stimulate the development of housing societies and lend to them. The Corporation would also have powers to buy land for societies and assist in development. The housing developed under its auspices was designed to fill what had been identified as an emerging gap in the housing market associated with the decline of the private rented sector. This was not affordable housing as might be expected today, but housing for middle- or higher-income groups who wanted neither to buy nor to rent from the council, but could not find modern housing matching their choices within the rented sector. Because the assumption was that this did not involve a need for subsidised housing, an innovative approach involving mixed public and private finance was involved. Cost rent or co-ownership housing would be planned and promoted by housing societies and two thirds of the finance would be provided by building societies, with the government, through the Housing Corporation, providing the balance. As the government's loan would be a second charge, the risk borne by the building societies was very low.

The Housing Act 1964 built on the experience of the 1961 experiment to support new activity by housing societies. Although the failure of the National Federation of Housing Societies to impress ministers with its operation of the 1961 experiment may have been important, Lewis and Harden (1982) state that, when it was suggested that the experiment become a new continuing scheme, the NFHS requested the establishment of a new institution to run it. Consequently, the Housing Corporation was created to fulfil that role under the Housing Act 1964. The Corporation was constituted by its board (initially of nine members), whose members were appointed by the housing minister to part-time, salaried positions. The chairman and deputy chairman were also appointed by the minister. Malpass (2000: 138) states that the NFHS was given assurances that the Housing Corporation would be independent, not an offshoot of the ministry, and issues of independence have been a continuing feature. The objective was to secure the formation of strongly organised housing societies in the main centres of population, the Corporation operating throughout Great Britain (but not Northern Ireland).

The legislation establishing the Housing Corporation had been proposed and passed under a Conservative government but the general election of October 1964 returned a Labour government for the first time for thirteen years and Labour remained in office until 1970. Labour's stance in opposition had been much less favourable to the private landlord than had the Conservative government's. Between 1952 and 1961 the Labour Party had developed a policy of municipalisation for the private rented sector although there was a moderation of this position after 1961 (Wicks 1970). The Housing Corporation survived changes in government in 1964 and again in 1970. However, the nuances of what ministers wanted changed. The original agenda of stimulating new investment in rented housing by private landlords was overlaid with reference to the promotion of co-operatives or new rented housing for lower-income groups: the Corporation started by meaning different things to different people and the need to resolve these differences came to a head with the new policies introduced by the Conservatives in 1970. The Corporation's early years were also affected by the economic turbulence marking the period. Inflation and high interest rates affected the viability both of cost rent and co-ownership housing. At the same time the concern with older inner-city housing generated pressures for action from a new generation of housing associations and changing government priorities. The ability of the Housing Corporation to adopt a wider remit meant that it represented a valuable resource in a new context and the transition to a more sustainable role closer to the heart of housing policy consolidated its position.

Establishing the organisation

The White Paper proposed the establishment of the Housing Corporation with powers to make loans to housing societies, which would be required to be registered as industrial and provident societies. Many of the cost rent associations which had been formed to take advantage of the pilot scheme under the Housing Act 1961 were expected to extend their activities as soon as the Corporation was functioning. However, there was a considerable gap between the time when all the money made available under the pilot scheme had been committed and the time when the Corporation began operation. Inevitably this meant some loss of momentum and although valuable lessons had been learnt about cost renting, very little practical experience of co-ownership had been gained.

The Housing Corporation commenced operation on 1 September 1964. Its board and key staff had already been appointed and its early actions were to locate their headquarters in central London, initially at 55 Park Lane, on what were described as 'very favourable terms'. The staffing of the Corporation in this first phase is the subject of comment by some of those recollecting the early years. The creation of the Corporation almost exactly coincided with the formal end of empire and the closure of the Colonial Office. A number of experienced colonial civil servants were available for other duties as the residual responsibilities of the Colonial Office passed to the Commonwealth Office. While this experienced cohort of civil servants included some who proved extremely successful in their new roles others found it less easy to adapt. The emerging culture of the organisation reflected this recruitment, as did the membership of the board, and its style generated some antagonism especially from the more radical elements within the housing association movement and among lobbying groups.

The first meeting of the Corporation was held on 14 September 1964 with Admiral of the Fleet Sir Caspar John in the chair and Herbert Ashworth as deputy chairman. Thereafter the board met fortnightly to draw up the main lines of policy and to settle procedural arrangements. It referred to consultation with the minister of housing and local government and a long list of agencies: the Registrar of Friendly Societies, the Building Societies Association (BSA), the Valuation Department of the Inland Revenue, the National Building Agency, the NFHS and various other official and professional bodies. At an early meeting with the minister of housing, Richard Crossman, who seemed very much on the Corporation's side, John and Ashworth had a cordial reception and discussed tax, interest rates, control of urban building land, rent restriction and the financing of projects by loans from the Exchequer and from building societies (HCBM 23/11/64).

Work went ahead with furnishing and equipping the Housing Corporation's offices, recruiting and training staff, drafting formal documents such as model rules and mortgage deeds, and preparing a brochure giving general information about the work of the Corporation and its relationship with housing societies.

A more detailed practice note for housing societies was also drafted and systems operating in Scandinavian countries were considered by the board (HCBM 9/11/64). By the beginning of January 1965 the Corporation was able to announce through the press that it was ready to do business. Copies of its brochure were sent to government departments, local housing authorities, Citizens Advice Bureaux, the NFHS and numerous institutions and private persons who had made preliminary enquiries. Arrangements had been established for the provision of legal advice, finance, a common seal, meetings and liaison with building societies. The chairman stated that he was extremely anxious to maintain public interest in cost rent and co-ownership housing until the Corporation was ready to do business in a practical way. It was essential to 'keep the kettle on the boil' – launch a publicity campaign, set up regional offices and develop advisory services for embryo societies.

The early reports of the Housing Corporation are distinct from the flamboyant and colourful documents of later years. They were printed as House of Commons papers in exactly the same format as others presented to Parliament. They were published by Her Majesty's Stationery Office as black print on white, octavo paper with no illustrations or diagrams. The first report, for the period 1 September 1964 to 31 March 1965, was presented to the minister of housing and local government, the secretary of state for Scotland and the secretary of state for Wales.

Duties

Any assumptions that the Housing Corporation would merely act as a conduit for finance and as an advisory and promotional body were misplaced. The Corporation used its position to ensure that housing associations registered under rules drawn up with the Registrar of Industrial and Provident Societies. The first report of the Corporation stated that its efforts would be directed to ensuring that the housing society movement played a significant part in the provision of the country's housing. It saw its main duties as:

1. to promote and organise cost rent and co-ownership housing societies and through them to stimulate the building of houses and flats to let or for co-ownership;
2. to help the societies in every way and more particularly to assist them with their development schemes, giving advice where necessary on legal, architectural and other matters;

3. to join with the building societies and other financial institutions in providing finance for housing society schemes.

The Housing Act 1964 placed a general duty on the Corporation to promote and assist the development of housing societies. These were societies registered under the Industrial and Provident Societies Act 1893, not trading for profit and established for the purpose (solely or among others) of constructing, improving or managing houses. There were two distinct types of society: one which kept houses available for letting – cost rent societies – and one which provided houses exclusively for occupation by its members – co-ownership societies. The latter had two different forms: founder societies, which built and developed for co-ownership and could also be involved in cost rent housing, and successor societies, formed by their members once dwellings were occupied. The Corporation had been given power to make loans to a cost rent or a co-ownership society to meet the whole or any part of any expenditure incurred by the society in carrying out its objects. There was provision for up to £100 million of Exchequer money to be placed at the disposal of the Corporation for this purpose. This figure was increased periodically in subsequent years. The plans were for mixed public and private finance. Normally it was expected that building societies or other financial institutions would lend two thirds of the capital required to finance housing schemes, the remaining third coming from the Corporation on a second mortgage. In effect this was a mechanism designed to encourage building societies to lend on cost rent and co-ownership housing by reducing the risk associated with such lending.

As the Housing Corporation's mortgage would be a second mortgage in the event of any problems, the building societies would have the first claim and their investment would consequently be secure. In considering these arrangements it is important to recognise that the regulation of building societies at this time restricted their lending to housing and excluded personal or other loans for wider purposes. Building societies' capacity to lend was also directly related to their ability to attract investment from the retail sector – the individual account holder. They were not able to borrow on the wholesale market – from other institutions. This was the era of mortgage rationing, where lenders were driven by the flow of investment rather than the demand for borrowing. If the demand increased it made no difference – the amount lent was determined by the flow of investment funds. In this context a commitment to lend to housing societies meant fewer funds available for mortgages sought by individual households and investors with the lender.

The Corporation had received ministerial directions setting out the terms under which it could make loans to societies under the Housing Acts and receive Exchequer advances and the arrangements for repayment of loans it made. Such loans would bear interest at a rate of 0.25 per cent per annum above the rate recommended by the council of the BSA to its members for advances made to owner-occupiers, and the loan rate would vary with that rate. Any loans were repayable with interest over a period not exceeding forty years.

The Act of 1964 also provided reserve powers to acquire land and to build and manage houses. Compulsory purchase powers were also available as a last resort. Although they were rarely used, they were of critical importance, for example in Scotland. The Corporation's main job, however, was to develop a strongly organised movement of housing societies which would search out and acquire land, prepare schemes and build houses to let at cost rents or on the basis of group ownership without profit and without subsidy. The target group for these societies was people who wanted a modern house and were able to pay what it cost. They were people who would not normally be looking to local authorities to provide them with a house and who for various reasons did not seek individual home ownership. This was a clear view of a distinct part of the market that had shrunk as part of the more general decline of the privately rented sector and the transfer of the better stock within it to owner occupation. This had left a privately rented sector that did not include modern or desirable houses attractive to people who did not wish to, or perhaps were not able to, access council housing or, permanently or temporarily, become home owners.

The Corporation's first report set out its approach to forming and registering housing societies. For non-profit-making cost rent landlords, the founder members comprised the management committee and it was seen as advisable for them to have access to specialised knowledge in order to draw up housing schemes, work out the costs, get the contracts, arrange the building work and then deal with lettings and management. For that reason the Corporation advised embryo societies to include professional and business people (including architects, surveyors, lawyers and accountants) in their management committee. When an application for registration was made, the Corporation would call for particulars of the proposed founding members, including their occupations, professional qualifications, commercial and financial interests and similar information, before deciding whether the society was suitable for registration under the Act and to receive loans (HCAR 1964/5).

The first report also identified the wide variety of people to be catered for by cost rent schemes as including those whose work necessitated their moving from place to place for relatively short periods of duty and who found it an expensive and tiresome business to be buying and selling properties each time they moved. For a co-ownership society, membership would ultimately be determined by the people who would collectively own and manage the dwellings they occupied as individuals. In the early stages it was recognised that it would be useful for the society to have members with professional skills, and provision was made in the rules for these members to drop out if they did not wish to take up the lease of a house when it became available. The drafting of the co-ownership rules presented a large number of legal and technical difficulties and the model rules were not formally approved by the Registrar of Friendly Societies until shortly after the end of the financial year. No societies were registered during the period covered by the first report but numerous groups had been interviewed and were ready to proceed as soon as the documents were ready (HCAR 1964/5).

The Corporation also set out whom it believed co-ownership would appeal to. This included many kinds of people, including those nearing retirement who were not adequately provided for by existing arrangements, who wanted the security of a permanent home but found it difficult or impossible to get any mortgage at all, let alone one of forty years, and who might have insufficient capital to be able to buy in the ordinary way. The man or woman who wanted advantages similar to those of private ownership, without the problems and expense of buying and selling, could find that co-ownership was the answer. Sir Caspar John set out the position clearly:

> I should like to emphasise that it is no part of our business to encroach on the preserves of either the local authorities or private builders. Our job is to supplement, not to supplant, existing agencies, to fill the gap between the council house for rent and the private house for sale. We shall certainly work in close co-operation with the local authorities, and we hope that where they can they will make land available for housing society schemes. (John 1965: 112)

Setting out

The first meeting of the Housing Corporation board was attended by three representatives from the Ministry of Housing and Local Government and one from the Scottish Development Department. The first part of the meeting included a discussion of what was expected of the Housing Corporation, led by the government officials present. The direction given by the minister would be general in character and the day-to-day work would be in the Corporation's hands. The Corporation was expected to encourage the development of cost rent and co-ownership housing schemes at roughly equal rates. In the early stages it might be necessary to devote more time to co-ownership since it had not been possible to get more than a few of these societies going under the £25 million pilot loan scheme. The view was expressed that the Corporation need have no doubts or fears about the demand for both forms of housing provision. In the ministry's view it would be preferable to have assurances from a building society that a loan would be forthcoming right from the start of an approved housing scheme, and that advances were being paid to a housing society as the work progressed, rather than for the Corporation to finance the project through to completion and then ask a building society to make a loan on it. There was, however, no legal bar to this. The final draft of the financial directions that the ministry would issue to the Corporation were under consideration by the Treasury and it was hoped they would be available within a week or so. (HCBM 14/9/64).

The Corporation would be expected to encourage the new housing societies to build to high standards, commensurate with the rents needed to service the costs and the demand from people willing to pay the rents of better-quality houses. The Corporation would serve Scotland as well as England and Wales. Because of the low rents charged by local authorities in Scotland, it could well be that the main emphasis there would be on co-ownership societies. The Housing Act 1964 provided for the Scottish Special Housing Association to act as agent for the Corporation and it was thought that the services of its technical staff could be used for the architectural examination of building projects. It would be essential, however, to set up a Scottish office of the Corporation to deal with publicity and enquiries, the formation of societies, the financing of schemes and liaison with the Scottish Development Department.

The Corporation could make advances only to the new types of society defined in the Act. It would be necessary to draft new model rules on which a society could be registered and these would need to be agreed with the Registrar of Friendly Societies, the BSA and the Ministry of Housing. The cost rent rules would follow the model drawn up for the pilot loan scheme and it should be possible to clear them quickly. The registrar had said, however, that he was not satisfied with the model rules drawn up for the experimental co-ownership associations and the drafting of an acceptable model might take longer.

At the end of March 1965, thirty-one housing societies had been registered and others were in the process of formation. The practice notes published by the Housing Corporation stated that societies should be concerned primarily with new building in well-populated and expanding areas where there was a need and a demand for housing accommodation. There were no rigid limits to the size of developments, but cost rent societies were advised to think initially in terms of estates of forty to sixty units. For co-ownership societies, smaller estates of ten to thirty dwellings were referred to because these schemes were for people who would be responsible for managing collectively the houses that they occupied individually. All housing societies were expected to aim at high standards of layout, design, building, internal finishes and fittings and to follow the recommendations made by the Parker Morris report in 1961 (see Chapter 2). Once a society had found a site suitable for development, the advice of the district valuer would be sought about the current open market value and the likely demand for the accommodation at the level of rents proposed. The development proposals would then be drawn up in consul- tation with the district valuer using the standard form provided by the Housing Corporation and including proposals related to the building society or other financial institutions to which it was looking for two thirds of the capital cost. If the district valuer and the prospective first mortgagees confirmed that the proposals were *prima facie* acceptable, a formal submission would be made to the Corporation to approve the scheme for loan purposes. The board subsequently agreed (HCBM 10/1/66) that standards of housing promoted under the Corporation's aegis should aim to be as far above the Parker Morris minimum as was commensurate with the economic viability of the individual scheme under consideration. Particular attention should be given to standards of finish and to the sort of extras that would convert an ordinary dwelling into a deluxe model. Some interested parties required education about the type of housing the Corporation wanted to see built and the sections of the com- munity for whom it was intended to cater.

As well as the Corporation distributing its own brochure, the Ministry of Housing and Local Government provided all local authorities with information about the Corporation through Circular 41/64 in July 1964. A leaflet had also been prepared in conjunction with the Central Office of Information under the title *Building to Let and for Co-ownership*. The initial organisational arrangements included the first regional offices, established in Cardiff and Edinburgh, and the first report referred to the intention to set up other regional offices in Manchester, Leicester and London.

In these early years it is evident that the board considered whether it could do more than the limited activities asked of it. It agreed that there was no objection in principle to the Corporation's entering into the acquisition and modernisation of older property. This did not imply that the Corporation was ready to assume a commitment to become involved in the purchase and modernisation of the whole range of existing property, but simply that the proposition should be looked at in collaboration with the ministry. The board also considered a cost sale scheme, but came to the conclusion that this had nothing to commend it. The Ministry was believed to share this view and to be unlikely to press the Corporation to give this matter further consideration.

The board agreed that the Corporation should lay down guidelines for societies to follow in the exercise of their responsibilities for the letting and management of completed estates. It was further agreed that future staffing requirements should take into account the need to extend the functions of headquarters and regional office staff to include inspection of sites under construction and completed estates, and to carry out enquiries, where necessary, into the organisation and administration of societies. A separate management branch had been set up at the Corporation's headquarters to give specialist advice and assistance on all aspects of housing management. There was also some move to rationalise activity. Societies which managed a small number of dwellings were joining forces to make their organisations more efficient and economic, or were transferring their management functions to more substantial societies which had already achieved economies of scale. The expected pattern was of a relatively small number of strong management groups and this was beginning to take shape.

Difficult cases

Setting up new housing societies was not straightforward and a series of problems was experienced at an early stage. There were general difficulties encountered in Scotland, where schemes were floundering (HCBM 13/9/65). Scottish building costs were above the average for England and Wales and very much higher than for the north-east of England. The board was advised that there would be insufficient demand for accommodation at the rent levels needed to cover these costs. The economical cost rent in Scotland was also way above the rents charged by local authorities. The board agreed that it might well be necessary in Scotland to concentrate more on co-ownership than on cost rent. There was no justification, however, for amending the rules and procedures so as to give more favourable treatment to Scottish co-owners. The suggestion that the Corporation should consider applications from Scottish societies for finance to acquire and modernise existing dwellings was also rejected (HCBM 8/11/65).

The Housing Corporation also wrestled with a succession of problems associated with individual societies – usually related to membership or the independence of organisations. For example, the problems of conflicts of interest are illustrated by one society that was asked to broaden its management committee by admitting two members who were independent of a named private company. They were also asked to investigate a firm linked with that company (HCBM 28/6/65). A decision on another society's application was deferred while action was taken to persuade it to achieve a better balance in its membership (HCBM 3/12/65). Other housing societies, including the Park Housing Society and the Second Cathays Housing Society, were having problems in meeting their financial obligations (HCBM 16/10/67). It was later reported that the chairman and secretary had resigned from the Park Housing Society (HCBM 11/12/67). The management of Park's estate had been taken over by the Plan Housing Society and steps were being taken to put the estate in order and let vacant dwellings. The chairman of Plan had taken over the chairmanship of Park, a Plan nominee had been appointed secretary and three members had joined the management committee. The issues related to Park and Second Cathays continued to be reported at subsequent meetings (HCBM 13/5/68). Elsewhere problems were reported in relation to the condition of estates and variation orders issued by societies' architects without consultation with the Corporation. In some cases, in order to offset costs, this resulted in standards that were below the Parker Morris minimum. There was concern about whether these were isolated or more common situations and whether more than occasional checks by regional staff, with or without technical support, would be sufficient (HCBM 16/10/67). Examples of later difficult cases included the simultaneous disappearance from the Newton Garth Housing Society of the secretary and £10,000, and the option of reporting the Anglo-Scottish Group architect to the Architects Registration Council for failure to respond to letters (HCBM 19/4/71).

The ways that the management and board handled these early cases influenced its later practice. The problems associated with Park and Second Cathays were not isolated ones, other examples including the letting of properties in Maidenhead through the Swanston Housing Society. The experience of all of these generated new proposals for supervising societies and schemes. A regional office would initiate remedial action or, in appropriate circumstances, call for advice and assistance from headquarters if a society was found to be failing to meet any requirements set out in the checklist. The form of annual return to the Registrar of Friendly Societies was also redesigned to meet the needs of housing societies and it was agreed that the new edition of the practice notes should include reference to the sort of books, accounts and records to be kept by housing societies.

By July 1968, the board minutes had begun to include a section referring to 'cases for report'. Questions related to supervision continued to arise. The list of cases, and the problems giving rise to difficulties experienced by the Corporation's officers, included a number of societies under close surveillance (HCBM 8/12/69). New model rules, including Corporation consent to remuneration of committee members and officers of cost rent societies, were introduced and the board was presented with a note about the statutory powers of the Corporation to deal with an ailing housing society. The existing powers of direction applied only to the disposal of land in a housing society's ownership, and it was agreed that the Corporation should consider and submit draft legislative provisions designed to enable it to give direction of a general nature concerning the administration and management of housing schemes. The board subsequently agreed to continue to press for legislation to provide powers of direction for ailing societies (HCBM 13/7/70).

Different issues arose related to the Corporation's own use of its land purchase powers. The Corporation had used these in some cases for land assembly – buying land with the intention of identifying an appropriate housing society to develop it at a later stage. In some cases this began to generate losses. Land purchased in Warlingham, Surrey was subsequently affected by road widening proposals that reduced the potential for development. This was resolved by sale at a loss, with the agreement of the ministry that 'there was nothing untoward about this' (HCBM 11/11/71).

Making progress

The early years of the Housing Corporation coincided with a brief period of expansion of housing activity. With the new priority accorded to housing by the Labour government, total output expanded, exceeding 400,000 in both 1967 and 1968. However, wider economic problems led the government to cut the programme as part of the package of public expenditure reductions following the devaluation of sterling in November 1967. Following this, public-sector completions fell away sharply after 1968, reaching a low of 88,000 in 1973.

In the five years following its formation, the Housing Corporation saw a steady build-up in the number of dwellings completed but began to experience fluctuations in proposals and approvals for projects, associated with changing interest rates and the shortages of mortgage funds. Table 4.1 indicates that projects approved by the Corporation rose steadily up to 1968 and then fell back dramatically. The lagged effect meant that completions increased to a plateau in 1970 and 1971 but then fell away. By 1969/70 record high interest rates, an acute shortage of mortgage funds available for lending to housing societies by building societies and restrictions on capital expenditure generally put a firm brake on the promotion of new housing society schemes and there was a declining trend in the rate of development projects coming forward (HCAR 1969/70). Table 4.2 sets out the government advances received in this period and the same pattern is apparent. Until the Corporation broke away from the confines of co-ownership and cost rent and accessed public subsidy for fair-rent housing its initial surge of growth was not sustained and it had only drawn down some £60 million. The success of the Corporation in funding new housing provision appeared likely to be short lived, an adverse economic environment having encumbered it in its infancy.

The expectation that the 1964 Act would result mainly in the provision of cost rent housing was replaced as co-ownership housing outstripped cost rent in popularity. Building societies' own traditions meant that they were more willing to lend for co-ownership schemes and the fact that co-owners became eligible for option mortgage subsidy (see below) added to this. Nevertheless a small group of four building societies dominated lending and the larger the scheme was, the more difficult it was to find a lender (Campbell 1970). At the same time higher construction costs and interest rates made it almost impossible to let houses affordably at unsubsidised rents to the kind of people who wished to rent rather than buy. It was argued that, however attached to long-term renting sections of the middle classes may be on the Continent, Britain offered no significant market for unsubsidised higher-rent homes. Such people wanted at least a part-share in ownership and probably individual home ownership. While the new arrangements for co-ownership were being presented to housing societies, the concerns about cost rent continued. The board agreed that they were no longer seeking a subsidy for cost rent housing,

Table 4.1: Housing Corporation approvals and completions 1965-74

Year ended 31/3	Approvals		Completions
	Schemes	Dwellings	
1965	18	1,100	–
1966	96	4,180	–
1967	216	8,427	600
1968	202	8,099	1,900
1969	83	3,317	4,169
1970	52	1,174	6,346
1971	117	3,480	6,006
1972	165	5,353	3,961
1973	221	9,581	3,370
1974	366	15,379	3,926
Total	1,536	60,090	30,278

In 1974 there were 303 additional approvals for acquisitions, conversions or improvements of dwellings and 713 approvals under arrangements with the GLC.

The breakdown between different types of investment is not clear from the annual reports but for the whole period 1965 to 1974 approvals had been made for 11,381 fair rent dwellings and 48,119 co-ownership dwellings (HCAR 1974). It seems likely that any cost rent dwelling approvals are included in the latter figure. The same report refers to completions of 30,278 co-ownership dwellings and again this seems likely to include cost rent dwellings completed. The 1968 annual report refers to approvals for 8,874 cost rent dwellings but this was a reduction on the figure given in the previous year and some of these approvals were subsequently switched to co-ownership.

Source: HCAR (1971-4).

Table 4.2: Government advances received, £ thousands

	England	Scotland	Wales	Total
1/9/64–31/3/65	22	0	0	22
1/4/65–31/3/66	2,558	0	104	2,662
1/4/66–31/3/67	6,120	75	188	6,382
1/4/67–31/3/68	12,000	585	408	12,994
1/4/68–31/3/69	11,450	260	250	11,960
1/4/69–31/3/70	12,200	750	150	13,100
1/4/70–31/3/71	5,900	760	100	6,760
1/4/71–31/3/72	8,900	1,900	1,500	12,300
1/4/72–31/3/73	23,550	1,170	600	25,320

Source: HCAR (1965-73).

Individual figures have been rounded to the nearest thousand. Totals are derived from unrounded numbers and may not equal the sum of the rounded numbers.

but were simply asking the ministry to accept that occasions would arise when it would be prudent and sensible to be flexible in the arrangements governing the repayment of loans on approved schemes (HCBM 6/2/67).

The challenges created by rising and high interest rates both for the Housing Corporation's programme and for housing societies involved in co-ownership schemes were addressed by the introduction of option mortgages in 1968. Option mortgages were introduced as a subsidy to home owners with a mortgage but with incomes that left them below the threshold for income tax and so unable to benefit from mortgage interest tax relief. Where home owners buying property would not fully benefit from tax reliefs on mortgage payments, they could opt into an arrangement whereby the payments they made to the lender were reduced and the government contributed to their mortgage payments. Option mortgages in effect provided an interest rate subsidy and co-ownership societies qualified as if their members did so individually. The ministry had agreed to discuss in detail the method by which the option mortgage subsidy would be applied to co-ownership housing societies. The initial draft of the statutory instrument from the ministry had included a condition that housing societies would be required to declare, in the option mortgage notice, that its members were ordinarily resident in the United Kingdom. This had not been anticipated and it was not easy for housing societies to give this assurance. The ministry was urged to give special dispensation in this particular case (HCBM 13/11/67), subsequently changing the statutory instrument draft and excluding this requirement. While option mortgages helped with co-ownership, the ministry had insisted that there was no prospect of extending them to cover cost rent societies. In this context it was difficult to prevent or discourage a cost rent society from changing to co-ownership if this were the unanimous wish of its members and tenants (HCBM 13/11/67). By the end of 1972 there were 442 registered cost rent societies and 953 co-ownership societies and the Housing Corporation had effectively become a specialist co-ownership promoter.

Later in 1969 the government recognised that increases in mortgage interest rates had reduced the value of the option mortgage differential, as compared with tax relief, and a new sliding scale was introduced which allowed the subsidy to vary with the rates of interest payable on mortgages. The new scale was effective from January 1970 and this meant that the earlier increase of ⅞ per cent was cut back to ⅝ per cent for co-ownership schemes. This was seen as a welcome encouragement for co-ownership housing societies. At the same time steps were taken to insure part of the building societies' share of the loan finance in order to protect them against any potential loss. This indemnity insurance was hoped to encourage hitherto uncommitted building societies of appropriate size and resources to become involved although there was little evidence that it would do so (HCBM 6/10/69). In March 1970 the minister of housing, Anthony Crosland, also announced an additional funding commitment of about £10 million for the Housing Corporation. With the participation of building societies this was expected to lead to a total additional commitment of at least £20 million in 1970/71.

The introduction of the sliding scale of option mortgage relief alleviated the interest rate problem for most co-ownership societies and created something approaching a stable base on which their rent structures could be projected with greater confidence. In contrast, however, no such relief was extended to cost rent schemes and they continued to be priced out of the market in most parts of the country.

Working with others

The Ministry of Housing and Local Government did not intervene in detail during this period. For example, the Housing Corporation board was informed in 1967 that the ministry had raised no points of substance on the draft practice circular related to lettings and management. But there were indications of an instinct for more detailed management from the ministry. For example, at the end of a meeting with the board on 22 November 1967, the minister, Anthony Greenwood, said that he felt that an 'early warning system' should be considered with a view to the Corporation consulting with the ministry before committing itself to high-cost schemes. This was followed up with exploratory talks between the management and ministry officials. The board generally agreed that if a figure of some kind was to be the basis of an early warning system, it must be realistic and should relate only to land cost per unit with a limited amount of regional differentiation. Figures were discussed and agreed as a basis on which further talks between the management and ministry officials could be held.

More confusingly, correspondence exchanged with the ministry stated that it had always been intended that Exchequer money should be lent only in respect of schemes providing accommodation for tenants of modest means. This statement was challenged by the board, and the management were instructed to refer back to the ministry on this and to enquire about the reasons for Greenwood's rejection of a proposed scheme in Liverpool (HCBM 13/5/68). This is an interesting indication of the changing perception, within the ministry, of the Housing Corporation's role. It indicates a drift away from a view that the Corporation was intended to house better-off people and towards a view that it should be more concerned with those of modest means. The Corporation at this stage was adamant. It stood up to the ministry and remained inflexible.

A strong working relationship with building societies was a prerequisite for success and, during their first meeting, members of the board had indicated their willingness to use their contacts to make an approach to the Halifax Building Society – the largest building society at that time. By the third meeting one month later, the Halifax had passed a resolution expressing its willingness to co-operate with the Corporation and agreeing in principle to make loans to cost rent and co-ownership societies. A more general liaison with the BSA was also proceeding. The National Building Agency agreed to provide architectural and other technical services required by the Corporation.

While there were continuing debates about payments to residents who left co-ownership schemes, there were also issues about approval of the terms for such schemes, both from the Registrar of Friendly Societies and from the BSA. Liaison with building societies also had some associated problems, although thirty-nine building societies had indicated their willingness to earmark funds for housing society schemes by February 1965. There was little information on the scale of financial support forthcoming, although there was some indication that a limit of £100,000 was likely to be imposed on any one scheme: This would make it very difficult for any but the smallest cost rent schemes to get off the ground. A consortium of lenders would be an alternative but this matter created some anxiety at an early stage.

By the end of March 1965 the five largest building societies were reported as happy to accept the position requested by the Housing Corporation and although there was concern to involve a larger group, the worries about building society participation began to decline. Liaison with building societies was a continuing matter of importance and in a period of rising interest rates, the anxieties of the building societies movement were clear. Proposals for government guarantee of loans gave way to mortgage indemnity insurance and were one response to these concerns, but differences relating to the method of valuation of schemes and their viability remained.

Co-ownership and co-operative housing

Co-ownership societies were not expected to play a major role in the development of housing societies initially. Whereas cost rent societies would develop more than one larger scheme and employ professional staff to build and manage schemes, co-ownership developments would generally be small and societies would initiate only one scheme, to be run by its residents (CHAC 1971). Following the limited uptake of co-ownership under the Housing Act 1961 experiment, action had been taken to give the members of approved co-ownership societies tax relief on mortgage interest payments in the same way as owner-occupiers. In other respects arrangements were unchanged: individuals made an initial contribution of some 5 per cent of cost and the rest was borrowed collectively, repayable over forty years; residents were responsible collectively for repayment of the loan, management and maintenance. In practice these matters were often the subject of a management agreement established by the founding organisation and continued by residents once they took up occupation.

The arrangements relating to co-ownership included that outgoing members of societies sponsored by the Corporation would receive a premium payment in addition to the return of the original deposit. The premium payment was designed to reflect, but not exhaust, any appreciation in the capital value of the property during the term of occupation and should take into account the contribution made by the outgoing member; but it should not be pitched so high as to place the incoming member in the position of a person buying in the open market. The premium payment would have to be financed by the incoming member and should not make membership any less attractive than applying to a brand new co-ownership society. In October 1966, changes were made in the model rules and the mortgage deeds so that a simplified form of co-ownership tenure could be adopted. The normal length of leases was reduced from ninety-nine years to no more (and sometimes less) than three years (CHAC 1971) and deposits, which had been equal to 5 per cent of the cost of the dwelling, were reduced to six months' rent in advance or 5 per cent of the value of the house, whichever was the less, as security against rent arrears, damage and other contingencies. Co-ownership societies could be offered 100 per cent, rather than 95 per cent, mortgage finance. It was also agreed that anyone leaving a co-ownership scheme should qualify for a premium payment after three years instead of five years, which had applied hitherto (HCBM 16/2/66). These changes 'had an immediate impact and, as rising interest rates militated against the promotion of cost rent schemes, co-ownership marched ahead in terms of projects approved and the total loan commitment ... until the building society interest rate moved to the record high level of 7⅞ in May 1968 and the Corporation's interest rate was raised automatically to 7⅞' (Housing Corporation evidence, quoted in CHAC 1971: 57). The increases in interest rates 'amounted to a ban on cost rent' and also had a 'very dampening effect on co-ownership' (CHAC 1971: 57–8) and it was not until option mortgages were put on a sliding scale that there was even a slight revival in the latter.

Some 16,000 co-ownership dwellings had been completed by 1970. Co-ownership housing societies have been presented as 'the first mainstream model of co-operative ownership of property in Britain' (Clapham and Kintrea 1987). While this may be technically accurate, it is evident that not many of those involved perceived it in this way; and none of the Housing Corporation, the co-owners or the sponsors and managers saw it this way. They saw it as a mechanism to achieve housing development, as providing some choice and as a stepping stone – usually to home ownership. In this early phase it is striking that very little homage was being paid to co-operative ideas. Although Lewis Waddilove, who had commented favourably on Scandinavian experience (Waddilove 1962; see also Clapham and Kintrea 1987), and Herbert Ashworth (who was vice-president of the Co-operative Permanent Building Society) were both Corporation board members (and Ashworth was chairman from 1968 to 1973), it is not possible to trace a strong co-operative emphasis in the board minutes or annual reports of the Housing Corporation until Harold Campbell joined the Board in 1967. Even then the impression is that the majority of the board had no enthusiasm for or commitment to developing co-operatives. Co-ownership, which can be presented as a form of co-operative housing and which had been promoted by some in this guise, was more commonly presented by the government and the Corporation as a pragmatic gap filler for middle-income groups who found the choice between social renting and owning insufficient. The White Paper in 1961 referred to co-owners as follows: 'In their collective capacity they are in a position of owner-occupier.' And the taxation arrangements followed this logic. There is no evidence of any intention to develop a third arm of co-operative housing as an alternative to traditional renting or owning.

Although it is possible to focus on different attributes of co-ownership there does not appear to have been a shared or even widely held view that it formed a distinctive alternative tenure embracing co-operative principles. It was not regarded as a path-breaking innovation to be proud of and to be defended once other priorities and difficulties came along. Nor did the practical experience of the foundation of co-ownership societies by estate agents and other property professionals strengthen its co-operative credentials. The Cohen committee (CHAC 1971: 58–62) provided the clearest account of how far the practice diverged from the rhetoric of co-operative housing. Very few co-ownership societies were started by their members, an approach that would take two or more years; most co-owners were more like owner-occupiers moving onto a new housing estate than partners in a co-operative venture. Out of the 800 co-ownership societies registered with the Corporation at the end of 1970, 750 were 'subsidiary' rather than 'original'. The initiative to set them up had been taken by a cost rent society. The incentive to promote a co-ownership society, for the professional members of a cost rent committee, was the fees paid for design, land acquisition, building and maintenance (and subsequent management). In their evidence to the Cohen committee, 'the Housing Corporation refute the suggestion that schemes sponsored by professionally based societies are not "genuine co-ownership", whatever that expression may mean'.

The Corporation encouraged sponsoring or parent societies with professional skills as the most effective way to expand co-ownership.

> An established society may sponsor any number of co-ownership developments provided that the offshoot co-ownership society is registered in time for the site to be purchased in its name. Once the design and development work is completed and lettings begin, the role of the sponsoring society changes from that of the promoter-developer to that of a property manager for the resident co-owners so that there is the necessary continuity of administrative and management expertise. (CHAC 1971: 59–60)

The Corporation had encouraged the merger of promotional societies and in 1970 there were fewer than 200 such societies. The sponsoring society normally provided administration and management services for co-owners on an agency basis for at least three years after a scheme had been completed. The research carried out for the Cohen committee referred to some of the weaknesses connected with arrangements for professional management of co-ownership societies:

> There were a number of complaints over 'wilful refusals to clarify agreements', failure to divulge the initial value of dwellings, or to give a detailed breakdown

of accounts, and insensitive treatment of people, taking advantage of their lack of understanding ... The net result of such actions is to make co-owners feel like tenants having to fight for their rights ... and to create ... an escalation of accusations that the agents are just out to draw their fees and do not care how they treat the residents, and from the other side that co-owners are in it for financial gain too and not prepared to behave responsibly. In such an atmosphere mutual understanding becomes less and less likely. (Quoted in CHAC 1971: 60)

Clapham and Kintrea (1987) refer to studies of specific co-ownership schemes and indicate that access to such schemes was often on the basis of good fortune or word of mouth: there was no widespread knowledge of housing opportunities provided, nor any formal waiting lists, and sponsors advertised schemes through newspapers and site billboards. They also argue that control of costs and standards was ineffective and examples of low standards and profiteering were encountered. The involvement of architects could lead to costly one-off designs. Finally the Housing Corporation's detailed control of financial and management arrangements were insufficiently sensitive to the nature of these organisations, while the Corporation was reluctant to provide assistance or advice for societies that were in difficulties, because they were self-determining organisations.

While this account of the practice adopted in relation to co-ownership does not refute the argument that co-ownership technically was a form of co-operative, it cautions against building an image of co-ownership as a co-operative in any broader sense. Co-ownership was promoted for profit, treated for tax purposes as home ownership, and designed, developed, marketed and managed within the practices of the private sector. In letting property there was a concern for the financial status of applicants but none for their interest or commitment to any co-operative principle. The members of co-ownership societies were predominantly young, salaried and higher earners, and the house rather than the tenure had influenced their choice in deciding where to move. Clapham and Kintrea (1987) report other research that led them to conclude that in co-ownership 'management was often remote, unaccountable and inefficient', 'a sense of residents' control was almost totally absent'. Many co-owners 'failed to appreciate that they actually owned the houses themselves and management existed to serve them' and had not known that the housing they had applied for was co-ownership, regarding the tenure as a form of renting and the sponsoring society as akin to a landlord. Turnover was high and the implication is that many did not understand what they were taking on and, because they would move on quickly, were not concerned to address their rights and responsibilities. The culture of the operation very rarely connected with ideas of co-operatives and was indistinguishable from cost renting. Unsurprisingly, many co-owners appeared to regard the tenure as a staging post on the way to home ownership rather than as a long-term place to live with a different ownership and management philosophy.

Birchall (1991) offers a more damning verdict on the Housing Corporation's operation of co-ownership. He states that while the Scandinavian model and the similarity to earlier co-partnership schemes might have been expected to guarantee the development of a genuine co-operative housing approach, 'the civil service drafters of the scheme failed to understand what made the Norwegian and Swedish co-operatives so successful, and it is unlikely that they had even heard of co-partnership'. He also criticises the Housing Corporation for adopting a 'hands off' approach with little cost or quality control. Many schemes proved costly, with cost overruns that were passed on in high rents; they were badly designed (for instance with flat roofs) and used inferior materials; and there was inadequate site supervision. By the end of the 1970s some schemes had to be demolished, and others were saved only by vigorous legal action by members who successfully sued architects and builders. The Housing Corporation's guidance notes also expressed distrust of resident co-owners and betrayed a greater belief in the private sector professionals in the sponsoring societies. Many managing agents ran schemes for years without informing the co-owners that they were anything other than tenants of the agent; members discovered their true status when there were defects needing remedy, whereupon they found that they were paying fees to the agents that the latter had negotiated for themselves as founder members; they had to rely on these agents to seek remedy for defects or sue the architects that the agents were associated with! Birchall shows that the Housing Corporation was content to let the 'professionals' operate at arm's length, but was uncomfortable with the whole idea of elected resident committees that controlled management. In its guidance notes and model documents for co-ownership housing, published in 1972, the Corporation recommended that 'the Managing Society should be permitted to carry out the duties in the Agreement without pettifogging interference, or being required to report on the minutiae of its tasks' (quoted in Birchall 1991: 13–14).

Agents were to be left to exercise detailed control over management but societies had to obtain approval from the Corporation for rent setting, premium payments and any change of managing agent. This latter made it all the more difficult for members to wrest control from managing agents imposed at the beginning of the scheme by founder members, who had entered into long-term contracts usually of seven years.

When they finally took on self-management, members found they had an overcomplex form of tenure that was difficult to administer, with five sets of model rules that remained hard to understand, dubious legal status, no right to rent allowances or some grants that were available to home owners; yet they were unable to deal effectively with co-owners who defaulted on payments (Birchall 1991: 13–14). Rather than acquiring the best elements of other tenures they appeared to have acquired the worst.

Both cost rent and co-ownership had emerged following scrutiny of co-operative housing in Scandinavia and co-ownership had been seen, by some, as a type of co-operative housing. The Co-operative Party and especially Harold Campbell had actively advocated co-operative housing schemes and with the advent of a Labour government in 1964 had hoped for positive action. Campbell's appointment as a Housing Corporation board member in March 1967 should be seen in this context. He had become secretary of the Co-operative Party in 1964 and had voiced his dissatisfaction with the lack of action on co-operative housing (Carbery 1969: 177). In June 1967, Campbell expressed the view to the board that the true participating spirit of co-ownership might be lost if cost rent societies were regarded as the prime sponsoring agents. The Corporation was an appointed body, and Campbell suggested that the promotion of the co-ownership concept might best be undertaken by an elected body, a federal society to which all co-ownership societies might be affiliated. Other members of the board found this unacceptable on the grounds that the Corporation was the government's chosen instrument to undertake promotional responsibility and that it would not help to interpose yet another body. The Corporation had encouraged cost rent societies to make full use of their professional expertise in sponsoring co-ownership as a matter of practical politics dictated by experience. The success of this policy was reflected by the results achieved to date. It was felt that the spirit of participation would have more fertile ground in which to take root once the dwellings were built and occupied. The pattern might change when a number of schemes had been completed and the idea of co-ownership was more firmly established but it was agreed that existing methods and policy should be continued for the time being at least (HCBM 5/6/67).

At this same meeting, Campbell raised questions about student housing and the possibility of its provision under co-ownership arrangements. A preliminary view had been sought from the Ministry of Housing; its advice was that if housing accommodation, other than self-contained units, were intended, it should not be within the Corporation's powers to provide the finance. Secondly, the ministry did not see how a student co-operative could be said to be analogous to owner occupation and so be eligible for tax relief within the scope of Section 43 of the Finance Act 1963. The Corporation's solicitor had advised that it had power to lend only to a housing society whose objects were those set out in the Housing Act 1964 and which provided separate dwellings. Other difficulties mentioned included the limiting of membership to those aged twenty-one or over, the question of sub-lettings during vacations and administrative complications and expense arising out of the transitory nature of a student's occupancy. While the board expressed sympathy for and appreciated the difficulties facing students in obtaining suitable accommodation, it was agreed that the responsibility for finding the solution to their problems rested with the Department of Education and Science and the universities, and it would not be appropriate for the Corporation to intervene on students' behalf. The Corporation's powers were directed to the provision of houses for the general public and it would be undesirable for it to seek legislative changes in favour of one particular section of the community (HCBM 5/6/67). This position was to change with the expansion of the Corporation's vision in the early 1970s; for example in early 1973 there was a scheme to lend to Student Co-operative Dwellings for a co-ownership scheme in Lewisham that would be approved for option mortgage subject to certain conditions. The Corporation's approval for option mortgage was instrumental in this decision.

These exchanges highlight the lack of consensus within the Housing Corporation (both at this stage and later) over any underlying philosophy of housing provision. Campbell in later written material represented co-ownership housing as 'none other than a co-operative housing society well-known and well-tried in Scandinavia and to be found elsewhere' (Campbell 1970: 326). But this verdict is at odds with any more detached evaluation and with subsequent evidence. For example, Campbell's expectations of who would be living in co-ownership (the elderly and late middle aged; the young who have not yet acquired sufficient capital resources of their own; the widow and the single woman) (Campbell 1970: 327) did not square with the reality of a much younger, transient and affluent group. While Campbell and some others saw an opportunity to build on co-ownership and create a large and distinctive co-operative sector, he recognised that this would require a greater contribution from others (banks, pension funds and trade unions). But his vision and enthusiasm were not shared by others who had a much more instrumental approach. For them cost rent and co-ownership – indeed the Housing Corporation itself – were simply mechanisms to achieve more house building or mobilise private and public finance and fill a gap in the market. There was no aspiration to produce a different type of housing. The interest in developing co-operative housing schemes remained within the Corporation for some time and is referred to later in this book. Although the remit to develop co-operatives was at best ambiguous and at worst non-existent, there were energetic advocates and it is one area where the Corporation can be regarded to have failed. The privatisation of co-ownership housing sealed the failure but the story otherwise is unimpressive.

The first transition: 1970–74

The most fundamental challenge to the long-term role of the Housing Corporation became evident less than four years after its establishment and was related to the effect of the rise in interest rates on rents (HCBM 11/3/68). Concern was expressed over the difficulties likely to be encountered in letting dwellings in completed, or near-completed, schemes where the rents chargeable were already close to the level at which market resistance was felt. In the home ownership market generally the minister for housing, Anthony Greenwood, had asked building societies to deal with rising interest rates by maintaining current repayment rates for owner-occupiers but, where possible, extending the mortgage term. This was not feasible in the case of the forty-year loans to housing societies. However, it was remarked that it would be helpful in the short term if participating building societies followed the lead of the Woolwich Equitable and postponed increasing the rate to existing borrowers until 1 January 1969. It was suggested that an informal approach might be made to the BSA on the grounds that it would be not only consistent with government policy, but also of administrative convenience to the Housing Corporation, if all building societies postponed raising their interest rates to housing societies until 1 January 1969. Alternatively, and if high interest rates persisted, it might be necessary to seek ministry consent for housing society dwellings to be offered at less than the economic rent, in order to secure full occupation initially and until the situation improved (HCBM 13/5/68).

Subsequently it was reported that the BSA was not prepared to make a general recommendation to its member societies to postpone the increase in interest rates. It suggested that the Corporation might like to approach individual building societies directly concerned. It was agreed that the Corporation could not properly make such approaches without the prior knowledge and consent of the ministry. And the general manager of the Corporation undertook to consult Greenwood immediately (NCBM 8/7/68). In the event, it was agreed that difficulties created by the rise in interest rates should continue to be dealt with on an ad hoc basis.

After five years the apparently simple and straightforward role of the Housing Corporation as the orchestrator of a niche within the housing and housing policy system had begun to appear unsustainable. Although the Corporation had successfully established itself and its key procedures, economic changes were destabilising it. In particular cost rent housing had hit a brick wall – high interest rates made the rents too costly and anyone able to afford them would immediately be aware of the relative advantage of buying a home and offsetting some costs against the mortgage interest tax reliefs that were available. Co-ownership struggled on and was helped by the availability of option mortgages and their effects in reducing mortgage costs. However, this left the Corporation on the fringes of housing policy rather than in a central position highly regarded by any of the interested parties.

At the same time the housing policy agenda was changing. The 1960s had seen the rediscovery of homelessness and there was more concern about urban renewal and alternatives to slum clearance as a means of addressing problems of the older housing stock and inner-city problems. A new cohort of housing associations, including many that have subsequently become major players (for example the Notting Hill Housing Trust and the Paddington Churches Housing Association), were established. They provided subsidised rented units for lower-income tenants and received funding from the national housing charities, Shelter in particular. They were part of a shifting political debate about a new housing crisis and homelessness. The new associations shifted the main focus of the voluntary housing movement away from the areas occupied by the Corporation and from cost rent and co-ownership schemes. The Housing Subsidies Act 1967 and the Housing Act 1969 confirmed this by providing new subsidies to encourage housing associations to rehabilitate homes by arrangement with local authorities. Local authorities were made responsible for checking and certifying costs and the Housing Corporation at this time took no part in the increasingly important rehabilitation work that was to form such a large part of its activity in later years.

The Housing Act 1969 signalled a shift from slum clearance to area improvement as well as the improvement of individual properties and it is evident that this would change the role of housing associations and the Housing Corporation. However, in 1970 a new Conservative government led by Edward Heath was elected and this brought a new element into the mix. The new government pursued what was at the time seen as an uncompromisingly right-wing agenda. In housing this involved not just promoting home ownership but also reorganising council housing and changing the basis of housing subsidy.

Municipal housing itself was changing. The shift from building for general needs to slum clearance had required changes in the way of working as well as in who moved into council housing. The increasing involvement in improving rather than clearing older property required a shift towards a more comprehensive approach to housing and the leading local authorities modernised the way they worked to address issues across all tenures. The process of urban renewal was often led by the housing department, but included significant roles for environmental health officers who assessed house condition, valuers involved in buying property and staff from the treasurer's department and the town clerk's or chief executive's department involved in financial and legal aspects of the comprehensive housing service.

Some signs of the Housing Corporation's wish to respond positively to changing circumstances were apparent early in 1970. The government had recognised that increases in mortgage interest rates had reduced the value of the option mortgage when compared with mortgage interest tax relief and introduced a sliding scale that took account of this. The indemnity insurance scheme was also put in place and Greenwood committed additional resources, stating: 'We are also anxious to encourage the work of co-ownership housing societies, operating under the Housing Corporation [HCAR 1969/70].' The Corporation announced that it would be in a position to take on some £20 million of new business over and above the 1969/70 level of approved schemes (HCBM 13/4/70). It was also suggested that for the time being housing societies could accept a loan of half the capital cost of a scheme as the minimum advance from a building society, although an offer of up to two thirds (with an indemnity guarantee where appropriate) would still be welcomed. The board discussed actions to expand activity in 1971 (HCBM 9/11/70), and the parliamentary under-secretary of state for the environment, Paul Channon, hoped the Housing Corporation would have an important role to play in the future of the voluntary housing movement, whose expansion the government wished to see. He invited the board to submit its written views on how this expansion could be achieved, and on the legislation it would like to see enacted in the forthcoming Housing Bill with this end in view (HCBM 14/12/70). Following this the Corporation began to plan for expansion, with proposals to divide the South East region into two with a new regional office outside central London (HCBM 8/2/71).

From this point on the nature of the debate shifts to a more expansionist agenda envisaging greater variety of activity. The publication of the White Paper *Fair Deal for Housing* prepared the Corporation as well as others in the housing sector for a different environment. The Housing Corporation was nevertheless concerned that there was a significant number of schemes, completed or under construction, lacking firm offers of support from building societies. In August 1971 Parliament approved the Housing Corporation Advances (Increase of Limits) Order. This raised the limit on Corporation borrowing from £75 million to the full £100 million authorised under the Housing Act 1964. The board had been previously advised that there had been 'encouraging comments from both sides of the House as to the future role of the Corporation and the voluntary housing movement generally' (HCBM 19/4/71).

Both of the major political parties, however, were competing to be seen as the party of home ownership, with the Conservatives' abolition of Schedule A tax in 1963 and Labour's introduction of option mortgages in 1968 as real additions to the package of measures designed to encourage and reward home ownership. Against this background the debates of the late 1960s indicate that alternative roles for the Housing Corporation were being considered. Arguably the Corporation had to take on a wider role or its marginality would put its long-term future in question.

The Cohen committee, set up in 1968 to consider the role of housing associations and societies in the light of the developing housing situation, was disbanded by the incoming Conservative government in 1970, but ministry officials pulled the considerable body of evidence together, which formed the basis for a report from the Central Housing Advisory Committee (CHAC, 1971). This identified the problem of the proliferation of small, inexperienced associations heavily dependent upon their local authorities for finance and managerial support. The Housing Corporation was seen as quicker and more efficient than local authorities; the committee discussed the view that the Corporation should fund all new-build work by associations but that local authorities should continue as the sole source of public finance for rehabilitation. This proposed division of labour was not adopted in the Housing Finance Act 1972, nor the Housing Act 1974, and the Corporation was given responsibility for both kinds of work.

The Housing Finance Act extended the Corporation's powers to enable it to lend to all associations and allowed it, for the first time, to provide loan finance for subsidised housing intended for lower-income tenants. However, the Act's complex subsidy arrangements were to be administered by the Department of the Environment (DoE), created in 1970 from several former ministries, including the Ministry of Housing, and not until 1974 did the Corporation begin to act as the department's agent in this task. The Act included provision for increasing the advances from the National Loans Fund available to the Corporation from £100 million to £300 million. A further provision would empower the Corporation to make loans to housing associations in addition to the housing societies included within the meaning of the Housing Act 1964. While the secretary of state had responded favourably to the Housing Corporation's views of the likely impact of the Housing Finance Act (HCBM 13/3/72), the Treasury opposed the proposal that building societies lend direct to the Corporation (HCBM 8/5/72). The minister for housing and construction, Julian Amery, later explained that the government had come to the conclusion that the objections to this proposal outweighed the likely advantages (HCBM 3/7/72). However, the Housing Finance Act widened the Housing Act 1964 to include the charitable trusts and to facilitate lending by building societies to housing associations. Such lending would be governed by the special advance rules that already existed.

All of this set the background for the Housing Corporation's role to expand. The Corporation was able to consider applications for loans to all types of society, including associations engaged in new building for letting at fair rents (HCBM 14/8/72). This included loans for purpose-built accommodation for special needs such as those of elderly persons, on the understanding that the schemes would need the prior approval of the department for subsidy purposes. At this stage it was still considered impracticable for the Corporation to make loan finance available for the conversion and improvement of individual houses; it was, however, possible to consider assisting societies and associations with schemes for area improvements which would embrace the modernisation of a substantial number of houses.

While the likely shift in direction of the Housing Corporation could be identified in the late 1960s, the transition to a new role was slow. Details of the government's proposals for involving the Corporation in the improvement and conversion of existing property took a long time to emerge (HCBM 8/1/73). The sensitive finances of co-ownership schemes meant that some societies were only able to meet payments to outgoing members by borrowing, although the DoE agreed that the Housing Corporation could make such loans to housing societies. But the financial complications of this arrangement continued to create problems and the board agreed that housing societies should be constantly reminded of the need to raise rents on relets as a matter of course in order to build up reserves to pay premiums from (HCBM 12/2/73). Nevertheless the atmosphere of change was pervasive. Expanded staffing had been proposed in anticipation of the Housing Finance Act 1972 (HCBM 13/12/71). A year later (HCBM 11/12/72) there were proposals to restructure the Corporation's organisation to deal with the additional workload arising from new duties and responsibilities. Opportunities opened up to consider other innovations: Lewis Waddilove, as a board member, suggested that the Corporation should examine the problems of students and mobile young people in the light of impending wider powers (HCBM 13/9/71). Other suggestions related to developing activity in new towns (HCBM 18/10/71) and Harold Campbell noted that, whereas the Corporation could not previously finance shared accommodation, the new legislation would allow this and would make it possible to look at young people's housing.

The government's position was also slowly becoming clearer. Paul Channon, who had recently succeeded Amery as minister for housing and construction, had been a member of the board of the Guinness Trust between 1959 and 1970 (Malpass 1998). He decided that, broadly speaking, the NFHS should be the 'trade association' and the spokesman for the movement, while the Corporation should be the instrument for the promotion and financing of housing societies and associations. He was looking for a considerable increase in the number of dwellings produced through new construction, but also for improvement and conversion of existing property (HCBM 11/12/72). The secretary of state for the environment, Geoffrey Rippon, stated in Parliament that he wished to give as much encouragement to the voluntary housing movement as possible (HCBM 12/2/73).

The continued increase in both building costs and interest rates had begun, by the early 1970s, to make even co-ownership schemes, with their personal share in the equity of the buildings, an unattractive proposition. The Corporation's work was kept alive by its power to lend to subsidised rented projects, but even these were hard hit by rising costs. The subsidy provisions of the 1972 Act, which tapered off support, did not protect associations. In this context the new grant regime introduced under the Housing Act 1974 effectively guaranteed the financial viability of schemes once approved. It was the final, and arguably most important, component enabling the Housing Corporation and housing associations to embark on a different and expanded role closer to the mainstream of housing policy although still much less prominent than the role of local authorities.

The new era was also marked by a new chairman for the Housing Corporation and new members of the board. Sir Herbert Ashworth resigned to take up a new appointment as special advisor to the environment secretary on land and housing in new towns in England and Wales. He was replaced by Lord Goodman, whose inimitable account of his appointment as the chairman of the Housing Corporation gives some flavour of the time:

> Some time in March 1973 my telephone rang and I was asked if I would call on Mr Geoffrey Rippon, the Secretary of State for the Environment, the following day. Being of a courteous disposition and more prone to say yes than no to most things I agreed willingly, particularly as I liked Mr Rippon. That evening, prior to the meeting, I ran into Mr Paul Channon, another very agreeable man. He said to me, 'You are seeing Geoffrey tomorrow and you are to do whatever he asks.' Again, although not quite prepared to accede to a commitment as open ended as that, I intimated that any reasonable request would obtain my willing consent.
>
> When I saw Mr Rippon the next day he asked me if I would chair the Housing Corporation and at the same time assume the chairmanship of the National Building Agency. I have to admit now with shame that I had never heard of either of them. The secretary of state explained with the assistance of a couple of civil servants what they were all about, but what he failed to explain was why he thought I was possessed of the qualifications necessary to discharge such duties. I was left with the flattering impression that he regarded me as a general purpose animal capable of discharging in reasonable fashion most duties that did not involve excessive physical exertion, particularly running at high speed. He offered me a stipend for the two jobs to be agreed, but I waived this aside loftily without telling him that since I earned a moderate sufficiency as a lawyer it was folly to assume any government mantle without the independence of being unpaid unless you actually needed the money.
>
> The next day I set off for the Housing Corporation (and the National Building Agency). At the Housing Corporation I discovered an atmosphere of deep, bleak gloom. It was an organisation which had become conscious in a relatively short space of time of its own futility, and it plainly did not believe that ordinary human exertions could correct this situation. The building of houses was by a general consensus of opinion as near an impossibility as the human

imagination could conceive. There was, I was told, no land; there were, I was told, no building materials; there were, I was told, no builders; and the possibility of rectifying this situation was one that only a demented optimist would entertain.

I must confess that even my sanguine disposition was mildly discouraged. The absolute certainty of non-achievement exceeded anything that I had met among the pessimists holding Olympic medals. Moreover the press were equally discouraging. This time, they said with some glee, he has bitten off more than he can chew. 'It is doubtful', announced the *Financial Times* (I believe), 'whether the problems can be overcome by the utmost determination and vigour.' (HCAR 1976/7)

Conclusions

The Housing Corporation set out as a specialist niche enabler working at the edge of mainstream housing policy and operating a mixed public/private sector funding model. Its role was prescribed by legislation and direct approval from the Ministry of Housing and Local Government as the sponsoring department. Nevertheless even at this early stage the image and actions of the Corporation were affected by how it set about its job. The old-school civil servants who staffed it brought what some felt was a style more in keeping with the Colonial Office, and there is little evidence of a desire from within to play a more central role in housing policy or to develop a distinctive new culture within housing associated with co-operative ideas, let alone new approaches to the refurbishment of older housing or provision for lower-income households. There was, nevertheless, considerable energy in setting up the new organisation and establishing a track record with government, building societies and others.

While the Housing Corporation embarked on the serious, intensive business of registering and scrutinising its small empire of housing societies that had sought or received funds, the economy and public finances were not standing still. And the problems arising from the continued restructuring of housing tenures and new demands for homes stemming from demographic and economic changes were becoming more pressing. This was the era of property speculation and gentrification, illegal evictions and winkling, scandals associated with private landlords exploiting and abusing tenants, a rising awareness of homelessness and the failure of post-war prosperity to deliver quality, choice or security in housing for a significant part of the population. It was the era of Rachman, Milner Holland, *Cathy Come Home* and the foundation of Shelter and other housing pressure groups. It also saw the formation of new inner city housing associations motivated by a concern to address the dramatic failure of housing policy and of the post-war welfare state to create a housing system that responded sufficiently to housing need and demand. The Housing Corporation had been discussing strengthening powers relating to ailing or misbehaving housing societies and further stretching option mortgages. This and the progress (albeit halting) in developing cost rent and co-ownership housing are testament that the Housing Corporation was doing more than fiddle while homes burned but also demonstrated its marginal position. The mechanisms that the Corporation had were being rendered ineffective by economic and financial changes. High interest rates undermined the viability first of cost renting and then also of co-ownership. Arguably the value of the Corporation continuing in its current role was coming under question and the Corporation needed to move more to the centre of the contemporary policy agenda or it would fall off the edge of the policy map. Looked at in another way, policy makers concerned to respond to the evident crisis in housing had an existing reputable organisation at hand that could be asked to take on a wider role.

5

From renewal to crisis 1974–80

Introduction

When it was set up by the Housing Act 1964 the Housing Corporation had the task of promoting cost rent and co-ownership housing by housing societies. The limited nature of this task and the financial and economic environment as well as a changing housing policy debate made review of the Corporation's role unavoidable. The Corporation emerged with further powers under the Housing Finance Act 1972. The White Paper *Widening the Choice: The Next Steps in Housing*, published in April 1973, had announced the government's intention to strengthen the Housing Corporation and provide it with additional funds so that it could play a leading role in promoting the expansion of the voluntary housing movement. All of this meant a significant change in the role of the Corporation. The Housing Act 1974 is regarded as a watershed in the development of housing associations (Gulliver 2000) and it was also for the Housing Corporation. It increased the amount that the Corporation could borrow for lending to housing associations. More importantly, it provided for a new subsidy, the housing association grant (HAG), so that housing associations could meet the gap between the actual costs of new house building and the fair rents as set by independent rent officers and intended to be fair to both tenants and landlords. HAG was restricted to housing associations registered with the Housing Corporation and backed by two other discretionary annual grants (the revenue deficit grant (RDG) and the hostel deficit grant) designed to address problems on housing association balance sheets. The Corporation was given the statutory duty to register and supervise those housing associations that wished to receive grants. It also was given supervisory powers enabling it to conduct enquiries into the running of associations, to wind them up or to freeze their assets.

The Housing Corporation had moved from a niche player on the fringe of mainstream housing provision to a position closer to centre stage. It also entered a public sector phase that required new financial arrangements. These were not changes it had envisaged from the outset or was entirely comfortable with and a new leadership was needed for new directions.

The Housing Finance Act 1972 had repoliticised the housing policy debate. It had introduced a degree of controversy and conflict into housing policy that had largely been missing in the post-war period as governments had competed first to achieve the highest levels of house building and then to be identified with home ownership. The new policy agenda marked a sharp division between the parties in their attitudes to council housing. The Housing Finance Act 1972 would involve significant rises in rents for many council tenants and there was strong opposition to this. The refusal of Clay Cross council in Derbyshire to implement rent increases and the consequent surcharging of councillors was the tip of the iceberg (see Lowe 1986: 94ff). The antagonism of the Labour movement to the Housing Finance Act meant that legislative provisions on rents were likely to be reversed by a Labour government if elected. What was less certain was how far such a new government would change other aspects of policy, including those related to the future role of the Housing Corporation.

The continued increase in both building costs and interest rates had begun, by the early 1970s, to make even co-ownership schemes, with their personal share in the equity of the buildings, an unattractive proposition. The Corporation's role was broadened by its power to lend to subsidised rented projects, but these were also hard hit by rising costs, and the subsidy provisions of the 1972 Act, which tapered off support, did not protect associations. The real change came with the introduction in the Housing Act 1974 of HAG and the RDG, which together effectively ensured the financial viability of any scheme once approved. This legislation and the appointment of a new leadership of the Housing Corporation led to the closest thing possible to a cross-party decision. The new Labour government endorsed the approach set out by its Conservative predecessor in respect of these matters while reversing policy on rents. There was a green light for the Housing Corporation with more money and a dramatic increase in activity. The total allowance to associations in the period 1974–9 amounted to £1,360 million, of which £400 million was lent in 1978/9.

The massive commitment of resources to making the voluntary sector a significant third force in housing provision was accompanied by the conferment on the Housing Corporation of stringent powers to ensure adequate control through legislation and supervision of associations. The development of new housing strategies and investment programmes (housing plans in Scotland) also signalled the intent to co-ordinate and plan the contribution of housing associations and local authorities and others more effectively at a local level. However, as in the previous period economic and public expenditure problems led to a cutback in activity, and the framework of cash limits added new tensions. Finally the election of a new Conservative government (in 1979), determined to reduce public expenditure further, to reduce municipal housing provision and not enamoured of any publicly subsidised housing, called the whole activity of the Corporation into question.

Changing leadership

Rather than the Housing Corporation it was the housing association movement nationally that had been re-energised by the new concerns about poor housing and homelessness and the need to find alternatives to slum clearance. More community and locally accountable associations were set up, often with charitable support – sometimes augmented by grants from the new national campaign for the homeless, Shelter, established in 1966. The new generation of housing associations did not initially find the Housing Corporation responsive. They were addressing the needs of people who were affected by the overall housing shortage, the cost of housing, the unscrupulous behaviour of some private landlords and the fact that there was inadequate legal protection against their behaviour. For example, the Paddington Churches Housing Association in London was set up in 1965 by a group including local church leaders and businessmen involved with Paddington Borough Council. The association received a grant from Shelter to enable it to survive and obtained funding from Westminster City Council and the Greater London Council. When it contacted the Housing Corporation in the run-up to the 1974 Act it discovered that the Corporation had never funded rehabilitation, emphasising its concern with co-ownership schemes for middle-class people who had no social problems.

As part of the revival of the housing association movement the National Federation of Housing Societies (NFHS) also changed. It had been dominated by traditional and respectable associations. It had come out of the Octavia Hill tradition and was seen by some as lacking dynamism and 'not at the cutting edge of anything'. The new generation of inner city associations committed to rehabilitation had set up their own pressure group called the

Improvement Action Committee as the equivalent of a trade body and had appointed Richard Best (at that time working to set up associations for the British Churches Housing Trust) to administer it. Following the 1974 Act the NFHS reconstituted itself to make itself more widely acceptable. It became the National Federation of Housing Associations (NFHA) and Lewis Waddilove, its chairman, paid off the incumbent chief executive and installed Best. The new housing associations were beginning to assert themselves at the same time as a new leadership created a more receptive atmosphere in the Housing Corporation.

The ethos of the Housing Corporation was quite separate from that of the newer inner city housing associations across England and it would have to be dragged into the new era rather than leading others. Effectively the Corporation in 1974 was faced with an externally created revolution. In response, and in anticipation of a more prominent role closer to the centre of housing policy, Lord Goodman was appointed chairman of the Housing Corporation and of the National Building Agency (NBA), as we saw in Chapter 4 (HCBM 16/4/73). He was charged with reviewing the functions of the Corporation and the NBA and their relationship to enable them to make the most effective contributions to the new initiatives. As a first step towards establishing closer working relations, the NBA was represented at Corporation meetings and John Baker, assistant secretary at the Department of the Environment, who had been assigned to Goodman by the department as liaison officer, was also invited to attend.

The transformation in the activities of the Housing Corporation meant that in 1974 there was a total increase in staffing of some 40 per cent, and the Corporation took a number of steps to reorganise itself to deal with its changing tasks. It strengthened its structure and staffing at headquarters level and in the regions especially to cope with wider responsibilities for strategic planning and the promotion of the voluntary housing movement as a whole. It carried out detailed examination of its regional organisation, developed a new grading structure of posts to provide younger staff with a clear career path, recruited twenty-five new graduate trainees and additional surveyors, extended arrangements for consultation between staff and management, appointed a training officer and started to develop a range of far better training facilities for staff at all levels (HCAR 1974/5). While the 1974 Act provided the legal infrastructure, the Housing Corporation liaised with the DoE and some of the innovations that were to increase the effectiveness of the legislation emerged. These included the development of funding to train potential chief executives of housing associations (HCBM 8/4/74); those among them who ended up nurturing new associations were affectionately referred to as the 'flower pot men'.

Preparations for improvement

The White Paper *Better Homes: The Next Priorities*, published in June 1973, envisaged a large role for the Housing Corporation in helping housing associations improve and convert older property in the worst stress areas. As preparation for this the position of general manager was replaced by that of chief executive, whose incumbent became a member of the board. A deputy chief executive was also appointed. Dick Madge, then an under-secretary at the Department of the Environment, was made the first chief executive, while his predecessor as general manager, Roger Lloyd Thomas, was appointed to the new post of director of administration, with special duties relating to co-ownership. These changes in the senior staff were part of the overall change in leadership and marked a break with the past. The original staffing of the Housing Corporation had not involved recruitment of people with knowledge of housing associations or housing policy. In contrast the new leadership had policy expertise and experience. Tony Collinson, who was appointed in 1974 as deputy chief executive, was recruited from local authority housing in Lambeth, which had a reputation as a front runner in the development of a modern approach to comprehensive housing management; and John Baker, who was appointed as a second deputy chief executive in 1975, had been closely involved in preparing the HAG system and the legislation that extended the role of the Housing Corporation. Operationally the Corporation was split into two parts: one dealing with investment and one with regulation or operations. The two parts under the two deputy chief executives worked together on any application for funding, pooling their knowledge.

Lord Goodman later described the appointment of key staff and a board of directors who believed in housing possibilities and were firmly convinced of their priority of human affairs. He went on to describe how

> this group of people and the zeal and vigour that they imparted had started to shape a movement that has to a notable extent already changed the face of the country's housing policy, and can, given its head and the appropriate degree of support, make an historic change that could endure for generations. (HCAR 1975/6)

For the housing association movement as a whole, however, these changes did not signify too much. The main staff of the Corporation remained the same and housing associations regarded it as a very weird and alien animal. It is instructive to refer to Ken Bartlett's experience when he was appointed the Corporation's policy officer in March 1979. He moved from the Paddington Churches Housing Association, which he had helped to found, and received a series of sorrowful and vitriolic letters from luminaries in the housing association movement, expressing incomprehension at the decision to join the organisation and regarding it as some kind of betrayal. In retrospect it was the recruitment from a wider pool of expertise over a lengthy period which was effective in changing the perception of the Housing Corporation, at least to some extent. In practice the role of the Housing Corporation was fundamental and unless housing associations could influence that role, then the organisation would not be as effective as it could otherwise be.

The last period of Conservative government in 1973–4 was marked by active debate about the option mortgage scheme, changes in legislation to deal with ailing societies, proposals related to Scotland, financial assistance for London housing associations to make finance available for the acquisition of property in the capital, and a regional dimension to the Corporation's strategy (HCBM 15/10/73). In preparing for a more active role in urban renewal it was agreed that most property acquired should be expected to have a life of thirty years or more, but short-life property could also be considered for loans where redevelopment rights could be retained by the association (HCBM 12/11/73). The chairman and chief executive met the minister for housing and construction to discuss the housing of key transport staff in London and how surplus British Rail land might be brought into use for this purpose (HCBM 14/1/74). As a result British Rail signed an agreement with the Corporation to make land available for development by fair rent housing associations, in return for nomination rights over a proportion of the dwellings. Finally there was consultation with DoE officials on the government's planned new legislation. The Housing and Planning Bill, published on 25 January 1974, proposed legislative changes concerning the Corporation and the voluntary housing movement, and was well received on both sides of the House (HCBM 11/2/74). However, it was overtaken by the announcement of the general election, to be held on 28 February. Although the Corporation's planning could reasonably proceed on the assumption of the continued expansion of its role, hard decisions had to await confirmation of the policy of an incoming government.

As anticipated, the antagonism aroused by parts of the Housing Finance Act 1972 was such that the new Labour government reversed policy on rents, immediately prohibiting any rent increase during the period 8 March–31 December 1974 for any dwelling let on a regulated or controlled tenancy (HCBM 11/3/74). This included housing association tenancies but not co-ownership. It would cause financial difficulties for associations with existing fair rent schemes, subject to phased withdrawal of subsidy, and it was hoped that early legislation on the lines of the defunct Housing and Planning Bill would be introduced to address this. The environment secretary, Anthony Crosland, advised the Corporation at the end of March that the voluntary housing movement would be supported by the new government and that it was intended to introduce legislation on the lines of the lapsed Bill at an early date (HCBM 8/4/74).

Against this background the Corporation pressed ahead with its expanded programme and plans for the future. The government backed its commitment to the Housing Corporation and Parliament approved the Housing Corporation Advances (Increase of Limits) Order 1974 and increased the limit on borrowing from £150 million to the maximum of £300 million prescribed under the Housing Finance Act. Two years later the Housing Corporation Advances (Increase of Limits) Order 1976 was approved by Parliament and the limit on borrowing raised to the maximum of £600 million prescribed under the Housing Act 1974 (HCBM 8/3/76).

The change in the leadership and environment for the Housing Corporation was indicated by the different format for the 1974/5 annual report and a contribution written by the chairman. Goodman's preface was a brief and entirely personal introduction that made plain the progress which the Housing Corporation had made in the year under review. This referred to 37,000 approvals for new or improved homes for the year, or 47,000 if local authority-financed schemes were taken into account, and this was 'an achievement of which the movement can rightly be proud'. In Goodman's view 'it demonstrates beyond argument that provided the appropriate money remains forthcoming from the government and successive governments, the voluntary housing movement is now already an established and valuable institution in the provision of homes for people whose incomes makes some degree of public assistance necessary' (HCAR 1974/5: 1).

The Corporation's expanded role led to a move to new premises on 8 November 1976 at Maple House in Tottenham Court Road, where it remained until it was wound up. All of the schemes that associations put forward were considered at the regional level. In England the Home Counties South regional office was in Croydon, Home Counties North was in Potters Bar, South West in Exeter, East Midlands in Leicester, West Midlands in Wolverhampton, North West in Manchester and North East in Leeds. The Welsh regional office was in Cardiff and there were two offices in Scotland, one in Edinburgh and one in Glasgow.

Registration and monitoring

The new and expanded task of the Corporation included, for the first time, a statutory requirement to register housing associations. To be eligible for support from the Corporation housing associations must be registered; the Corporation would maintain the register and decide whether or not to accept an application for registration. This created a critical process for all housing associations and Lewis and Harden (1982) indicate that the NFHA fought successfully on behalf of its members to prevent the 1974 Act containing restrictive registration provisions. The context for this was a view indicated by the considerations of the Cohen committee (CHAC, 1971) and others that voluntary housing was composed of a vast number of bodies of a bewildering variety of types, mostly small and without considerable assets: the case for simplifying arrangements was evident. Against this background the board considered two options: whether to have a blanket system in place to cover all but the few associations which could not satisfy criteria of probity and financial stability, but leaving the Corporation itself to operate selectively, subsequent to registration; or whether to have a more positively selective system based in part on policy criteria.

In the event and following the representations of the NFHA, any restrictive registration option was discarded. Instead the Corporation was given power to establish criteria in consultation with a statutory advisory committee appointed by the minister for housing (the Housing Associations Registration Advisory Committee (HARAC)). Harden and Lewis (1988: 169–70) argue that the government wanted to see success and co-operation after the 1974 Act and did not want conflict with associations. Consequently it was best to adopt a policy that would result in the registration of almost all associations in the shortest possible time. The initial registration process would represent a 'coarse sieve' and reliance was placed on post-registration supervision to prevent impropriety in the use of public funds. The HARAC consisted mostly of NFHA members and the agreed criteria were devised and published to structure the process of registration rather than to result in exclusion. This does not mean that all applications for registration were successful. There were rejections and there were instances where the Corporation did not simply approve registrations but required a more robust proposal before doing so. In effect, however, the NFHA, the government and the Corporation arrived at a set of arrangements that suited each party at the time but has left a legacy of burdensome monitoring, continual form filling and a long list of post-registration supervision.

When the minister for housing, Reg Freeson, formally set out the criteria he wanted to see adopted for the proposed registration of housing associations under the new legislation, they were seen to be in line with the Housing Corporation's own thinking (HCBM 8/7/74). There would be no formal appeals machinery, but the Corporation would be required to consult the HARAC before establishing the criteria for registration. Following this consultation the criteria were established in December 1974. They were sufficiently detailed to effectively define and structure the basis on which decisions would be made and referred to matters of probity, viability and efficiency. They were intended to ensure that registered associations, which were not directly accountable to the public, were seen as serving the public as distinct from private interests. The registration criteria were sent to all housing associations registered under the Industrial and Provident Societies Act 1965 and to all those registered with the Charity Commission. All of these associations were invited to notify the Corporation if they intended to apply for registration. The register of housing associations was opened on 20 March 1975. By the end of March 2,900 associations had said that they intended to apply and 1,423 had made formal applications to register, mostly at the end of the month. Green folders, each containing all the data on a particular association, were numbered and went to a panel of the board, which, as the registration committee, decided whether they would allow them through. A schedule of those approved was then ratified by a full board meeting.

Goodman referred to a process of careful registration 'to sift from the ranks of the associations the small number whose activities may give rise to doubts and even suspicions' (HCAR 1974/5: 2). He urged patience if the registration process took time and referred to the question of the control of housing associations through their committees of management:

> To us, a genuinely voluntary association is one which achieves the coming together of a committee of a number of private persons, set on performing the important task of improving the nation's housing without consideration of personal benefit or private reward. Many such have always been but there have been others where the committees and management have been controlled by people, not infrequently professional men, who have been able to use their controlling position to provide themselves with income from professional fees or other forms of contract and remuneration. Again, many such men have operated with the highest of motives for little return and not the least suspicion of impropriety but it has become clear that the handling of a vast investment programme financed substantially by the tax-paying public requires a separation between those who, as committee members, control the distribution of these resources and those supplying as contractors to the association goods and services financed by the same resources. (HCAR 1974/5: 2)

By the end of March 1976, 1,561 associations had been registered out of the 2,796 that had applied. Only seventy-one applications had been rejected on the grounds that the criteria for the registration established by the Housing Corporation had not been fully satisfied. In some cases rejected applicants were advised to resubmit applications after making significant changes. Of the thousand or so applications remaining at the end of the year 372 had been withdrawn and a further 400 were awaiting more information for completion. The Corporation's annual report reflected upon the process of registration and concluded that the spur that registration gave to associations was to take a fresh look at their style and quality of management:

> The main gain from registration has, we believe, been to enable shortcomings to be put right and to ensure that they are. The result has been to strengthen the quality, efficiency and accountability of many associations and to confirm the confidence that may be placed in registered associations supported with public money. (HCAR 1975/6: 11)

At the same time the Corporation stated that registration was not an end in itself: the Corporation had the duty to continue to monitor the efficiency and probity of registered housing associations. The annual report stated: 'We hope to develop this not only as a means of checking on associations but as a method of advising them on management and policy issues [HCAR 1975/6, p. 11].'
Registration had demonstrated a range of problems arising from the

number of small individual associations operating in one area. Although small associations had advantages, particularly in being able to concentrate on local problems and on small schemes in the most sensitive way and being able to call on more voluntary help, they might not find it possible to employ or command development and other skills needed in the complicated world of housing regulations and procedures.

The process of registration was not straightforward and the Corporation was sometimes put under considerable pressure. For example, all local authorities were asked in 1976 to give the Corporation their views on the registration of housing associations. One of the registration forms (HAR2) required the local authority to comment on individual named housing associations that were seeking registration. Occasionally local politicians sought to block registration without giving good reason or attempted to insist that any registered associations would be required to give the local authority rights to nominate all the new tenants for housing association properties (100 per cent nomination rights). This was incompatible with a government circular which required that local authorities could only ask for a reasonable number of nominations and certainly not 100 per cent. The refusal of the Corporation to acquiesce could lead to further attempts to bully or coerce its officers. In at least one case it seems likely that local politicians retained a suspicion of housing associations because of the involvement of key individuals in earlier co-ownership schemes that had been lucrative for their founders. The assumption was that if the same people were involved in housing associations at a later time, they were still benefiting personally in the same way as previously; and if the Housing Corporation was registering these associations, there was an assumption of corrupt practice.

By 1976/7 the Corporation reported that it had substantially completed the massive task of registering some 2,400 housing associations. The emphasis then shifted towards monitoring. New co-ownership schemes on the lines the Corporation originally promoted were no longer an economically viable proposition for the people co-ownership was intended to help. Monitoring proposals raised their own concerns at this stage and a meeting was held with representatives of the NFHA and the Scottish Federation of Housing Associations (SFHA) in relation to monitoring. This removed a large degree of misunderstanding. It had been accepted that monitoring must be a checking-and-audit process, but it was to be conducted in a manner that was helpful rather than inquisitorial (HCBM 8/11/76).

Once the initial registration exercise was virtually completed, the Corporation, in consultation with other interested bodies, considered how to ensure that the register contained an up-to-date record of all registered associations and how to demonstrate that all such associations were still adhering to the criteria, conditions and understandings under which they had been registered. It was felt that matters such as the total and geographical location of housing stock, total staff and disclosures of interests were appropriate for public record and that there was also a need to fill some gaps in the basic data held about registered associations. The most practical way of achieving this was to ask associations to complete an annual return, which would provide a natural successor to registration documentation. The general layout of the annual return, HAR10, was consequently modelled on the application form for registration, HAR3. The format of this annual return had been discussed with associated bodies, including colleagues in the sponsoring government departments in England, Scotland and Wales, the NFHA, the SFHA and the Council of Co-ownership Housing Societies. This set up the system of annual reports through HAR10 returns with a separate annual return for Housing Corporation-funded co-ownership societies. Both returns were to be completed at the end of each financial year.

Because of the eligibility for subsidy through HAG and the RDG, the detailed scrutiny of associations' projects had increased. Once an association was registered the key task was to scrutinise and consider approving its actual schemes. They received detailed scrutiny by both the Corporation and the DoE but against a general background of cost limits determined by the department. These limits were intended to give prior guidance to associations as to whether any particular scheme should proceed at all. In order to qualify for HAG an association should normally work within the cost and design yardsticks laid down. The most striking aspect of this system is that both design and cost checking were operated by the Corporation and the DoE. In principle both examined the scheme at the feasibility and tendering stages, the Corporation also examined at completion, and there was further scrutiny by the DoE before payment of the grant was authorised. This double scrutiny was later identified as unnecessary duplication and removed in 1980 but at this stage it was deemed necessary by the department.

While the registration panel would continue to meet as normal, the supervision panel would adopt a separate role related to greater supervision of those housing associations in receipt of public funds. Annual spot financial audits of such associations combined with a switch of emphasis towards on-the-ground supervision of associations' business and a streamlining of the monitoring process would constitute a more efficient form of control. There would also be a wider use of capital sanction in cases when associations' performance was unacceptable. There was another streamlining process where associations of proven performance were excused external scrutiny altogether provided they operated within the cost yardsticks. However where yardsticks were exceeded the system of double checking remained and this continued to be regarded as a source of delay, which in turn increased costs, particularly building costs.

In developing its approach to registration a number of difficult issues concerning conflicting interests and the membership of management committees arose. The first of these was the issue of professionals on committees, which particularly affected societies set up to promote co-ownership (and having professionals involved in this on their committees) but wishing in the post-1974 environment to convert to landlord organisations. Traditional associations were not faced with the same problems and did not sympathise with them. The HARAC felt very strongly that, as a condition of registration, the Corporation should require management committees to divest themselves of any members, particularly professionals, who were in a position to take out fees for themselves or their firms. However, the Corporation feared that if this approach was adopted immediately new business might be affected. The HARAC view also directly contradicted the policy and practice pursued over the previous ten years by both central government and the Corporation, while their targets related to a different part of the market and different types of landlord. But it would be difficult for the Corporation to be seen publicly to be at odds with the HARAC. Initially a compromise formula was sought – accepting the principle that committee members should not benefit financially from their membership, but securing sufficient breathing space to enable the orderly transfer of power in their committees. When the draft criteria for registration of a housing association (accepted by the HARAC) were considered, however, there was concern that they could be unacceptable in view of amendments that had been made to the Housing Bill in the House of Lords (HCBM 9/9/74). Counsel's opinion was that it would be *ultra vires* for the Corporation to require associations to arrange their affairs so that a member could not be elected to and serve on the management committee if he received fees for professional work done for the association, or otherwise gained financially from any contract with the association. The HARAC was informed of this and made representations to the secretary of state to introduce amending legislation if considered necessary. Pending the outcome of these representations, the introduction of the registration procedure was deferred and the Corporation adopted a neutral attitude. The secretaries of state for the environment, Scotland and Wales subsequently agreed in principle that amending legislation should be introduced at some later date, to meet the representations by the HARAC in relation to the membership of committees (HCBM 11/11/74).

In a similar context the Corporation considered whether it was appropriate to have members of other statutory bodies on the committees of housing associations (HCBM 14/10/74). The Association of Municipal Authorities was consulted over the propriety of local government officials and elected members serving on the management committees of housing associations, operating in areas where development schemes might be referred to them for adjudication. The preliminary reaction was that there was no reason why local councillors and officials should be debarred from serving on management committees. However, it was expected that the HARAC would suggest new criteria to prevent an association's management committee from being unduly controlled or influenced by any other statutory authority which had its own housing powers and responsibilities. It was understood that the establishment and early publication of such criteria, by the Corporation, would be welcomed by the Department of the Environment (HCBM 8/12/75). Reg Freeson subsequently accepted the need for amending legislation to prohibit members with a pecuniary interest from serving on the committees of management of registered housing associations (HCBM 18/4/77). Later in 1977 he acknowledged and encouraged individual initiatives taking place within the voluntary housing movement but also expressed concern that there was slow progress towards achieving full democratic accountability (HCBM 10/10/77). There was also discussion of the issue of payment to members of housing association management committees (HCBM 11/10/76); the Corporation recommended to ministers that any future legislation on the subject might be worded to allow the Corporation discretion to approve payment in exceptional cases.

The development of registration and monitoring was surrounded by tensions with the NFHA and individual housing associations. Put simply, while the Corporation regarded itself as beholden to the central department and was developing its very strict criteria for development and other activities, housing associations wanted a completely free hand to do exactly as they preferred. Once housing associations had found a site, identified the need and agreed it with the housing authority, they wanted to move ahead – to get their hands on public money without any strings whatsoever. They did not always appreciate the Corporation's ways of scrutinising proposed schemes in detail.

There were different issues when associations started buying properties off the shelf from builders, and these related to the standards to which properties were built. There were also tensions about what were seen as inconsistencies in expenditure – expensive cars for chief executives. And there were tensions about the effects of the Corporation's zoning policy and the impact of this on the plans of some of the larger associations. The Corporation used its central team of surveyors and a surveyor in each regional office to scrutinise individual schemes and assess whether it was a good scheme to lend money on or not. Their view was that they were dealing with vast sums of public money and had to be sure they were putting it in the right places.

The Corporation, in developing this approach, was working within a broad brief from the DoE rather than a detailed one. The DoE in liaison and other meetings indicated where they felt the Corporation ought to be putting money and the Corporation developed the processes to determine how this was achieved in detail. Changes of government tended to mean a shift in emphasis between the south-east and the north. The broad nature of the department's brief also meant that the Corporation carried out and used research to develop innovations. For example, it is argued that the support for specialist housing for older people grew out of a research-based recognition that an ageing population with smaller households had needs that differed from those of other households, but people living in three-bedroom houses who no longer needed them would not move out unless they were offered something attractive. From this the Corporation developed and funded proposals with housing associations for sheltered housing schemes. Funding for hostels for single people developed from a similar recognition of need rather than through pressure from the DoE. This variety of activity also meant that the Corporation was funding a wide range of specialist as well as a diverse group of more general housing associations.

Delivery

The number of fair rent housing association schemes and the number of dwellings involved in 1974 had already outstripped the co-ownership pro-gramme for that year and the cost rent programme had effectively vanished. That year there were also a very small number of conversion schemes and some schemes under arrangement with the GLC. In effect the Housing Corporation had begun to change tack. Table 5.1 indicates the growth in new building and rehabilitation. Between 1975 and 1980 new building increased by over 75 per cent in England (and more in Scotland and Wales) while the contribution to rehabilitation rose from almost nothing. Table 5.2 indicates an uneven pattern of activity across England but with the greatest activity in the London, North East and West Midlands regions.

Table 5.3 presents data related to improvement grants for a longer time period and highlights the absolute as well as relative growth of importance of housing association activity in this area. In 1970 housing associations accounted for less than 3 per cent of improvement grants. The steady growth in their activity in relation to older housing stock, as well as the decline in both private sector and local authority activity, meant that in 1979 they were responsible for almost 14 per cent of improvement grants. While housing associations were still very much the junior partners of local authorities in all of these areas, they were increasing their contribution significantly.

Following the Housing Act 1974 the Corporation concentrated on funding schemes for homes to let at subsidised rent, both through new building and increasingly through the acquisition and improvement or conversion of older homes. This represented a radical transformation. While new building for rent was the dominant activity, improvement and conversion of existing houses, including those under the partnership arrangement with the GLC, had

Table 5.1: New-build and rehabilitation completions 1975/6–1979/80

	England	Wales	Scotland	Great Britain
New build				
1975/6	7,579	191	462	8,232
1976/7	10,329	429	565	11,323
1977/8	16,243	523	626	17,392
1978/9	13,301	797	908	15,006
1979/80	13,331	1,350	800	15,481
Total	60,783	3,290	3,361	67,434
Rehabilitation				
1975/6	214	0	71	285
1976/7	887	29	435	1,351
1977/8	4,617	121	519	5,257
1978/9	10,510	260	1,548	12,318
1979/80	7,926	196	1,059	9,181
Total	24,154	606	3,632	28,392

Source: HCAR (1979/80: 24, 1980/81: 25).

Table 5.2: New-build and rehabilitation completions in the regions of England 1975/6–1979/80

	New build	Rehabilitation
London	6,496	11,060
South East	13,854	1,143
South West	5,661	868
East Midlands	6,143	953
West Midlands	10,417	2,348
North East	10,417	3,679
North West	7,795	4,103
England	60,783	24,154

Source: HCAR (1979/80: 24).

Table 5.3: Dwellings approved for improvement grants 1965–79, thousands

	Private owners	Housing associations	Local authorities	Total
1965	85.2	*	37.8	123.0
1966	77.5	*	30.2	107.7
1967	82.6	1.7	28.8	113.1
1968	81.1	2.1	31.0	114.2
1969	76.4	3.2	29.4	108.9
1970	110.5	4.1	42.0	156.6
1971	130.2	6.2	61.1	197.5
1972	208.4	6.8	104.0	319.2
1973	238.0	5.1	117.9	361.0
1974	149.3	5.3	77.3	231.9
1975	84.5	5.3	37.1	126.9
1976	72.8	13.9	39.0	125.6
1977	68.5	19.8	37.6	125.8
1978	62.3	14.7	50.9	127.8
1979	64.7	19.0	52.3	135.9

* Included with private owners before 1967.

Individual figures have been rounded to the nearest hundred. Totals are derived from unrounded numbers and may not equal the sum of the rounded numbers.

Source: Holmans (1987: 160).

increased dramatically. In addition there were significant portfolio acquisitions. The combination of a falling property market and rents failing to keep pace with inflation had led or forced many owners of large property portfolios to put their older or less profitable holdings on the market. Housing associations were keen to purchase this type of property in order to improve it, to keep it within the rented sector and to protect existing tenants from the uncertainties and difficulties that attend speculation in property (HCAR 1974/5). From 1974 onwards the major element in programmes was refurbishment and some of the key players experiencing the most rapid growth were the newer inner city housing associations initially established with grants from Shelter.

The Corporation supported two housing associations as central buying agencies for the acquisition of portfolios. The United Housing Associations Trust and the United Kingdom Family Housing Association negotiated the acquisition of portfolios and property companies. The expectation was that properties so acquired would be passed on to experienced housing associations, which would become responsible for the improvement and ongoing management of the housing. While this usually transpired it did not always do so. In 1974/5 the Corporation referred to the approval of the purchase of ten major portfolios comprising more than 4,000 units of accommodation centred mainly on London, Manchester and Liverpool. The annual report also referred to its desire to support housing associations' activities in housing action areas and their contribution to meeting special housing needs.

In the early part of 1974 the slump in the market for new homes left many builders with new or partly built developments which they were unable to sell. The government agreed that local authorities and to a lesser extent housing associations should be able to take the opportunity of adding to their stock of rented housing by purchasing such developments where they were in places with a high demand for rented housing that could be used to relieve housing pressure. During the year the Corporation approved a number of schemes of this kind, the largest being for more than 500 houses to rent in the London Borough of Sutton. This responsive housing market intervention was less dramatic than the Housing Market Package of 1993 (see Chapter 7) but demonstrated the same advantages for the government of having an agency that could help in situations of market difficulty.

During the year 1976/7 the Housing Corporation obtained Reg Freeson's approval for a limited pilot programme of equity-sharing schemes designed to extend the co-ownership concept and fill a gap in the housing market. Two principal versions were agreed, co-ownership equity sharing (CES) and community leasehold, and pilot projects were planned for these in England and Scotland. The key to CES was HAG. Under CES around half the capital cost would be financed by a block building society option mortgage, around a third would be funded by HAG, and the remainder financed by the

Corporation on second mortgage. The Corporation would retain the freehold of the landlord property and that part of the equity funded by HAG would always remain in social ownership, but outgoing tenants would qualify for 50 per cent of any appreciation in the value of the property provided they had lived there for at least a year. Community leasehold came in two forms. The initial form designed primarily for young couples in housing need involved the individuals obtaining a building society mortgage to cover the purchase of a lease. Leasehold schemes for the elderly involved sheltered housing where some contribution from the occupier, usually as a result of the sale of their previous home, was used to purchase the lease. In both schemes the part of the costs not raised by the individual's contribution would be covered by public funds and the occupier would pay rent for this portion.

The annual report for 1976/7 continued to refer to co-operative housing and self-build schemes, but its major focus was upon housing associations' role in rehabilitation; it referred in particular to the Liverpool Housing Trust, to the activities of Shape in Birmingham and to Brent Housing Association Ltd. There were other examples related to the south-west of England and separate emphasis was placed on Scotland and Wales. The Corporation also referred to its activities in Scotland and Wales. In Scotland the major associations were stated to have moved successfully into the field of subsidised housing for rent. Scotland was poised for major expansion with particular emphasis on rehabilitation work. Although there was less activity in Wales the Corporation also referred to the increasing range of housing schemes there.

Management matters

A priority for the Corporation was to lead a drive to strengthen and improve the quality of housing association management (HCBM 13/1/75). It was essential to build up a pool of people with enthusiasm and management skills who were willing to make themselves available to serve on management committees. It was also necessary to reduce the delays in realising schemes. While many delays were due to shortages of suitable staff within the associations themselves, the Corporation, local authorities and government departments, it was important to find ways and means of operating more quickly and efficiently within these constraints. It was hoped that as partnerships developed with local authorities and larger housing associations on a programmed basis, delays would progressively be minimised.

The guidance given to housing associations on the selection of tenants involved discussion with local authorities and others of the extent and nature of housing need and ensuring that housing association homes went to those in greatest need who, for a variety of reasons, had little hope of being housed elsewhere (HCBM 31/3/75). The guidance was intended to facilitate the mobility of labour by housing key workers. Housing associations were urged to make arrangements with the local authorities to identify those people who had greatest claim to housing association properties, but this did not mean that they should simply take people off the local authority waiting list. On the contrary they should use their flexibility and independence also to house people who as yet were not being catered for by local authorities, particularly those who might not have qualified for municipal housing on residential grounds. The Corporation opposed the sale of nomination rights (HCBM 8/3/76), followed up its advice on tenant selection with advice on tenancy agreements, and suggested that associations should consider how they could bring their tenants more actively into the affairs and management of their association. These were things that were to become much more important in future years.

Concern had been raised about the payment of unacceptably high salaries to senior housing association staff. The NFHA was informed of the Corporation's anxiety and pressed to take more of a lead on this subject and to generate self-discipline and a feeling of public responsibility within the movement. It was also asked to notify the Corporation of any problematic cases which did emerge and where any particular salary could not reasonably be justified. The board agreed that it would not hesitate to use the sanction of withdrawing financial support from the association in question (HCBM 8/3/76).

At this stage, in accordance with the recommendations of the Working Party on Housing Co-operatives, Reg Freeson asked the Corporation to assume overall responsibility for sponsoring and advising co-operatives under the guidance of an advisory committee. He also announced that he had been considering additional forms of social ownership and tenure and had asked for a new working group, chaired by Harold Campbell, to consider new forms of social ownership, tenure and management and methods by which wider opportunities might be provided for individuals to share in the ownership and management of their homes (HCBM 8/12/75).

During this period, while there was no right to buy in the local authority sector, local authorities had powers to sell council houses subject to the secretary of state's approval (set out since the 1950s in the form of a general consent). In this context the Housing Corporation, mindful of the government's purposes in giving it powers, normally refused consents to major disposals by housing associations although there were exceptions of a technical nature (HCBM 10/4/74). This policy was supported by the Welsh and Scottish Offices (HCBM 11/11/74) and subsequently the DoE also confirmed its agreement. The board expressed itself generally antagonistic to the sale of properties to sitting tenants and, subject to the proviso that the views of the relevant local authority should be obtained, there would not normally be any such sales (HCBM 14/11/77).

Alongside this the Corporation considered its role in relation to home ownership. Local authority building for sale and equity sharing (shared owner-ship in today's terminology) had been pioneered in Birmingham, Plymouth and elsewhere and the Corporation was developing approaches to equity sharing. By November 1976 there was discussion of a pilot programme to develop equity-sharing systems; following discussion with a number of local authorities, schemes offering homes for sale under arrangements which provided for the local authority to take over any not sold within a reasonable period were proposed and the first scheme completed in Birmingham.

Balancing programmes

The Housing Corporation's early experiences had all related to new building and in the debates about widening its remit it had not shown great enthusiasm for grappling with problems of older housing. However, in its new guise and in its discussions with central government, the question of the balance between acquisition, improvement and conversion of existing older houses and new build, and questions about regional balance had to be addressed (HCBM 13/1/75). The Corporation was provided with programmes which reflected existing ministerial decisions and these set the ceilings on its activities but at the same time it kept the DoE informed of realistic projections of what might be achieved, given additional funds (HCBM 10/2/75).

The approach to programme planning set out in the annual report for 1975/6 saw the Corporation working closely with local housing authorities. The regional offices discussed their housing strategies, the particular needs outstanding in their areas and the role which housing associations could best play. From those discussions and from a central view of national priorities, the total resources allocated to the regions of England and thence to individual housing associations were developed. The proposed programme for each region was discussed with housing associations in a series of regional conferences and regular liaison was maintained with local authorities throughout as programmes grew into specific schemes. The three main stages of scheme approval remained in place: planning and district valuers' approval, DoE yardstick approval and letting the contract.

In addition to focusing upon the quantity of housing, the Corporation and housing associations had been concerned about issues of the quality of housing, including design and maintenance, of efficiency and of accountability and quality of management. These matters were discussed with the NFHA, for whom the Corporation provided financial support to help it employ officers for research and training. This included a specific scheme for selecting and training a small number of potential housing association directors needed to work on rehabilitation in urban stress areas.

In order to provide the right homes in the right places for people who most needed them the Corporation identified three broad priorities:

1. To support the drive to improve housing conditions where they are worst, particularly in housing stress areas, but remembering that the problems in these areas cannot entirely be solved by development and improvements within their boundaries.

2. To promote a substantial increase in new housing for rent throughout the country, but concentrating on those places where the demand for rented housing is greatest or when new rented accommodation would help related stress areas.

3. To support in particular more housing for groups of people with special needs such as the elderly, the handicapped and single people.

The Corporation's annual report for 1974/5 referred to the year as 'one of intense activity, turmoil and inevitably some exasperation. We've all had to develop and learn new ideas, new ways of doing business, new procedures and in the meantime we have all learnt to improvise.' There was a considerable growth in approvals of new housing projects, mainly in fair rent activity. High interest rates and rising costs meant that co-ownership housing was no longer the halfway house between full owner occupation and renting that it was intended to be. In contrast and buoyed by HAG, the combined ambitions of the housing associations were for far more schemes than the Corporation and the local authorities could fund. Talks were being held to fix realistic budgets, but it was sometimes difficult to persuade associations to face the monetary facts. Proposals to decentralise decision taking on housing projects at various stages of approval were also being considered (HCBM 19/3/75).

There was also concern about moving resources wholly across to rehabilitation programmes. While the Corporation had to put its main weight into stress areas, unless some financial resources were reserved to maintain a modest programme and presence throughout the country, the vast majority of housing associations would be denied support and the movement as a collective force could wither (HCBM 12/5/75). In December 1975 the chief executive was authorised to adjust allocations between regions and to transfer some units back from rehabilitation to new build, if this was essential during the last quarter of the financial year, to meet the overall target for the year (HCBM 8/12/75).

The Corporation had begun to take the national and regional dimension much more seriously. It worked closely with the Scottish Development Department and the Welsh Office and acknowledged the different pattern of activity there (HCBM 12/5/75). By the end of 1975, the board began to change its practice in the reporting from Scotland and Wales. In future the Corporation's activities in Scotland and Wales were to form the subject of brief written reports for issue with the other agenda papers, but would not necessarily be discussed (HCBM 10/11/75). A review of the London situation endorsed revised allocations of new build and rehabilitation units, and the Corporation supported initiatives for the promotion of federations of housing associations, with early examples in Leeds and Surrey. The Corporation was actively involved in nurturing new associations where there was not a strong existing presence. With its increased funds and role since 1974, the ability to deliver a programme evenly across the regions was limited by whether the housing associations existed to do the job. Where there were not felt to be enough housing associations to deliver the base load needed, new housing associations were created and newly trained staff put in to lead them. For example the Leeds Federation of Housing Associations was brought together by creating an umbrella organisation from a number of smaller ones.

By this time the Corporation had begun to have doubts about its previous direct acquisition of land and about the future of co-ownership schemes. It had commissioned a review of the latter and the final report was completed by May 1974. At the same time it began to consider the sale of parts of its land bank in view of the current restraints on finance, agreeing that it should review all the land in its ownership and sell off that which no longer fitted in with development priorities (HCBM 13/10/75). Alongside this there were various innovations. Papers were presented to the board on physically handicapped and single-person housing in London, on essential staff (HCBM 10/3/75) and on self-build societies (HCBM 14/4/75). New arrangements for monitoring and model forms of accounts, which had implications for RDG applications, were also introduced (HCBM 13/10/75).

Riding the storm

The newly relaunched, refitted Housing Corporation very quickly ran into the problems associated with high inflation and interest rates, a balance of payments problem and an economic crisis only resolved by the government accepting loans from the International Monetary Fund in 1976. These loans were negotiated on terms which included action to control and reduce public expenditure. The IMF cuts were initially more severe for local authorities but affected housing associations because of cuts in local authority allocations to them. Subsequently the Housing Corporation's own budget was cut. This environment had a profound impact across local authority and voluntary sector housing. In an attempt to control public expenditure at a time of high inflation and high, volatile interest rates, the Labour government introduced new arrangements for housing capital expenditure. Cash limits to fix the maximum level of spending by each authority replaced the 'volume' targets related, for example, to numbers of dwellings built or improved. A system of annual local authority bids and central government allocations was introduced through Housing Investment Programmes (in England and Wales) and the similar Housing Plans (in Scotland), beginning in 1977/8. These involved all local authorities in preparing an annual programme for the next four years; there would be an annual capital allocation, which established the cash limit within which the local authorities could spend, with much less detailed scrutiny of individual schemes by the centre. Although presented as a way of increasing local autonomy, encouraging better working between local authorities and housing associations and the private sector, and achieving better decisions about what activities (local authority new building, improvement activity, housing association activity) to spend money on, the system developed in practice as an extension of central control and was used to bring about substantial cuts in investment.

In Lord Goodman's terms, in 1976 'we are sailing into and hopefully through a financial storm of unprecedented violence. Every timber in the ship is rattling and there never was a time when we were more dependent on the seamanship and skill of the crew for survival.' Goodman went on to emphasise the importance of house building and to assert the success of the housing association movement in building 37,000 homes in the year. This was still not as large as it should be but 'is a gratifying total against the predictions of the Jeremiahs who do not believe in the voluntary housing movement'. The resources available for housing were now insufficient to enable the supply to keep pace with the demand. Local authorities in the previous year had backed far more new housing association schemes than expected, but in the coming year they would have a reduced allocation of resources; although the Housing Corporation's allocation was increased, it was not sufficient to make up the shortfall. In addition, capacity may have been further reduced by the diminishing value of money. Goodman considered that the result had not so far been too injurious to the voluntary housing movement but the bite was already being felt and could have serious repercussions upon housing associations' ongoing programmes.

When the general objectives of the programme for 1976/7 were agreed they involved a continuing shift of emphasis towards rehabilitation at the expense of new build outside London and most markedly in the West Midlands and the North East regions (HCBM 9/2/76). Three months later there was concern that the housing association programme was likely to exceed the cash ceiling of £369 million. Representations were made to the DoE in an endeavour to get the ceiling figures raised in order to avoid pruning approvals in London and other inner city stress areas, but by September it was apparent that there would be no increase in the cash ceiling for approvals in England that year (HCBM 13/9/76).

Running aground

In July 1976 the government required the Housing Corporation to take steps to achieve a saving of £15 million in England and £1 million in Wales in planned expenditure for 1977/8. This meant withdrawal of support from a number of schemes already approved. In December 1976 a further cut of £57 million in the budget for England in 1977/8 was announced, with yet another, even greater reduction the following year. Because of the expenditure already committed for 1977/8 and later years on existing schemes this cut meant a complete freeze on any new work in 1976/7, and a reduction of some 50 per cent in new work planned for 1977/8. A moratorium on new projects for the latter part of 1976 was introduced (HCBM 13/9/76).

The strategy and programme proposed for England for 1977/8 created one of the rare occasions when a board paper was referred back for further consideration. David Mumford, a Birmingham City councillor and chief executive of Copec, declared his interest in the allocation of rehabilitation units to the West Midlands region, but considered that the information provided was insufficient for the board to assess whether the possible cake had been cut into equitable slices (HCBM 11/10/76). A further paper was considered at a special meeting which agreed to a further switch from new build to rehabilitation and from other regions to the north, subject to its acceptability for the purposes of the Public Expenditure Survey Committee (HCBM 1/11/76). On Monday 20 December 1976 a further special meeting of the board considered the public expenditure cuts announced by the government on 15 December (HCBM 20/12/76). The severity of the cuts could undermine confidence and put the future of the voluntary housing movement at risk. It was felt that no attempt had been made to share out the cuts between housing associations and local authorities on any reasonable or scientific basis, or in accordance with the merits and priorities of individual housing schemes. Local authority building programmes had escaped unscathed and to that extent it appeared that housing associations had been discriminated against. It seemed further that the real implications of the expenditure cuts might not have been recognised and appreciated in relation to the cash profile of outgoings on past and present loan commitments.

Problems of financing and the economy did not go away. The minutes of board meetings in 1976 and 1977 are dominated by issues of uncertainty about the allocation of funds and about economic problems.

Private finance

Against the background of cuts, there was increasing activity to find private funding alternatives for housing associations. A separate company in which the Corporation had an interest was set up in 1976 to provide homes for sale (HCBM 8/11/76). This company, Housing Corporation 1974 Ltd, was to operate with private money made available by the banks with a guarantee from the Corporation. The Corporation initially had a nominal holding of ten £1 shares in Housing Corporation 1974 Ltd, in accordance with the consent given by the environment secretary under the Housing Act 1974. Other avenues for obtaining private finance were explored and the annual report for

1976/7 describes attempts to obtain private funding to replace the public expenditure that was cut. The secretary of state assured both the Corporation and the voluntary housing movement of the government's continuing support, and offered to provide guarantees if the Housing Corporation could secure up to £50 million of private money to replace public money and so mitigate in part the effects of the public sector cuts. The Corporation urgently set about looking for private money, and by the end of the financial year was hopeful of concluding arrangements with a consortium of merchant banks for a substantial loan.

Private finance was drawing closer. A group of eight housing associations investigated funding schemes during the construction period with money loaned by their own banks, backed by a Corporation guarantee (HCBM 17/1/77) but questions arose about whether this was possible in practice under existing Bank of England rules (HCBM 14/2/77). Nevertheless the Anchor Housing Association had, subject to a guarantee from the Corporation, negotiated an overdraft facility with its bankers for £20 million and the board agreed to support this. The board also noted that the Orbit Housing Association was soon to complete negotiations with its bankers for an £8 million overdraft and again it was agreed that it should be possible for the Corporation to provide the necessary guarantee (HCBM 18/4/77). Although the secretary of state had agreed in principle to make available the public sector guarantee sought by the joint stock banks (and so enable them to provide working capital for cost sale by Housing Corporation 1974 Limited), formal confirmation of the terms was awaited from the department, together with its endorsement of the proposed arrangements for the local authority to take over, for renting, any unsold houses. At the same time Morgan Grenfell had supplied the Corporation with fairly detailed terms and conditions of a possible inter-bank loan of up to £50 million. These had been examined by the Corporation's financial advisors and the details transmitted to the department, which had in turn passed them to the Treasury, where they were under consideration. Later it was reported that loans had been made by Morgan Grenfell and the possibility of a syndicated twenty-year loan from nationalised-industry pension funds was also referred to (HCBM 22/5/78).

With Sir Lou Sherman having succeeded Lord Goodman as chairman of the board in 1977, the preoccupations remained those of restricted finance, struggling with cash limits and exploring with the DoE additional guarantee powers and private finance options. At the end of 1978/9 it was feared that the annual cash limits would not be achieved (HCBM 12/3/79). In the event, after a last-minute rush the cash target was fully taken up, while in Scotland it was exceeded and in Wales the unit target was missed by just 150 dwellings (HCBM 23/4/79).

Scotland

The Housing Corporation's initial remit embraced Scotland as well as England and Wales. Activity in Scotland started slowly but the Corporation developed a very active and distinctive role. Tenements with significant house condition problems and with mixed ownerships presented a very different challenge for public policy than houses and the community-based housing associations promoted by the Corporation in west central Scotland were an important, innovative response.

From the outset the Housing Corporation reported to the secretary of state for Scotland and received funds from the Scottish Office as well as departments in England and Wales. It opened an office in Edinburgh but its early activities were limited. The Edinburgh office was regarded in Scotland as 'an awfully nice office dealing with co-ownership but never with poor people's housing'. Differences in the housing market had made cost rent even more unattractive than it was in England. The greater proportionate size of the council sector and lower rents also presented a different environment for the development of co-ownership. It was not until activities related to the improvement of older property developed that a Scottish programme took off.

In these early years there were some indications of restricted communication between the Corporation in London and Scotland. By 1971 difficulties peculiar to Scotland had given rise in some quarters to expressions of dissatisfaction and there were discussions related to this (HCBM 8/11/71). In the same year it was noted that in the absence of different directions from the Scottish secretary, the Corporation had no alternative but to assess the viability of schemes in Scotland on the same criteria as for those in England and Wales. These expressions of concern coincided with the opportunity created by the Corporation's expanding ambitions after 1972. They also coincided with Glasgow seeking to expand the tenement rehabilitation budget. Clapham and Kintrea (1992) refer to the significance of the backlash against slum clearance in Glasgow and experiments with alternatives. They credit the idea of community-based housing associations to a group of student architects from Strathclyde University, who set up the Tenement Improvement Project (later known as ASSIST) in Govan in 1970. Their method of co-ordinating improvement was to set up a local residents' group and the first community-based housing association, which bought its properties from private landlords and owner-occupiers who were reluctant or unable to carry out improvement. At the same time Glasgow Corporation was using compulsory purchase to achieve the same improvement outcome.

The Housing Corporation's interest in Glasgow is said to have come directly from Lord Goodman. After his appointment as chairman, Goodman asked for two maps to be hung on the wall. One was a map of housing need in the UK and the other showed where the housing associations were. He looked at these maps and said: 'Hold on, Glasgow has a greater housing need and yet there's virtually no housing associations. Why is that?' He was assisted by David Astor, who visited Glasgow on his behalf. Glasgow had hitherto been quite antagonistic to partnerships with any other organisations but there had been a change in its political leadership and the new council leader, Geoff Shaw, knew Astor well.

Goodman followed Astor's visit with one of his own and this resulted in the setting up of a working party, in collaboration with Glasgow Corporation, to identify stress areas in the city where housing associations might play a major part in acquiring and refurbishing older property (HCBM 10/12/73). There were doubts amongst those developing improvement programmes in Glasgow that the Housing Corporation would respond in the way needed, but following a number of meetings in Glasgow with Dick Madge and John Baker, the Corporation identified Glasgow as a special case needing a different approach and the idea of community housing associations was adopted. Regular reports on activities in Scotland and especially in the Glasgow area became a feature of board meetings. Raymond Young, who had set up ASSIST in the existing improvement programme with Glasgow Corporation, was persuaded to apply for the job of heading what would be a new Glasgow office. He would theoretically report through the regional chief officer for Scotland, based in Edinburgh, but in reality there was a direct line to Madge and Baker. Rather than work from the Edinburgh office the Glasgow team worked from the Planning Exchange until their own premises were obtained.

In March 1974 the Housing Corporation set out to establish a Scottish panel to advise it on the development and expansion of its role and the voluntary housing movement in Scotland (HCBM 11/3/74). Although the Corporation agreed a proposed membership, this was not approved by the

Scottish Development Department until after the second general election of that year – almost a year later. The panel first met in January 1975. By then an interim report had been received from the joint working party considering activities in Glasgow, and the Corporation had agreed to finance the purchase of properties by nominated housing associations within three areas selected for immediate action and with a pilot improvement project in each area if suitable property could be obtained (HCBM 8/4/74).

The Housing Corporation through its Glasgow office promoted a series of new housing associations based in the communities where rehabilitation was being undertaken, and established special stockpiling, acquisition and improvement procedures, all as part of progressing the major partnership with Glasgow City Council, as Glasgow Corporation had become in 1975, for the improvement of older tenement properties in the city. The whole arrangement was publicly launched by Goodman and Sir William Gray, the lord provost of Glasgow, in November 1974 (HCAR 1974/5).

Because of Young's knowledge of tenement improvement issues and existing contacts in the Scottish Development Department, the Glasgow office developed its approach. The community-based housing association model did not appeal to the existing housing societies in Glasgow and involved 'fewer cars and deep pile carpets'. It appealed to a different breed of architect and professional who wanted to work with communities. A big problem was ownership and to deal with this the Corporation set up an acquisition process. The Glasgow office of the Housing Corporation in Scotland (HCiS) developed its own acquisition department on behalf of housing associations and bought from owner-occupiers who could not afford their share of improvement costs as well as from private landlords. Many landlords and owner-occupiers were pleased to sell because they would get some money from the sale. Glasgow factors were a major stakeholder group, as they were the key people to persuade landlords to sell up. The extent to which the HCiS shaped the process is illustrated by the establishment of a special group of housing associations, under the Glasgow Fair Housing Association, which existed solely to buy properties on behalf of community-based associations that had just been set up and where the registration was being processed. Effectively the HCiS was putting a gun to the head of the registration department in London and saying to them: 'This is part of our strategy. We need this organisation [housing association] and you will register it.' This strategy only worked because the HCiS was also quick to move and effective in dealing with any questionable activity.

Where voluntary acquisition did not work compulsory purchase powers were used. The Corporation had compulsory purchase powers but it had been agreed that any decision to seek consent to the exercise of these powers in individual cases should be made by the board as a whole. At the board meeting of 9 June 1975 there was agreement in principle that the Corporation's powers might be used in Glasgow, should it prove to be necessary. Agreement had been reached with Glasgow City Council to set up a committee comprising members of the council's rehabilitation, clearance and redevelopment committee and this was a useful adjunct to the working party of officials (HCBM 8/9/75). By February 1976 it was evident that it was not possible to acquire property in Sauchiehall Street and Derby Street in Glasgow by voluntary agreement and plans in relation to these would not go ahead without the use of compulsory purchase powers (HCBM 9/2/76). Glasgow City Council had made it clear that the area fell within that allocated to the Housing Corporation for development by registered housing associations and that they desired and expected the Corporation to invoke its powers of compulsory acquisition. The board accordingly approved the execution of the Sauchiehall Street and Derby Street, Glasgow Compulsory Purchase Order and instructed that all the required action be taken to secure its confirmation by the secretary of state for Scotland. Other compulsory purchases were approved in Glasgow at later dates (HCBM 10/10/77).

In its annual report for 1975/6 the Housing Corporation drew attention to its activities in Scotland and Wales. It stated that the housing situation was markedly different in Scotland and in Wales than in England. The individual decisions on particular schemes were delegated to the officers for Scotland and Wales, which was intended to cut out a potential source of delay. The activity highlighted in Scotland was the partnership described above with Glasgow City Council to rehabilitate tenement buildings in Glasgow.

> The partnership has gone from strength to strength; experience has shown that the tenements, soundly built but lacking in amenities, can be rehabilitated to provide good homes for the people who live in them. In the special circumstances in Glasgow the Housing Corporation has itself, through its Glasgow office, undertaken the acquisition of flats in existing tenements, community-based housing associations formed from people living and working in the areas have been set up progressively to take over the improvement and management of flats from the Corporation area by area.

Sixteen such associations had been established and 1,272 flats acquired (HCAR 1975/6). Some measure of the significance of the work in Scotland is provided by the fact that in the year ending 31 March 1977 Scotland had the largest rehabilitation programme of any region other than London.

Some existing accounts of community-based housing associations in Scotland emphasise their co-operative credentials and refer to a subsequent history associated with the improvement of municipal housing neighbourhoods. They emphasise, however, that these organisations built on earlier experience from the tenemental improvement of the 1970s. Clapham and Kintrea (1992: 106) state that central government played no direct role in initiating co-operatives in Glasgow and while they refer to Scottish Homes' subsequent role they ignore the role of HCiS in the formative phase. While the political environment and the role of residents and the local authority were critical, the success of the early Glasgow community housing associations also derived from the real freedom that was given to the Glasgow office of the Corporation (and the support received from the key lead officers in London), their link with Glasgow City Council and the Scottish committee set up by the Housing Corporation, and support from the Scottish Office. The joint liaison committee between Glasgow City Council and the Housing Corporation symbolised a very close partnership.

Initially the Glasgow office was only concerned with Glasgow city tenement rehabilitation and anything else was managed by the Edinburgh office. Over time it took responsibility for the whole of Strathclyde, in the first instance for tenement rehabilitation, but by 1978 for all Housing Corporation activities in the region. By then a new chief officer for Scotland was in place in Edinburgh, working with two deputy chief officers – one in Glasgow and one in Edinburgh. In terms of resource distribution Strathclyde generally was allocated 60 per cent and the rest of Scotland 40 per cent. While Edinburgh did not take quite the same approach to community-based associations as Glasgow, there were a number of housing associations which were run by the local community and in effect the HCiS shaped a distinctive set of organisations which have had a long-term impact on urban Scotland and especially the west of Scotland. This was contentious and reflected a different strategy from England.

The HCiS was actually promoting housing associations – physically going out and saying to a community: 'You could do with a housing association here.' The Corporation worked with local authorities, but as the junior partner concerned with delivery while the local authority set the strategy.

Although there was a mutual influence through an effective partnership with the council, the essential stance for communities that wanted houses improved was that their landlord was not likely to do it for them, the council had insufficient resources, but the Housing Corporation could help if a housing association was set up. A group of people were put through a training programme of twelve weeks or so for each of these housing associations. The HCiS also trained people who would become housing association staff: it brought them into the Corporation office, trained them in running housing associations and then passed them out to a housing association. The development of the SFHA, separate from the NFHA, added to the resources available and the capacity of the housing association sector. It had strong relationships with and was supported by the HCiS. The HCiS always attended the SFHA annual conference, having a slot that was regarded as a kind of annual general meeting, and always produced an annual Scottish report for the conference. The development of an employers' group (Employers in Voluntary Housing) was also established with support from the HCiS.

All of these are examples of the HCiS pursuing a strategy to create a distinctive set of organisations and a new movement, and that movement had to be supported. Establishing new organisations and enabling them to stand on their own two feet was crucial. The culture within the HCiS was of working very closely with housing associations at all hours of the day and night – definitely not the arm's length relationship that obtained in much of England. No doubt this was facilitated by the smaller size of the Scottish 'village' and the extent to which people knew one another. It may have benefited from the absence of existing associations when Lord Goodman's two maps demonstrated that there was a huge need and a lack of resources there to meet it. Unlike, say, Liverpool, there were few existing organisations to negotiate with or around and it was possible to set out to fill a vacuum. This enabled a different strategy that was not just about improving houses but was about using the housing associations as part of a community development process. This became even clearer after 1986, when the HCiS was asked to become involved in public sector housing through three co-operatives in Glasgow. In earlier schemes different types of ownership had made the development of co-operatives problematic but in the peripheral estates it was possible to talk about them.

Co-operatives

Previous chapters have argued that while the development of co-ownership schemes may be technically seen as co-operative housing, they were never developed in that manner or spirit. However much the Scandinavian experience was set out as an exemplar, the Housing Corporation adopted co-ownership in a pragmatic way and the key role of sponsoring societies imbued with a private sector professional philosophy meant that in practice co-ownership fell far short of a co-operative model. By the end of 1970 just 16,000 co-ownership dwellings had been built (CHAC 1971: 58). This limited success may be taken as indicative of the weakness of the co-operative lobby in housing but there was still debate about developing real co-operatives.

In 1974 Reg Freeson had become minister of housing in the new Labour government. He remains the only such minister with any ambition to develop co-operative housing, having been involved in founding three small co-operatives in north-west London during the 1950s (Birchall 1992: 13). Freeson commissioned Harold Campbell to consider the prospects for co-operative development and this resulted in amendments to the Housing Rents and Subsidies Act 1975 enabling common ownership co-operatives to register with the Corporation and tenant management co-operatives to be formed. Later, short-life co-operatives were also allowed to register and obtain 'mini-HAGs' for repairs, while secondary co-ops (which were set up to provide management and other services to co-operatives) and housing associations could obtain funds to set up co-operatives. The result of this was a rapid growth in common ownerships formed out of squatting groups, private tenants wanting to take over mansion blocks and others (see Birchall 1992).

The Working Party on Housing Co-operatives, chaired by Campbell, had recommended that a national organisation be set up to act as a forum for co-operative housing development and promotion (DoE 1975). Following this the government invited the Housing Corporation to take on responsibilities for promoting and advising housing co-operatives. During 1975–6 the Corporation lent its support to an increasing number of housing schemes developed by co-operatives and in December 1976 the Co-operative Housing Agency (CHA) was launched with particular support from Freeson. It had a limited budget and a small staff in premises near the Housing Corporation's headquarters, and its aim was to help to create an alternative form of housing tenure in Britain based upon co-operative principles. The agency was to work with and through co-operatives to achieve four aims:

1. to create a legislative and administrative framework which would enable co-operatives to develop in response to local needs;
2. to help make available financial resources for co-operative development and help members exercise proper financial control;
3. to promote the principles and techniques of co-operative housing nationally and provide a national resource centre for co-operative education in housing;
4. to provide some direct assistance for co-operatives and co-operative development groups relating to legal and financial education and housing management development.

The government had removed stamp duty as an obstacle for the transfer of property from a registered housing association to a co-operative formed by tenants and had promised further legislation to deal with other problems. The Corporation stated that it would like to see up to 10 per cent of its capital resources go to co-operatives, both new build and rehabilitation, provided that the schemes met the normal criteria of relieving housing stress or meeting special needs and showed good value for money. In spite of these good intentions and the establishment of an agency, such a level of activity was never achieved. Looking back, perhaps with the exception of community-based housing associations in Scotland, the 1970s appears as the final serious attempt to promote housing co-operatives in Britain; but they did not emerge as a major feature of the housing system (McCafferty and Riley 1989).

The view subsequently articulated to the Housing Corporation was that the CHA had attempted to perform several functions which fitted uneasily within one organisation (HCBM 19/1/79). It had been acting as a controlling and sponsoring body for co-operatives in association with the Corporation's headquarters; it had tried to be a sounding board for the movement and had been performing an educational and evangelising role; its controlling and sponsoring activities had got in the way of its pressure group function and, coupled with a rather rigid approach to its duties, had led to a lack of success in the promotional field too. The alternative was for the Housing Corporation itself to act directly as the controlling and sponsoring body using its wide resources and regional organisation. In its arm's length role the CHA had not been in a position to make full use of these resources. There would be a real advantage in integrating the central part of its work with that part of the Corporation which dealt with policy issues, including the whole spectrum of tenures and ways of giving tenants a greater say in their housing affairs. The Corporation would then staff its regions as necessary to give practical help to co-operative groups. This would be a practical move to achieve greater efficiency and speed of action and to cut out unnecessary procedures for co-operatives seeking registration and funds.

Freeson effectively suggested that there should be revised arrangements for the promotion of co-operative housing, leading to greater take-up by co-operatives of the allocations the Corporation had earmarked for them. This meant restructuring work related to co-operative housing, joining together the work done by the CHA with that done in the Corporation's headquarters, dealing with a whole spectrum of tenures and ways of giving tenants a greater say in their housing affairs. It also meant strengthening the Corporation's regional offices to give practical help to co-operative groups and promoting the development of an independent representational body for co-operatives which, when established, could fill both a consultative and representational role, so replacing the advisory committee on co-operatives. Whether this exchange would have resulted in a new and effective approach to co-operatives, and in the context of constrained finances, must be open to doubt. The CHA was formally integrated within the Corporation's Housing Policy Division on 1 April 1979 but in practice the election of a Conservative government the following month meant the replacement of an enthusiast for co-operatives by an advocate of privatisation.

Lord Goodman's assessment

Lord Goodman appears as the first dominant personality associated with the Housing Corporation, its emergence from the shadows and its successful transition to adopt a much wider role than envisaged in the first decade. By 1976 Goodman had formed the view that

> the voluntary housing movement is now an established success. Only very partially would we want to claim any credit for this at headquarters. The success is due to the bursting out into blossom all over the country of voluntary energy and effort by those who are persuaded that self-help is the best help.
>
> The pullulation of housing associations brings its problems, but it has been in almost every respect a healthy and beneficial phenomenon. (HCAR 1975/6: 1–2)

His assessment at the end of his tenure as chairman, when he was moving on to other tasks, is also instructive:

In the four years of my chairmanship and, more important, in the four years of the splendidly synchronised activities of my team, the movement really achieved near miracles. When we arrived and started the Housing Corporation was supervising or responsible for the building of less than 5,000 co-ownership houses a year. These had started with great enthusiasm, but the enthusiasm waned as circumstances changed, building costs rose and interest rates escalated to astral heights. But the 1974 Housing Act gave us a new virility and a new springboard, it was an interesting demonstration that bipartisan government is by far the best, or in another word non-party government is by far the best. The Act had been prepared and was introduced by Messrs Rippon and Channon in the Heath government. When the government was defeated and the Labour government returned to power there was an awkward period of indecision and the fate of the Housing Act remained unknown, and with it of course the fate of the Housing Corporation. Several weeks elapsed before there finally emerged from the office of my friend the late Anthony Crosland an intimation that the Act would be adopted by the new government, and the Housing Corporation encouraged to become a third limb in the housing movement.

And we did indeed. From under 5,000 houses per annum that were being approved, planned and built in the early years using new powers and the housing association grants, we built houses in an almost Walt Disney-like frenzy ...

Over 2,000 associations were registered in little over a year. Including Scotland and Wales a figure approaching, if not exceeding, 50,000 units was achieved in one year including the units of renovation. (HCAR 1976/7: 1)

Goodman also referred to the reduction in hostility and jealousy with which the Corporation and housing associations were regarded by local authorities; by the end of my day this had diminished almost to vanishing point. The local authorities and the Corporation both exercised great tact in their relationship. He also noted that the curtailment of capital during the year, which fell most heavily on voluntary housing associations, had led to improvisation and that the Housing Corporation had obtained the agreement of the DoE for borrowing from private sources, on the basis of a statutory guarantee.

Conclusions

While Lord Goodman's assessment serves as part of an effective summing up of the Housing Corporation in its second phase, other elements are important.

The Corporation had a much wider responsibility than earlier but, despite Goodman's assertion, was neither universally liked nor trusted by the housing association movement and especially the 'young Turks' who had risen to prominence through energetically engaging with the challenges of the inner city and urban renewal. Its registration role was disliked by some especially where it was imposing a new view of probity and accountability. A slow accretion of standards and practices related to governance and housing management performance was apparent. Recruitment of staff from the housing association sector began to break down barriers and build greater empathy and collaboration between the centre and the coalface. The investment in training would also help to change relationships as well as competences. What was happening has been described by Mullins and Riseborough (2000) as a process of incorporation of housing associations by the state. The 1970s saw considerable expansion in the work of housing associations supported by Corporation funding and local authorities. Associations were increasingly dependent on the state and subject to regulatory mechanisms and these arrangements came to form and strengthen the sector's identity and its networks. Mullins and Riseborough also use the term 'regulatory capture' as a description of the ways in which housing associations actively used policy networks such as trade associations to shape this regulatory regime.

With a larger programme and closer to the centre of the stage the Housing Corporation began to struggle with the twin uncertainties that were to dominate its role thereafter: the economy and the politics of housing policy. Taken together these exposed the Corporation and housing associations as well as local authorities to unpredictable and sudden shifts in the availability of finance. The management of a large number of complex housing programmes to meet an annual cash target required considerable skill and quick-footedness. But if the goalposts moved, if there were sudden cuts, the coping strategies were inevitably more brutal and inefficient and included moratoriums, although opportunities were created that enabled acquisitions from the private sector in times of market downturn. While these issues dominated the Housing Corporation in this period it is also important to note that some of the innovations associated with later years had their roots in this period. Private finance and low-cost home ownership were being mulled over and experimented with and a stronger, distinctive approach had developed in Scotland. This was attributed to various factors but was not replicated in other regions. The distinctive Scottish approach was less bureaucratic and more able to develop solutions that matched its needs, much more committed to developing small community-based organisations and resistant to pressures related to economies of scale and large developments. The English regions were never able to articulate their distinctiveness in the same way and appeared more suffocated by the London bureaucracy. There was no support from government in the English regions equivalent to that from the Scottish Office, whose view was that Scotland was different and whose support made a huge difference throughout.

The continuing struggle against economic turbulence and cuts in public expenditure did not prevent the Corporation from making progress. Indeed, it stimulated consideration of ways of drawing in private finance. But it also drained energy and resources. The failure to develop distinctive regional approaches in England, to develop the co-operative housing schemes commensurate with the stated support for them and to bring tenants to the centre of the debate may be partly attributed to deep-seated reservations about or lack of enthusiasm for these directions. But the immediate economic, financial and political climate also made it easier to neglect them.

6

From bust to boom 1980–88

Introduction

The Housing Corporation had started the 1970s in some disarray and ended it in crisis. While it had successfully reinvented itself to play a role at the centre of housing policy and worked with a larger and more diverse set of energetic and committed housing associations, it had not yet proved itself to them and was treated with some suspicion. At the same time it had been battered by the uncertainties of the economy and the inconsistency of financial and political support. In this environment it had struggled to maintain control over its programmes and its reputation. A new Conservative government elected in 1979 had a vigorously anti-municipal housing policy but was no more enamoured of housing associations, which were equally tainted by their shared dependence on public funding. It had no commitment to the Housing Corporation, which was left in a constant state of uncertainty about its future. There are anecdotes about Margaret Thatcher having instructed her ministers to close down the Corporation and while these are unsubstantiated it is clear that finance was always uncertain, ministers committed themselves to outcomes and expected the Corporation to conjure up delivery and there was always a sense of crisis. Hugh Cubitt, chairman of the Corporation throughout the 1980s, was asked at the end of his term what he would regard as the single most important achievement of his time at the Housing Corporation, and he replied: 'That it still exists,' which shows how tenuous the Corporation felt its survival was. The feeling was that 'during that time the politicians were endlessly trying to get rid of us. We didn't feel they had a huge confidence in us.' At the same time the housing associations themselves expressed considerable antagonism towards the Corporation.

The new government adopted a market-based approach to housing, and providing council tenants with the right to buy would both expand the home ownership sector and diminish the public sector. While tax reliefs associated with home ownership increased, the government promoted low-cost home ownership, deregulated the housing market, reduced tenants' rights and further cut back direct public expenditure on housing. The Conservatives were re-elected in 1983 and again in 1987, and the right to buy, coupled with the effective termination of new building by local authorities, meant a continuing and rapid decline in the council housing sector. Housing associations were operating in an environment that had not existed for sixty years. Local authorities still had large stocks of dwellings although these were being eroded by the right to buy. But they were no longer the favoured plannable instruments of the past and housing associations' ambitions were no longer to be crowded out by the government's attachment to an alternative builder of rented housing. At the same time deregulation of building societies and private lettings further changed the shape and functioning of the housing sector and created a new environment for the Housing Corporation.

After a period of rising unemployment in the first half of the 1980s, increasing social and income inequality generated high house price inflation and a housing market boom associated with affordability problems in the second half. The social rented sector was increasingly associated with disadvantage and failure to invest in the sector was recognised as a problem in the inner cities and elsewhere. Housing associations emerged from this environment with new financial arrangements but were increasingly seen as an alternative to municipal landlordism and, by enabling further dismantling of that sector, were seen variously as potential predators and agents of privatisation or as the key agencies able to maintain active investment in new affordable rented housing.

Reviewing non-departmental bodies

After the 1979 general election the incoming Conservative government set itself the task of increasing efficiency and this included culling quangos. Some of the flavour of the quango discussion emerges from a contemporary publication by a Conservative MP (Holland 1981: 17). This asserted that there were some 600 quangos that could be abolished with savings to the public purse and reductions in unnecessary government bureaucracy and patronage. Holland did not suggest that the Corporation's activities were unnecessary but argued that they could be carried out directly by the Department of the Environment or by local authorities, acting as agents. In either case those responsible for handling the funds would be directly responsible to the general public with their activities subject to public audit annually.

The government's formal *Report on Non-Departmental Public Bodies*, published in January 1980, reflected its concerns that there was a plethora of organisations that were sources of patronage and costly to the Exchequer. In some cases there was no need for these organisations to exist at all, and in other cases they should be replaced and the tasks would be better carried out directly by different ministers and departments. The Housing Corporation was one of the most significant non-departmental public bodies in England. In terms of expenditure in 1978/9 it was the fourth largest quango in operation behind only the aggregate for the regional water authorities for England and Wales (of which there were ten), the combined new town development corporations in England and Wales (seventeen) and the Manpower Services Commission (MSC). On this basis it could be argued that the Corporation was the second largest single quango – almost as large as the MSC. Because it was so important the Housing Corporation received special attention. It was identified (Prime Minister's Office 1980: 17) as the instrument for a rapidly expanding programme of government grants to housing associations; when compared with the alternative of direct government intervention there were advantages in promoting the growth of housing associations but disadvantages because of duplication of detailed paperwork, which did not improve safeguards on the use of the public money. A number of steps, some already planned, could secure less duplication and better safeguards. The verdict was that it would be inappropriate to abolish the Housing Corporation but that perhaps it and its sponsor department could do the job more efficiently or at lower cost.

It is instructive to note the overall view taken of the Housing Corporation by the report as indicative of the government's view at this time. The report devoted more space to the Corporation than any other single organisation with the exception of the MSC. The Corporation was seen as a vehicle for transmitting funds to housing associations, not only from the DoE in England but also from the Scottish and Welsh offices, and it had been doing this at a rate of more than £400 million a year. On average over 80 per cent of that money was in the form of housing association grant and the balance was provided as loans. The reason given for the high proportion of grant in the capital financing of housing associations was that the amount they could charge for accommodation was limited by fair rents. After the initial capital financing operation, if rent proved insufficient to cover current outgoings, including servicing loans, housing associations could receive revenue deficit grant direct from the department. *The Report on Non-Departmental Public Bodies* stated that broadly speaking, local authorities and housing associations provided accommodation of much the same standard, governed by the same cost yardsticks for people in much the same income groups, though the tenants of housing associations tended to be rather poorer than local authority tenants and include a rather large number of people with special needs. The report also stated that the DoE and the Corporation considered that there was no significant disparity when the cost of new work carried out by local authorities and housing associations were compared. A comparison of rents charged was complicated by the fact that local authority accounts benefited from significant amounts of older housing, carrying relatively low loan charges. Housing association rents were broadly comparable with local authority rents but, on average, about 15 per cent higher.

The case for these arrangements was that the Housing Corporation and the housing associations which it financed provided an alternative to the local authorities as a landlord and one 'close to the tenants and capable of giving more personal attention to their particular needs' (Prime Minister's Office 1980: 34). Since the whole of the initial capital and a degree of revenue subsidy were provided by central government they should be subject to the safeguards appropriate when taxpayers' money is being spent. While it would have been simpler and more suitable for departments to deal directly with the associations, and this would have obviated some of the problems which arose from using the Housing Corporation as an intermediary, the case for retaining the Corporation as a chosen instrument was that it was not simply a channel of finance but had a function to promote registered housing associations: the Corporation was better suited than either central or local government for mobilising a great deal of voluntary effort and personal initiative. It could also operate side by side with local authorities in the same areas without raising the issues of relationships that might arise if central government were more directly involved.

The report identified the need to reinforce the safeguards on the use of money but added to the view that the existing dual scrutiny arrangements were not effective in this respect and were unnecessary duplication. The Corporation was audited by a commercial firm but Exchequer and audit departments had access to the books of the Corporation and, within limits, housing associations. The Corporation's staffing arrangements had always been subject to the supervision appropriate for a body whose expenses are wholly met from public funds. It was intended that the Corporation's administrative costs should be financed by grant in aid, which was to be confined to that expenditure and separate from the grants for capital purposes. Enhanced provision was made for the Corporation in turn to monitor the administration of the housing associations and formal safeguards were introduced against duality of interests on the part of housing association members and officers.

The operation of these safeguards had so far involved the disadvantage of substantial duplication of work in the Housing Corporation, whose administrative cost was running at about £5.5 million a year, and in the DoE and the Scottish and Welsh offices, which had administration costs of about £1 million a year arising from functions in relation to the Corporation. These departments were studying the scope for simplifying procedures and eliminating or reducing duplication of effort. The report argued that simplification could not be pursued by forgoing safeguards on public money, but it should be possible to reconcile the two objectives. The fact that senior officials of the departments were the accounting officers for this money, were signing the appropriation accounts and were answerable to the Public Accounts Committee (PAC) appeared hitherto to have inhibited any reduction in the checks carried out by the departments. However, the Corporation's chief executive had appeared with the DoE's accounting officer before the PAC and it was the chief executive and not the accounting officer who was directly responsible for effecting the disbursement of capital finance to the housing associations. This situation was understood and accepted by the PAC and it was regarded as feasible to work out a clear delineation of responsibilities, between the department and the Corporation, that would meet the requirements for safeguarding public funds and reduce the total administration costs involved. The combination of commercial audit and the comptroller and auditor general's right of access would provide a satisfactory arrangement for public scrutiny of the Corporation's accounts. There was no need to displace the arrangements for commercial audit by switching the audit responsibility to the comptroller and auditor general.

A new regime

Accounts of British housing policy place considerable importance on the election of a Conservative government in 1979. While there were continuities with the legislation, patterns of cuts in public expenditure and operation of cash limits associated with the previous government, there were also major breaks. There had been significant sales of council housing in England under previous discretionary policies, but the introduction of the right to buy removed local discretion and increased the levels of discount involved (see Jones and Murie 2006). This represents a good example of policy based on populist, electoral or ideological considerations rather than being evidence based. In the light of subsequent evaluations, the levels of discount offered were excessive and did not represent good value for money. At the same time the failure to invest the capital receipts generated by the sales of properties was a direct rejection of arguments made at the time and apparently supported by both the Housing Corporation and the DoE. Further cuts in public expenditure left local authorities reducing their new building activity but also unable to invest what was deemed necessary to prevent the deterioration of their ageing housing stock. Concerns about the build-up of a backlog of disrepair as well as of rising levels of homelessness were expressed repeatedly. Legislation to strengthen tenants' rights had been presented to Parliament at the beginning of 1979 but fell with the general election. However, the legislation of 1980 largely incorporated the same measures as part of a wider strengthening of tenants' rights and added the right to buy.

Neither housing associations nor the Housing Corporation could be sure of their position under the new regime. The right to buy was initially planned to apply to tenants of housing associations as well as of local authorities, and it was only effective lobbying by the National Federation of Housing Associations (NFHA) in the House of Lords that altered this intention. The Corporation appointed a new chairman, Hugh Cubitt (later Sir Hugh), in 1980. A Conservative, Cubitt had not previously been a member of the board; he was a chartered surveyor and a former lord mayor of Westminster. He was at least initially regarded with considerable suspicion both by the movement and by the staff – 'because they did not think that the Tories knew much about housing or cared too much about it'. His tasks were to persuade the housing association movement and the Housing Corporation staff that 'Tories were not all dyed in the colours of Genghis Khan'. Equally important, he had to 'persuade Tory MPs that housing associations were not all in it for the make and to address their strong feeling that a lot of housing associations had sticky fingers'. The new chairman adopted a strategy later imitated by others of visiting the regions, having dinner parties and entertaining the regional chairmen. While the Corporation's chief executive had a very easy channel of communication to the chief executives of the associations, there was not the same communication with the members of boards, particularly the chairmen, and an effort was taken to improve that communication and to be available to MPs.

The Corporation's annual report for 1980/81 reflected the preoccupation with the effects of cuts in the programme and in expenditure. The year had been dominated by three issues: managing programmes at a time of scarce resources, developing and introducing the new initiatives opened up by the Housing Act 1980, and restructuring the organisation and staffing of the Corporation and its procedures to ensure that the minimum was spent on overheads and the maximum on housing. In a hostile environment, efficiency was very much the buzzword.

The incoming Tory government thought that there was a lot of inefficiency around and the chairman was told to slim down the whole operation and smarten it up. The sense of being under scrutiny and at risk was greatest in this early period and up to 1985. The Corporation persuaded Michael Heseltine, the environment secretary, that it should develop its own system similar to the DoE's Management Information System for Ministers (MINIS). The Corporation's version (referred to as CORPIS by some) was adapted to its particular functions, to enable it to review its manpower needs and achieve the efficiencies to be achieved elsewhere in government. While this gained some plaudits there was opposition to attempts to amalgamate the Glasgow and Edinburgh offices and, even more so, to suggestions that North Wales should be administered from Liverpool and South Wales from Bristol.

There was disquiet within the board at selling co-ownership properties, at the impact of the right to buy on small housing associations (particularly over staffing) and at giving tenants the right to a mortgage from the Corporation (HCBM 4/6/79). There was also concern about the interpretation of the exclusion from the right to buy of special needs housing and about vendors' liability for structural repairs (as a secondary measure to ask for financial provision to be included to enable associations to meet such a liability). The Corporation also pressed for the legislation to preclude officers or employees serving on the committee of their associations. The subsequent ministerial response was that generally associations should be treated the same as local authorities on the question of vendors' liability for structural repairs, though it was conceded that expenditure on this account would be eligible for RDG; and the preclusion of officers or employees serving on the committee of their association was not acceptable to ministers (HCBM 28/4/80). The Corporation was receiving fairly short shrift. Although many housing associations were eventually excluded from the legislation even charitable housing associations were to experience the longer-term consequences of market restructuring.

In July the minister for housing, John Stanley, affirmed his faith in the voluntary housing movement and satisfaction with the Corporation's work and, in the interest of staff morale, consented to the chairman informing staff of a continuing role for the Corporation (HCBM 16/7/79). However, there would have to be a change of emphasis and an acceleration of equity-sharing and conversion-for-sale programmes, and Stanley would require public bodies to dispose of any unwanted land holdings as quickly as possible. He also made it clear that he favoured financing the Corporation through grant in aid (HCBM 10/9/79, 22/10/79). The final decision that double scrutiny was to be abolished from 1 April 1981 was communicated to the Corporation in April 1980 (HCBM 28/4/80) and formally announced in September. Prior to this both the Corporation and the DoE had been required to approve individual housing association schemes – afterwards departmental approval was no longer required. This formed part of an attempt to reduce bureaucracy and controls and to concentrate decisions on the key issues of whether a scheme met the priorities within the programme and how much money should be invested in it. The outcome was said by the Corporation to minimise the number of occasions on which associations needed to obtain its prior approval before taking the next step in progressing a scheme, and to avoid the need for one professional to go over the technical work of another. The new procedure would clarify responsibility, improve accountability, save time and, as a consequence, reduce the interest cost on schemes.

Prior to the implementation of this change and following the earlier discussions with Stanley on the grant in aid budget and on the reduction in the capital programme, the Corporation's structure and organisation had been reviewed along with the procedures for scheme scrutiny, supervision and control. The outcome of the review indicated possible staff savings in the region of 110–135 on a current establishment of 657 in England; the annual report referred to a new structure in England that would reduce the number of posts from 657 to 517, a saving of 140 (HCAR 1980/81: 21). On supervision and control it was proposed to make more use of commercial auditors in the supervision of financial stewardship. The Corporation's role in monitoring would be concentrated on the detection and elimination of serious weaknesses or misconduct in the running of associations' affairs. The Corporation would no longer be able to provide what amounted to a management consultancy service. Procedures would be simplified, with a revised division of labour between the Corporation and the associations and between the Corporation's HQ and its regional offices. The responsibility for design and construction work in individual schemes would be placed on the associations themselves, with minimal approval stages by the Corporation. Greater delegation of scheme work to regional offices was also proposed.

In spite of these changes the Corporation remained under pressure. In 1981 Stanley summoned Hugh Cubitt and told him that he was not happy with the Corporation's performance; procedures were far too complex, he was getting complaints from everybody and he was minded to do something else with it. The Corporation worked intensively to respond to this, including undertaking a project called Operation Aberdeen to rewrite the procedures within three weeks, resulting in a number of redundancies. The pressure continued throughout this period although the riots in Liverpool and elsewhere in 1981 meant some recognition by the government that they could not wholly neglect housing or the inner cities and the Housing Corporation was needed to develop a response.

Cash limit crisis

The imperative at a time of economic difficulty and pressure on public expenditure was to operate within strict cash limits. The Corporation did not have the funds needed to pay for existing commitments and new programmes of the size possible in previous years. It had to adjust within the year to cash limits implying a programme operating at a lower level than in the past. In order to fund work in progress it had to limit the level of new commitments.

The government, with its preoccupations with efficiency and controlling public expenditure, was, as late as January 1980, unable to provide any information on the allocation to be made to the Corporation for 1980/81, nor could it give any indication as to when an announcement might be made (HCBM 28/1/80). In the light of this the Corporation could not give advice to the housing association movement and prepared contingency plans based on a range of reductions in the programme. The eventual allocation to the Corporation was a cash limit of £420 million total expenditure in 1980/81, but subject to a limit on commitments during the year of £368.4 million. The latter figure was intended to permit about 20,000 approvals as against 33,000 in 1979/80, but John Stanley hoped that the allocations would be stretched as far as possible by introducing schemes of shared ownership and rehabilitation for sale (HCBM 10/3/80).

As the year 1980/81 progressed it became clear that a programme of 20,000 dwellings could not be met within the cash figures available and continued uncertainty about expenditure dominated affairs (HCBM 14/7/80). Projections from the first quarter's expenditure figure for England (£121.2 million) suggested that the limit of £420 million would be exceeded. The Corporation discussed with Stanley the possibility of a longer-term programme for associations but a three-year programme was not regarded as possible at the time. By September it had become clear that the cash limit of £420 million for 1980/81 was not enough for the programme intended (HCBM 15/9/80). Stanley had requested adjustments to reduce projected expenditure by £30 million. This might be achieved by cutting tender approvals by two thirds and loan approvals by about a half. In addition Stanley had asked the Corporation to sell more of its land quickly (the receipts from sales could be added to its expenditure limit) and to examine schemes for possible conversion to shared-ownership or improvement-for-sale projects, so allowing the funds to spread further.

Against this background and the pressure on programmes the Corporation launched two major initiatives, one on hostels and the other on improvement for sale. In September 1980 Stanley announced that £12 million of the Housing Corporation's programme for 1981/2 would be allocated to a new initiative to provide more hostel accommodation. The hostels initiative in England was launched in 1981 and involved the closure of some old institutions and the building of new hostels that would provide homes and care for many groups of people with the emphasis on the homeless and rootless (especially young, single homeless people) and people with mental disabilities. In London the urgent needs of single homeless people were emphasised and the DoE and the Department of Health and Social Security acted together to give practical and financial support and encouragement, enabling housing associations to provide 985 bedspaces for the single homeless. This was partly to address the consequences of the planned closure of the Camberwell resettlement unit. Some 200 of the new bedspaces would be specifically reserved for men who would be rehoused from Camberwell. Revenue funding for the projects would come from the two departments and hostel deficit grant would cover the deficits on housing management. Some additional topping-up finance to cover the additional costs of caring would also be provided by DHSS approvals, but to be spread over five years, and the whole programme was expected to be completed by 1987.

An additional £5 million was allocated for housing associations to launch a pilot programme of improvement of older houses for sale. This programme was worked up with thirty-seven associations to improve houses, mainly in the north-west and north-east of England. The Abbey National and Nationwide building societies agreed to provide mortgages for people buying the improved homes in this programme, and the pilot programme was regarded as a success. The annual report also referred to another smaller-scale initiative to develop a pilot programme for the frail elderly; this would complement the long-established tradition of providing for the housing needs of elderly people by providing more supportive accommodation for frail elderly people. The first leasehold schemes for the elderly in England had been built in the 1970s but legal and technical problems had prevented further development. The Housing Act 1980 removed the major impediments and a modest programme of leasehold schemes for the elderly was reintroduced during 1981/2. The Corporation also made progress in developing approaches to housing for disabled people, encouraging the inclusion of mobility units on the ground floor of new-build developments and suitable rehabilitation schemes.

Alongside these initiatives, in September 1980, Stanley asked the Housing Corporation to hold back expenditure during the second half of the year, and the Corporation cut back on loan approvals and introduced new procedures to ration the invitation and approval of tenders. A circular was issued to all housing associations on the administrative arrangements that should be followed to minimise further cash expenditure and the Corporation identified ways to save some resources in its administrative budget. Nevertheless, expenditure on schemes already in progress remained heavy. In December a halt was called on all new loan approvals for fair rent schemes for the rest of the year. Approval stopped for more than two months. By the end of the year the Corporation had approved new schemes for a total of 10,544 homes for fair rent, but 25,988 had been completed and building or improvement work had started on 17,081.

In this atmosphere of cash crisis and moratorium on new approvals, the Corporation expressed concern to Stanley about the consequences for the voluntary housing movement. The levels of expenditure and commitment through new approvals in 1980/81 also made it likely that the approvals for 1981/2 would be substantially reduced below 20,000 units. In spite of these difficulties Stanley had not announced the cash allocation for the 1981/2 programme, but indicated in December 1980 (only four months before the start of the financial year) that he would like to have proposals based on options of £420 million, £400 million and £380 million (HCBM 8/12/80). The problems of managing the housing programme in the environment of inflexible annual cash limits were continuous. The shrinkage of the programme in 1981/2 meant that there was difficulty in putting enough new work in the pipeline in 1982/3, to ensure a continuing and stable programme for 1983/4 and beyond. If approvals in 1982/3 were held back too drastically it would be difficult to sustain a significant programme of work in 1983/4 when work from the larger programmes approved in earlier years ran out. One possibility would be to give more approvals in the last quarter of 1982/3, incurring little expenditure in that year, but establishing a steadier flow for the future (HCBM 14/9/81).

The continuing problems related to annual budgets remained difficult to manage and budgets continued to be cut and/or notified at a very late stage. In this respect the Corporation proved both flexible and successful. In 1981/2, despite the vagaries of the winter weather and the volatilities of the construction industry, the actual expenditure in each of the three countries was almost exactly the same as the cash limits of £605 million plus receipts of £33 million. The receipts were largely associated with the proceeds from co-ownership sales and to a lesser extent voluntary sales and right-to-buy sales. These generated early repayment of loans and provided the opportunity for the Corporation to develop new approaches. In November of 1981 Stanley authorised the Housing Corporation to use receipts from co-ownership sales to boost the home ownership programme. These receipts had to be spent by the end of the financial year, 31 March 1982, and the Corporation mounted a programme of off-the-shelf purchases, normally purchase of completed houses in a new estate for onward sale on a shared-ownership basis. By the end of the year the Corporation had approved schemes worth some £33.3 million and spent over £26 million on 1,500 houses; in that way they increased the supply of shared-ownership purchases, consistent with government policy, but also helped the building industry to dispose of houses that were slow to market and encouraged it to go ahead with further new building. This approach can also be seen as consistent with the Corporation's response to urgings from the government to take a more active role in developing home ownership.

The shift in emphasis towards home ownership and the difficulties of managing within a restricted and cash-limited budget for fair-rented housing marked a significant change in direction. Major repairs to existing housing association projects continued to receive attention, but the limitations on expenditure were having an impact in this area, and there were particular problems where local authorities were unable to provide funding for what had been housing association schemes, for the Housing Corporation felt that it did not have the resources to take on the whole responsibility for this.

The general pressure on resources impacted on other activities. The Housing Corporation, having received consent from Michael Heseltine, became the sole shareholder of the Housing Corporation Finance Company Ltd (HCFC). HCFC had been incorporated as an associate of the Corporation in 1977 to introduce private finance and it became a wholly owned subsidiary (HCBM 10/3/80). It borrowed money from the private sector through a syndicate brought together by Morgan Grenfell and used this to buy from the Corporation an equivalent amount of loans which the Corporation had made to associations. This enabled the Corporation to lend additional money to associations without a net increase in public expenditure. Initially £50 million was borrowed in this way.

Policies and priorities in relation to housing co-operatives were reviewed to ensure that they properly reflected current pressures on resources and the opportunities for initiatives in alternative forms of tenure. Although there had been pressure from co-operatives urging continuing support, the pressures from elsewhere and from the government to be innovative in relation to home ownership and the overall reduction in resources squeezed out any potential initiatives in relation to co-operatives. The Corporation also decided that in future it would make regional allocations on the basis of the General Needs Index (GNI), which had been developed to measure the different levels of housing need across England. There was a close correlation between the Corporation's regional allocations for 1981/2 and the allocations which would have resulted using a modified GNI formula and this meant that making use of such an index could be more easily justified in future years.

The general election for 1983 saw the return of the Conservative administration led by Margaret Thatcher. For the Housing Corporation the election was followed by a tightening of the financial belt with the imposition of immediate cuts to capital and revenue budgets. Prompt action had to be taken to slow down the development programme for housing associations financed through the Corporation. The problems that the Corporation faced in dealing with cuts of expenditure were by now familiar. In 1983/4 the Corporation started the year with programmes amounting to £833.9 million (£690 million in England, £101.5 million in Scotland and £42.4 million in Wales). In July 1983, as part of the government's expenditure cuts, these cash limits were reduced by £11.8 million and to meet these reduced limits programmes were rescheduled to defer planned expenditure. At the end of 1983 the proposed cash limits for 1984/5 were announced and it was necessary yet again to reduce forward commitments for expenditure that year (while keeping within the expenditure targets for 1983/4) in order to avoid unmanageable fluctuations in the flow of business for associations. In the event all the money available was spent in 1983/4 in Scotland and Wales, and over 99.9 per cent of it in England. This small shortfall was not lost since the Corporation was now able to carry forward to the following year any underspend in England that did not exceed 5 per cent of the cash limit. The annual report for 1983/4 commented:

> While we recognise that we, and through us our associations, are at the mercy of the state of the economy and the availability of public sector funds it is nevertheless a time-consuming process, and one that can be neither efficient nor cost effective, to have to manage a capital development programme with a natural time span of three years on the basis of annual programmes, particularly when these are themselves liable to short term fluctuations. (p. 5)

By 1985 the Housing Corporation was expressing real concerns about the levels of funding. Sir Hugh Cubitt stated that '1984 was not an easy year for housing associations, and 1985 offers little prospect of improvement' (HCAR 1984/5: 3). He continued: 'The fact remains that resources available in both years fall very far short of those required to meet the all too apparent housing needs of the country.' And he concluded:

> We understand the difficulties which ministers face in taking decisions on the allocation of scarce resources, but in reporting to them on our stewardship in 1984/5 I would be shirking in my own responsibility vested in the Corporation by statute, for promoting and developing housing associations, if I fail to put on record our considered view that housing for those in the most dire need, for whom we provide, is now seriously under-funded. (HCAR 1984/5: 3)

While referring to reductions in the real level of resources available to it the Housing Corporation was also identifying increased need including home-lessness. The scale of the housing problem, the limitations and unreliability of public sector resources and the search for alternative ways of financing and expanding the Corporation's role in funding housing were continuing themes throughout the 1980s. The annual report of 1985/6 referred to the report of the Inquiry into British Housing, chaired by the Duke of Edinburgh, and *Faith in the City*, published by the Archbishop of Canterbury's commission. It stated that these two reports showed the extent of the housing issues which now confronted the nation. There was evidence of a clearly rising housing need but the government was not prepared to commit increasing resources and at best resources were likely to remain constant (HCAR 1985/6).

While housing associations in Wales and Scotland continued to benefit from rising public expenditure the situation was much more fraught in England. Budgets had not been restored to levels that had previously existed and although receipts were higher than forecast, the level of funding was not rising in real terms. In 1986/7 it again declined in real terms, and the requirement that resources were concentrated in the eighty local authority areas with the highest levels of multiple deprivation was a considerable constraint. In Scotland, gross expenditure in 1986/7 was at £113.8 million the highest ever achieved by the Corporation and the continuing emphasis on area renewal and community-based housing associations maintained a distinctive Scottish programme. In England there was a noticeable investment in black and minority ethnic (BME) housing. The Corporation's annual report acknowledged that minority ethnic groups suffered a disproportionate share of Britain's worst housing, and identified the need to promote a movement with strong local roots and a tradition of local community involvement. A race and housing advisor began work in July to improve communications, encourage new associations and co-operatives and administer grants to support this work. By the end of the year 1986/7 the Housing Corporation had registered ten new BME associations, bringing the total to thirty-three, and there were special training funds available to support these organisations, to bring issues of concern to the attention of the Corporation, and to identify ways forward.

The right to buy and home ownership

The right to buy had been a key part of the Conservative Party's election campaign in 1979. Although it was couched in terms of the sale of council houses, it is evident that the government also intended the right to buy to apply to housing association tenants. The legislative proposals presented to Parliament applied equally to council and new town tenants and housing association tenants in England. The Conservative majority in the House of Commons fully accepted the Prime Minister's view that 'thousands of people in council houses and new towns came out to support us for the first time because they wanted a chance to buy their own homes' (Hansard 1979). They saw the right to buy as key to their electoral success and could see no reason to deny housing association tenants the opportunity to buy. Although arguments for various modifications to the proposed legislation were advanced, including some related to housing associations, these had no impact and the House of Commons approved the proposals that would make no distinction between council, new town and housing association tenants. In the event, however, the housing Acts of 1980 did distinguish between different landlords. In Scotland housing association tenants did not have the right to buy and in England tenants of charitable housing associations were excluded. These exclusions arose not because of some late conversion or second thoughts among ministers but because of amendments tabled and passed in the House of Lords – and these amendments reflected the capacity of the housing association movement (largely through the NFHA) to mobilise support in the upper chamber of Parliament. The issue was to safeguard the right of charitable organisations to hold their assets in perpetuity. The House of Lords included Conservative peers who were strongly associated with housing associations, including two trustees of the Guinness Trust. They could see that the right-to-buy proposals would decimate their stock and they, with the NFHA, spent all summer of 1980 campaigning with their Conservative colleagues to overturn the proposals for the right to buy to apply to housing associations. John Stanley had insisted that the dying and wounded were assembled in the House for the vote in order to win it. When told of the result he apparently said: 'Thank goodness for that,' but he had evidently misunderstood because the vote was 286 against and 186 for. When this was pointed out to him, it is said he 'went ballistic and was unapproachable for two hours'.

The decision of the Lords was accepted and was very important for the subsequent development of housing associations. The insulation of most of the sector from the right to buy further separated it from the municipal rented sector. Tenants of non-charitable housing associations had a right to buy their homes and to obtain a mortgage from the Housing Corporation but the exclusion of charitable associations meant that the proportion of housing association stock sold under the right to buy was very much less than for local authorities. The adoption of assured tenancies after 1989 and the new financial regime discussed later in this book meant that these housing association tenancies fell outside the right to buy and reduced the erosion of the sector. At the same time the development of stock transfer after 1986 put the housing association sector on a growth trajectory in sharp contrast to the decline in the council housing sector.

The government pursued its ambitions to expand home ownership by encouraging both local authorities and housing associations to participate in a series of low-cost initiatives. In June 1981 Stanley had agreed that discounts of up to 10 per cent could be offered to housing association, new town or local authority tenants wishing to buy property that had been improved for sale. And the progress with this scheme, especially in the Midlands and the north, was assisted through a loans facility with Barclays Bank. By January 1982 the first rush of right-to-buy sales was over but the boom in co-ownership sales continued with the receipts used to finance shared ownership. There were 446 units already on site for shared ownership schemes at an acquisition cost of £10.7 million, with expectations of more to follow (HCBM 25/1/82). Shared ownership policy and procedures were moved forward with detailed consultation between the Housing Corporation, the Building Societies Association and leading building societies. The arrangements allowed people seeking homes to buy 25 per cent, 50 per cent or 75 per cent shares immediately and to increase their stakes whenever they liked by 25 per cent stages up to 100 per cent. If they increased their share, public money was returned and the receipts from that could be used for other schemes.

Do-it-yourself shared ownership (DIYSO) was launched experimentally in England and Wales in January 1983, described as the most spectacular initiative in low-cost home ownership in 1983/4. Under the initiative people could themselves choose a house that they liked and which was for sale and ask a housing association, with the Housing Corporation's support, to fund the purchase of that house on a shared ownership basis. By June 1983 all of the money earmarked by government for the scheme had been committed. As no more money was available the scheme halted in its tracks, to the expressed disappointment of the Corporation, having funded 3,108 purchases.

Programmes to promote home ownership continued, however, alongside rehabilitation and new homes for rent. The Housing and Building Control Act 1984 paved the way for a new scheme to help tenants of charitable associations who did not have the right to buy their homes. Rather than test the housing association movement and the House of Lords again about their determination to protect the charitable housing associations from the right to buy, the government opted to generate alternative routes for housing association tenants. Under the new scheme the Housing Corporation was responsible for providing discounts roughly equivalent to those available under the right to buy to help tenants of charitable associations to purchase a home on the open market, either outright or through shared ownership. The new scheme introduced in August 1984 to enact this was developed out of the previous experience of DIYSO. In 1984/5 a new form of shared ownership in England was established by the Corporation and the Nationwide Building Society called Open Door, which involved index-linked mortgages for people buying their housing association home in stages through shared ownership.

Dismantling co-ownership

The early 1980s saw the effective termination of the co-ownership housing that had been the distinctive product of the Housing Corporation in its early years. Although not strictly embraced by the right to buy, the expectations and rhetoric associated with that legislation marked the death knell of the co-ownership societies. Members of co-ownership societies raised questions about why they were excluded from the right to buy and the Council of Co-ownership Housing Societies is said to have directly raised this with the Prime Minister, Margaret Thatcher. The powers to dispose of properties with the Housing Corporation's consent were included in the Housing Act 1980 (perhaps as an afterthought) and these were applied to facilitate the sale of co-ownership dwellings.

Prior to the Housing Act 1974 there was no requirement for any association to register with the Housing Corporation before receiving public capital funding. The 1974 Act introduced the requirement to register not only before receiving any public funding for new developments, but also in order to continue to receive public funding for developments which were already underway. Co-ownership associations which had completed their developments and received all their capital funding before the enactment of the 1974 Act did not have to register with the Corporation, and most chose not to do so. Those which were part way through their developments in 1974 had to register in order to receive the money to complete them, and any co-ownership associations or co-ownership equity-sharing societies which came along after 1974 had to be registered before they could start their schemes. However, with the advent of the 1980 Act they, along with societies which had received funding under the 1961 Act, had to register if they wanted to sell to members.

Initially the consent to sale of co-ownership dwellings required agreement from all members of an individual society. While in many cases all such members wished to buy, or were persuaded to, there were cases where the desire of many co-owners to buy was frustrated by the few who did not wish to. As these cases emerged there was pressure from those wishing to buy and other options were introduced by the Housing Corporation. This meant that, where some co-owners did not wish to buy, the properties they lived in could, with their agreement, be sold to a new management company or a housing association. The co-ownership society would be wound up and all of the properties sold – but not all to their occupiers. In effect the co-ownership societies – their members collectively – could apply to dissolve their societies and for the power to sell, and the Corporation would approve the sale if the proposal fell within the terms of the options it set out. For the individual purchaser the terms of sale were enormously attractive – often more attractive than in the right to buy as applied to secure tenancies. All that was required was to clear the outstanding loan and any other debts and this meant sales well below the market price. Effectively it was a sale at historic cost and no account was taken of the use that had been made of government funds or other support. In some more complicated cases an additional loan might be taken out, or an amount added to the purchase price, to meet any need for major-repairs expenditure or to remedy any defects.

Under Section 122 of the 1980 Act the Corporation introduced procedures through which, with its consent, societies could exercise the power to sell their properties to their members. The Corporation's concerns were to ensure that the process complied with the law and was fair to all co-owners, and that each co-owner should be able to take free and fully informed decisions on whether or not the society should sell its properties and whether or not he or she wished to buy. The first application from a society wanting to sell was received immediately after the Housing Act came into effect, at the beginning of October 1980.

The first procedures permitted sales only where all the members wished to purchase. The problem with this was that unless all members of a society were willing or able to buy, nobody could do so. This led rapidly to problems within some societies and to pressure on the Corporation to enable partial sales. A series of options was devised for co-owners who did not want to or were unable to buy and by 1982/3 these were in place. All the alternative options were dependent upon the free and fully informed consent of the co-owners concerned and it has always been the case that a single non-purchasing co-owner who is unwilling to accept any of the alternatives offered could stop the whole sales process altogether.

Table 6.1 sets out annual figures for initial applications to the Corporation for permission to proceed with sales. These applications occurred after the co-owners received details of estimated purchase prices and resolved in a general meeting that the society should sell its properties, but before each individual had to indicate whether or not he or she wished to buy.

Table 6.1: Co-ownership societies – applications for permission to proceed with sales

1980/81	242	1995/6	0
1981/2	417	1996/7	0
1982/3	73	1997/8	2
1983/4	28	1998/9	5
1984/5	18	1999/2000	1
1985/6	15	2000/2001	0
1986/7	7	2001/2	1
1987/8	9	2002/3	0
1988/9	4	2003/4	1
1989/90	12	2004/5	1
1990/91	18	2005/6	1
1991/2	3	2006/7	1
1992/3	0	2007/8	0
1993/4	1	2008/9	0
1994/5	1	Total	861

Source: Housing Corporation

By the time of the Housing Act 1980 there were around 900 co-ownership and co-ownership equity-sharing societies on the Corporation's books. More than 70 per cent of societies had received approval to sell up by the end of March 1982. There was a headlong rush to dismantle co-ownership and this confirms the absence of any strong co-operative principle embedded in the thinking of the great majority of societies. By mid-2008 approval had been given for 861 societies to sell up and 860 had completed sales. Sales could take various times to complete – between nine months and twenty-two years (where one dissenting co-owner eventually moved out of the scheme and this finally enabled sales to proceed) from initial application to the Corporation to completion of sales to members. Co-ownerships were originally dealt with, including sales (subject to initial approval and overview by headquarters), in the regions, but by the early 1990s there were so few left that it was decided to take all the casework into headquarters, where it was dealt with by a dedicated team. As the work continued to dwindle, so did the original team of four, until by the late 1990s co-ownerships were the responsibility of just one person.

By the end of March 1984 only some 9,000 co-ownership homes remained in schemes that had been funded by the Housing Corporation; 26,717 had been sold since 1980 and the receipts had been drawn upon for other purposes. This was the final end of the initial era in which the Corporation had sought to provide a distinctive product within the housing market. This product had now been absorbed into mainstream home ownership and ceased to retain its distinctiveness.

Because of the generous terms of sale of co-ownership tenancies these sales were not generating the capital receipts that they could have done. There were substantial capital benefits to be reaped by co-owners who purchased their properties and a number of fairly difficult cases had arisen. There were some other more embarrassing issues for the Corporation: concerns were raised about staff who had recently obtained co-ownership tenancies and were making an unreasonable gain from their purchase. The implication was of a form of 'insider dealing' where greater knowledge of the potential gain than was available to outsiders was influencing action. However, it was extremely difficult to prove any intention to deal in property, rather than a genuine desire to find a home. This was especially so where a member of staff had informed his chief officer about moving to a co-ownership property. It would also be difficult to prove any mischief if the co-ownership had been acquired by a relative of staff (HCBM 14/10/81). What was really being highlighted was the excessive advantages to be gained through the purchase of a co-ownership property, especially if someone had only recently become a co-owner. Within the Corporation thirteen cases of staff recently joining co-ownerships were investigated and in one case an area manager was dismissed following a disciplinary hearing.

Birchall's comment on the effective termination of the co-ownership experiment is instructive:

> The death of this tenure form might be seen as a disaster for co-operative housing in Britain, but its effect was limited. It had never really been co-operative enough in practice to damage the idea of co-operative housing. There had been no attempt at screening prospective members for commitment, and so democratic participation had generally been low. There had been virtually no education in co-operative principles and practices, and so the co-operative nature of the tenure had been left hidden. Disowned by the Housing Corporation, forgotten by the policy-makers, the co-ownership tenure has gradually merged into the tenure to which it was always meant to be a stepping stone – owner occupation. (Birchall 1992: 14)

Building for rent

The general political and public expenditure environment in the 1980s was unfavourable for rented housing. The government's preoccupation with home ownership and its anti-municipal stance combined with a determination to cut public spending. Housing was an easy target for cuts and took more than its fair share. However, rather than emphasising cuts, this period has been presented as one of reorienting public expenditure: the housing capital expenditure programme was severely cut; the very considerable and continuing capital receipts generated from the exercise of the right to buy by council tenants were not invested back in housing; increased rents as well as restrictions on management and maintenance expenditures by local authorities began to reduce the general assistance subsidy for council housing; but tax reliefs associated with the encouragement of home ownership grew and the expenditure on housing benefit (established in 1982) took the strain associated with rising rents and increased. So the reorientation was from council housing to home ownership and from general assistance or bricks and mortar subsidy to subject subsidies related to individual household needs and incomes. A lesser part of the reorientation was from council housing to housing associations. As has been outlined above, housing associations were being treated far from generously in the early 1980s – but local authorities faced even more severe pressures.

Table 6.2: New dwellings for rent made available by housing associations in England and Wales with subsidy from the Housing Corporation and Tai Cymru 1974/5–1991/2

	England	Wales
1974/5	242	4
1975/6	4,288	105
1976/7	10,260	355
1977/8	20,521	644
1978/9	23,782	1,057
1979/80	20,693	1,534
1980/81	25,956	1,173
1981/2	20,014	2,328
1982/3	21,637	2,115
1983/4	20,658	1,535
1984/5	25,335	1,487
1985/6	21,329	1,520
1986/7	19,981	1,424
1987/8	18,183	1,767
1989/90	17,728	2,442
1990/91	19,843	3,060
1991/2	25,815	3,548

Source: Wilcox (annual).

Table 6.2 sets out the numbers of new housing association dwellings built for rent (or released by grant-assisted moves to owner occupation) in this period. It highlights the steep increase after 1974 associated with the development of HAG. The peak year for new rented housing was 1980/81, reflecting schemes approved and started before that. In England, in spite of the decline of local authority completions that peak figure was not reached again in the 1980s.

Table 6.3: Housing association stock and lettings in England 1980/81–1989/90, thousands

	Stock	All lettings	of which:	
			New tenants	Existing tenants
1980/81	410	51	42	9
1981/2	423	52	43	9
1982/3	432	55	45	10
1983/4	447	58	47	11
1984/5	464	60	49	11
1985/6	483	62	51	11
1986/7	495	64	52	12
1987/8	512	67	54	13
1988/9	534	70	57	13
1989/90	567	76	60	16

Source: Wilcox (annual).

Table 6.3 indicates the growth in the stock of dwellings owned by housing associations and the numbers of lettings made by them. Over the course of the 1980s housing association stock expanded by 38 per cent but remained small in comparison with local authority stock. Even so, by the middle of the decade it was accommodating 50,000 new households each year.

Table 6.4 provides data comparing rent levels across tenures over this same period. Local authority average rents in 1980 were well below the fair rents determined in the housing association and private rented sectors. Although local authority rents rose faster over the period than those charged in the other two parts of the sector, they were still well below them in 1990. Local authority rents also increased more rapidly than average earnings, increasing from 7 per cent of average earnings in 1980 to 8.9 per cent in 1990. The respective figures for housing association fair rents were 11.3 per cent and 11.2 per cent and for private rented sector fair rents 10.1 per cent and 11.0 per cent. These figures lend support to the perception that the reorientation of rented housing programmes away from council housing and towards housing associations was part of a wider privatisation agenda involving higher rents. It was not difficult to suggest to tenants and prospective tenants (and those considering tenants' choice or stock transfer options) that housing associations were higher-rent landlords and part of a privatisation agenda.

Table 6.4: Housing association and local authority rents in England 1980–90, £ per week

	Local authorities average rent	Housing associations fair rents	Private landlords fair rents
1980	7.70	12.52	11.18
1981	11.42	13.98	12.99
1982	13.48	15.63	14.51
1983	13.97	17.19	15.21
1984	14.66	18.69	17.25
1985	15.54	19.75	18.11
1986	16.36	21.44	20.91
1987	17.20	22.86	21.69
1988	18.82	25.00	25.58
1989	20.70	26.83	25.40
1990	23.74	29.94	29.21

Figures relate to the average across all properties. Local authority average rents are for the April of each year. 1988 housing association and private fair rent figures are for the second quarter of the year. Private sector rent figures are presented for all lettings at time of compilation, including the small proportion of unfurnished lettings.

Source: Wilcox (annual).

Merseyside

The development of the Housing Corporation's activities in Liverpool and Merseyside highlight different dimensions of the way it worked and its relationship with government. Housing association activity had been strong in Liverpool in support both of co-operatives and of associations involved in refurbishment in the inner city. This had included associations purchasing considerable property portfolios from existing private landlords. In these cases housing associations tended to drive the agenda, approaching the Corporation with proposals. In August 1981, following the civil disturbances in Liverpool and elsewhere, new processes began to drive activity. The secretary of state for the environment, Michael Heseltine, took on special responsibility as minister for Merseyside and established a Merseyside task force. The smallest Housing Corporation region received disproportionate attention from ministers and senior civil servants and over the following period there were a series of initiatives driven by the government but using the Housing Corporation and housing associations. These included the transfer of the Cantril Farm estate in Knowsley to the new Stockbridge Village Trust and the creation of the Eldonian Community Housing Association. The absence of any effective working relationship between the local council in Liverpool and the Conservative government also affected how these initiatives were developed. For the first time ever the Corporation was involved in reclaiming land and the government created a mechanism that enabled it to use its grant for this purpose. The government recognised that in the Corporation it had an agency at its disposal that it could use to deliver things it wanted to see rather than working through local government, with which there were increasing difficulties over the years.

The clearest example of this is the request for the Housing Corporation to work alongside the Merseyside task force to help with the development of potential initiatives. While the government could have gone direct to housing associations, it was more comfortable working with its agencies, which it could control. The effect of this was to change the Corporation's role: it became much more central to the development of initiatives and actively sought housing association partners to come and deliver aspects of government plans. The Housing Corporation's national programme after 1982 included 'an additional amount' that was 'the Merseyside special allocation', to develop and deliver the projects that had come out of the Heseltine period in Liverpool. It was initially granted for three years, but many of the schemes were longer term. David Edmonds, later to become chief executive of the Corporation, was Heseltine's principal private secretary at this time and was seen to be a strong believer in what the secretary of state had promoted in Merseyside. In effect the Housing Corporation was delivering projects almost in the face of severe opposition from local government, and it appears that ministers became more and more convinced that the Corporation was a vehicle it could work with in Liverpool or wherever else it was: it became a trusted delivery agent, which itself had its trusted delivery agents in housing associations, and therefore the government was getting delivery for the programme that had been voted through Parliament. One project operated in this environment was to develop a symbolic regeneration site alongside the Anglican cathedral in Liverpool, and Heseltine asked the Housing Corporation to mount a competition for this development. This site of some 18 acres had been vacant for many years and its development was seen as potentially catalytic for the regeneration of the area. A panel of assessors was appointed to judge the competition, for architects linked with developers who would build the winning entry. The competition was launched in January 1982 and resulted in eighteen entries, from which the winners were announced. They went on to develop the site.

At this time there was no national regeneration agency equivalent to English Partnerships, which was formed in 1999 by an amalgamation of the Commission for New Towns and the Urban Regeneration Agency, itself established in 1993. Housing associations and the Housing Corporation were able to move various projects forward and pioneer approaches that were later incorporated in other government initiatives such as housing action trusts and the City Challenge programme. The Corporation was working at regional level directly with senior civil servants from the Department of the Environment and the Treasury, and with backing from the chief executive and the chairman of the Corporation there was a situation in Merseyside more like that in Scotland than in the other English regions. The Merseyside example is one where the Housing Corporation proved able to supply a flexible and effective framework for the development of a new policy initiative, enabling central government to develop new initiatives in an area where it had particular concern. The reality is partly, however, that it needed to be able to work around the local authorities in Merseyside.

The second transition

While the first three years of Hugh Cubitt's chairmanship had been active ones of adjustment to a new regime and new policy priorities, the next three were ones in which it was made absolutely clear that housing was a very low priority for the government. It was in the middle of this period that the key players in the Corporation changed. As in 1973, the rehabilitation of the Housing Corporation was entrusted to people who had been involved in drafting the new legislation that was designed to shape the next phase of policy and were highly regarded by civil servants at the DoE. This change of leadership marked a break with the previous regime. John Baker had left in 1978 and he was followed by Tony Collinson in 1983 and Dick Madge in 1984. The new chief executive was David Edmonds with a former brigadier, Brian Ridley, as his deputy. These appointments changed the atmosphere. Edmonds was a senior civil servant in the DoE and was in charge of the Inner Cities Directorate at the time that he applied for the post. He had previously been principal private secretary to the then secretary of state, Michael Heseltine. Edmonds's knowledge of, and commitment to, voluntary housing from his early days as a member of the management committee of a new housing association had been critical in his decision to apply for the post and was important in his approach to it. He was also close to Terry Heiser, who became permanent secretary at the DoE and had been closely involved in preparing the Housing Act 1980. He presented a different face for the Corporation and worked hard to improve communication and relationships with housing associations. Alongside him Ridley is presented as an 'engaging character who used to perch on the table addressing the serried ranks of the Housing Corporation, most of whom were women, and say "Well, men", and it went down a storm'.

Edmonds had empathy both with the government and with housing associations and set out to alter relationships. Members of the board also had connections with housing associations and felt uncomfortable at the way the Housing Corporation was perceived by them. The Corporation presented itself as a partner in the housing association movement. If there were to be arguments it wanted them to be arguments within a family rather than shouting across the airwaves, as they had been recently. A lot of time was spent simply talking to housing associations, with consultation meetings in each NFHA region, and the chief executive attended them all. In contrast, in the previous period the leadership of the Corporation had rarely been seen outside Tottenham Court Road. A quite different relationship was built with the NFHA, firstly with Richard Best and then Jim Coulter: to talk, to consult and to listen. The first objective as chief executive was to build a different relationship with the housing association group. This was a key focus for the next four or five years because it made no sense to have the major supplier, deliverer and executor at daggers drawn with the funder. The existing relationship was not working and had to be changed to make it work.

Alongside this the new team set out to rearrange the organisation. New people were brought in at the regional director level and more able people brought into the centre, putting emphasis on younger people. There was also an emphasis on delivery. For the first time the Corporation produced a mission statement and a strategic plan. The strategic plan covered periods of three and five years whereas previously the Corporation had simply presented a series of annual bids to the department. The chief executive took the view that the Housing Corporation had statutory objectives of its own, which it had the right to pursue. He built strong relationships with civil servants and, coming from within them, knew the right people to talk to. But he also created an atmosphere which gave a degree of independence that had never previously been apparent.

This independent style does not appear to have been resisted by the government, perhaps because of the skill with which it was pursued but perhaps also because by the mid-1980s ministers had been persuaded that more capital investment was needed in housing. They could see a much more efficient and effective Housing Corporation emerging and hitting all its targets. The development of proposals for private finance consolidated the position, in effect involving a different way of doing things but also resulting in more housing investment. Between 1985 and 1987 the Corporation worked with the DoE in devising what became the Housing Act 1988, the move to assured tenancies, the massive switch in the level of HAG and the ability of housing associations to borrow on the market. The Housing Corporation had 'a monumental achievement' in persuading the department and the Treasury to sign up to it.

The most notable development in this period involved drawing in private finance to fund social housing. This marked the final and most significant element in the second transition for the Housing Corporation – from disburser of public funds to the key agency operating at the interface between government and private finance and enabling a new mixed finance model to become the norm for new social housing investment. The new financial arrangements also facilitated a programme of housing stock transfer and commenced the process through which housing associations were to become the main providers of social housing rather than the lesser partner behind local authorities.

In the enthusiasm to associate the governments of Margaret Thatcher with privatisation, there is a tendency in the housing policy literature to represent the new private finance approach, which was to underpin the growth of the housing association sector after 1986, as a product of new right or Thatcherite thinking or a Treasury-led initiative, part of a wider privatisation and marketisation strategy. The reality appears to be different. The initial thinking relating to private finance and the detailed preparatory work was carried out within the Housing Corporation and grew out of the tentative steps that had been taken in earlier years. The DoE and the Treasury were sceptics and delayers, emphasising problems and, in the Treasury's case, concerned about the moral hazard that would exist if there were no risk associated with lending. It appears that the Corporation persisted in pressing the case, persuaded key stakeholders and individuals including some in the financial sector and finally persuaded ministers

– and it was ministers that persuaded their cautious civil servants. In this process Edmonds's credibility with the DoE and strong working relationships with the key ministers, secretary of state Nicholas Ridley and housing minister William Waldegrave, were very important. The Treasury rules barred the use of private finance for public purposes and the Treasury ruled. The new approach involved changing the whole basis and methods of financing and Ridley's ability to persuade the Treasury was critical. When Ridley was appointed secretary of state 'the housing association movement were horrified because he was considered to be ultra-right wing but, having been a Treasury minister, he was much more effective than his predecessor Kenneth Baker, who did not have clout at the Treasury'.

Reference has already been made to the record of housing associations and the Housing Corporation in using private finance from 1964 onwards. Although HAG and the associated public subsidy had come to dominate the sector, actions to access private finance had continued. These activities were speeded by the enactment of building society deregulation in 1986 and the greater scope this gave the societies to lend to housing associations. The Corporation's 1984/5 annual report had strongly asserted that the resources being made available by the government fell very far short of those required to meet the all too apparent housing needs of the country (HCAR 1984/5: 3). It linked this directly with the initiatives related to private finance:

> We recognise that in the current economic climate additional finance is unlikely to come entirely from the public purse, so this year we have devoted a considerable energy to attracting private finance. Associations and the Corporation have tested new initiatives and under the auspices of the Secretaries of State for England and Wales two private finance working parties with wide membership from public and private sector organisations have been meeting on a regular basis. (HCAR 1984/5: 10)

The initial outcome was the launching of the Open Door shared ownership scheme referred to earlier. Mortgage financing from the Nationwide Building Society for this scheme totalled £30 million and this released public funds to meet unexpected VAT expenditure and maintain the programme of homes for rent in England. This was seen as illustrating what could be achieved through the marriage of public and private sector funding.

The annual report went on to say that associations were well placed to attract private finance. Although publicly funded they were essentially independent private sector organisations, with records as efficient developers and appreciating assets attractive to private institutions wishing to invest in housing. They had official approval through registration with the Corporation, which was well regarded by the private sector, and were in a strong position to negotiate on its behalf. However, for private investment to have real significance the principle of partnership between public and private funds had to be backed by government: it should serve to increase housing investment and not result in a corresponding reduction in public funds. In this context the report stated: 'We hope the government will feel able to give us the support we need so that we can use our public funds wisely to augment the resources available for homes to the lasting benefit of those of our fellow citizens who are in housing need [HCAR 1984/5: 10].'

Because of this the Housing Corporation devoted much time and effort to finding ways of bringing private finance to the support of public funds. Its corporate plan had stated that it was 'well placed to create a regular channel for private sector investment in low-cost housing' and the annual report stated: 'This is not just a wish, it is a view supported by building societies and other investing institutions.' Using private finance would mean that increased investment in housing could be achieved while still containing the overall level of public expenditure. The housing programme could be expanded to help meet the undoubted problems of homelessness and poor housing. In this context the Housing Corporation's private finance working parties had launched a number of initiatives primarily related to index-linked or deferred-interest loans: the Alliance and Leicester Building Society had joined Nationwide in making index-linked finance available for Open Door, and the Halifax Building Society raised £15 million of index-linked cash on the money market to lend to housing associations and the Milton Keynes Development Corporation for up to 1,300 new homes including rented housing. Although adverse interest rates prevented take-up of a further £35 million, the Corporation hoped that more would be raised in that way as interest rates fell.

The deregulation of building societies was seen as providing an opportunity to build a relationship between them and housing associations. The importance of attracting private finance also led to different emphasis in relation to rents. To attract private funds there must be a reasonable return for investors' money. There were restrictions on rent increases associated with the fair rent formula and it was easier to attract private funds to the care-in-the-community schemes, where rents were not fixed, or to homes for sale than to the provision of homes to let at a fair rent. Progress was dictated by Treasury conventions and controls and the Corporation hoped that the government would be able to support its efforts by introducing greater flexibility in funding rules.

From 1985 onwards the government encouraged housing associations to make more use of private finance in funding the development of housing and in longer-term financing. A part of the Housing Corporation's development programme began to be devoted to schemes under which HAG was fixed at 30 per cent of scheme costs. Normally HAG was calculated as the residual after rents had been set by a rent officer independently of scheme or management costs and it often formed a much higher proportion of scheme costs. The 30 per cent HAG programme aimed to get more units from the same amount of HAG, while still keeping rents at affordable levels. This was to be achieved in various ways: through additional subsidy inputs such as land provided free by a local authority or donated through some other source; through the use of index-linked loan finance to reduce debt charges early in the life of new schemes; or by making use of revenue grants and allowances (such as those paid by the Department of Health and Social Security to particular groups) which would permit an economic rent to be recouped. A few associations with large, debt-free housing stocks were also able to use their stock as security on loans from the private sector to facilitate such developments. Despite some successes the 30 per cent HAG programme proved difficult to sustain and expand and there were doubts about how much scope there was for it to do so without steep increases in rents.

In the same context, in 1985/6 the Corporation referred to new initiatives with health authorities and local authorities and, following the successful transfer of Central Lancashire Development Corporation properties to housing associations, referred to the possibility of further transfers. A wider agenda relating to stock transfer and private finance was already under discussion. The year 1986/7 was seen as the one in which the breakthrough occurred. In autumn 1986 the Treasury gave consent to the first rented housing scheme involving a combination of index-linked mortgaged finance from a building society, public investment in the form of land provided by a local authority, and housing association grant made available by the Corporation. The breakthrough scheme was at St Mellons in Cardiff, where the Halifax Building Society was the private funder and Cardiff City Council provided land and infrastructure. The significance of the scheme, however, was not in the detail but in the principle and the acceptance by the Treasury that this was the direction that the Housing Corporation was taking.

The lead-up to new legislation that established the basis for mixed financing in 1988 involved the Housing Corporation developing other private finance initiatives: the Coventry Churches Housing Association devised three new forms of low-cost home ownership, none of which required any public funds, and the Corporation signed its first joint venture agreement with them in November 1986 to promote the schemes with other associations; the Abbey National Building Society lent money to the North British Housing Association to acquire 3,200 properties, formerly owned by the Greater London Council, from its successor, the London Residuary Body – these were seaside and country homes built for older people and distributed around the country in different locations. At the same time the Housing Finance Corporation was launched to provide a vehicle for raising loans for housing associations. The expectation was that a new financial regime would create different opportunities. The chairman in the annual report for 1987/8 stated that the opportunities for associations to extend their activities were comparable with those which followed the Housing Act 1974: 'Our hope and expectation is that they will grasp these and thereby will justify the confidence which government is clearly showing in them.' A period of frustration and restriction seemed likely to give way to one of much greater opportunity for innovation. Mixing public and private finance was still in its early stages, but had crossed the threshold from a possible idea to a practical reality levering in private funds that did not count as public expenditure.

The Housing and Planning Act 1986 had also recognised the potential role of housing associations working in partnership with others. Associations in England and Wales could be managing agents for local authorities, receive revenue grants and pay for the costs of helping tenants' associations and co-operatives get underway. Building on the success already demonstrated in Scotland, one of the outcomes of this was the development of Care and Repair, an independent charitable housing association sponsored by the Housing Associations Charitable Trust and Shelter. The Care and Repair scheme was able to operate under the new legislative environment and take action in relation to homes owned by elderly people and in need of major repairs. Care and Repair could provide advice, grants and financial support to enable arrangements to be put forward that would lead to improvement of housing without the existing owners being required to give up their homes.

These significant changes were occurring twenty-five years into the life of the Housing Corporation. They also involved the handover of its responsibilities in Wales and Scotland to two new agencies, Housing for Wales

(Tai Cymru) and Scottish Homes, and there is no doubt that the loss of responsibility in these two areas was unwelcome at least for some in the Corporation who had valued the work carried out in Scotland and Wales and the innovation especially evident in Scotland.

Demunicipalisation

In the mid-1980s there was a shift in emphasis in the Conservative government's thinking from enabling public sector tenants to become home owners to dismantling public sector housing. This was important in the measures contained in the Housing and Planning Act 1986 to facilitate demunicipalisation and expressed by John Patten, the minister for housing, urban affairs and construction, in introducing that legislation:

> The problem in public sector housing does not lie with money alone. Of course, there is a continuing role for public sector housing, but in the rest of this century and the next century it will be different. It will be smaller and more specialised. The old bureaucratic and paternalistic monopoly which has characterised public sector housing for too long must go ... The keynote is not doctrinaire privatisation but diversification and an end to bureaucratic control. (Hansard 1986)

The next step was to establish a process so that the powers enabling demunicipalisation were put to use. It is in this context that the Conservative manifesto for the general election of 1987 referred to choice of landlord under the heading 'Rights for Council Tenants' and stated:

> We will give groups of tenants the right to form tenant co-operatives, owning and running their management and budget for themselves. They will also have the right to ask other institutions to take over their housing. Tenants who wish to remain with the local authority will be able to do so.
> We will give each council house tenant individually the right to transfer the ownership of his or her house to a housing association, or other independent, approved landlord. (Conservative Party 1987: 14)

Following the election the government embarked on incorporating this choice of landlord in legislation, which would become the Housing Act 1988.

The Act's other major objective was to achieve the deregulation of the private rented sector. Nicholas Ridley, the environment secretary, stated that together these elements would mean 'a long-term transformation of the rented housing market in Britain'. He went on to state: 'Our aim is that the emphasis of local authorities' role should shift from that of landlord towards that of facilitator, with a responsibility to encourage and co-ordinate the activities of all those with the resources capable of meeting local housing needs [Ridley 1987].'

This new emphasis in housing legislation can be interpreted as a logical progression in the move towards a more privatised housing market. The revival of private renting had always occupied a prominent place on the Conservative Party's housing policy agenda. The right to buy could be seen as a response to consumer demand and the success of local discretionary policies and was justified as enabling tenants to become home owners. Various social surveys had shown an overwhelming and growing desire for home ownership among tenants but there was no evidence of a desire for a change of landlord and private renting was the least popular tenure (see for example BSA 1983; BMRB 1986; Gallup 1988). Without evidence, the government believed that tenants would transfer and that an independent rented sector could deliver an improved quality of rental service.

The Housing Act 1988 included detailed proposals to tighten the right-to-buy arrangements. Important changes in the privately rented sector meant that all new private lettings would become assured and/or shorthold, and rents would be freely negotiated between landlord and tenant and would move towards market levels. There were also new provisions regarding recovery of possession by landlords. Housing association rents would also move towards market levels and all new lettings would be assured tenancies. Local authorities would perform a reduced role in the supply or management of housing although they would continue to assess local housing needs and demands. In their new strategic and enabling role, they would be expected to encourage innovations by other housing institutions and organisations to maximise private finance and to encourage interest in the revival of the privately rented sector.

Initially the agenda for demunicipalisation involved providing all tenants with a choice − Tenants' Choice − to transfer to any private landlord, but as the Bill progressed through Parliament the government gave assurances that would discourage traditional profit-seeking landlords from participation. In effect the demunicipalisation agenda was channelled into a programme of transfers to responsible landlords, and the presence of the Housing Corporation and its role both in regulation and investment made this option easier to implement.

William Waldegrave stated that he could see no arguments for generalised new build by councils and expressed the belief that there should not be much property in council ownership at all:

> It is an oddity confined largely to Britain amongst European countries that the state goes landlording on this scale. The next great push after the right to buy should be to get rid of the state as a big landlord and bring housing back to the community. If you want to buy and can buy, so much the better; if, for example, flats are more likely to continue to be rented, then the landlords should be the sort of social housing organisations we see overseas. They can represent tenants more closely; they are not caught up in the electoral swings and cycles of party politics; they can be single minded about housing and as skilful about it as only specialists can be; they can in many cases be smaller and more local. The British housing association movement can provide these organisations, either directly or as foster parents. Meanwhile the councils can concentrate on their front-line housing welfare role, buying the housing services they need, or subsidising those who need help, and undertaking the wide range of regulatory enforcement, planning and other tasks which are the essence of the public sector. (Waldegrave 1987)

The White Papers outlining legislative proposals for England, Wales and Scotland emphasised the dominant role of local authority housing in the rented sector and acknowledged that the growth of municipal housing since the war had been effective in increasing the total housing stock and in clearing slums. But it was argued that the concomitant system of ownership and management was often not in the tenant's best long-term interest. In some areas the system provided good-quality housing and management but in others insensitive design and bad management had alienated tenants and left housing badly maintained, and a wide range of social problems had emerged. It was necessary to move forward to give tenants a greater positive role in securing the housing conditions and quality of community life to which they aspired by giving most public sector tenants rights to form co-operatives with their neighbours if they wished and to transfer to a new landlord of their choice (see DoE 1987; Scottish Development Department 1987).

The White Papers indicated that tenants who wished to transfer would identify a new landlord willing to take them on. Landlords would be formally approved on the basis of their suitability and viability and there would be arrangements to put tenants in touch with prospective new landlords. Many approved landlords were expected to be established housing associations, but some would be commercial landlords and some tenants might wish to form a co-operative with their neighbours. Once they had a tenant's agreement, the legislation would give prospective landlords the right to negotiate the transfer on legally defined terms.

The consultation paper on Tenants' Choice published later in 1987 reiterated the options and elements of choice and elaborated on the requirements related to landlords. They might be registered housing associations, co-operatives or other independent housing bodies, or private firms, but they would have to be approved before they could take on tenants under Tenants' Choice. The approval process would aim to ensure that new landlords were financially stable and capable of managing their homes to a high standard while giving value for money. At this stage it was not clear who the 'appropriate' authority for approval would be, but the exclusion of local authorities and other public sector landlords from being 'new landlords' under the scheme was explicit.

The period following the publication of the consultation paper was one of considerable speculation about predatory private landlords gearing up to take advantage of the transfer opportunity. Fears about 'pick-a-tenant speculators' were reported in the media (Mullins et al. 1993). Partly to head off this possibility a number of local authorities began to review their best strategy and initiate a process of transfer that they would regard as satisfactory. This contemplated sale to established housing associations or setting up new housing associations. This appears not to have been anticipated by ministers and initially they did not welcome these initiatives. By August 1988, however, papers were published setting out the government's position on two proposed schemes to transfer local authority housing to private bodies, tenant-initiated Tenants' Choice and landlord-initiated Large-Scale Voluntary Transfer (LSVT) (DoE 1988a, 1988b).

The minister acknowledged that since the Bill had been published a great deal of further thought had been given to how the social rented sector would operate in future and to the contribution that private landlords could make. First, those who took over council housing could not strip the assets; housing provided, usually with public subsidy, to meet particular needs left unmet by the market should not be sold for other purposes at the first opportunity. The new owner must maintain the housing for its original purpose or a comparable one – normally in the rented sector. The government or the Housing Corporation would want to see that the new landlord was committed to doing this by its articles of association or other legal documentation. To make this commitment stick, landlords who later wanted to dispose of property which had been transferred to them would need the secretary of state's consent to do so. Second, there must be a proper guarantee of standards of service. Third, the procedures for exercising Tenants' Choice must give tenants real choice and proper information with which to exercise it. Fourth, the new landlord must not be indirectly controlled by the council, and must not be so large as to have an undesirable local monopoly of rented housing.

The Housing Corporation was placed at the centre of the procedure for Tenants' Choice and in response to this set up a special unit to develop its approach. This approach was initially set out in two consultation papers (Housing Corporation 1988a, 1988b). Tenants would contact the Corporation for information and where they wished to take matters forward, the Corporation would arrange informal consultations and establish which of any competing potential new landlords had the clearest support from tenants. The Corporation would have powers to prevent formal applications proceeding where there was no significant support for transfer or where it withheld its approval of the applicant. The Housing Corporation's role also included promoting the Tenants' Choice scheme with suitable potential applicants. The criteria for approval required new landlords to be

- committed to normally reletting vacant dwellings at rents within the reach of those in low-paid employment;
- prepared to include basic tenancy terms, open about lettings policy and responsive to housing demand in the area;
- controlled by persons with appropriate skills and experience;
- organised so as to acquire and manage rented housing effectively including management, maintenance and financial skills and experience;
- financially viable in terms of capital and revenue.

The criteria implied rents being set in sympathy with housing benefit arrangements. This, the restrictions on disposal and the overall scrutiny represented a strong framework that restricted opportunities for profit and reduced the scheme's attractiveness to unsubsidised bodies. It was to be some time before the government opened the case for subsidy to be available to unregistered organisations. The criteria effectively reduced the likelihood of new landlords being other than housing associations and the likely result of Tenants' Choice became a transfer from one public body (local authorities) to another (housing associations). As well as approving landlords, the Housing Corporation had the role of monitoring applicants during the transfer procedure and powers to revoke or suspend any uncompleted application. Where the approved new landlord was a registered housing association the Corporation could also monitor and supervise.

LSVTs would be subject to the consent of the secretary of state, but in principle were welcome and 'accord well with the enabling role which the government envisages for local authorities in housing'. The secretary of state would consider each application for consent on its individual merits but would be unlikely to give approval unless the acquiring body was

- independent of the local authority;
- able to demonstrate that it was a stable and responsible organisation with a long-term commitment to the provision of rented housing for those who need it;
- committed to providing a good service to tenants.

It was emphasised that council membership of or shareholding in new landlords should not exceed 20 per cent; that while a council could enter into contracts to fulfil statutory housing duties (primarily in relation to home-lessness) it would be inconsistent for it to operate waiting lists or retain nomination rights; that a council should not specify staff selection, but should obtain undertakings relating to various aspects of operation including that 'normally' vacant dwellings would be relet and that rents would be at levels within the reach of those in lower-paid employment. Furthermore, consent would be unlikely to be given to disposal to a single purchaser of more than 5,000–10,000 properties and authorities within that range would need to demonstrate the advantages of doing so.

The secretary of state, Nicholas Ridley, did not wish to see large public housing monopolies converted into large private housing monopolies. To ensure that the management problems which beset overlarge housing organisations were not perpetuated, he would in principle prefer local authorities to dispose of their stock to more than one purchaser. This was in line with the objective of providing a wider choice in rented housing. Even in the area of a small housing authority, it would be undesirable if a disposal created a single new predominant landlord in the area. Beyond these issues, large-scale transfers would largely follow the principles and procedures set up for Tenants' Choice. The one significant exception related to the requirements for voting systems. Under Tenants' Choice the result of the ballot was to be determined by a majority but abstainers were to be counted as votes for and those who voted 'no' would not be subject to transfer. While there was no explicit legislative requirement for a ballot in relation to LSVT the local authority was required to demonstrate that a majority of tenants favoured transfer and effectively the secretary of state would be convinced of this only if there had been a ballot. Where there was a ballot, and assuming a 50 per cent turnout or more, a simple majority determined the outcome and if there was a majority of votes cast in favour all tenants, including any who voted 'no', would be subject to transfer.

One of the barriers to private investment in stock transfer or other housing association development had been the inflexibility of rents under the fair rent system. The new finance system for housing associations changed this. All new housing association tenancies (including relets) were removed from the fair rent regime and became assured tenancies at rents set by the housing associations themselves. All existing tenants with fair rents lost their entitlement to rent phasing, which had meant that any increase in their regulated rent was phased over two years to prevent the landlord from imposing a sudden burden on the tenant. Under the new arrangements rents would be determined in line with a notion of 'affordable rent'. The determining factor was that rents should be high enough to enable housing associations to balance their books when using HAG paid at a specified level of estimated scheme costs. HAG levels were to be set by a matrix of fixed-level grants, arranged by dwelling type for different areas of the country, but the average level was expected to be in the region of 60 per cent. This would avoid the need for housing association rents to rise as much as had been anticipated: the government accepted that rents for the new housing association assured tenancies would be lower than market rents where dwellings had been taken over from local authorities or otherwise provided with public subsidy. The grant levels would be calculated assuming affordable rents and the use of index-linked finance. Because no rental surplus was generated using index-linked funding, there would be no grant redemption fund contribution expected from these new lettings. There was no entitlement to apply for RDG, nor was there any HAG for major repairs.

The whole approach meant higher rents and higher housing benefit costs. It involved a shift in public expenditure with a new financial system levering in private finance to supplement public money and with housing benefit taking the strain. The next cohort of tenants of housing associations, including stock transfer associations, would pay higher rents, have less security protected by law and would not have the right to buy. The desire to demunicipalise seemed to have overridden the desire to improve tenants' rights. In the context of a government wishing to demunicipalise but recognising that some continuing scrutiny and control would be needed for any successor landlord, housing associations and the Housing Corporation provided a convenient and necessary solution. The government, seeking an alternative to the local authority sector, welcomed housing associations because they were independent organisations controlled by volunteers, because many had developed entrepreneurial and financial skills, and because in comparison with the traditional private landlord they were much more competent developers and managers of their stock. In addition they were attractive because they could be more easily encouraged to follow particular policy initiatives than local authorities, which were subject to local political influence.

The Housing Act 1988 carried through the deregulation of lettings of housing association properties. Most new housing association lettings would no longer have their rents determined by the rent officer and would be assured rather than secure tenancies. The rents would be determined by the landlord. This deregulation of rents provided a framework which would enable lower rates of subsidy, assuming, that is, that rents went up compared with fair rents, but it was a framework which would prove much more viable in a mixed funding context: the ability to increase rents would give private lenders greater certainty that housing associations could take appropriate steps to meet their financial obligations. The 1988 Act also introduced the framework for the new grant system for housing associations made possible by the deregulation of rents. Most secured tenants of local authorities and new town development corporations were provided with the opportunity to change their landlord under Tenants' Choice arrangements. The Act also widened the Housing Corporation's powers to pay grants to associations for activities other than the provision of new housing. Alongside the Housing Act, a new Local Government and Housing Bill had begun its passage through Parliament and this would affect the revenue and capital positions of local authority housing and its position relative to the housing association sector.

Transfer actions

Powers for local authorities to dispose of properties with the consent of the secretary of state were long established although not widely used. Westminster City Council's notorious programme of sales of empty properties with its gerrymandering dimension was atypical although it had been carried out with Nicholas Ridley's approval. The transfer to Stockbridge Village Trust of the 3,000-unit Cantril Farm estate in Knowsley in 1983 acted as a pioneer for a new phase – with a new trust created for this purpose and charged with raising finance to improve and remodel the area. The Housing and Planning Act 1986 signalled the government's greater interest in such procedures and introduced the need to consult with tenants before seeking ministerial approval for transfer. Usher (1987; 1988) refers to the pressure felt by local authorities to make use of these powers to dispose where their capital programmes were insufficient to modernise a dilapidated stock – or, less commonly, where disposal to the private sector formed part of wider privatisation strategies. He identifies thirty-nine local authorities in England, three in Scotland and one in Wales that had disposed of or planned to dispose of properties to the private sector. Even at this stage, however, such proposals were relatively small scale and more of an extension of the trickle transfer associated with disposal of individual dwellings as they became available.

A new phase of stock transfer followed the Housing Act 1988. In addition to Tenants' Choice, the legislation provided for setting up housing action trusts (HATs). These involved stock transfer for estate improvement and came with a large public expenditure commitment based on what had been required for Stockbridge Village Trust. The areas that the government initially selected for HATs uniformly rejected this development. However, some local authorities saw opportunities and made alternative proposals that resulted in six HATs being set up. Alongside this, Tenants' Choice remained an almost wholly unused provision. LSVTs, however, began to be pursued in rural and suburban locations. The first transfer, in the Chiltern district of Buckinghamshire in 1988, pre-dated the implementation of the Housing Act and other early transfers involved considerable negotiation with the DoE and the Housing Corporation to clarify many grey areas including stock valuations and the calculation of catch-up repairs (Mullins et al. 1993). During 1989 the Corporation set out further guidance. The LSVT model matured into a managed programme and found favour with both Conservative and Labour governments. In the period 1988–2000 there were 449,972 dwellings transferred from 101 local authorities as part of the LSVT programme.

Malpass and Mullins (2002) argue that between 1988 and 1992 central government was largely reacting to ad hoc local proposals for transfers of dwelling stock from local authorities to housing associations but in 1992 a new phase for stock transfer policy was launched. An annual transfer programme enabled the government to recapture the initiative that had been lost by the failure of Tenants' Choice and the refocusing of HATs. The government was also able to take into account the findings of research on the early transfers. The new transfer programme involved:

- a limit of 5,000 dwellings in any one transfer, thus requiring authorities with larger stocks to split their estates between two or more new landlords;

- an annual cost-limited disposals programme, a levy of 20 per cent on the capital receipt accruing to the local authority, i.e. after repayment of outstanding housing debt;
- a requirement for tenants affected by stock transfer proposals to receive independent advice reflecting research evidence of unbalanced information provided in the early transfers.

The scale of the programme was later increased under Labour, with almost 200,000 dwellings transferred in the period 1998–2000, nearly as many as in the previous ten years. Transfer became a more important source of depletion of the council stock than sales under the right to buy and a more important source of growth of the housing association sector than new development. Mullins and Murie (2006) state: 'From 1988 onwards whole stock transfer was the dominant process in the formation of new housing associations. In addition there were smaller scale transfers, mainly of rundown estates to existing and new associations, pump-primed by public subsidy, notably the Estates Renewal Challenge Fund.'

Large-scale transfer of council housing to housing associations created a new group of big professional associations and usually carried a long experience of council housing management across into the new organisations. To this extent it embodied the merging of municipal traditions with new independent financial and governance regimes. The new large-scale landlords presented a challenge for the Housing Corporation. Initially they were under pressure to register and regulate organisations with large housing stocks and considerable local authority participation but also with high ratios of debt to assets, new inexperienced boards and senior management teams that were often inexperienced in the ways of the housing association movement. This is an example of the Housing Corporation accepting the need to play its part in enabling government to deliver its policy. It had to be flexible and willing to move quickly to facilitate transfers and while it may have had reservations in relation to detailed aspects of the registration of stock transfer associations, it operated the process of scrutiny and registration in such a way as not to derail the government's programme. While some stock-transfer landlords subsequently encountered episodes of Housing Corporation intervention and supervision and there have been governance problems reflecting the inexperience and different culture of boards, most transfers have not encountered major regulatory problems and have significantly outperformed their business plans.

Scotland

Although Scotland was affected by the restrictions on expenditure in the early 1980s and its programme was smaller than in previous years, the difference between the Scottish operations of the Housing Corporation and those in England became clearer. Unlike in England and Wales, no housing association tenant in Scotland had the right to buy – although associations were encouraged to deliver a positive sales policy. In addition the board of the Housing Corporation formalised the position of the Scottish Committee, which had operated as an informal committee comprising board members from Scotland and the chief executive and oversaw the work of the Corporation in Scotland. The more formal arrangement extended the Scottish Committee's responsibilities to include advising the Corporation on the policies it should pursue in Scotland. The committee met regularly in Edinburgh and had quarterly meetings with the Scottish Federation of Housing Associations. None of the English regions had an arrangement as robust as this. The Housing Corporation's annual report stated:

> The management of the Corporation's Scottish affairs is largely carried out in Scotland and we have developed a distinctive Scottish style, including a separate series of guidance notes for associations, *Scottish News*, and other publicity material, reflecting the different nature of the housing problems, legislation and housing associations themselves in Scotland. (HCAR, 1981/2)

The emergence of a distinctive approach and strategy to build up a Scottish housing and community development movement has been discussed in the previous chapter. This special arrangement links with subsequent debates about devolution and was, indeed, overtaken by it. Scottish solutions for Scottish problems were a feature of the pre-devolution era. As the chairmen and chief executives of the Housing Corporation changed, it was also necessary to re-establish that Scotland was different. Between 1978 and 1989 the Housing Corporation in Scotland was run as a chiefdom, unlike the English regional offices. It ran its own procedures, agreed with the Scottish Office. While registration and supervision were dealt with by London (but with an outpost in Edinburgh), there was a chief officer of Scotland, two regional directors and a management team, which in some ways paralleled what was going on in England.

The pressure to streamline the Corporation following John Stanley's concern that it was too complex did raise the question of whether it should 'get rid of Scotland', which 'would just become a region'. At this time the first strategic plan for the HCiS was being written. The plan emphasised a distinctive Scottish approach through community-based organisations and a subtle shift in emphasis to self-help was made, to appeal to Conservative ministers. Nevertheless some within the Housing Corporation in London regarded costs as high in parts of Scotland and were more willing to question value for money there than, say, in London. There was a fear that the Thatcherite agenda would have severe repercussions on housing in Scotland. In this context the Scottish members of the Housing Corporation board met with the secretary of state for Scotland, Malcolm Rifkind, and expressed concern at being pressurised into being 'Anglified' and not doing the right thing for Scotland. This expression of concern coincided with the Scottish Office looking at the future of the Scottish Special Housing Association (SSHA). The opportunity to make the Housing Corporation accountable in Scotland – to 'bring it home' – and amalgamate it with the SSHA began to emerge as attractive. From the Scottish perspective this would defend an organisation with an annual budget that had grown from something like £1.2m in 1974 to £165m in 1988. It was a fast-growing organisation with partnerships all over the country and doing all sorts of things that were different from what was being done in England. Within the politics of the Thatcher era it was not enough to assert national difference, it had to be evidenced; but the differences in Scotland associated with tenements, geography and local authorities worked for Scotland.

People were beginning to say: 'Why should that money be channelled through London when it could be dealt with in Edinburgh?' Although the Conservatives had ruled out devolution, there was a mood around for much more Scottish things, culminating in Rifkind's indirect successor Michael Forsyth bringing back the Stone of Destiny as an attempt to fend off demands for devolution. It was on that basis, then, that Rifkind pulled all things together and proposed to amalgamate the HCiS with the SSHA to form Scottish Homes. Inevitably Scottish Homes was a different agency and the housing management legacy inherited from the SSHA made it a much bigger organisation. However, the majority of the senior managers came from the HCiS and there was considerable continuity.

Conclusions

The continuity of a tight cash-limited public expenditure regime and the specific housing policies brought in by Conservative governments after 1979 presented a different environment for the provision of affordable rented housing. With the municipal sector in decline and a belief in the capacity of the market to meet need, affordable rented housing could be seen as reaching the end of its policy career. There can be no doubt that the Housing Corporation was at risk altogether or at risk of remaining on the sidelines as an interesting but largely unimportant example of a passing approach to policy making and delivery. Further deregulation of the private rented sector and plans to make it possible to provide grants to registered private landlords could render the legacy of earlier public sector subsidy regimes redundant. The next phase of demunicipalisation would then put private landlords at the heart of the provision of rented housing – at the expense of both local authorities and housing associations.

By 1988, however, a new formula offered a new lease of life. The Housing Corporation reverted back to earlier attempts to access private finance and create a new mixed-finance model. The detail as well as the initial thinking behind this new model came from within the Corporation and it developed an approach that prolonged the life of the sector and offered an acceptable alternative to both a municipal sector that was too dependent on public funds and a private rented sector that could not be presented as meeting the guarantees that tenants should expect and that government offered.

But all of this involved tensions. It had involved the development of a new relationship between housing associations and the Housing Corporation and, while this served both for some considerable time, it was the source of later criticisms that it had become too cosy. The new formula had also required the abandonment of fair rents and that left the package open to being represented as privatisation and exploitation. At the same time the emerging English regime was unattractive to Scotland and Wales and, in a political environment where devolution was being debated, the Corporation's territorial reach was reduced. The development of the private finance package, the move to high rents and then stock transfer were all conducted in a fraught political environment where privatisation was seen by some as an attack on tenants and local authority staff. The mechanisms that enabled housing associations to continue to receive investment to provide additional affordable housing also pushed the associations and the Corporation into controversial privatisation territory. There was concern about predatory landlords seeking to profit from demunicipalisation and privatisation and while the eventual Tenants' Choice and Large-Scale Voluntary Transfer procedures were likely to exclude the worst predators, the motives of more responsible and properly regulated housing associations were not unquestioned. The Housing Corporation was now in a critical position and was seen alternately as facilitating and legitimating the dismantling of accountable municipal housing and replacing it with a higher-rent 'privatised' culture, or wrestling effectively with a government that thought the private sector would meet all housing need if it was left to get on with the job and convincing it that the culture and capacity represented by housing associations could be used to draw in private funds that otherwise would not be invested in the housing sector.

7

From growth to downturn 1988–2000

Introduction

After 1988 the Housing Corporation's operations were restricted to England, as its functions in Scotland and Wales were taken up by new agencies. The new private finance-based model presented the opportunity for unprecedented growth of the housing association sector, operating outside the severest constraints of the public expenditure system and acting as the preferred vehicle for building new social rented housing and increasingly also for low-cost home ownership. At the same time the new finance system provided the opportunity to develop further demunicipalisation through large-scale stock transfers of housing from local authorities to a new generation of housing associations. Some local authorities, without the resources to manage and maintain their stocks effectively and sometimes without the political will to continue as housing providers, were attracted to stock transfer and the receipts it would generate to pay off debt and fund other activity.

The growth of the housing association sector was further enhanced by increased public expenditure, which transformed the social rented sector as the relative share of housing association providers began to converge on that of municipal landlords. However, the new system was introduced in the context of continuing inflexible management of public finances and a rapidly changing economic situation. Initially this generated a new crisis of planning and delivery of the housing programme that damaged the credibility of the Housing Corporation. The high interest rates and housing market problems associated with the early 1990s presented new challenges and the Corporation's ability to respond to government through the Housing Market Package had mixed consequences for the sector. In the ensuing period the Corporation was preoccupied with avoiding anything that would damage its credibility in the future but reductions in its budget again generated tensions. The election of a new Labour government in 1997 did not entail dramatic changes in policy although there was increased expenditure and a new impetus for stock transfer.

A new start

In 1988 the government announced a significant growth in the Housing Corporation's Approved Development Programme, and indicated an even greater growth in the subsequent two years. The original allocation for 1988/9 had been £727 million and this was increased to £815 million in 1989/90, £1,036 million in 1990/91 and £1,328 million in 1991/2. In addition there were capital receipts of £57 million in 1988/9, principally from buoyant house sales by housing associations. All of this amounted to a very considerable rise in expenditure and there was also expected to be a rapid increase in the use of private sector loan finance. The atmosphere for housing associations and the Housing Corporation had changed dramatically. Although local authorities were unlikely to continue to be a major source of funding for housing associations the growth in the Housing Corporation programme and in private finance would more than outweigh this.

Private finance institutions had increased their investment in housing associations through 1988/9 and by the end of the year the Housing Corporation had made contact with more than eighty lenders including merchant banks, foreign banks, clearing banks and brokers and building societies. There was optimism about the number of organisations that would participate and the level of resources that would be forthcoming. The Corporation's annual report stated that 'housing associations are the main engine of social housing and are being funded accordingly' and it described what the new framework did as follows:

1. Removes rent control making it easier for associations to raise private loan finance – this is not public expenditure and means that more homes are funded for a given amount of public funds;

2. Fixes grants in advance, giving associations a strong incentive to control the costs of developments since extra costs fall upon associations and ultimately on their tenants;

3. Reduces Housing Corporation control of association schemes.

It went on to say that the new systems were more complicated than had been wished. While ways to simplify systems would be sought, detailed controls were needed and the growth of mergers and joint arrangements among associations and between associations and other partners suggested a pattern for the future.

In Scotland and Wales the transfer from the Housing Corporation to new bodies was accompanied by increased funding through the Scottish Office and the Welsh Office. In Wales the transfer was to be to a new agency, Tai Cymru (Housing for Wales). A steering group was established with the Welsh Office and a support task force planned the shape, structure and budget of the new body. This ensured that the Corporation's knowledge of the work which would face the new body was carried forwards. The new chairman and board were recruited in advance and arrangements were made in both Cardiff and London so that a smooth handover of business was achieved for 31 March 1989. The annual report said:

> Naturally we are sad to have lost our direct contact with housing associations in Wales. However, we were able to leave at the end of the year two substantial assets. The first is a vigorous and diverse housing association movement tuned into the new financial realities. The other is our staff team in Cardiff, committed to the housing needs of Wales and the work of the movement. These together represent a rich resource on which Tai Cymru will be able to build. (HCAR 1988/9: 19)

A similar account was provided in Scotland. The transfer of the Housing Corporation in Scotland to Scottish Homes was achieved while managing the largest and most varied programme ever mounted in the country. Legislation to establish a unified housing agency in Scotland had received royal assent in November 1988 and Scottish Homes came into being on 1 December 1988. It had wider housing responsibilities reflecting the different constituent bodies that had been brought together – the HCiS and the Scottish Special Housing Association (SSHA). On 1 April 1989 it assumed those responsibilities. It inherited from the SSHA a stock of 70,000 public sector homes, and from the HCiS a strong, locally developed housing association movement with 210 registered housing associations and some 45,000 homes. More than 90 per cent of these had been funded by the HCiS. Scottish Homes would mainly be an enabling body with economic and environmental improvement powers as well as housing responsibilities. It would be able to make improvement grants to owners and make grants to private developers as well as to housing associations. The legislation required Scottish Homes to offer employment to every member of the Corporation based in Scotland and all were appointed to posts in the new agency.

The annual report commented on the winding up of the HCiS:

> We handed over to Scottish Homes on 1 April 1989 a strong housing association movement in Scotland developed over the last 15 years in a distinctive and local way. At transfer there were 210 registered associations, many of which were directly promoted by the Corporation in partnership with local authorities. We have lent over £2 billion to these associations and with that they have provided over 40,000 new and improved homes, some 2 per cent of Scotland's housing. Under Scottish Homes they are poised for future expansion and a wider role. We also handed over to Scottish Homes a highly motivated and skilled staff. They have a successful record. We wish them and the new organisation well. (HCAR 1988/9: 22)

While operations in Scotland and Wales were winding down, the Housing Corporation was vigorously promoting housing associations for black and minority ethnic (BME) groups. The need to prioritise these issues derived from legislation and more immediately the inquiry into the allocations policy of a housing association by the Commission for Racial Equality. This had first been raised at the board in 1979 and it considered various methods by which the Corporation might cater for ethnic minorities (HCBM 19/1/79). The real pressure for black housing associations came from a group of housing and community activists located in London and Liverpool. They realised that the needs of black communities were not necessarily being met by so-called white, mainstream housing associations and these associations were not recognising or responding to the issue. The receptiveness of government to this view was increased by civil disturbances in 1981 and 1985 in Toxteth and Handsworth and in 1985 in Tottenham. These disturbances included action by members of the black communities against the police and against a range of different conditions, one of which was housing.

David Edmonds as chief executive brought a greater energy to this agenda and from 1984 onwards the Corporation embarked on an explicit strategy to promote black housing associations and to work with the Federation of Black Housing Organisations. The Corporation's first BME strategy was produced in 1986 and was about empowering black people in housing through supporting and developing black-led housing associations. It was very much a producer-based strategy in the first phase and led to more than forty housing associations being formed. The Corporation gave BME organisations registered status as well as funding. In the mid-1980s, the Corporation, its chief executive and its chair were very receptive to issues of race equality and were seen as being fairly radical for a quango at that time.

What the strategy the Corporation adopted failed to do was to upskill people sufficiently, or else it feared such action would be seen as tokenistic and patronising. It was easier to register somebody and give them funding and then regulation would take care of everything else. In addition, especially in London, there were too many new associations registered and not enough money to go round. Ten years on there was success in having a large independent BME housing sector but there were also problems; too often they emerged in supervision actions, which arose because the associations were failing in some way. This explains why the early activity did not achieve more in the long term. By the time of the second BME strategy (for 1991–6) the agenda had shifted, with more attention given to consolidation. There were still registrations of black-led associations, but because of the importance of private finance, the Housing Corporation had less freedom than in the first phase of the policy to really promote black-led associations.

The Corporation also became concerned with general promotional issues. Its annual report stated:

> Among the public, awareness of the housing association movement remains too low. Organisations which are the main providers of new subsidised housing should be better known. Knowledge of and information about the work of associations is essential both to allow fair access to the homes they provide and to assist public scrutiny of how public money is spent. (HCAR 1989/90: 5)

As a result of this the Corporation determined to work with housing associations and with the NFHA to promote wider awareness and understanding of the movement.

The Housing Corporation addressed how it distributed resources within England. It stated that housing needs varied considerably across England and began a revision of the housing needs index, which had come to be used to determine the broad regional allocation of resources. The revision attached increased weight to homelessness – reflecting government concern to at least appear to be worried about the very high levels of homelessness. In the same context David Trippier, a minister at the Department of the Environment, asked the Corporation to encourage associations to examine their lettings policies, to ensure that priority was given to those in the greatest housing need, especially the homeless, and said: 'The greatly expanded overall programme for the Housing Corporation and the improved targeting of resources to areas of greatest need should help provide much needed homes for the homeless [Hansard 1988].' At the same time emphasis was placed on the needs of those in rural communities. Allocations of investment funds to individual associations were determined not by formula but rather by which associations shouted loudest and one perspective is that the largest associations bullied Corporation staff at regional level.

A new visual identity for the Corporation was launched on 1 April 1989, to coincide with the devolution of its work in Scotland and Wales. The new identity included the first version of what became a familiar logo, representing a three-storey house with eight windows (later reduced to two storeys and five windows), a front door, a pitched roof, a chimney stack and a rising or setting sun behind it in red to match the red roof. The Corporation's new identity was said to have two main aims: to reinforce its role in its new England-only responsibilities and to help focus greater attention on the work of housing associations and their contribution to the provision of good-quality social housing. An example of this was the increased emphasis on the use of sign boards on Corporation-funded housing association sites, aimed at promoting a consistent image for publicly funded housing association schemes. Although there was some initial resistance to what was seen by some as a bureaucratic requirement, this approach appears to have achieved widespread acceptance relatively quickly.

A new financial crisis

The new financial arrangements contained in the Housing Act 1988 came into force on 1 April 1989 and the ensuing twelve months were ones of considerable difficulty for the Housing Corporation in achieving programme targets with the accuracy of previous years. The new financial arrangements transformed the fundamental principles of HAG. The key ingredient of the new capital funding regime was the concept of a limited, in some cases fixed, grant, combined with the freedom to set rents to cover costs.

Under the previous system rents were determined by the rent officer and this dictated the size of the long-term mortgage an association could afford. The grant was the residual element required to meet the full costs associated with development expenditure and with any cost overruns, design changes or other factors. There were cost norms and checks and balances which compelled a proper regard for cost control, but they were largely external to associations, rather than being internalised as part of their own interest. Public accounting practice required tendering to ensure value for money, even though that meant forgoing some apparent bargains.

Within the new framework all of the risk was borne by housing associations and they were left to decide the method they used to procure their new properties. As it was in associations' interest to keep costs down various forms of negotiated package deals, including off-the-shelf purchases, became much more attractive. They were not necessarily the cheapest deals, but they offered certainty of cost and averted the possibility of cost overruns. Under the new system the grant came in fixed percentages, according to the location, type, design and other characteristics of the scheme. Cost overruns or savings would carry the same grant percentage so that the proportions of grant and long-term mortgage remained constant provided costs did not exceed the specified ceiling. But this meant that the size of the long-term mortgage varied, according to the actual cost of the scheme. As the rent required to cover costs was no longer constrained by the rent officer, the cost and size of the mortgage directly affected the rent charged. Overruns that took the total cost beyond the prescribed ceiling were financed wholly by the association or by rent as there was no extra grant available to help fund any such excess costs.

Associations generally took advantage of the more flexible rules, with some poor consequences for Corporation cash flow. Risk was transferred largely to housing associations and public money was used to lever in private funds, so producing more social housing for government cash. In 1989/90, 69 per cent of the rented programme and 100 per cent of the low-cost home ownership programme used mixed funding. All of this was very welcome to the government but left the Housing Corporation with problems of managing its programme in a much more flexible environment and one that it had no prior experience of.

There were other implications of the changing financial regime. The effects of rising rents, coupled with fixed loan repayments, meant increasing levels of surplus for associations. Under the old system such surpluses were recovered annually through a grant redemption fund. Following the Housing Act 1980 there was in effect a 100 per cent tax on rental surpluses, which were recycled through the Corporation's Approved Development Programme. The Housing Act 1988 converted the grant redemption fund into the rent surplus fund. Seventy per cent of rental surpluses were to be set aside in provision for future major repairs and this would gradually reduce the call on the 100 per cent major repairs grant over time. Of the remaining 30 per cent half was paid over to the Corporation as before and the rest passed to the association's reserves, for use at its own discretion. Schemes completed under the new regime were exempt from rent surplus fund, partly in recognition of the likely increase in debt repayments through the use of low-start, long-term, mortgage finance, and partly to enable associations to maintain adequate provisions for major repairs which were ineligible for major repairs grant. The new schemes were also ineligible for RDG, which had been a longstop for associations previously. Once completed, associations would now stand on their own feet and be independent of future public support. However, they would be able to build up reserves and to make surpluses without repaying them. Inevitably special transitional provisions were needed to cover schemes conceived under the previous system but not reaching tender stage by 31 March 1989. An additional grant (the development deficit grant) was available to assist associations with schemes whose costs, through no fault of their own, had gone so far over budget that the schemes would not be viable at any rent affordable by the appropriate client group.

All of these new arrangements required the Housing Corporation and housing associations to learn a new approach. There were concerns that rents emerging from the grant matrix could be too high and there was a need to monitor these closely. It proved impossible to introduce a version of the new regime tailored to the requirements of special needs and especially shared-ownership housing during the first year. More importantly the Corporation found itself unable to manage the programme as tightly as it had in the past. The government had announced an increased level of public investment in housing and by bringing in some private finance this would result in an even greater expansion in the size of the programme. The programme for 1989/90 and the following two years was seen as enabling the Housing Corporation to approve schemes in the first year providing about 17,600 homes for rent, rising to 24,400 new approvals in 1991/2, over 50 per cent more than the expected number of approvals in 1988/9. David Trippier said:

> This will be possible not only because of the greatly increased level of public resources being made available, but because of the wider opportunities for private finance opened up by the Housing Act 1988. It is planned that by 1991/2 schemes providing about 80 per cent of new homes for rent will be approved on a mixed funded basis, combining grant from the Corporation with private loan. (Hansard 1988)

Substantial public subsidy would remain available to ensure that rents were within the reach of those on low incomes. Mixed funded grant rates would vary in different parts of the country because of the significant regional differences in development costs, but the average grant rate in England in 1989/90 was expected to be 75 per cent. Provision of housing for sale under the Corporation's low-cost home ownership programme would also expand and the whole of this programme was planned to operate on a mixed funded basis from 1989/90. By 1991/2 the housing-for-sale programme would have nearly doubled.

The new financial regime was introduced on 1 April 1989, four months after the Housing Act 1988 became law. The Corporation had consulted widely and had closely involved the NFHA in setting up the new grant regime. It had also used management consultants to undertake a review of its systems. Their report made a number of recommendations on points of detail, but it did not identify a risk of cash control problems of the kind that emerged soon afterwards. What no one predicted was the scale of problems which caused the Corporation severe cash management difficulties throughout 1990/91.

As expected, scheme approvals under the new regime were slow in coming and after six months only 3 per cent of the annual schemes had been approved. However, by October 1989, it became apparent that the Corporation's expenditure was going too fast. There was higher than anticipated spend on schemes already in process as the year opened but there was also evidence that schemes under the new system moved more rapidly. There was less time between acquisition and start on site. In addition the slump in house-building programmes in the market as a whole meant that there were more off-the-shelf purchase opportunities and available money was used more quickly (HCAR 1989/90: 8–9).

These factors, combined with the bigger initial payments to housing associations to start schemes (grant was paid in tranches that provided associations with 80 per cent of the grant on a scheme by the time the main contract began), had an impact on the Corporation's cash flow and became a matter of concern. There had been no general body of evidence available to enable accurate aggregate forecasting and so the Corporation's regional offices gathered what information they could, virtually scheme by scheme. By mid-December, it was apparent that the Corporation would probably have spent all of its cash limit by mid-February. In early January 1990 the Corporation asked the DoE if it could bring forward £120 million from the next financial year, 1990/91, to enable it to meet its contractual liabilities as they fell due.

The government acquiesced in this and at that stage the evidence did not indicate insuperable problems in 1990/91.

The Corporation had, with ministerial agreement, reduced the scale of its new rented programme for the next year, from 24,500 planned to 19,550. With similar reductions in low-cost home ownership, this took into account the current overspend and would bring the whole programme back into line. However, during the final three months of 1989/90 it became clear that the scale of expenditure already committed for 1990/91 was far more than anticipated; it was so substantial that it threatened to absorb virtually all of the cash available, depleted by the £120 million brought forward. Between 70 per cent and 80 per cent of public cash committed to new schemes was being spent within one year of approval, compared with between 20 per cent and 35 per cent under the old regime.

This unanticipated crisis reflected badly on the Housing Corporation's competence. In view of all this, the Corporation took action on two fronts. Firstly, approvals in 1989/90 were reduced from the level of original allocation by rigorous review of applications for project approval and by not replacing schemes that fell by the wayside. Secondly, the level of new programme to be approved, against the 1990/91 Approved Development Programme, was substantially reduced. The Corporation expected to reduce the public programmes over the two periods by some 14,000 rented and sale homes – about 31 per cent. This was aimed at getting the Corporation back on track for 1991/2. Because homes were being completed more quickly, there was not an overall reduction in the number of new dwellings being built, just in the number of approvals in each time period.

In previous years the Housing Corporation had become a centre of real expertise in the control of finance. Even though it was working with between 500 and 600 developing associations, the money committed to the programme was all spent by the afternoon of 31 March, and some 98.5 per cent of the money was spent each successive year for five years. The new finance system was introduced by the DoE with no chance to pilot it. The consequence was a serious overspend of £100 million and 'all hell broke loose', with little realism about the likelihood of hitting the target accurately without a trial run. Although the DoE understood the complexity of the management of finances, it had no sympathy with the situation and did not understand how difficult it was. While the DoE was subject to the same kind of financial framework, what it typically did was to underspend dramatically and hand the money back to the Treasury. The Housing Corporation had been under different pressures for years – to avoid underspending – it had a different culture and did not intend to hand back anything.

The programme management difficulties of the second half of 1989/90 caused the Corporation to advance by one year the original plans to devolve cash management to regional offices and then to associations. The greater choice in procurement methods open to associations, combined with the tranche system of grant payment, resulted in variations in cash flow. Staff involved in project-level decision making in the Corporation's regional offices and in associations had to take account of cash flow. Cash planning targets were introduced in 1990/91 for all developing associations, and they planned their development programmes accordingly. The Corporation's regional officers also worked to cash limits, with the whole process overseen at headquarters.

This framework was constructed rapidly during the last quarter of 1989/90, to deal with the failures in that year. New computer systems and monitoring information were drawn up. While the new framework and systems worked they also indicated the extent to which the Corporation had failed to anticipate how the change in financial arrangements would affect the way in which it and housing associations operated. The overspend in the programme and the continuing rumbling crisis associated with this was extremely damaging to the Corporation. The problems that had been associated with the introduction of the new financial regime had a continuing impact on the Housing Corporation. Although it is now possible to see that the actions taken within the first year and the introduction of a regionally based cash limit system proved effective, the damage done to the Corporation's reputation by its failure to control its spending had been profound.

The problems experienced by the Corporation were discussed in Parliament both in general terms and in relation to the problems they had generated for individual associations and developments (Hansard 1990a). Parliamentary debates referred to examples of the consequences of 'what some call the current crisis, but which is officially called a dislocation'. A site in Lambeth had been sold to a housing association for rapid development to provide much-needed homes for rent because the borough council was said to be too slow in developing it, but the consequence of the crisis was that the housing association could not develop the site because money would not be available to start during the current financial year. A co-operative that had acquired land in Kent for phased development had completed phase 1 and acquired the land for phase 2, but had been told by the Housing Corporation that work on the site could not be started. Interest charges were accruing on the money paid for the site and building costs could rise during the next year. If the accumulated costs exceeded the maximum allowable total the scheme might have had to be abandoned. It is another example of a delay in starts that year leading eventually to a reduction in the number of completions in later years. There were also concerns that successful housing association development teams would have to be disbanded because of the break in the flow of work; and there were concerns about employment. 'The end result is that building firms will shed labour and homeless people will not get homes [Hansard 1990b].' The Birmingham Friendship Housing Association's plan to build four five-person houses on a site in Sparkbrook through a package deal with a local builder who owned the site was at risk although it was included in the draft Housing Corporation programme for 1990/91. Birmingham Friendship did not know whether it would get an allocation for work that year; the builder, who had held the price for the scheme, was anxious to get on with the work. This 'sums up the hardships and disappointments suffered on the ground because of the cash crisis. Homes for local Asian families will be lost. Work in an area of high unemployment will be lost to a firm of multi-ethnic builders which has held its costs for a year, waiting on the promise that it was in the draft Housing Corporation programme' (Hansard 1990b).

Ministers responding to these concerns reaffirmed the government's confidence both in the Corporation and in the ability of the housing association movement to take the lead in the provision of low-cost homes for households in need. They reiterated the view that housing associations had avoided the mistakes of local housing authorities, as relatively small-scale providers, had not allowed bureaucracy or professional vested interests to get between them and their customers and that on average, their tenants were better satisfied than those of local authorities. 'That is the main reason why over the past few years we have reversed the traditional roles and made associations, not local authorities, the lead providers of new low-cost housing. In doing so, however, we have found it necessary to recast the basis for funding their development [Hansard 1990a].'

Ministers referred to a revolution in the financing of housing associations and restoring to them the freedom to set their own rents provided that they kept them within the reach of their own clients, tapping private sources of loan finance, and giving them full financial responsibility for their successes and failures. The government had provided the framework for the funding revolution and the expansion of the movement in the Housing Act 1988 but, as Christopher Chope, a minister at the DoE, acknowledged:

Most of the hard grind of devising the detail of the new grant arrangements and all the complex transitional machinery, putting the systems and people in place to run them and educating the movement about the implications and opportunities of the new regime, fell on the Housing Corporation. It had, too, to prepare itself and the housing association movement for a massive expansion in the capital programme. I pay tribute to its immense achievement in getting everything ready to roll in April 1989.

The strain on management, systems and staff throughout the organisation was enormous, and it would be altogether astonishing if everything had run with clockwork precision and smoothness from day one. If anything has gone wrong, it is that the housing association movement has mastered the new arrangements and responded to the challenges and opportunities that they offer even more quickly and impressively than we and the corporation had expected ... That has upset some of the key assumptions on which the Corporation's plans for its capital programme in 1989/90 and 1990/91 were based. (Hansard 1990a)

In spite of this official understanding, another minister was heard to say 'heads must roll'.

Recovery

The fallout from the crisis of 1989/90 included changes in key personnel. Sir Christopher Benson replaced Sir Hugh Cubitt as chairman. Cubitt had served three full three-year terms plus a further year and was the longest-serving chairman in the Corporation's history, longer than would have been expected. Benson was appointed in May 1990 following the crisis of overspending. He already had developed a close working relationship with government as the chairman of the London Docklands Development Corporation (LDDC) and through that knew Terry Heiser, the permanent secretary at the DoE, and Sir George Young, minister of state at the department. Although Benson was not seen as a housing expert, the LDDC had been involved with housing associations and tried to encourage them to work in an area that had no history of successful residential development. He moved from the LDDC to the Housing Corporation in a seamless way: as he gave up one he moved to the other.

Benson was involved in the appointment of Anthony Mayer as chief executive when David Edmonds left the Housing Corporation in March 1991 to join the National Westminster Bank. Mayer was a former civil servant who had worked in the Central Policy Review Staff and in the Department of Transport but had since been working in the private sector for N M Rothschild Asset Management. The appointment was made by the Housing Corporation, which 'was not leant on', and then approved by the DoE.

The overspend in 1989/90 had scarred the Housing Corporation internally and it had lost confidence. It also severely damaged the reputation that Edmonds had built and the task of his successors was to re-establish credibility. The independent style of operation was difficult to retain or rebuild in this environment and from the 1990s onwards the Housing Corporation was managed as an adjunct of Whitehall rather than an agency with independence, fight and a responsibility to argue a different case. In effect its strategy was put in reverse – rather than assert independence the strategy was 'spend the ackers, run an orderly house' and as long as it achieved 99.9 per cent spend in line with government targets and housing associations were run in an orderly fashion without dreadful supervision cases, without systemic failure, without tenant revolts, it would be listened to. In that environment the Corporation would be able to contribute to developing policy – and it built the capacity to contribute to research-based policy debate.

This more restrained approach enabled it successfully to attract government funding and use the opportunity created by the Housing Act 1988 to deliver an increased programme. The Corporation went to a huge amount of trouble to get from the civil servants great clarity as to what they wanted by way of a housing investment programme. It was participative but owned by government and helped by very good inter-personal relationships with key civil servants.

The primary task in 1990/91 had been to eliminate the cash problems flowing from the 1989/90 overspend and to deliver the programme. In the annual report for 1990/91, the chairman, Sir Christopher Benson, was able to say: 'We were successful. On a programme involving 730 associations, over 20,000 new schemes and a £985.5 million budget, we secured a 99.9 per cent spend against our allocation. We thereby re-established the precise degree of expenditure control, which over recent years has been the hallmark of the Corporation [HCAR 1990/91: 2].'

Continuing government support for the Corporation was made easier by these signs of a return to normality and during the year a major increase in capital funding was announced – rising by almost 100 per cent over three years – to £2 billion in 1993/4. The Approved Development Programme for 1990/91 totalled more than £1.1 billion: for the first time, the Corporation's investment in housing associations exceeded the £1 billion mark. The background to this was the collapse in the housing market nationally and the problems in the economy associated with high interest rates and the mismanagement of the economy by the government. The Housing Corporation also remained as the essential vehicle for further demunicipalisation and so had made itself an indispensable body for delivering the government's policy. During 1990/91 the government carried out its five-yearly review of the Corporation's internal organisation, which was completed successfully and resulted in the regrouping of responsibilities within headquarters, the appointment of a second deputy chief executive and a continuing search for efficiency and effectiveness (HCAR 1990/91:13). Transfers of stock from local authorities continued to be important. In 1989/90 nine new associations, promoted by local authorities, brought some 35,000 homes into the sector and in 1990/91 six local authorities transferred their homes to new housing associations (see the section 'Large-Scale Voluntary Transfer' in this chapter).

All these activities required the support of private finance and there is some evidence of concern that the level of support needed might not be forthcoming. The annual report for 1990/91 stated that in that year the Housing Corporation did much to inform the private lending sector of the work of housing associations and to persuade lenders of their needs: 'During the year we gave consent to over £1 billion in loans to associations. This included some £625 million to fund the transfer of housing stock from local authorities. Some 37 institutions were directly involved in lending to housing associations, with a further 30 in syndication.'

Most lending was from banks and building societies and it remained difficult to interest long-term lenders such as pension funds and insurance companies. There was concern that private finance for associations was getting tighter. One of the ways in which the Corporation sought to increase the likelihood of private finance being forthcoming was to insist on changes to housing associations' baffling registered accounts. This appears to be an example of where the private finance expertise at board level, particularly that of Benson, directly influenced the approach. Government statutory accounts were not felt to be something that a lender would have been satisfied with. They did not make sense to a business community and were not fit for purpose if you were going to seek business support and private finance. While housing associations had not realised that they needed different accounts to raise private finance, they, as well as the Housing Corporation, were quick to see the point of them. The Corporation referred to the need to ensure that association accounts and asset valuations were comprehensible to private lenders. In addition it was stated that no registered association should undertake speculative activity where risks could not be underwritten without loss to the public purse; no organisation, registered or unregistered, related to a registered housing association should incur debts which it could not honour. In this context further changes to supervisory methods were needed and planned, including the effective combination of financial supervision with the existing monitoring function. To facilitate these changes, on 1 April 1991 the responsibility for financial supervision was transferred to the Corporation's Registration Division, as part of the major reorganisation of headquarters during the second half of the year.

Throughout the early 1990s the Corporation sought to maximise the use of public funding by drawing in private sector finance and it recognised that the more it achieved this the more it would help its overall reputation within the key policy community. At the same time the preoccupation with meeting cash limits was evident. No doubt this is partly a reflection of the concern to avoid any repetition of the unfortunate 1989/90 situation, but more importantly, it was a recognition of the importance of the housing programme in the economic environment of that time. For both reasons – its own effectiveness and government concern about the economy in the housing market – the Corporation saw a considerable and continuing growth in expenditure and with the adoption of the private financing approach, public sector expenditure levered in private sector expenditure. Successive annual reports refer to achieving over 99 per cent of budget spending, new highest figures ever, exceeding targets for new home completions and approvals, and introducing new initiatives. They refer to greater value for money and government confidence in the Corporation, evidenced by its willingness to commit larger public expenditure amounts.

In 1991/2 the Corporation progressed with introduction of the Tenants' Incentive Scheme (TIS), a new DIYSO scheme offering shared home ownership opportunities to existing council and housing association tenants and targeting activities on homeless people. The annual report referred to a welcome growth in confidence among private lenders in housing associations. The Housing Finance Corporation continued to be regarded as successful, raising more than £115 million in fixed long-term financing in 1991/2.

While the investment programme dominated attention, the Corporation continued to develop in other ways. During 1989/90 it addressed its new powers in relation to the promotion of racial equality and the elimination of racial discrimination. Existing programmes were aimed at improving participation by ethnic minority communities but the new powers would generate increased activity. At this time the Corporation also introduced its CORE continuous recording system to establish the characteristics of incoming tenants. This was set up through the NFHA and became one of the key information sources for the sector over future years. The Corporation's responsibilities in relation to Tenants' Choice gave it an explicit direct concern for the needs and welfare of tenants for the first time and prompted wider action including the promotion of tenant participation (HCAR 1989/90: 4).

The Housing Market Package

In 1992/3 a measure of how far the Housing Corporation had succeeded in re-establishing confidence with the government was found in its ability to deliver its Housing Market Package (HMP) for the government. The package arose in the context of the housing market recession following the unprecedented high interest rates of 1990, the ensuing collapse in the volume of sale transactions and the fall in housing prices that generated negative equity on a large scale and left a lack of demand for new construction, with large numbers of unsold dwellings. In addition to the annual development programme for 1992/3, £577 million was allocated to the Corporation in the Chancellor of the Exchequer's autumn statement to enable housing associations to purchase new, empty and repossessed properties by 31 March 1993, thereby providing around 17,000 extra units of social housing. In addition the Corporation was given £20 million for additional TIS grants to housing association tenants. This was expected to enable up to 2,000 new first-time buyers to enter the housing market, releasing the same number of units of social housing for reletting.

The HMP stands as a clear example of the Housing Corporation acting as an agency but it also demonstrates that the government was dependent on the Corporation and could not have achieved the same result without its co-operation. The Corporation was advised by the DoE and two Treasury officials that the Chancellor, Norman Lamont, wanted to announce a boost to the housing market the day after his autumn statement and it was told that it would have until 31 March to spend £594 million on unsold houses. The Corporation accepted the task subject to two conditions: that it would select the housing associations and would allocate to them and not invite a bidding war; and that there would only be monthly (not daily) reporting back on how things are going. In other words, 'I'll do it, I'll report back to you every month but neither the DoE nor the Treasury should interfere.' The package was designed to stimulate the stagnant housing market by buying up empty properties, and the annual report referred to the successful implementation of the HMP: 'In just 93 working days between 13 November and the end of March, 81 housing associations spent £577 million on the purchase of 18,430 vacant homes, over 2,400 more than the original target. This was achieved by associations negotiating deals offering excellent value for money [HCAR 1992/3: 8].' The package was organised rapidly and in addition to the planned Approved Development Programme, which still met its target.

By buying up empty properties the HMP scheme showed the dynamism and flexibility of the sector in operation in a way that it would not have done and been able to do in the past. A selected group of associations purchased more than 1,800 homes in satisfactory condition from builders and developers, private sellers and mortgage lenders. This provided a major boost to the housing market, but it also provided rented homes earlier than would otherwise have been the case. The aim of the package was first and foremost to help revitalise the private housing market, but it had the effect of providing good-quality homes for families and others in housing need. Almost half of the homes bought were acquired from builders or developers; over 40 per cent came from private treaty sales. In addition purchases from mortgage lenders for repossessed properties amounted to 6.7 per cent of the total. Almost all local authority areas benefited from the package, and a number reported the eradication of their need to house families in bed and breakfast accommodation because of the homes released through the package.

In the East Midlands region more than 100 family homes, for sale as a result of the departure of the US Air Force, were bought by the Suffolk Heritage Housing Association, needing less than £13,000 grant per property. Nationally the average amount of HAG put in was £32,067 while the total cost per property bought was £50,489. The funding made available through the HMP was supplemented by almost £328 million of private finance and almost £12 million from other public subsidy. More than 40 per cent of HMP funding was targeted at the London and Home Counties regions, where the problems in the property market were greatest, but there was also a significant impact beyond this. In the North East region almost 60 per cent of the 1,860 homes purchased were bought from individual owners, making a significant difference to the local housing markets. In particular the Yorkshire Metropolitan and Bradford and Northern housing associations were instrumental in breaking a number of housing chains to get the market moving.

In 1992/3 some £1.8 billion was channelled through to housing associations from the Corporation's Approved Development Programme (ADP) to provide homes for people in housing need. The additional £577 million made available under the HMP meant that the Corporation spent £2.3 billion overall in relation to more than 60,000 homes, the biggest programme in its history. Some 99.97 per cent of the ADP was spent achieving all the separately identified ministerial targets, except for the TIS and DIYSO, which were both demand led. The remainder was held back as a safety margin. Well over half of the programme was targeted at meeting the needs of homeless people. The level of interest shown by private lenders in the housing association market continued to rise and private sector lending amounted to £627 million, including the £328 million coming in to supplement the HMP. This overall programme could be seen as representing a complete recovery from the problems of earlier years and demonstrating the value of the Corporation to the government, in enabling it to inject significant new resources into the housing market and the economy, at short notice.

There were criticisms and alternative perspectives on the HMP. It was rushed and in some cases the choices made may not have been the best ones. The pace and nature of the purchases of properties were not always ideal. There were some housing associations that would have liked to have been included but were not. The associations that participated also often purchased properties in localities that they had not worked in before. This added to their territorial expansion (and provided a platform for some housing associations to expand geographically later) but may not have resulted in the best or most responsive services to tenants. There were questions about whether money was spent on the highest-priority properties, whether the prices paid were the lowest achievable or whether the long-run outcomes were the most desirable. There was also severe antagonism in some quarters where associations acquired properties in newly built estates; this raised objections from home owners who had purchased properties in what they assumed would be wholly private estates. Government ministers were subjected to a barrage of criticisms passed on by fellow MPs over this latter issue. But whatever these reservations were, the Housing Corporation had passed the test of meeting the government's objectives to inject resources into the housing market and to overcome some of the problems that were seen as creating a national and regional crisis.

New questions

By the end of the financial year 1993/4 Sir Christopher Benson was coming to the end of his period as chairman and his statement in the annual report referred to the changed role of the Housing Corporation in the five years since the Housing Act 1988. Housing associations had become major risk-taking businesses, responsible for the stewardship of very sizeable sums of public and private investment. They had taken on these increased financial responsibilities without any major failures in the most depressed property market since the war. In effect the Corporation had enabled the government to achieve key policy objectives, had made associations the main providers of new social housing with a rapidly increased programme, had maximised the output of new homes, and value for money for the taxpayer, by levering in unprecedented levels of private finance to housing associations. This ensured that for each pound of public funding there was also significant private finance and meant that the growth lay outside the public sector borrowing requirement. Housing associations had taken on a greater share of risk in both the development and the management of housing activities. The change in financial regime and an increasing proportion of funds coming from the private sector resulted in a major realignment in the regulatory approach to ensure that associations performed in a prudential, business-like manner.

A more strategic relationship between the Corporation and the DoE was also referred to, which had enabled the Corporation to carry out its responsibilities and manage its business with greater efficiency and effectiveness. The Corporation had streamlined systems and procedures and improved the quality of its services without increasing staff numbers. It had reinvented itself as the lead agency in a new mixed-funding, public/private sector housing initiative. It had also been able to demonstrate its effectiveness in delivering the HMP and reviving the stagnant housing market.

Alongside all of these successes there were a new set of questions. The opportunism associated with the HMP had generated antagonisms and criticisms within and outside the housing world. At the same time the dominant role of housing associations in providing new social housing and their increasing role in taking over stock from local authorities heightened concerns about accountability and governance. Increasing merger activity within the housing association sector went ahead largely without reference to tenants and cemented the view that there was a cosy relationship between government, the Housing Corporation and housing associations. Elsewhere questions were being asked about what housing associations were doing about governance and accountability.

The Housing Corporation had not altogether neglected governance issues in its capacity as regulator and matters related to membership and payments to committee members have been referred to earlier in this book. The NFHA had also taken initiatives, producing its first code of conduct in 1979 and updating it periodically. Nevertheless housing associations had entered the new financial regime after 1988 with management committees that

> had been recruited in, and were used to, a very different and less demanding environment. In the past questions had arisen as to the competence and accountability of committee members, but this was generally in relation to allegations of isolated cases of fraudulent or inept behaviour. Now the demands of the new financial regime ... put a premium on both competence and accountability. (Malpass 2000: 255)

This chimed in with the mood of the times. The early 1990s also saw the publication of the Greenbury and Cadbury reports, recommending better corporate governance practices for Stock Exchange-listed companies, and the formation of the Nolan committee, which pursued a wider agenda in relation to standards in public life.

The question of how well-equipped housing associations were to operate in a different financial environment were exemplified by problems uncovered in the Focus housing association in 1995. An internal investigation prompted by three anonymous letters alleging improper conduct in the property services department was carried out with the association's auditors, the police and the Housing Corporation fully briefed. The investigation related to the purchase of properties in the period that included the HMP, 1990 to 1995.

> The nub of the investigation was that a small number of Focus' staff in its property services department had been overpaying local property dealers for properties acquired for refurbishment. The implication was that these staff had made financial gains from these fraudulent activities. Two staff were suspended and later convicted of fraud. (Gulliver 2000: 189)

Both the general political environment and specific cases imparted an urgency to debates about governance. The NFHA set up a committee, chaired by Sir David Hancock, a former permanent secretary at the Department of

Education and Science, to carry out an inquiry into the governance of housing associations – perhaps partly to head off more antagonistic views (see Malpass 2000: 258). The Hancock committee recommended the adoption of the term 'board' for the governing body of housing associations and made recommendations related to turnover of board membership and the roles of the chairman, the board and the chief executive. Although the report may be seen as 'a rather bland document' it provided a forum for the discussion of critical issues and was a milestone in the development of later advice on governance and accountability and training for board members.

The atmosphere of the time began to alter the emphasis in regulation. The new performance review system, which came into effect in April 1994, enabled the move away from a prescriptive, hand-holding, regulatory style to one in which the Housing Corporation allowed associations to make their own decisions as established risk-taking businesses. Yet, at the same time, the further requirements on associations to provide accurate, regular and detailed financial information were achieved through the introduction of measures such as quarterly financial returns and plc-style accounts. As a result the Corporation had a better picture of housing associations' overall financial health than ever before, even though it had a less prescriptive, regulatory style. Both the House of Commons Public Accounts Committee (PAC) and the National Audit Office, in its inquiry into the financial management of associations, recognised the strides the Corporation had made in adding to its regulatory armoury over the past five years (HCAR 1993/4). To quote the PAC's report: 'We attach great importance to the safeguards which the Corporation's regulatory framework provides for the proper conduct of business within associations and ensuring value for money.'

The Commons Environment Select Committee had also looked at the Housing Corporation in 1993 and made a number of recommendations. They regarded it as unacceptable for the housing association ombudsman to be located within or serviced by the Corporation, as there was an implied restriction on autonomy. They also recommended open and transparent procedures for appointing members to the board of the Corporation (House of Commons Environment Committee 1993). The DoE took steps to act on the recommendations of that report, in particular the introduction of twice-yearly, regional consultative meetings, to achieve better and more informed feedback on the exercise of the Corporation's funding and regulatory responsibilities, and the realignment of regional office boundaries to more closely match those of the DoE's regions. This came into effect in April 1995.

The issue of co-terminous DoE and Corporation boundaries also related to integration of the Corporation's ADP and the DoE's Housing Investment Programme (HIP) for local authorities. The demand to integrate these better created anxieties in the Corporation. The HIP process was dealt with by the regional controllers in the DoE and it was argued that duplication through two separate processes was wasteful. This represented a threat to the Corporation. The antagonism of local authorities at this time and the weakness felt by the Corporation led to a fear that takeover rather than integration was planned. The compromise achieved was that the Corporation's regional boundaries should align with DoE regional boundaries, that there should be much more strategic co-ordination of programmes. Local authorities should have an earlier say in the allocations process but the institutional framework should only change to be co-terminous.

The shifting interest in accountability also explains why it was at this time that the Housing Corporation published its strategy document for the next three years, *The Housing Corporation's Plans and Priorities 1994–97*, and launched the Housing Association Tenants' Ombudsman Service, as a free-standing organisation under the overall aegis of the Corporation, to resolve tenants' complaints.

New tensions

The Housing Corporation managed a declining budget after 1994. The slow recovery of the housing market meant that the housing programme fell back into the low-priority doldrums that had applied before. The 1993 budget of £2.2 billion fell in each of the following years: to £1.7 million, £1.4 million and then £1.1 million. These cuts were not, as in earlier periods, associated with economic crises but with plans to cut taxes – culminating in the 1997 Budget, which cut 1p off the basic rate of income tax.

There was no implied criticism of the Corporation in this decline. It was reviewed in 1995 as part of the government's programme of regular five-yearly finance management and policy reviews (FMPRs) of non-departmental public bodies. The prior options stage of the FMPR was completed in June 1995. The purpose of this stage was to assess whether the Corporation's functions remained necessary for the achievement of the government's policies, and whether there was scope for privatising, contracting out or transferring all or part of its functions to another body.

This first stage identified issues to be examined in the second stage of the FMPR, including the Corporation's approach to registration and regulation in the context of the prospective introduction of new registered social landlords (RSLs); the procedures for the appointment of Corporation board members and for dealing with potential conflicts of interest arising from board members' involvement in other housing-related activities; arrangements for liaison between the Corporation and government regional offices; and the scope for contracting out or market-testing support services within the Corporation (Hansard 1995). The second stage of the FMPR in 1996 reinforced the positive conclusions about the continuation of the Corporation's role signalled in the prior options stage, which had seen the continuing co-location of regulatory and investment functions as inextricably linked in the effective use of public resources.

The government accepted the conclusions of the prior options stage: that the Housing Corporation should continue to be responsible for the funding and regulation of housing associations in England; that it should take on responsibility for payment of grant to and supervision of the proposed RSLs, including landlords receiving transferred local authority stock; and that non-departmental public body status remained appropriate to the Corporation's functions. The review also recommended that the Housing Association Tenants' Ombudsman Service (HATOS) should be put on a statutory footing. The initial location of the ombudsman within the Housing Corporation had been criticised by the House of Commons Environment Select Committee and by many of those submitting evidence to that committee. It was not surprising that these arrangements gave way to a wholly independent housing association ombudsman. The prior options review recommendation was accepted and subsequently incorporated in the Housing Act 1996.

The Housing Corporation accepted a number of operational recommendations in the report, in particular those related to the promotion of housing associations, liaison with county councils over care in the community and other issues, future monitoring of housing associations' employment practices and exposing activities to competition from the private sector, where relevant. It accepted these conclusions against the background of the White Paper *Our Future Homes*, which indicated the government's commitment to a social rented sector and set out plans for other landlords to provide social rented housing, alongside housing associations. Systems for allocating government subsidy, monitoring the provision of dwellings and overseeing the operation of RSLs continued to be needed although there were proposals that other organisations should be able to access grant and subsidy. In 1996/7 all housing associations were required to make a performance return, fulfilling the commitment to the PAC to review all housing associations' performance annually.

The Housing Act 1996 established the independent Housing Ombudsman Service to replace the HATOS, run by the Corporation. It also introduced the power to register and regulate not-for-profit local housing companies (LHCs), including those set up by local authorities to receive a transfer of their existing housing stock. The NFHA relaunched itself as the National Housing Federation in order to be able to include the new providers within this regime. From April 1997 social housing grant, which replaced HAG, would be open to all housing associations including not-for-profit, non-charitable companies. The rising costs of housing benefit since the introduction of assured tenancies were also to be addressed by taking prospective average rents into account in value for money assessments. Other activities related to work on developing performance indicators, a regulatory framework for risk management in larger housing associations and efforts to facilitate good practice in the social housing sector, especially through innovation and good practice grants. A primary aim in this was to develop the partnership and regeneration agendas including activities which became identified as Housing Plus and involved housing associations taking an interest in the needs of tenants and communities beyond those associated with the landlord function itself.

In 1996 the Housing Corporation adopted a new mission statement: 'Working to improve quality of life through social housing'. Five overall aims underpinned its functions. These were:

- to secure the effective and efficient delivery of new social housing which creates and sustains healthy communities;
- to promote the interests of tenants in the housing services they receive and their full involvement in the provision of those services;
- to protect the interests of taxpayers in their investment in social housing by ensuring the financial and management viability of RSLs;
- to secure the long-term maintenance and improvement of existing social housing provided by RSLs;
- to encourage innovation and best practice in the delivery of RSLs' services.

At this stage, in early 1997, the Corporation sold its outstanding loan portfolios to the private sector (Hansard 1997a). The then secretary of state, John Gummer, had previously (Hansard 1996) agreed in principle to sell the loans provided to housing associations by the Housing Corporation and Housing for Wales, subject to satisfactory final bids from the private sector for the portfolios. Following negotiations NatWest Markets was chosen as the preferred bidder for both the English and the Welsh portfolios.

The decline in budgets and the different elements referred to above had the effect of turning the Housing Corporation inwards. It reviewed its administrative funds over the three years from 1997 to allow itself to live within its reducing budget while keeping staff cuts to a minimum. The outgoing chairman, Sir Brian Pearse, at the end of his three-year term of office referred to the continuing downward pressures on resources, along with major shifts in the policy environment. Because of this 1996/7 was a year of reassessment and refocusing of strategic direction. The Corporation again spent 99.9 per cent of available resources. Almost 32,000 new homes were completed for rent and more than £1.3 billion of finance from the private sector allowed housing associations to almost double the value of every pound of public subsidy. Some £11 billion of private funding had been raised since 1988 – an achievement which outstripped any other sector involved in private finance initiatives. On the regulatory side, the track record of protecting taxpayers' money and tenants' homes continued. Since 1989, when the mixed public/private funding regime for housing associations was introduced, no public investment had been lost, there had been no insolvencies among housing associations and no tenant had lost their home. The regulatory system had reassured the private sector sufficiently for it to invest £11 billion, complementing the £20 billion public subsidy already invested. However, Pearse wrote, 'we faced a substantial reduction in our resources for investment in social housing for 1997/8. This reduction, on top of that in 1995/6 and 1996/7, was a major disappointment for all of us.'

Against the background of success, the further reduction in the programme for 1997/8 to fund tax cuts was seen as disproportionate and Pearse indicated that he wished to stand down when his term of office ended on 31 March 1997. This resignation was not anticipated and a stop-gap arrangement was put in place. Effectively, and for the only time in its history, the chairman of the Housing Corporation had resigned – and not because of any row with the housing minister: indeed the absence of any policy-based rationale for the cuts and the disproportionate share of cuts being borne by the housing programme had made them harder to take. In February 1997 Gummer announced (Hansard 1997b) that Peter Cooke, who was then deputy chairman and had been a board member for nine years, had agreed to take over as chairman for six months from 1 April. This would provide proper continuity for the Corporation at a time of change.

Changing relationships

The various developments referred to above began to change the established relationships between the different parties in the housing association sector and it is valuable to reflect on the discussions of these changing relationships. The concerns about the Housing Corporation compromising its regulatory role and being more demanding in relation to efficiency and effectiveness meant that its role in promoting housing associations was questioned and after 1996 it no longer had a duty to do so. At the same time Mullins (2000) states that the last years of Conservative government were a period of sustained conflict between local authorities and the Corporation over local investment priorities for housing associations and he identifies this as one of the developments which marked a paradigm shift from social democracy to liberalism. The increasing emphasis on private funding of housing associations and the ability of some housing associations to draw on accumulated surpluses appeared to indicate their growing independence from the state and their emergence as a third sector consistent with the liberal model rather than as a sponsored state-dependent sector in the social democratic model.

During the mid-1990s housing associations acted to a significant extent as contractors of the state, channels for state subsidy into the provision of new housing rather than as an independent sector. The increased funding for the non-profit sector had not come from philanthropic or charitable sources, nor from the expansion of charges met in full by users, although rental income was a very important source of funding for housing associations; rather, the expansion had been facilitated by the state. The increasing importance of indirect subsidy through housing benefit paid to tenants in financing associations' rental income streams had also been significant. Numbers of housing association tenants claiming housing benefit grew from 210,000 in 1981 to 840,000 in 1988, from 48 per cent to 73 per cent of all association tenants (Mullins 2000). Despite significant reductions in state contribution to the capital funding of new development, and withdrawal of major repairs funding, the sector remained highly dependent on the state. Notwithstanding the increasing use of private finance by associations and the use of accumulated reserves, the scope for new development for low-income groups without state subsidy remained severely limited.

Mullins (1999) identifies one of the responses to the new environment among housing associations as a move towards mergers. Between 1993/4 and 1997/8 a total of 101 transfers of engagements were reported to the Housing Corporation. These mainly involved the winding up of very small associations. Alongside this was the formation of group structures, organisations consisting of a parent undertaking and subsidiary undertakings. The growth of these was marked in the period after 1994/5: in that year there were only two group structures, while in 1997/8 twenty-three were identified. The increase in scale of the larger not-for-profit housing providers has been seen by some observers as involving an abandonment of the values and distinctive identities that shaped the voluntary housing movement. Mullins quotes the submission of the NFHA in 1995 to the Nolan committee:

> The first of our core values is that of independence, and the importance of this point cannot be over-emphasised. Housing associations are independent voluntary organisations, representing a tradition going back many hundreds of years; they have this in common with a great range of charitable, self-help and community organisations.

Mullins describes a process which began to move towards more professional and larger organisations and perhaps involved some abandonment of these core values and of localism. The factors that Mullins identified as motivations for merger in the non-profit sector at this time reflect the tensions referred to above – the wish to spread central overhead costs, achieve economies of scale, increase the asset base and borrowing capacity, achieve geographical and sectoral expansion, eliminate competition and respond to taxation changes. He suggests that housing sector mergers echoed the efficiency and monopoly drive found elsewhere in the non-profit sector and states: 'In these respects it is difficult to detect significant differences in the behaviour of non-profit and profit distributing businesses. Merger activity in both sectors may be seen as an attempt to influence operating environments to reduce uncertainty and to manage resource dependency.' The increasing size of associations gave clear advantages in negotiating and obtaining better terms for private borrowing and the steady process of transfer of engagements and group structures is evident.

The Housing Corporation presented itself as neutral in relation to these trends and Mullins quotes Baroness Dean, Peter Cooke's successor as chair, in 1998: 'In recent times we have become concerned about the growing evidence of so called mega-mergers in a sector that came out of local initiatives. The evidence is that there seems to be a chief executive-driven motivation that big is beautiful, but I think mixed is beautiful.' However, the Corporation's position remained ambiguous. The rhetoric was that mixed was beautiful and there were clear objections to the excessive salaries and severance payments associated with some mergers. At the same time the Housing Corporation was participating in meetings with larger associations as part of a new lead regulator regime in which closer dialogue and understanding were sought between regulators and regulated; and as part of these discussions associations were encouraged to consider the possibility of mergers and group structures (Mullins 1999).

In 1998 the Corporation issued new guidance which declared that it was 'neutral about the principle of any proposed partnership' (quoted in Mullins 1999: 360). The new guidance was important in emphasising the interests of stakeholders other than chief executives and paid directors and that boards should have access to independent advice. But the new provisions were less strong in relation to the role of tenants and did not propose a ballot, independent advisors and a guaranteed package of improvements for tenants similar to those associated with stock transfer from local authorities. Amalgamations, mergers and other new arrangements for housing associations did not require the tenants to be directly balloted or provided with guarantees. They would have to be consulted on the implications for services, access, maintenance and complaints, and there should be an expectation that any proposal enhanced or at least protected the interests of current and future tenants; but they would not be directly involved in the decision making.

Mullins (1999: 361) comments: 'New regulatory guidance places some constraints on "mega-mergers", on anti-monopoly, local accountability and tenant involvement grounds; however, these would appear not to be enormous challenges and a continuing erosion through merger would be likely.' The changes in the environment of the non-profit housing industry in the 1990s made it more difficult for organisations to continue to grow through publicly funded development activity. This stimulated the investigation of mergers and other inter-organisational links which might be expected to produce a greater degree of concentration in the industrial structure.

Mullins comments on the blurring of terminology: key actors were reluctant to use explicit business vocabulary smacking of the private sector, preferring more cuddly terms such as 'partnerships', 'alliances' and 'group structures'. He says: 'This ambiguity is resonant of underlying conflicts in the purposes of non-profit organisations as they respond to pressures to be more competitive and efficient yet retain the social purposes of public service and local accountability.' He also suggests that the actors involved were sensitive to these dilemmas and were actively engaged in the management of ambiguity.

New Labour

Most accounts of the impact of the election of a new Labour government in 1997 stress the absence of any major immediate change in policy. Nick Raynsford, who had been the Labour housing spokesman in opposition, was not given the housing portfolio in government. Hilary Armstrong, as the minister with direct oversight of housing within the new Department of the Environment, Transport and the Regions, showed no inclination towards innovation: the new government's commitment to working within its predecessor's expenditure plans meant that there was a significant period of marking time in relation to housing.

The new government's view appeared to be that the Housing Corporation did a good job but was a quiet sleepy backwater and not very close to its key stakeholders (local authorities and tenants in particular). Presented with the opportunity to appoint new board members, the Corporation intended to have people that were closer to the tenant community. Sir Brian Pearse had resigned from his role as chair of the Housing Corporation in protest at the scale of reductions in their budget. The impact on the Corporation and housing associations was unacceptable to him especially in view of cuts in earlier years and the disproportionate cuts in England when compared with Scotland. His resignation had pre-dated the election of the previous government and without the reversal of cuts would not be rescinded. While Peter Cooke was chairman for a short period, the new Labour ministers preferred a new chairman, and Baroness Dean (Brenda Dean) was appointed. Dean was a former trade union leader and Labour Party loyalist close to the deputy Prime Minister, John Prescott. She brought energy and a strong personal style to the post of chairman and an inclination to have much greater visibility than her predecessors.

There was a view that the Corporation needed to become 'more transparent' and to reverse tendencies to discourage getting close to local authorities or working with tenants' associations. These issues became a priority and, for example, regular consultative meetings were set up with tenants, housing association chief executives and people linked with BME housing associations. This became known as the 'Brenda agenda'. It is unclear how widely this agenda was welcomed within the Corporation. At the end of her period as chairman Dean stressed that the Corporation was a more transparent and effective organisation, better equipped to respond to the challenges of today's modern business environment. She also expressed an important view about its role: 'I believe that the Corporation, as the regulator for the sector, should never be regarded as its "friend or representative" but seen rather as independent and coming to evidence-based decisions and policies. In other words, telling it as it is.' This reflected a shift from a period in which the Corporation and housing associations had sought to increase effectiveness by building a closer relationship to one of more formal and guarded partnership.

The shift in the political landscape with Labour's election in May 1997 was the most important change for the Corporation. The annual report referred to a new set of policies but, whereas in previous eras there was new housing policy or legislation, this time there was reference to government's wider policy programme – to the New Deal and its aims to ease the transition from welfare to work. The report asserted that the Corporation's task had been to respond to this new agenda, while continuing to deliver its investment programmes and protect the interests of tenants and taxpayers through the regulatory regime.

The five key areas of activity identified by the Corporation contrasted with those of the previous year. In view of the later identification by Martin Cave, this can be presented as passporting of policy – using the Housing Corporation and housing associations as vehicles to promote and develop wider government policies in addition to core housing activity.

1. Meeting the needs of the consumer

Landlords needed to deliver services that were efficient and effective and that met the needs of their tenants. This could only be done by involving tenants and listening to their views – on repair services, improving homes, or making sure their area was kept clean, tidy and crime free.

Having tenants on boards was identified as one way of encouraging participation but landlords also had to explore other ways of ensuring that tenants were involved in setting standards and providing services. The revised performance standards set out what was expected from housing associations in relation to accountability to residents, consultation, information, opportunities for participation and influence and complaints procedures and compensation. The Corporation wanted to see housing associations and tenants working together towards participation models 'which can contribute to other government policy objectives including Best Value, social exclusion and Welfare to Work and the New Deal'.

2. Influencing the level of rents

The need for downward pressure on rent levels and rent increases was linked to the Green Paper on welfare reform. This had signalled that the current national bill for housing benefit was unsustainable in the long run and that rents that were not affordable to those on lower incomes acted as a barrier to the success of the government's Welfare to Work strategy and made it more difficult for tenants to access the jobs market.

The established condition for allocating grant for new schemes (that housing associations should not only meet the stated level of the starting rent but also restrict subsequent rates of increase to 1 per cent above inflation) was to be continued and the regulatory regime used in this direction.

3. Changing priorities for housing

The pressure to contain future housing growth to urban areas by using brownfield, recycled land was encouraged by making it possible for housing associations to recycle grant when they demolished properties instead of repaying it to the Corporation. In future more investment resources would also be targeted on areas with above average levels of economic and demographic growth. Wider measures of community regeneration would involve an approach that tackled all housing tenures, not just social housing, and would consider whether some unpopular locations had a future.

4. Building sustainable communities

This referred to the positive steps housing associations could take to make communities work better and help meet the government's objective of tackling social exclusion. The Corporation had previously embraced this agenda through its Housing Plus initiative, launched in 1996, and had encouraged housing associations to participate in the government's New Deal to help people, particularly young people, to enter work.

5. Openness and freedom of information

The Corporation accepted the need for accelerated change to exhibit greater openness in the way it operated and referred to its close work with local authorities to ensure that schemes funded through the ADP were closely related to local housing needs and that money was spent cost-effectively. It referred to developing an alternative to the yearly bidding round for funding, in which housing associations competed for grant in an often unco-ordinated fashion. It also referred to the success of 'joint commissioning', which involved a partnership between the Corporation and local authorities in agreeing a longer-term investment perspective and should produce a more collaborative approach to housing investment than the existing bidding and allocation framework.

Housing associations had built up resources arising from rental surpluses on their pre-1988 Act stock in their rent surplus funds (RSFs), a designated fund which by law could only be spent as directed by the Corporation on behalf of the secretary of state. These had been 'locked up' until required for specific qualifying properties but the Corporation introduced measures to convert existing RSF reserves into a reinvestment fund and unlock them for immediate use. This would provide a cash injection for reinvestment over the next four years of some £350 million accumulated funds, plus a further £80 million to £90 million annually.

In the 1997/8 annual report Baroness Dean referred to the huge cut in investment (from £1,062 million in 1996/7 to £702 million in 1997/8) carried over as the new government retained its predecessor's programme. Overall, the Corporation's investment programme had been reduced by more than 50 per cent in the previous five years and it was stated that this cutback in resources had limited the contribution made to meeting the need for social housing, both in the provision of new and in the refurbishment of existing homes. Dean stated:

> This need is not going to diminish. Whatever the figure is for the growth in households in the period up to 2015 – whether 4.4 million as is often quoted or another figure – we face the fact that for a substantial number of people, the housing market is not going to provide an affordable or appropriate option …
>
> The need is not simply for new houses, important though that is in many localities. Regeneration, and the huge task of building communities where people want to live, is the real challenge which we all have to address in the future. (HCAR 1997/8: 3)

A performance review system had been introduced in 1994 and was made up of three elements: a desktop review of the information collected from each RSL; an investigatory process to follow up any concerns arising from the desktop review; and a visit (on a sample basis) to validate the integrity, accuracy and completeness of the information supplied. Performance standards had been introduced to reflect the increasing government focus on housing association rents, the changes introduced in the 1996 Housing Act which stressed greater accountability to tenants and the emergence of local housing companies, which posed new challenges in terms of governance and risk management. More streamlined processes and increased self-certification of compliance with standards by RSLs were designed so that statutory regulation responsibilities could be carried out effectively without being overly prescriptive and imposing undue amounts of paperwork on housing associations. The new standards came into effect on 1 April 1998, the secretary of state having approved statutory housing management guidance known as Social Housing Standards under Section 36 of the Housing Act 1996. This followed consultation on proposals to amend the performance standards. While the majority of the regulatory requirements were unchanged, the importance attached to rent-influencing policy was reflected in the revised standards, which were designed to secure downward pressure on housing associations' rate of rent increases and on the rent levels they charged.

During 1997/8 a new approach to mergers between housing associations was formulated. The Corporation worked on proposals for criteria to inform decisions on whether and how to exercise statutory powers to give consent to various types of arrangement, including mergers, group structures, transfers of engagement, stock transfers and amalgamations, and there was also some renewed interest in co-operatives.

Issues of governance very quickly came up the agenda, initially with questions about the pay of housing association chief executives. Normally the Corporation would not have commented on that because housing associations were independent bodies and the issue was outside the Corporation's remit. However, backed by the minister for housing, the Corporation took a different view, issuing a press release which expressed surprise and asked people to remember that they were working in the social housing sector. This issue confirmed a view that the corporate governance of the sector was not as strong as it should be. As a result the Corporation began to look at corporate governance. Alongside that, the policy related to supervision cases changed. The new approach was more transparent and less friendly, with a press release issued referring to the organisation that had been put under supervision.

The themes identified in 1997/8 continued to be important in subsequent years. For example, in 1998/9 the chairman's introduction to the Annual Report emphasised residents' charters, meeting the challenge of Best Value, enhancing tenant participation, increasing openness and managing risk. The emphasis on the rights of consumers of social housing was reconfirmed in the proposals for a national housing policy for people from BME communities.

The policy, built on the two earlier strategies for BME-led housing associations stretching back to 1986, was that all housing associations should promote a culture which would empower BME communities; encourage the career development of BME staff; and actively involve BME people in identifying housing need, delivering housing services and improving accountability and tenant involvement.

At this stage the shift in emphasis towards tenants and standards was more than an adoption of the language of the times. It also reflected Dean's feeling that the relationships in the sector were too comfortable and the interests of tenants were not given sufficient attention. The performance indicators system showed that RSL performance between 1995/6 and 1997/8 had declined in a number of areas, including average rent arrears, average rent losses and average time to relet properties (HCAR 1998/9: 15). While some of this reflected the increasing problems associated with a changing housing market (and underlying trends contributing to low and changing demand) rather than simply management failure, it inevitably raised questions about whether housing associations were sufficiently aware of what their customers valued. The period in which regulation had been strongly influenced by the regulated and housing associations actively shaped the regulatory regime (what has been referred to as regulatory capture) gave way to one of regulatory competition. The emphasis on service delivery as well as investment performance was increasingly marked by the Housing Corporation, which adopted a neutral stance rather than a laudatory one. This was consistent with the debates within government and the DETR, but for some key parts of the housing movement it communicated a diminution in interest, commitment or support on the part of the Corporation. The appointment in 2000 of Norman Perry as chief executive added to the shift in emphasis and perception (see Chapter 8). Perry was a former civil servant who had more recently worked as a local authority chief executive. He was not a housing insider and had no prior view about whether the Corporation was worth keeping in the form in which it had existed up to that stage, with the co-location of investment and regulation. The focus of the Corporation shifted to the introduction of modern management systems. There was a reaction against the perception of how the Corporation operated – while both the regulatory and funding systems worked, were understood and were certainly not corrupt, the cosiness of relationships meant that there were favourite organisations and people; you could work out how to do well out of the Corporation. Managerial restructuring, putting in new systems, overhauling the IT networks, which were collapsing, were all designed to change this. Existing proposals for a regionalisation of the structure which Simon Dow, as the acting chief executive until Perry's appointment, had put into place were implemented, creating a parallel regulatory and funding regional structure with two directors.

Delivery

The statistics relating to the delivery of programmes associated with the Housing Corporation between 1989 and 1999 present a clear picture – of a rapid expansion of activity up to the mid-1990s and then of decline. Starts by housing associations in England peaked in 1993 and 1994 but by 2000 were running at less than half that level (see Table 7.1). For completions the profile is the same but lagging by one year (see Table 7.2). With public sector starts and completions having declined to historically low levels by 1990 and continuing to decline the housing association programme dominated new building for rent. Throughout the period private sector starts and completions remained relatively stable – but they did not expand to fill the gap in output when the other providers had smaller programmes.

Table 7.1: Housing starts in England 1970–2001

	Total public sector	Housing associations	Private sector	All dwellings
1970	112,235	8,111	148,318	268,664
1975	125,957	18,768	129,777	274,502
1980	33,634	13,154	84,123	130,911
1985	18,818	10,362	144,301	173,481
1990	6,641	14,111	112,717	133,469
1991	3,058	16,437	114,305	133,800
1992	1,601	28,111	99,586	129,298
1993	1,198	33,574	116,458	151,230
1994	450	33,585	131,401	165,436
1995	592	25,232	110,409	136,233
1996	492	22,629	121,590	144,711
1997	310	21,191	136,069	157,570
1998	98	17,375	131,887	149,360
1999	166	16,895	130,898	147,959
2000	106	13,021	131,389	144,516
2001	183	11,104	136,322	147,609

Source: Wilcox (annual).

Table 7.2: Housing completions in England 1970–2001

	Total public sector	Housing associations	Private sector	All dwellings
1970	130,181	8,176	153,436	291,793
1975	116,325	13,652	131,481	261,458
1980	74,835	19,299	110,232	204,366
1985	23,284	11,298	135,457	170,039
1990	14,015	13,821	136,063	163,899
1991	8,126	15,295	131,174	154,595
1992	3,509	20,789	119,533	143,831
1993	1,422	29,779	116,634	147,835
1994	1,094	30,848	122,699	154,641
1995	787	30,888	125,466	157,141
1996	511	27,025	121,550	149,086
1997	290	20,966	128,237	149,493
1998	243	19,901	122,855	142,999
1999	54	17,775	123,467	141,296
2000	87	16,681	118,330	135,098
2001	160	14,502	114,845	129,507

Source: Wilcox (annual).

Table 7.3: Housing association gross investment expenditure, including use of private finance, in England 1986/7–1999/2000, £ million

	Housing Corporation	Local authorities	Private finance	Total
1986/7	809	145	0	954
1987/8	864	156	25	1,045
1988/9	881	128	125	1,134
1989/90	1,034	308	250	1,592
1990/91	1,234	193	250	1,677
1991/2	1,732	179	700	2,611
1992/3	2,369	286	1,100	3,755
1993/4	1,843	388	1,275	3,506
1994/5	1,530	331	1,475	3,336
1995/6	1,183	354	1,475	3,012
1996/7	1,078	327	1,475	2,880
1997/8	684	363	1,175	2,222
1998/9	607	335	1,025	1,967
1999/2000	638	328	875	1,841

Individual figures have been rounded to the nearest million. Totals are derived from unrounded numbers and may not equal the sum of the rounded numbers

Source: Wilcox (annual).

Table 7.4: Housing association gross investment expenditure, including use of private finance, in Wales 1986/7–1999/2000, £ million

	Housing for Wales	Local authorities	Private finance	Total
1986/7	52	0	0	52
1987/8	63	2	8	72
1988/9	66	7	8	80
1989/90	73	17	22	112
1990/91	102	14	33	149
1991/2	115	17	53	186
1992/3	163	11	73	247
1993/4	131	10	70	211
1994/5	122	5	68	195
1995/6	100	6	76	183
1996/7	92	7	75	174
1997/8	66	2	45	116
1998/9	68	0	42	109
1999/2000	68	0	42	110

Individual figures have been rounded to the nearest million. Totals are derived from unrounded numbers and may not equal the sum of the rounded numbers.

Source: Wilcox (annual).

Table 7.5: Housing association gross investment expenditure, including use of private finance, in Scotland 1986/7–1999/2000, £ million

	Communities Scotland	Local authorities	Private finance	Total
1986/7	114	0	0	114
1987/8	132	0	0	132
1988/9	164	0	0	164
1989/90	203	0	5	208
1990/91	195	11	43	249
1991/2	220	8	42	271
1992/3	255	3	63	321
1993/4	263	10	73	346
1994/5	269	0	81	350
1995/6	279	0	118	397
1996/7	256	0	92	348
1997/8	174	0	74	248
1998/9	165	0	85	250
1999/2000	172	0	105	277

Individual figures have been rounded to the nearest million. Totals are derived from unrounded numbers and may not equal the sum of the rounded numbers.

Source: Wilcox (annual).

Table 7.6: Housing Corporation Approved Development Programme 1989/90–1999/2000, £ million

	Housing for rent	Housing for sale	HAG on deferred interest	Other capital expenditure incl. Challenge Fund	Gross capital expenditure	ADP capital receipts	Non-ADP capital receipts	Net capital expenditure
1989/90	826	107	99	2	1,034	127	0	907
1990/91	1,006	65	158	3	1,232	78	0	1,154
1991/2	1,525	87	118	2	1,732	93	0	1,639
1992/3	2,199	124	45	1	2,369	63	0	2,306
1993/4	1,539	290	14	1	1,843	48	0	1,795
1994/5	1,246	280	3	1	1,530	43	0	1,487
1995/6	948	234	1	0	1,183	31	0	1,15
1996/7	851	216	1	0	1,068	37	500	531
1997/8	541	160	0	1	702	17	654	31
1998/9	506	115	0	0	621	4	0	617
1999/2000	558	79	0	0	638	1	2	634

Individual figures have been rounded to the nearest million. Totals are derived from unrounded numbers and may not equal the sum of the rounded numbers.

Source: Wilcox (annual).

Tables 7.3, 7.4 and 7.5 paint a similar picture in terms of expenditure in England, Wales and Scotland respectively. In England the Housing Corporation's direct investment more than doubled between 1989/90 and 1992/3 but by 1999/2000 it was significantly lower than ten years previously. Total investment expenditure was, however, higher in 1999/2000 than a decade before because of the massive impact of private finance. Although Wales and Scotland experienced relatively less dramatic reductions and private finance remained less important, the pattern was similar.

Table 7.6 sets out the importance of different elements of the ADP. Although home ownership programmes increased in importance, the rental programme dominated throughout and further details of this are presented in Table 7.7. Table 7.7 also indicates the importance of the HMP in boosting the size of the rental programme in 1992/3.

Table 7.7: Projected output from the Approved Development Programme – completions

	Housing for rent				Sales and incentives			Total all
	Mixed and public funded	Short life (mini-HAG)	HMP	Total	TIS	Low-cost home ownership	Total	completions
1990/91	17,610	990	0	18,600	2,270	780	3,050	21,650
1991/2	21,190	1,610	0	22,800	2,690	1,280	3,970	26,770
1992/3	32,160	1,380	18,430	51,970	4,780	5,380	10,160	62,130
1993/4	38,393	1,924	0	40,317	6,450	7,990	14,440	54,757
1994/5	38,506	1,098	0	39,604	6,525	11,066	17,591	57,195
1995/6	40,583	1,482	0	42,065	6,400	10,471	16,871	58,936
1996/7	29,386	2,000	0	31,386	7,029	6,966	13,995	45,381
1997/8	22,843	2,777	0	25,620	4,262	6,336	10,598	36,218
1998/9	22,330	1,500	0	23,830	2,900	6,100	9,000	32,830
1999/2000	19,768	1,194	0	20,962	503	4,032	4,535	25,497

Source: Wilcox (annual).

Table 7.8 shows that the stock of housing association dwellings more than doubled in size over the decade and that lettings almost doubled. Because of stock transfer a considerable part of the growth of stock did not create immediate new lettings but the role of the sector in housing homeless households and others in housing need increased significantly.

Finally Table 7.9 shows that housing association rents remained relatively high throughout this period. They were well above local authority rents, although well below private sector rents. The view that housing associations

Table 7.8: Housing association lettings in England 1989/90–1999/2000, thousands

| | Stock | Lettings | of which | | of which | | Lettings to homeless as % all lettings to new tenants |
			existing tenants	new tenants	existing LA tenants	statutory homeless	
1989/90	567	76	16	60	0	0	0
1990/91	608	77	15	62	0	9	14
1991/2	646	86	17	69	0	15	22
1992/3	714	109	19	90	0	23	26
1993/4	779	134	22	112	0	28	25
1994/5	857	132	21	111	0	26	23
1995/6	942	136	22	114	0	26	23
1996/7	985	139	32	107	27	18	17
1997/8	1,040	145	33	112	29	13	12
1998/9	1,146	146	34	112	27	13	12
1999/2000	1,273	148	36	111	26	13	12

LA: local authority.
Individual figures have been rounded to the nearest thousand. Totals are derived from unrounded numbers and may not equal the sum of the rounded numbers.

Source: Wilcox (annual).

(and stock transfer to a housing association) meant high rents was supported by these types of data.

While the conventional measures of delivery remained positive there were issues arising associated with increasing levels of empty social rented housing and evidence that the investment strategy was insufficiently informed by evidence about the nature of regional and sub-regional housing markets. For examples, homes newly built by housing associations in the north of England remained empty because there was insufficient demand, suggesting that the investment programme was not achieving value for money. Concerns about low demand in the north and excess demand in the south alternatively suggested switching resources between the regions or focusing on regeneration and other activities to stimulate demand in the north, and there was increasing concern about this in the Corporation during the mid-1990s. However, neither the DETR nor the Housing Corporation was well informed and there was some reluctance to admit that existing approaches were flawed. Two separate strands of work began to challenge this complacency. The government's Social Exclusion Unit commissioned research and considered the issue of unpopular housing through its Policy Action Team 7 (PAT7). PAT7 was chaired by Mavis McDonald, who was a

Table 7.9: Rents and earnings in England 1988–2000, £ per week

| | Local authorities | | Housing associations | | Private tenants | | Average earnings | Rents as % earnings | | | | |
	Subsidy guideline	Average rents	Fair rents	Assured rents	Fair rents	Market rents		LA rents	HA fair rents	HA assured	Private fair rents	Private market rents
1988	19.02	18.82	25.00	n/a	25.58	n/a	220.90	8.5	11.3	n/a	11.6	n/a
1989	20.97	20.70	26.83	24.50	25.40	n/a	242.70	8.5	11.1	10.1	10.5	n/a
1990	23.05	23.74	29.94	28.97	29.21	46.67	266.70	8.9	11.2	10.9	11.0	17.5
1991	24.89	27.29	32.73	33.93	32.02	54.50	288.30	9.5	11.4	11.8	11.1	18.9
1992	27.34	30.57	36.48	39.03	36.13	58.85	308.10	9.9	11.8	12.7	11.7	19.1
1993	29.40	33.62	38.50	44.87	38.92	62.27	320.90	10.5	12.0	14.0	12.1	19.4
1994	31.60	35.68	42.15	45.90	42.73	65.60	330.10	10.8	12.8	13.9	12.9	19.9
1995	33.88	38.31	44.46	48.42	45.63	68.62	340.60	11.2	13.1	14.2	13.4	20.1
1996	34.70	40.10	48.25	50.24	50.71	68.90	356.00	11.3	13.6	14.1	14.2	19.4
1997	35.36	41.18	51.35	51.40	53.69	71.75	372.70	11.0	13.8	13.8	14.4	19.3
1998	36.35	42.24	55.29	53.16	58.75	72.42	389.90	10.8	14.2	13.6	15.1	18.6
1999	37.81	43.82	56.65	53.84	60.77	74.19	405.40	10.8	14.0	13.3	15.0	18.3
2000	39.28	45.61	62.73	54.43	66.52	76.58	426.20	10.7	14.7	12.8	15.6	18.0

LA: local authority
HA: housing association

Notes: Local authority average rents are for the April of each year; the guideline rents refer to the financial year. Housing association assured rents exclude service charges. Private market rents are those determined by the rent officer when referred for housing benefit purposes. From 1996 onwards these rent figures are affected by the new limits on rents eligible for housing benefit. 1988 housing association fair rents, and private fair and market rent figures are for the second quarter of the year. Private sector rent figures are presented for all lettings, at time of compilation. Private sector rent figures are presented for all lettings, including the small proportion of unfurnished lettings.

Source: Wilcox (annual).

senior civil servant in the DETR; a range of departments was represented in the team as well as others from outside government, including Max Steinberg from the Merseyside region of the Housing Corporation. Many on PAT7 saw for the first time what others had been seeing for some years – described as 'private sector housing vandalism and housing sector abandonment', with council housing that had been built in the late 1980s and 1990s standing vacant or just boarded up. Private landlords were increasingly active in these areas and taking higher rents out of the areas without investing in them. The evident failure of policy 'created almost a furious argument' between civil servants who had begun to realise that there was a wider problem than the conventional wisdom of pockets of poverty or poorly managed estates suggested.

While the PAT7 report produced an interesting analysis, it failed to produce an effective set of recommendations. A second strand of research, funded through and supported by the Housing Corporation and individual housing associations, adopted a more effective methodology to inform policy and referred to the north-west and west Midlands (Nevin et al. 2001a, 2001b). This research, carried out by the Centre for Urban and Regional Studies at Birmingham University, established the methodology that was built on in subsequent work in other regions and for the eventual development of the Housing Market Renewal Initiative and the identification of nine Pathfinder areas included in the Communities Plan in 2003. Presented with this evidence, the department (by now the Office of the Deputy Prime Minister) had to respond but it is evident that the Corporation had been effective in leading the government towards a policy by preparing and presenting evidence.

Large-Scale Voluntary Transfer

The early stock transfers following the Housing Act 1988 had reflected the shift in government's thinking from Tenants' Choice to landlord guarantee, as outlined earlier. Applications for transfers came through the Large-Scale Voluntary Transfer (LSVT) route and applications to be included in the programme tended to be from Conservative-controlled shire districts with small stocks largely of houses, with few flats and without major problems of stock condition. Stock transfer created the opportunity to address any problems and still deliver a capital receipt sufficient to pay off housing and some other debt, pay a levy to government and leave a substantial sum that could be invested in other council priorities.

Table 7.10: Large-Scale Voluntary Transfer in England 1988/9–1999/2000

	Dwellings with positive values	Dwellings with negative values
1988/9	11,176	0
1989/90	14,405	0
1990/91	45,552	0
1991/2	10,791	0
1992/3	26,325	0
1993/4	30,103	0
1994/5	40,234	0
1995/6	44,871	0
1996/7	22,248	0
1997/8	24,405	8,577
1998/9	56,072	17,828
1999/2000	80,405	16,980
Total	406,587	43,385

Source: Communities & Local Government

Transfer activity started slowly and was restrained by public expenditure considerations – the size of the programme was linked with assumptions about the housing benefit consequences of transfer (Table 7.10). Only two transfers in the period up to 2000 were of 10,000 or more properties: Bromley in 1992 and Telford & Wrekin in 1999. While whole stock transfers were the norm until 1994, from then onwards partial transfers became common – including some transfers from a single local authority divesting itself of all of its stock but to more than one landlord. With the exception of Bromley and small transfers in Walsall and Manchester (in 1996) there were no obviously urban transfers until 1998. The criticism that stock transfer was only an option where positive values were involved – where the rental income stream more than outweighed the backlog in terms of repair and maintenance work needed – resulted in dowry payments made under the Estate Renewal Challenge Fund (ERCF), established in 1995. This did facilitate some transfers of stock with negative values and these began to come through in 1998 (along with some other urban transfers such as Bexley). Individual examples show that local authorities were able to secure concessions to make the terms of transfer more favourable than government's initial thinking had implied. The ERCF enabled the transfer of negative value estates by providing a dowry from private sector funding. The ERCF had a limited budget and only achieved limited numbers of transfers in urban areas. By March 1999 32,000 properties had been approved for transfer under the ERCF compared with the 323,000 transferred under LSVT. After three rounds of allocations the ERCF was discontinued. Because of the implications for public finances, local authorities applied for a place in the transfer programme – just as they did for the ERCF programme with its direct grant disbursement.

The election of the Labour government in 1997 did not lead to any reduction in transfer activity – indeed the opposite was to prove true. At the time of its election some sections of the Labour Party thought that the new government would redefine public expenditure or increase its level sufficiently to enable the severe backlog of council housing disrepair to be addressed and make further transfer unnecessary. However, the party in opposition had become more enthusiastic about a local housing companies model that would enable stock transfer and increased investment in the council stock. In the lead up to the general election, Nick Raynsford, as the opposition housing spokesman, had been involved in the development of proposals for the formation of local housing companies and had sought to identify a distinctive approach to stock transfers which would be acceptable to Labour supporters. Local housing companies were the acceptable New Labour vehicle for stock transfer – enabling the transfer that would provide access to private finance but building in local authority and increased tenant representation at board level to improve accountability.

The new Labour government took office with a commitment to improving all housing (but with more stringent targets for social than private housing) to a new Decent Homes standard. This standard broadened the concept of fitness to include energy efficiency and the standard of amenities such as kitchens and bathrooms. A decent home was one that met the then statutory minimum standard for housing (the fitness standard), was in a reasonable state of repair, had reasonably modern facilities and services and provided a reasonable degree of thermal comfort. This was a policy to modernise social rented housing and deal with the backlog of disrepair that had grown over the previous two decades, especially in the ageing council housing stock. At the same time government was committed to a mixed funding model and restrictions on public expenditure remained in place. The best chance of delivering Decent Homes was by transferring stock and accessing private finance.

Immediately following the election the government announced the release of housing capital receipts over a three-year period and so increased public expenditure by £5 billion. This was followed by a relaxation of the transfer rules to allow the Treasury to write off debt in whole-stock transfers with a negative or marginal value. However, the capital receipts initiative would not be sufficient to deal with the backlog of disrepair in the council housing stock and it soon became evident that the government would not redefine public expenditure to bring it more into line with the rest of Europe and to release local authorities from the capital restraints that they were working under. Although the government only maintained the ERCF until 2000, it used other ways of persuading urban and 'old Labour'-controlled local authorities to transfer. New governance regulations introduced local housing companies with increased local authority and tenant representation on their boards. Set up by local authorities to receive the transfer of run-down housing, often in inner city areas, they would have access to private finance. Under EU employment protection legislation most former housing department staff would be entitled to transfer to the new landlord and this could be expected to overcome some resistance from both employees and councillors. Local housing companies became the norm for all subsequent transfers and the boards of these housing associations, one third tenants, one third council nominees and one third independents, were distinctive, with much stronger tenant representation than elsewhere in the sector. In addition any associations set up following transfer of stock from local authorities were bound to retain some of the culture of local government – although changes of name and expansion beyond the boundaries of the local authority of origin reflected intentions to break away from that tradition.

The ERCF was discontinued and the first comprehensive spending review, completed in 1998, moved the capital funding of negative value transfers to the main HIP. The government adopted a new model stock transfer programme that emphasised flexibility and responsiveness to local authority preferences and councillor and tenant representation on boards. The new companies could have a high degree of accountability to tenants and manage very different numbers of properties with different kinds of group structure and federal arrangement.

During 1997/8 the Housing Corporation registered the first wave of local housing companies, stating:

> If local authorities feel they need to transfer stock in order to rehabilitate it, then the Housing Corporation will readily be of assistance and advise on the registration of new landlords. The government gave us a vote of confidence in this area when they asked us to take over responsibility for channelling the Estates Renewal Challenge Fund to transfer organisations. (HCAR 1997/8: 3)

Conclusions

By the start of the new millennium, the Housing Corporation and housing associations were firm fixtures in the housing policy community. The New Labour government had not reversed the demunicipalisation and privatisation favoured by its predecessor. At the same time it had failed to inject new resources and energy into the housing sector. While the Corporation had succeeded in rebuilding its credibility after the crisis at the end of the 1980s, it had continued to experience uncertainty and cuts. The extent of these cuts were such that the chairman resigned in 1997 – perhaps the Corporation had now lost its confidence in government and in the Treasury in particular.

The Corporation's flexibility in making the HMP work had left some antagonism within both the housing association sector and the wider community and had led to the build-up of some strong political opposition. The presence on the board of people with strong experience of the private housing and finance sectors appears to have been particularly important in this stage of recognising the need to adopt practices within the housing association sector which would provide comfort and confidence to private lenders, and it should not be underestimated how far this independent and private sector advice enabled a public sector body to read the market more effectively. By the late 1990s there was more concern with service delivery and governance issues. There was still support for race equality in housing, but the BME housing policy from 1997 to 2002 was less about BME-led organisations and more about changing the other 2,000 housing associations. The focus shifted from a BME producer-led strategy to meeting the needs of BME housing consumers.

By the end of the period, with a new Labour government and a chairman appointed by that government, the annual reports read more strongly as statements of government policy than at any other time. Without expressing significant concern over the level of funding, the emphasis was firmly on a managerial and social exclusion agenda that simply mirrored the government's priorities.

8

Preparing for the end 2000–2008

Introduction

It is widely accepted that by the end of the 1990s housing policy had become a very low priority for government. Housing did not have the prominence that it had had from the 1940s through to the 1970s and an electorate dominated by home owners was seen to be unlikely to be very interested in programmes for council or social rented housing. However, this was to change and the period following 2000 saw a significant revival of housing policy. The commitment to the Decent Homes agenda meant continuing investment to address the backlog of disrepair in the council sector. Renewed enthusiasm for stock transfer occurred, partly because of the need to draw in private finance so as to reinvest in run-down stock and meet targets related to the Decent Homes standard and partly to finance new development. Continuities in policy were apparent with the sustained operation of the right to buy, housing associations' role in new building for rent and the promotion of home ownership; but concerns about social exclusion, geographical concentrations of deprivation and neighbourhood renewal meant that problems associated with residualised social housing could not be so easily ignored. At the same time problems of low and changing demand in the Midlands and the north attracted more attention – not least from the Housing Corporation and housing associations. A housing Green Paper and the Sustainable Communities Plan captured the new priority afforded to housing and, followed by a series of high-profile reviews, marked a new active phase of policy, albeit not a return to the public sector-led strategies of fifty years earlier.

Ironically it appears that by this stage ministers and civil servants were actively considering whether the Housing Corporation was the right vehicle for the new era. In 2000 Anthony Mayer moved on and Norman Perry was appointed chief executive. Perry had previously been a civil servant but was unusual in having moved away to work in local government as chief executive first of

Wolverhampton and then of Solihull. The brief he was given by the Department of the Environment, Transport and the Regions was that the Corporation, after forty years of development, was being spoken about in terms of being wound up and he entered feeling that he could well be the last chief executive. The duty to promote housing associations had ended with the legislation of 1996 and against this background neither the chairman, Baroness Dean, nor the chief executive presented themselves as champions for the housing association movement. At the same time there were some in the Corporation who appear to have lost their appetite for carrying on as usual. The tensions around uncertain budgets and developing new approaches to regulation, inspection and investment introduced a strong sense that time was running out. A crisis over delegation powers added to uncertainty. While the Corporation embarked on another phase of expansion, the parallel agenda of termination was apparent.

New policy directions

As part of the government's programme of regular five-yearly finance, management and policy reviews (FMPRs) of non-departmental public bodies, the DETR conducted a thorough review of the Housing Corporation in 2000. The prior options stage assessed the extent to which the Corporation's functions were necessary for the achievement of the government's policies, and whether there was scope for contracting out or transferring all or part of its functions to another body. This stage of the review was completed (Hansard 2000) against the background of the government's housing Green Paper *Quality and Choice: A Decent Home for All*. The Green Paper, reflecting renewed energy in housing policy, affirmed the government's commitment to improving the quality of social housing and its management, supporting the transfer of larger numbers of dwellings from the local authority sector to housing associations and continuing to allocate funding to housing associations for new social housing. As a result there remained a need for a mechanism to regulate the housing association sector to protect public investment, to promote improved performance in the sector and to allocate funding for new social housing. Nick Raynsford, minister of state at the DETR, said:

> The government accept the prior options review conclusions, that the Housing Corporation should continue to be responsible for registration and regulation of RSLs in England; should continue to allocate funds for new social housing; and

that its status as a non-departmental public body remains appropriate to the Corporation's functions.

The Housing Corporation is already taking forward a number of recommendations in the report. In particular it is: strengthening its regulatory skills, especially in business and finance; working to establish a full Best Value regime to promote improved performance in the RSL sector; will set up an inspection process to support this regime; and will continue developing its funding arrangements and processes for making investment decisions.

The report identifies a number of issues to be examined in the second stage of the FMPR, including a review of the Corporation's organisational framework; exploring the options for an appeals mechanism for dealing with disputed regulatory judgments; the case for strengthening the Corporation's powers; agreeing a concordat between the department and the Corporation for joint working on policy development; and reviewing targets set for the Corporation. (Hansard 2000)

The Green Paper proposed a future transfer programme of up to 200,000 homes a year. In response to this the Corporation set up a dedicated Stock Transfer Registration Unit (STRU) and recruited new staff to the team, including senior staff from the housing association and commercial lending sectors. The new policy directions led the Corporation to recast its strategic objectives and radically overhaul the way in which it carried out its work. It stated that it would be encouraging a culture of compliance rather than enforcement, underpinned by a new attitude of trust and openness in order to develop a more mature relationship between itself and housing associations. The annual report stated:

RSLs are under just as much pressure to rise to these challenges. They must do more with less, meeting high standards while at the same time focusing on the individual demands of their customers. The proposals in the Green Paper on rent restructuring have consequences for all RSLs and for local authorities who are planning transfers.

Each part of the country has different needs and we want to target resources directly where they will have the biggest impact – in the north that will often mean investing in regeneration projects, in the south, new housing, with pockets of both in between. That means working even more closely than ever before with local authorities. They have a crucial role to play in working with us to identify the priorities for housing in their areas and also to look at ways in which we can better forecast what is going to happen in the future.

If we are to tackle problems such as low demand, we must look at developing better ways of predicting housing trends within localities and regions. That means we must work closely with government offices for the regions and agencies. They can help us look at the wider economic picture within a region and decide how best our investment can meet those needs. (HCAR 1999/2000: 2)

The annual report emphasised the importance of the relationship with private lenders and referred to more than £15 billion of private finance that had come into the sector in the past twelve years. Even more money would need to be raised from private lenders if stock transfer was to continue as planned. Reference was also made to regular meetings with civil servants at the Department for Education and Employment, the Department of Health and the Home Office as well as the DETR. These reflected the widening role of the Corporation in helping to build communities. Reference was also made to the Macpherson report and practical action to combat racism (HCAR 2000/2001).

Moving towards customer-driven services and policies was one of the main threads running through the housing Green Paper and the Corporation emphasised the role of its tenant consumer panel in developing policies and channelling views from residents and tenants directly to the centre. The development of a Best Value culture for RSLs was another major concern for the Corporation. Best Value principles and a focus on consumers meant that the old approach of resource rationing was no longer appropriate. There was also reference to a series of breakfast briefings – 'Brenda's breakfasts'– for small groups of RSL chairs to improve communication and feedback.

The widening agenda was also acknowledged. For a number of years, housing associations had been carrying out an increasingly diverse range of 'Housing Plus' activities, which involved them in working well outside a narrow housing brief. That process had accelerated, in many cases for sound reasons which recognised the growing need to provide housing solutions that were not simply about the homes themselves. At the same time, housing associations had to cope with an increasingly fragmented pattern of demand for social housing, coupled with restrictions in rent increases. The Corporation stated: 'As regulator, it is our responsibility to set parameters for diversification and this has involved us in a brisk debate with those whom we regulate [HCAR 1999/2000: 4].'

At this stage the Corporation was anticipating an expansion of its role:

The housing Green Paper signals that the Corporation will be developing inspection services to complement our regulatory functions. We are delighted that we are to be given this role and are now designing an approach to inspection that will focus on RSLs' Best Value techniques while checking with consumers to see what actually happens on the ground. (HCAR 1999/2000: 4)

The further development of regional housing statements resulted in a continuing move away from allocations predominantly based on the housing needs index (HNI):

Moving away from a formula-driven system has required us to develop new relationships and new styles of working as we apply more local judgements to the complex process of investing in housing markets.

Over the next two years, we aim to move away from the use of HNI at local level altogether. To see this process through successfully will require us to build on our new relationships with, for example, regional development agencies and regional political bodies, and to develop new skills to ensure that our funding decisions are transparent and justifiable. (HCAR 1999/2000: 4)

The government also expected the Housing Corporation to passport the very demanding targets suggested by the Egan report, *Rethinking Construction*, published in 1998 to improve the efficiency of the building industry and the quality of the homes produced. In 1999/2000 the Corporation was asked to achieve 10 per cent Egan compliance within the Approved Development Programme (ADP) and this was accomplished. The target increased subsequently and to help housing associations respond, the Corporation actively promoted greater use of standardisation and off-site pre-assembly techniques. At the same time it increasingly emphasised energy efficiency and green standards in dwellings.

During this period the Corporation was evangelical about low-cost home ownership. With support from John Prescott, the secretary of state, it set up a Home Ownership Task Force with Norman Perry as the secretary and Baroness Dean as chairman. While the report was ignored initially, it subsequently generated a response from the government, which accepted almost every recommendation. Against this background the Corporation had support from ministers to increase the proportion of the Corporation's budget that was spent on low-cost home ownership initiatives.

Modernisation

The housing Green Paper of 2000 provided the background for the Housing Corporation to set about 'modernising the way in which we provide services to the sector – and the way in which we manage ourselves' (HCAR 2001/2). The new-style Corporation set out to be a more transparent business, encouraging creativity, innovation and continuous improvement and with a 'can do' culture. This was expected to have a knock-on effect on the way in which associations operated their businesses, particularly in relation to the services they provided to tenants. Following the Green Paper the Corporation set up its new inspection system in 2002. Tenants were, for the first time, being consulted directly on the performance of their landlords, with their views incorporated in the final reports.

The Corporation was aware of possible vulnerabilities because it was investor and regulator, which influenced the decision to set up its own inspectorate and played into the inspectorate saga outlined below. This awareness also stimulated a different and less comfortable regulatory style in which housing associations would automatically be expected to comply with the standards set; if they did not the Corporation would apply sanctions. This would mean more periodical root-and-branch inspection rather than the routine annual tick-box regulatory process. This view was strengthened by an awareness both of the costs of inspection to the Corporation and of the fact that housing associations were getting bigger and bigger.

Mullins (2002) outlines how after 1999 the Housing Corporation and housing associations developed their approach to Best Value to achieve improvements in cost effectiveness. He presents this as part of a shift to a competitiveness or outcome regulation, the restriction on rents also being a key element in this process. The approach placed considerable emphasis on benchmarking, cost reduction, market testing, improved value for money from contractors, partnership and consortium building, and it was also associated with a reduction in the number of regulations and a more streamlined regulatory code introduced in 2001.

Alongside the developments in inspection the Housing Corporation continued to overhaul its own regulatory regime. It adopted a tailored approach to regulating different types of association, with less prescription, an emphasis on improvement and a new inspection regime focusing on tenants' experience of the service (Walker et al. 2003). The 2002 regulatory code reduced the number of performance standards to sixteen higher-level outcomes. While performance standards were not removed there was a shift of balance towards performance improvement, which was a development of Best Value and altered the emphasis to self-assessment and the adoption of quality improvement methods to meet each organisation's needs rather than conformance with external prescriptions of process. The emphasis on organisational ownership of continuous improvement involved a range of sanctions to deal with unacceptable performance. These included: continuing regulation whereby the association agreed to an action plan to remedy minor performance concerns; suspending funding while serious concerns were remedied; and enforcement status, which could involve a number of sanctions including suspension of funding, a statutory inquiry, appointments to boards and, ultimately, transfer of assets to another association. The spread of group structures also made it possible for a group parent to assist an ailing association with its strategy while the latter preserved its status as an independent association (Walker et al. 2003).

As well as reshaping the senior management structure and reviewing how the board worked, the Corporation set out its ambitions for the future in a three-year strategy document, *Building on Success* (March 2001). The Corporation emphasised working with local authorities and regional bodies to plan strategies which addressed entire housing markets and which allocated funds according to regional and sub-regional priorities. It referred to embracing the implications of the White Paper *Revitalising the English Regions*, and also working at the forefront of new initiatives such as affordable housing for key workers, restructuring of housing markets and regeneration. The regional structure of the Corporation was revised into five 'fields', each with a field director, and a review of policy and corporate services was undertaken. There is some controversy over these changes. Just at the time when the Labour government's regional agenda was at its height and following the establishment of regional development agencies the Housing Corporation chose to abandon the co-terminosity of boundaries that had been established in 1995. Not only did this send out a strange signal but it left the Corporation with some difficulty in later regional co-operation and planning. At the same time the decision to split the regulation and investment activities at field level (each field having separate investment and regulation heads reporting to separate investment and regulation divisions at headquarters) could be seen as likely to reduce the integration between the two.

In autumn 2002 the housing minister, Lord Rooker, announced the setting up of the Challenge Fund, a top slicing of the ADP aimed at tackling acute housing shortages in the south-east; within an eight-week deadline, the Corporation announced details of its successful launch. This programme was a precursor to the Sustainable Communities Plan for addressing the lack of affordable housing in the south while grappling with low and changing demand in the Midlands and the north. The Corporation announced that it was taking the lead in promoting the use of innovative and modern construction methods and would play a key role in the nine Housing Market Renewal Pathfinders established in the Midlands and the north. Collaboration with agencies including English Partnerships and the launch of a new joint unit, the Housing Partnership, that would identify potential sites for housing development were also emphasised.

The first setback: inspection

In view of later developments it is important to recognise that at this stage there was once again growing discussion about the co-location of investment and regulation within one agency and about the relative roles of the Housing Corporation, English Partnerships and the Audit Commission. The Audit Commission had been established in 1983 as part of the drive for efficiency at that time but had subsequently proved itself to the Treasury and was highly regarded within government. It had commented on different aspects of council housing from its earliest years and Duncan Campbell-Smith (2008), in his history of the Commission, describes the background to the development of the Housing Inspectorate. He indicates that, following his arrival at the Housing Corporation, Anthony Mayer met with Howard Davis, the head of the Commission, and they agreed that a team from the Commission would work with the Corporation on value-for-money projects. There did not appear to be any pre-conditions for the Commission's involvement although staff at the Corporation were surprised that an invitation had been made to the Commission. Following this a two-year agreement was made in 1994 for the secondment of staff from the Commission to the Corporation and the arrangement was sanctioned by the Department of the Environment with a letter from the secretary of state to the Corporation and the Commission asking them to work together on promoting value for money among housing associations. Campbell-Smith states that some high-quality analysis followed on profiles of the larger associations and on a series of six jointly prepared reports. While this was talked about as a joint studies programme the reports were actually written by the Audit Commission and were its responsibility (Campbell-Smith 2008: 399).

Since the funding for the programme came entirely from the Housing Corporation the partnership had its tensions. It was plain to ministers and their officials that the Commission had added a critically useful dimension to the Corporation's role. Before the two-year agreement expired the Housing Act 1996 consolidated the role of the Commission in relation to the housing association sector and the Corporation. The Commission rapidly developed its work on the housing association sector in 1996 and 1997. In July 1998 the Chancellor of the Exchequer, Gordon Brown, announced that he wanted to see an inspectorate set up for council housing. Initially there was no indication of where this inspectorate would be located. There was internal discussion in the Housing Corporation about whether this was an opportunity for it but it had no appetite to engage with the politics of local authority housing and, if there ever was an opportunity, it was not seized. By the autumn of 1998 John Prescott, the environment secretary, had made it clear that the inspectorate for council housing would be set up as a separate entity – a housing inspectorate within the Audit Commission. The Commission embarked upon setting up the inspectorate during the early months of 1999, aware that there was the possibility of expansion to the housing association sector (Campbell-Smith 2008: 452–3). The Housing Inspectorate, under Roy Irwin, began operations in July 2000. By March 2002 it had published 192 reports and, Campbell-Smith states, 'enjoyed a good reputation within the sector for the general quality of its work'.

With the exception of its agreement with the Audit Commission, the Housing Corporation appeared to be falling behind. When the New Labour government had introduced the Best Value regime for local government in 1997 it had not applied to housing associations but the Corporation was urged to adopt a parallel system. Best Value embraced continuous improvement, a closer relationship with customers and performance comparison with peers. Having consulted on this, the Housing Corporation announced that it did not intend to regulate to require housing associations to deliver Best Value in the way that local authorities were expected to. Instead it sought to encourage them to identify effective practice by piloting and by exchange of good practice through survey and review. Some associations saw this as a real opportunity to make policy and there was no shortage of applications for the pilot programme. The new inspection service went live in April 2002, at the same time as the regulatory code and organisational structures were radically redesigned to support the new approach. Through the regulatory code, associations were required to make a wider range of information accessible to the Corporation – including business plans, risk management strategies and black and minority ethnic and diversity plans. To support associations in complying with the code, an Internet-based Bank of Good Practice was established. Associations could find publications and examples to help them introduce new or strengthened ways of working, without having to reinvent the wheel. Inspection was designed to generate a more vivid 'real life' picture of associations' performance, and tenant inspectors were involved in developing the approach. Inspection was seen as starting to shift the emphasis from associations' achievement of standardised results, and the nuts and bolts of how they did it, to the direct impact of their actions on their tenants' quality of life. (HCAR 2001/2: 8)

Effectively housing associations were left to develop their approach to Best Value themselves and there was an explicit commitment not to regulate Best Value activities during a pilot period. There is little doubt that some saw this as the Housing Corporation dragging its feet and exposing its lack of commitment to tenants and service delivery – and perhaps too close an identity with the producer interest. The FMPR in 2000 concluded that the Corporation should build on what was being done by the Audit Commission for council housing, but the Corporation was convinced that it should adopt a different approach because housing associations were different. The housing association pilots were not published and the contrast between what the Audit Commission was doing and the Housing Corporation's approach was difficult to reconcile with notions that similar tenants in different parts of the social rented sector should get the same services.

Campbell-Smith (2008) states that the Housing Corporation was very slow to comply and there was an impression that it did not enter into the inspection business with enthusiasm. Rather than following what the Commission was doing it went off in its own direction, much to the displeasure of the Office of the Deputy Prime Minister, which now had responsibility for housing. It is possible that the relationship between the Housing Corporation and the National Federation of Housing Associations (NFHA) held the Corporation back from as rigorous an inspection system as applied in the local authority sector. There was a compromise around a cosier description of performance that was more confusing and intentionally less transparent. Perhaps this is one of the weaknesses of the process of regulatory capture and the closer relationship between housing associations and the Corporation. In this case it did not lead to the outcome that would have been desired.

The next stage in this saga was that in 2002 Brown announced the government's intention to have a single housing inspectorate in place of the two that currently existed, one belonging to the Audit Commission, the other to the Housing Corporation. When it came to considering which of the two existing bodies would take on the combined housing brief, it was the Audit Commission that succeeded. The decision appears to have been left to the ODPM. Campbell-Smith (2008) states that, given its tardy introduction of housing association inspections, there was no question of the brief passing automatically to the Housing Corporation, but Baroness Dean wasted no time putting a case to Prescott as deputy Prime Minister. How far he committed himself in private is not clear but officials at the Corporation were soon confident that their chairman had won him over. Prescott's local government minister, Nick Raynsford, was less committed. He thought it would be damaging to the local government comprehensive performance assessment process if housing inspection was carried out by a different body (the Housing Corporation) than was responsible for inspection of other services. He urged Prescott to reconsider and Campbell-Smith suggests that he had broad support from officials who respected what the Audit Commission's inspectorate had already achieved and that there was also support for this view from the Treasury. The Commission missed no opportunity to remind Treasury officials of the greater rigour that it would bring to the task. Campbell-Smith quotes Howard Davis: 'The Housing Corporation was both the funder and regulator of the HAs, which was crazy. I had been putting the argument to Treasury people that if they ever wanted to sort this out, they had to split the roles – and we would be available to do the regulation [Campbell-Smith 2008: 527].'

The Treasury publicly ruled out a new body in June but the final choice between the Corporation and the Commission was made following presentations to Prescott. In preparation for the 'beauty contest' the Corporation through its chair and chief executive presented plans to pass the investment function to English Partnerships. The Corporation would under these plans become the regulator of the whole social housing sector and not only retain the regulation of housing associations (and not lose it to the Commission) but would take over the local authority inspection functions from the Commission. Norman Perry had discussed this possibility with Irwin as chief housing inspector within the Audit Commission. Perry did not consider co-location as tenable and saw the future of the Corporation as a regulator. His view was that allocating investment funds was easy whereas regulation was difficult, intellectual work and that was where the future lay. Despite Perry's view, a review carried out within the ODPM had come to the conclusion that the two functions should continue to co-exist. Ministers separately decided that inspection of housing associations should go to the Commission.

Campbell-Smith provides an account of the presentation, made at its offices, by the Audit Commission:

> A slightly grumpy Prescott arrived at 2.30 p.m., straight from a lunch with the Chinese ambassador which he had not enjoyed. Accompanying him were seven officials from his department ... The meeting lasted an hour and a half. It seemed to go well. Irwin put this down to his team's readiness to explain how they would deal with the unfamiliar world of HAs. (The Housing Corporation scored poorly on this count, saying nothing about councils at its presentation the next day.) But Prescott also enjoyed hearing a little about the Commission's work with local authorities – and especially its audacity in ticking off the councillors of Sedgefield – Tony Blair's constituency – for their sub-standard housing policies. (Campbell-Smith 2008: 527–8)

Prescott announced his decision at the Labour Party conference in Blackpool at the start of October. From April 2003 the Commission would be responsible for a combined housing inspectorate. Campbell-Smith states this was a significant victory for the Commission, which added about forty people to its staff and around £2.5 million to its revenues in 2003/4.

Dean gave her reflections in the annual report:

> I think we were all taken by surprise by the Chancellor of the Exchequer's announcement of the creation of a single inspectorate for local authorities and housing associations, coming so shortly after we had introduced our new inspection service which looked for the first time at front-line delivery of services from the tenants' perspective. The Corporation was asked by the ODPM to take part in a so-called 'beauty contest' with the Audit Commission, which resulted in the transfer of the inspection service in April this year — just one year after we had introduced it. While we have made no secret of the fact that this was not the decision we would have wished for, we wasted no time in entering into a productive partnership with the Audit Commission to ensure a smooth transition to them. Our mutual aim was that those receiving our services would not notice any difference and we did not add to the regulatory burden for the sector.

The handover from the Housing Corporation to the Audit Commission went relatively smoothly and by the summer of 2004 a new inspection methodology was successfully agreed with the Corporation, which remained the overall regulator of the housing associations. The Housing Inspectorate within the Audit Commission still operated as a specialist unit rather than drawing on the general pool of inspectors of different services. The auditing of housing associations stayed with external commercial auditors and the Audit Commission focused on its role as a professional inspectorate.

Campbell-Smith notes that a poll of housing association chief executives in the autumn of 2004 found that many of them were still thoroughly confused over the respective roles of the Commission and the Corporation. The two bodies were pressed by the department to produce a fresh memorandum of understanding and to clarify matters and to remind housing associations that the Corporation retained responsibility for overall regulation. Nevertheless the whole process involved some fragmentation and complexity compared with arrangements in the past. It broke the cosy relationship between housing associations and the Housing Corporation, or at least moderated it. The relationship was no longer sufficient to act as a buffer between housing associations and their activities on the ground and central government. It would not be unreasonable to expect some further developments to occur subsequently.

The outcome of this episode was what at least some in the Housing Corporation regarded as an unsatisfactory hotchpotch. An active debate about the future shape of the Corporation and the co-location of regulation and investment functions would continue. Shortly after the inspectorate turmoil, in 2003, Dean retired as chairman, having completed her two terms. Her successor, Peter Dixon, made it clear from an early stage that he wanted to replace Perry with a new chief executive. Jon Rouse was appointed to this post in 2004.

It is important at this point to record the widely expressed view that by 2004 the Corporation had become distanced (at official level) from the sponsoring department. The confidence and trust that had been a hallmark of the relationship in the past had been eroded. There was a need to rebuild working relationships and address the expectation of some civil servants that at meetings with them the Corporation's representatives were first going to be unhelpful and then leak the outcome of discussions to the housing press. By 2004 the Corporation was seen by the ODPM as a reactive, belligerent and slightly incompetent organisation, and internally its morale was very low. The new leadership under Dixon and Rouse had to invest considerable time in rebuilding relationships. They were successful in this, for example in the co-operation between Corporation officials and the department on the spending review, and on issues including homelessness, worklessness and the creation of new low-cost home ownership products.

The changes to the location of the inspectorate had not dealt with the 'crazy' co-location of investment and regulation and the likelihood of this being changed appeared increasingly probable. At least some in government were concerned that regulation should be independent and it is interesting to note the views expressed by the Audit Commission in a discussion paper published in 2006, *The Future of Regulation in the Public Sector*. This emphasised the importance of independence to any worthwhile regulatory activity. Regulation must be delivered with unimpeachable integrity and authority by a wholly disinterested party. Regulators had to act as advisors to the government as well as agents of government.

The intellectual argument for splitting regulation from investment and using the different sanctions and incentives associated with both separately was becoming stronger and the rationalisation of the status quo, which had for years been defended both within the Housing Corporation and the central government sponsoring department, appeared to lack universal support and have less intellectual clout.

Delivering housing

Housing association starts and completions continued to decline until 2003 and 2004 respectively before increasing (see Tables 8.1 and 8.2). It is striking that the private sector followed a similar trajectory – rather than crowding out private sector activity an active housing association programme (along with other factors affecting both) seemed to stimulate the private sector. While housing association completions continued to rise in 2007, in the private sector both starts and completions fell. In the first half of 2008 private sector starts were only 73 per cent of the same period in 2007 and completions were 80 per cent. The credit crunch was beginning to bite.

Table 8.3 shows a continuing growth in housing association stock but a levelling out in the number of lettings. This is associated both with the importance of stock transfer in the growth of the sector and the relatively low rate of new building compared with the size of the stock. The housing associations were entering a mature phase where more of their activity was associated with existing stock and tenants rather than new building and new lettings.

Table 8.4 indicates a growth in public expenditure on the housing association sector so that by 2001/2 it was again more important for housing associations' investment than was private finance. By 2006/7 the housing association investment programme was almost twice as large in cash terms as it had been in 1999/2000.

Table 8.1: Housing starts in England 1970–2007

	Total public sector	Housing associations	Private sector	All dwellings
1970	112,235	8,111	148,318	268,664
1975	125,957	18,768	129,777	274,502
1980	33,634	13,154	84,123	130,911
1985	18,818	10,362	144,301	173,481
1990	6,641	14,111	112,717	133,469
1995	592	25,232	110,409	136,233
1998	98	17,375	131,887	149,360
1999	166	16,895	130,898	147,959
2000	106	13,021	131,389	144,516
2001	183	11,104	136,322	147,609
2002	162	11,726	137,176	149,064
2003	302	11,623	147,519	159,444
2004	170	14,278	162,153	176,601
2005	184	15,839	161,106	177,129
2006	288	17,498	160,118	177,904
2007 (provisional)	200	15,510	150,330	166,040

Source: Wilcox (annual), CLG.

Table 8.2: Housing completions in England 1970–2007

	Total public sector	Housing associations	Private sector	All dwellings
1970	130,181	8,176	153,436	291,793
1975	116,325	13,652	131,481	261,458
1980	74,835	19,299	110,232	204,366
1985	23,284	11,298	135,457	170,039
1990	14,015	13,821	136,063	163,899
1995	787	30,888	125,466	157,141
1998	243	19,901	122,855	142,999
1999	54	17,775	123,467	141,296
2000	87	16,681	118,330	135,098
2001	160	14,502	114,845	129,507
2002	177	13,309	123,317	136,803
2003	177	12,822	131,059	144,058
2004	131	16,604	137,330	154,065
2005	182	17,535	141,737	159,454
2006	277	20,752	139,732	160,761
2007 (provisional)	350	22,100	152,830	175,270

Source: Wilcox (annual), CLG.

The ADP continued to be dominated by rented housing although housing for sale increased more rapidly between 1999/2000 and 2006/7 (Table 8.5). The gap between housing association and local authority rents diminished only very slightly (Table 8.6).

Table 8.3: Housing association lettings in England 1999/2000–2005/6, thousands

	Stock	Lettings	of which			of which		Lettings to homeless as % all lettings to new tenants
			existing tenants	new tenants		existing LA tenants	statutory homeless	
1999/2000	1,273	148	36	111		26	13	12
2000/01	1,424	150	38	112		24	14	13
2001/2	1,467	159	41	118		24	15	13
2002/3	1,621	159	42	117		23	17	15
2003/4	1,665	144	40	104		19	17	16
2004/5	1,817	144	36	108		16	22	20
2005/6	1,850	128	32	96		13	21	22

LA: local authority

Source: Wilcox (annual).

In 2004, for the first time, funding was open to private developers and other organisations as well as housing associations. The Housing Corporation's biggest ever investment programme of £3.3 billion for 2004–6 would fund more than 67,000 affordable homes – 16,000 of them for key workers. During 2004/5, 28,756 homes were completed – against a government target of 27,000. Emphasis was placed on regeneration, energy saving, eco-homes standards, rural housing, the Decent Homes target and promoting the use of modern methods of construction (MMC). For 2004/5 the Corporation set a target that 25 per cent of the homes it funded should be built using some form of MMC. That target was exceeded: £784 million was provided to fund homes built using MMC techniques, 48 per cent of all homes in receipt of Corporation support. Between 2001 and 2008, the number of housing association-owned dwellings not meeting the Decent Homes standard decreased by 50,000, and housing associations were on track to meet the target for all their dwellings to meet the standard by 2010. The Corporation also continued to promote innovation and good practice across the housing association sector. Its Innovation and Good Practice programme in 2004/5 supported 369 projects across a wide range of themes including resident involvement, promoting modern methods of construction, tackling homelessness and anti-social behaviour.

Table 8.4: Housing association gross investment expenditure, including use of private finance, in England, Wales and Scotland 1999/2000–2006/7, £ million

	England				Wales			Scotland		
	Housing Corporation	Local authorities	Private finance	Total	Housing for Wales capital programme	Private finance	Total	Communities Scotland capital programme	Private finance	Total
1999/2000	638	328	875	1,841	68	42	110	172	105	277
2000/01	717	400	1,050	2,167	55	36	90	181	116	297
2001/2	775	410	600	1,785	58	36	93	193	119	312
2002/3	921	499	800	2,220	55	34	89	192	94	285
2003/4	1,817	249	1,600	3,666	52	32	84	235	131	366
2004/5	1,678	69	1,400	3,147	65	46	111	255	145	401
2005/6	1,600	0	1,200	2,800	78	56	134	360	224	584
2006/7	1,951	0	1,700	3,651	87	63	150	454	297	751

Individual figures have been rounded to the nearest million. Totals are derived from unrounded numbers and may not equal the sum of the rounded numbers.

Source: Wilcox (annual).

Table 8.5: Housing Corporation Approved Development Programme
1999/2000–2006/7, £ million

	1999/2000 outturn	2006/7 outturn
Housing for rent	558	1,495
Housing for sale	79	455
HAG on deferred interest	0	0
Other capital expenditure	0	2
Challenge Fund	0	0
Gross capital expenditure	638	1,951
ADP capital receipts	1	34
Non-ADP capital receipts	2	0
Net capital expenditure	634	1,918

Individual figures have been rounded to the nearest million. Totals are derived from unrounded numbers and may not equal the sum of the rounded numbers.

'Housing for rent' includes major repairs, mini-HAG, Rough Sleepers Initiative and City Challenge, but exclude ERCF. 'Housing for sale' includes purchase grant. Non-ADP receipts are loan receipts.

Source: Wilcox (annual).

The Corporation presented itself as working closely with the government through the ODPM, and contributing to achieving the government's social housing policy agenda by allocating funding provided by the ODPM to housing associations, enabling them to purchase, build or refurbish affordable homes. The Corporation outlined how the minister for housing and planning set targets for it to achieve over a two-year period, based on the work of the regional housing boards, as agreed in the regional housing strategies. The Corporation received grant in aid funding from the ODPM, based on the Corporation's own estimates. Grant in aid was transferred from the ODPM on a weekly basis to fund the Corporation's daily grant payments to associations and on a monthly basis to fund its administrative and capital costs. In January 2004 the Corporation changed its bank to the Office of the Paymaster General (OPG) and no longer invested surplus cash in interest-bearing short-term deposits as the OPG now performed this function centrally for the benefit of the Treasury.

Some sense of the scale and nature of investment activity is provided by the annual report for 2004/5:

This year our budget for capital investment was agreed at £1.7 billion. Approximately three fifths of capital grant was spent in the high demand areas of London and the south-east of England. During the year we commenced a

Table 8.6: Rents and earnings in England 2000–2006, £ per week

| | Local authorities | | Housing associations | | Private tenants | | Average earnings | Rents as % earnings | | | | |
	Subsidy guideline	Average rents	Fair rents	Assured rents	Fair rents	Market rents		LA rents	HA fair rents	HA assured	Private fair rents	Private market rents
2000	39.28	45.61	62.73	54.43	66.52	76.58	426.20	10.7	14.7	12.8	15.6	18.0
2001	41.18	47.87	n/a	55.46	n/a	88.32	451.50	10.6	n/a	12.3	n/a	19.6
2002	43.29	49.93	n/a	56.90	n/a	103.10	471.70	10.6	n/a	12.1	n/a	21.9
2003	45.46	50.96	n/a	58.11	n/a	104.90	483.40	10.5	n/a	12.0	n/a	21.7
2004	48.15	52.62	n/a	60.33	n/a	106.72	515.50	10.2	n/a	11.7	n/a	20.7
2005	50.89	55.11	n/a	62.76	n/a	111.47	527.70	10.4	n/a	11.9	n/a	21.1
2006	56.02	57.90	n/a	65.67	n/a	n/a	548.00	10.6	n/a	12.0	n/a	n/a

HA: housing association
LA: local authority

Source: Wilcox (annual).

new programme to subsidise affordable housing for key workers. This programme built on the lessons learned from the Starter Home Initiative programme which finished during the year. The new programme is restricted to confined geographical areas of high housing demand and a defined client group of public sector employees in essential services where there are difficulties in recruitment and retention of staff. The Corporation allocated grants totalling £15 million to ten RSLs specialising in homes for people from black and minority ethnic groups. This was a one-off programme that received ministerial backing in recognition of the vital role these associations perform and it was designed to relieve the associations from burdensome commitments that were impacting on their ability to implement target rents as required by the regulatory code.

In relation to regulation the Corporation continued to pursue its light touch and to develop a risk-based approach to regulation. In September 2004 it published *Regulating through Risk* followed by *How We Regulate: Risk-based Regulation*. The Housing Act 2004 had given the Corporation legal powers to pay grants to bodies other than RSLs and in 2004/5 work was carried out on selection criteria for these bodies.

New stock transfers

Labour had come into government enthusiastic about stock transfer under a local housing company model that was seen as different from that developed by the Conservatives. Chapter 7 of the housing Green Paper was entitled 'Raising the Quality of Social Housing'. It referred to investment in the social rented sector and especially to alternative approaches to stock transfer including the Private Finance Initiative and the introduction of arm's length management organisations (ALMOs). Stock transfer was seen as having a key role in regeneration and was to be part of an approach to better management and tenant empowerment: 'We want to see a step change in the performance of all social landlords and in the quality of social housing [DETR/DSS 2000, para. 7.51].' The new policy related to an increase in the proposed transfer programme and proposals for ALMOs for council housing but the process of transfer was unchanged. Local authorities still had restricted options and were required to go through an explicit options appraisal exercise.

The Green Paper noted that since 1988, more than 400,000 homes had been transferred from around 100 local authorities to housing associations. The government proposed:

> From 2001/2 we will support the transfer of up to 200,000 dwellings each year. If local authorities submit transfer proposals at that level, and if tenants support them, registered social landlords will become the majority providers of social housing from 2004 onwards. If the demand for stock transfer from local authorities and tenants greatly exceeds 200,000 homes each year, we will consider supporting the higher level of transfer. (DETR/DSS 2000, para. 7.19)

Stock transfers would bring more investment into the housing sector, but the case for housing transfer also rested on a more diverse pattern of dynamic and competitive organisations to run social housing:

> Transfer presents an opportunity to move away from large monopoly providers of social housing to a greater number of smaller bodies that are based in or closer to the communities where the homes are transferred ... Transfer also helps to separate out local authorities' strategic responsibilities from their landlord functions ... Increasingly, across the whole range of housing policy, there is a need for local authorities to play a more strategic role. (DETR/DSS 2000, paras 7.14–15)

The Green Paper went on: 'We are pleased with the success of the transfer programme to date and, against this background, we want to expand and modernise the transfer of housing stock [DETR/DSS 2000, para. 7.16].'

The transfer programme was seen to have established a new type of dynamic landlord, developing a wider role for themselves than simply delivering housing in a single district. The defence of council housing would not always mean the defence of the best interests of the tenants living in council houses. Indeed stock transfer tenants generally achieved a more rapid improvement in dwellings and services than tenants remaining in the council sector and they expressed rising satisfaction.

The Green Paper emphasised tenant involvement in the process of making decisions and set out criteria for approving future stock transfers consistent with the Best Value review criteria and with what had gone before:

> Future stock transfers should have evidence of support amongst tenants, be part of a coherent local authority strategy, provide value for money, contribute to

achieving other housing, social and economic objectives, deliver diversity and a better service to tenants, be based on a good relationship between the landlord and the local authority and address the long-term demand for social housing in the area.

The Green Paper also referred to the wider objectives of providing choice and tackling social exclusion. This involved a greater emphasis on community regeneration, particularly as more urban authorities contemplated transfer; a more strategic approach to tackling changes in demand; greater competition within the transfer process; ensuring that the transfer resulted in better services for tenants; and moving housing management away from large-scale monopoly landlords.

Against this background transfer activity continued at a high rate (see Table 8.7). By 2008 more than 1 million council homes had transferred to housing associations and the majority of these transfers had taken place since 2000.

Table 8.7: Large-Scale Voluntary Transfer in England 1988/9–2007/8

	Dwellings with positive values	Dwellings with negative values
1988/9	11,176	0
1989/90	14,405	0
1990/91	45,552	0
1991/2	10,791	0
1992/3	26,325	0
1993/4	30,103	0
1994/5	40,234	0
1995/6	44,871	0
1996/7	22,248	0
1997/8	24,405	8,577
1998/9	56,072	17,828
1999/2000	80,405	16,980
2000/2001	132,360	1,859
2001/2	35,390	0
2002/3	167,270	0
2003/4	38,635	0
2004/5	101,511	0
2005/6	46,653	0
2006/7	75,921	0
2007/8	93,594	0
Total	1,097,921	45,244

Source: Communities and Local Government.

Troubled associations

Throughout the history of the Housing Corporation there were issues concerned with housing associations that were failing in some way. In the early years the government actively encouraged housing societies where committee members directly gained from their involvement in development, design and other matters. The new financial regime after 1974 introduced new registration and regulation arrangements. At that stage the government, the Housing Corporation and the National Housing Federation preferred a 'coarse sieve' approach, letting almost any association register that wished to do so. Even without this there would have been associations that developed problems and the Corporation would have had post-regulation scrutiny and supervision issues. In the earlier days of the Corporation regulation was less important than investment but as the size of the sector grew, and as private finance increased after 1988, there was more emphasis on ensuring proper accounting for money. Alongside this, governance and service delivery moved up the agenda, the Audit Commission inspection system raised new questions and approaches to regulation began to change. The tenants' guarantee and stock transfer activity had formalised what tenants should expect and work was done to simplify this and make it more accessible, with performance standards tied in to legislation. Lighter-touch regulatory arrangements were developed for small associations, while group structures were increasingly encouraged as the way forward in the financial environment.

The new field teams set up in 2001 included specialists whose job it was to deal with supervision issues and to advise the field director and staff about how to respond to issues coming up locally. These specialists were supported by the central team, which would become more involved in really acute cases. The Corporation moved away from assessing process – whether associations had all the right processes and its own policies in place – and moved towards risk-based regulation. Where the old approach found a lot of associations that had failed to tick certain boxes, because they lacked certain policies, the risk-based approach was much more concerned with outputs, viability and services delivered.

The new approach was introduced with the Regulatory Code of 2002 and built upon with the move to risk-based regulation in 2004 and a shift towards self-assessment and self-regulation, coupled with more reliance on internal assurance and verification. The new less prescriptive approach identified fewer new supervision cases and the Corporation dispensed with its 'intervention' category, leaving the 'supervision' category as the only one where it was formally involved in enforcement action. Under this system the circumstances that had previously led associations to fall into supervision for failing to adopt the right processes no longer always did so.

The shift in approach meant that the numbers of associations in supervision came down quite dramatically from 2000 onwards. Supervision cases arose only where there were questions about financial strength, governance or service delivery. In this environment stock transfer organisations were more prone to hit problems than others. Such associations had relatively large stocks and started with an untried board and senior management team. Following this experience new stock transfers were much more closely monitored after registration.

Risk-based assessment was much more concerned with the underlying financial viability of the organisations and the capacity to take on more investment. While some such cases could be identified and monitored well before problems became too severe, others emerged out of the blue – occasionally associated with fraud but more commonly with failures of governance or issues raised during inspection. Failures by housing association boards were increasingly seen as being at the heart of problems. Consequently, whatever the presenting problem, the process of supervision would address governance failure – including where the controls, the management, the board and the business plan had failed. With this increasing emphasis there were fewer supervision cases and statutory inquiries but a consequence of supervision was often changes in governance – replacement of board members and senior executives. In some cases the association ceased to exist as an independent organisation and joined another group or merged with another association.

The Corporation's statutory powers enabled it to deal with supervision cases in different ways. When placed under supervision an association would not normally be able to receive transfers of stock from other associations or dispose of stock and it would be required to provide information. The Corporation had the power to make statutory appointments to the board for fixed periods – to fill vacancies or remove or replace existing board members. In more serious cases it could appoint an independent person to carry out a statutory fact-finding inquiry if it appeared that mismanagement or misconduct might be involved. The independent inquiry reported to the board of the Housing Corporation, which had strong powers if mismanage-ment or misconduct was found. The board could place financial controls on the organisation but it could also remove staff, remove board members and ultimately transfer the entire stock to another housing association. These processes were often carried out with the support of the board concerned, even where they resulted in merger or loss of independent status. However, on occasion the process was protracted and in some cases associations used judicial review. The most protracted case involved the Clays Lane Housing Co-op. This was the biggest co-operative in the country, with some 450 homes on one site in Stratford in east London. Its stock had major maintenance problems, which, with conflicts and high turnover on the board, were not being adequately addressed. The Corporation spent time trying to encourage and providing support but when it judged that there was insufficient response it established an inquiry and, after a long-drawn-out legal case, the stock was eventually transferred to another housing association.

Statutory inquiries were not common. In 2005/6 completed statutory inquiries led to the stock transfer of two associations and two new statutory inquiries were instigated during the year. In 2007/8 inquiries into the ARHAG Housing Association and the Black Roof Community Housing Association reported to the board but no new statutory inquiries were set up. Inquiries tended to result from cases of mismanagement, misconduct or failures by the association's board, or insolvency, and they were most common where there were problems in associations (see for example the three volumes published by the Housing Corporation under the umbrella title *Learning from Problem Cases*).

The supervision process was also used to address other problems. For example, it was used to prevent a proposed merger with another association where excessive severance payments for three senior staff appeared to be a strong motivating force for the merger to take place. In this case the Corporation set up an inquiry to look at how the proposed merger came about, who made the decisions and matters related to contracts allowing the payments to be paid. There were grounds for concern and the Corporation's intervention delayed the merger and applied enough pressure on the merger partners to renegotiate the pay-offs involved, reducing them by about £1 million.

An earlier and different case involved the West Hampstead Housing Association. Unlike most other associations this business was based on individual leases of properties from private landlords and it used these properties to house local authority homeless families, migrants and other groups of very vulnerable people. Some of the leases with private owners or landlords left the association paying more than it could recoup in rent. It had also failed to take full account of the costs of gas servicing and there had been mismanagement by the senior staff and board. In this case, if insolvency had been triggered, all the private leases would have been broken and there would no longer have been any protection for 2,500 tenancies. The private landlords did not want to manage them in the first place, preferring to lease to the association, and so the tenants would have been out on the street in a very short space of time with no chance of being rehoused.

The Corporation received a phone call on a Friday morning from the board of the association to say that it had met the night before and been advised that it was insolvent. The solution the Corporation offered involved a transfer into another housing association. The West Hampstead board agreed to this but the technicalities would take time to go through, and in order to trade over that time funding was needed through an overdraft guarantee to make sure the leases were not broken and that the tenants could stay in their homes. In this situation the Corporation went to the then housing minister, Nick Raynsford, and obtained a Treasury guarantee. This enabled the Corporation to go to Barclays Bank, who were the main lenders to the association, and reach agreement with them to carry on lending. The situation was finally resolved through the association being absorbed by a larger association (Genesis) which could see the long-term business opportunity. The assets were significant in the long term but Genesis had the short-term cash problem to deal with.

The Ujima Housing Association case arose late in 2007 and was unusual in that the financial problems associated with it were not resolved without the association technically being declared insolvent. In the Ujima case the Corporation had been alerted to problems, but investigation had not indicated that they were serious. However, the association made a series of major changes to senior management and adopted a very ambitious new business plan for an organisation of its capacity. In 2006/7 Ujima completely failed to deliver on its investment programme and, following assessment of its capacity to deliver in the future, the Corporation took away its partnership status and investment programme. A review was carried out to try and identify exactly what had gone wrong in Ujima's failure to deliver the investment programme, and this review indicated problems of management and governance. Consequently the Corporation made statutory appointments and, before very long, these appointees began to express major concerns about the underlying financial position and information available relating to this. In their role as board members they commissioned an independent financial review, which concluded that the underlying cash position was irretrievable. A proposed merger agreement with another association (London and Quadrant) was drawn up that would have resolved the financial position but this was narrowly rejected by Ujima's shareholders, who wanted to protect the history and the nature of the organisation. This left Ujima unable to trade, which triggered defaults on loans. The Corporation's powers automatically cut in and it declared a moratorium for twenty-eight days. In that time the Corporation, as regulator, was obliged to come up with some proposals for what should happen to the organisation and to obtain the agreement of all the association's secured lenders. With such agreement in place the proposal could be imposed on Ujima. This power had never been used before and the moratorium covered Christmas 2007. There were complexities especially related to poor records and whether there were still charges outstanding on small loans from twenty or more years previously. The negotiated proposal was for transfer of the stock to London and Quadrant. Because the lenders had already signed up to the previously negotiated voluntary transfer to London and Quadrant, they were ready to support this while the process worked through. The process was successfully completed and agreed by the secure creditors, one day within the twenty-eight allowed.

The report of the inquiry into the collapse of Ujima identified bad management, an ineffective board and the failure to control development. The Housing Corporation, confronted with an increasingly unco-operative association, faced difficulties. However this had tested the Corporation's systems and there were questions raised about the pace and effectiveness of Corporation intervention. The fact that failures in development were central to the case also led the inquiry to raise the possibility that the rigour of the Corporation's regulation was compromised by its responsibility for both regulation and investment.

The regulatory practice that had developed was no longer a simple bureaucratic one of form filling but underpinned the independence of associations and the confidence of lenders operating in the mixed public/private sector finance environment after 1988. The examples above indicate the variety of circumstances involved and the need to develop approaches tailored to each case. At the same time they indicate the capacity to work with other associations and with lenders and the government rather than such partners being unwilling to contribute to finding solutions. With small numbers of cases reaching a crisis point and effective advice and intervention at earlier stages the regulation regime worked for the industry, although it would be wrong to imply that it was not still regarded as burdensome by many associations.

The delegation crisis

In December 2005 the Corporation's chief executive, Jon Rouse, discovered that it had been acting outside its legal powers for its entire history. It had not had explicit power to delegate decision making to either sub-committees or officers, but its practice had been to do this. The discovery was initially made by an external lawyer preparing material for a training course for Corporation staff. It was reported to the company secretary, who reported it to the chief executive. Rouse recognised immediately how serious it was and what the full implications were: more than £40 billion of borrowing that had taken place on a completely illegitimate basis, supposedly sanctioned by the Corporation under seal – and it was worthless. Rouse was faced with a choice over whether to just stick it in a drawer and pretend he'd never seen it but knew this would be wrong – not because of the decisions made in previous years but because more decisions would be made on the same basis. Both he and his chairman, Peter Dixon, reached exactly the same judgement and they wrote to the ODPM. Initially the ODPM was unsure of what to do and probably did not understand the full implications of what it would let loose. A statement was issued to the market and the market, as expected, reacted badly. One view is that it was not the personnel of the banks and the building societies themselves who were most upset, but the lawyers who represented those banks and building societies: they felt that their own duty of care was in question and were concerned about accusations of negligence – they should have spotted this and therefore they panicked and this made it a very fractious period until emergency legislation was put through Parliament.

It is of course open to question whether previous chief executives of the Housing Corporation had discovered exactly the same issue and had chosen to hide it or whether it is possible that nobody knew about this previously.

Having taken the decision to disclose this uncomfortable discovery, the Corporation had to operate for six months (until the new legislation was passed) without any delegations. There were weekly board meetings and the board papers would go to 300 or 400 pages every week that had to be signed off. It was an industry just to keep the thing turning over. In the event the market continued to lend at the same rates throughout, the programme continued and there was no interruption in lending.

The ODPM and the Housing Corporation considered whether it was possible to remedy the problem without the need for legislation. When it became clear that legislation was the only thing that was going to save the day that the housing minister, Yvette Cooper, personally stepped in and decided she should consult the chief whip and the Cabinet Office about emergency legislation.

While this generated a more positive atmosphere and moved towards a solution the whole episode also caused a conversation at very high levels of Whitehall as to whether the Housing Corporation was an institution that had had its day. 'If its legislation is so flawed, it can't do the things it actually needs to do, is this just an institution that has been going on too long? Yes, it's performing; yes, it's meeting its targets; yes, it's keeping a regulatory clean sheet; but its powers are messy, there are probably better ways of doing this, it isn't agile and there are questions about regulation and investment being together anyway. Is this the moment at which we bite the bullet and go for something new?' That conversation went on for the best part of a year. It could be expected that such a conversation would have come at some point but it came a little earlier because the delegations crisis triggered it.

In February 2006, some two months after the problem was identified, Cooper announced to Parliament: 'The government will legislate to modernise the Housing Corporation's decision-making arrangements as necessary, at the earliest opportunity. This will clarify its ability to delegate decisions from the board to sub-committees and to officers [Hansard 2006a].' The Housing Corporation (Delegation) etc. Bill was supported by the opposition parties, which had met representatives of the Corporation and lenders in order to discuss the detail. In moving the Bill at the second reading Cooper said:

> This is a short, two-clause Bill, which is designed to deal with technical problems that have arisen due to an omission in the legislation governing the powers of the Housing Corporation. Those difficulties arose following recent legal advice to the Housing Corporation, which has subsequently been confirmed to the government. The advice makes it clear that the Housing Corporation board does not have any express power in legislation to delegate statutory functions below board level and that such a power cannot be implied by the terms of the statute.
>
> Prior to that advice, the Housing Corporation and everyone else believed that the board had an implied power to delegate its functions. Indeed, since its inception over 40 years ago, the Corporation has been acting on that basis in good faith. That means that the Bill needs to fulfil two functions. First, the Housing Corporation needs to be put on the same footing as other non-departmental public bodies and given the explicit power to delegate functions

below board level. Secondly, the Bill needs to deal with any uncertainty about historic decisions made by the Housing Corporation to ensure that no problems about past decisions arise inadvertently either for the Corporation or for housing associations and lenders.

The Bill gives the Housing Corporation board the express power to delegate its functions to members, committees and employees and it will have retrospective effect in deeming the Corporation always to have had such a power. The effect will be to restore the status quo, bringing the Corporation and other interested parties back to the position that they believed they were in before the problem was discovered. The Bill does not confer any new powers or functions on the Housing Corporation. (Hansard 2006b)

When it came back to Parliament for the third reading the minister stated:

We had considerable discussion in committee of a short Bill that enjoys widespread support in the House, both for its content, as I said, and because of the need for a speedy response from Parliament to the issue that has arisen for the Housing Corporation … The Bill's purpose is simple. It gives the Housing Corporation a power of delegation from board to below-board level, either to a committee of the board or to officials, with retrospective effect. It also deems the Corporation always to have had such a power, since it was founded in 1964. Over the past forty years the board had been acting, in good faith, on the basis that it had an implied power of delegation, until it was discovered at the end of last year that the board did not have that express power of delegation.

It was not just the Corporation that thought it had such a power, but everyone else with an interest, including the department, the lending community, housing associations and the residents of housing associations. When the Housing Corporation was created, it was common for public bodies and non-departmental public bodies not to be given an explicit power of delegation. At that time, powers of delegation were more readily taken to be implied. Since then, the majority of bodies set up without explicit powers have been wound up or have had their legislation modernised to confer such powers.

That did not happen in the case of the Housing Corporation because of administrative oversight on a series of occasions. Hon. members asked whether we were aware of any other NDPB being in the same predicament as the Housing Corporation, but we are not. (Hansard 2006d)

Later in the debate she stated:

> After extensive discussions with the Housing Corporation, the Council of
> Mortgage Lenders and other stakeholders, it became clear that it would be
> inappropriate for us to wait any longer, as the uncertainty was giving rise to
> significant concerns, especially among lenders, about the retrospective decisions.
> We did not want that uncertainty and anxiety among lenders to have an impact
> on the day-to-day decisions on the draw-down of loans or the rate at which
> housing associations can borrow, for example. Such uncertainty could have a
> serious impact on the viability of those decisions, should those problems start to
> escalate. (Hansard 2006e)

Cooper also referred to the possibility of a merger between the Housing
Corporation and English Partnerships:

> We are carrying out a consultation on the Housing Corporation and English
> Partnerships, but we have not made any decisions at this stage on the right way
> forward. Any further legislation in that area could therefore still be some way off
> – if it is to happen at all – and it would be inappropriate to leave the Housing
> Corporation, and those who depend on social housing held by housing
> associations, in a state of uncertainty. (Hansard 2006e)

Conclusions

The final phase of the Housing Corporation was marked by crises related to the
establishment of the Housing Inspectorate, the discovery of its lack of delegation
powers and issues related to individual associations, including the Ujima
Housing Association. It appears that the chairman and chief executive, in order
to secure the location of the inspectorate within the Corporation, went out on
a limb by suggesting that the co-location of regulation and investment be
brought to an end and there was also a serious weakening of the relationship
between the Corporation and the sponsoring department. However, it is wrong
to portray the Corporation as in decline or disarray. It had successfully managed
an increasing programme and was more involved in new regeneration and home
ownership initiatives than ever before. It was also rebuilding its relationship with
the sponsoring department and addressing the concerns that it was too closely

aligned with producers than consumers and was actively engaged in addressing issues to do with governance. It was moving away from the cosy relationship associated with regulatory capture and towards regulating competition.

All of these shifts in direction could be seen, however, to signal that it was time for a different structure. There was a changing orthodoxy from a view that co-location of regulation and investment was good to a view that it was undesirable. At the same time the sheer size of the tasks in either field suggested the need for some review. The ambitions to use the Corporation's investment to do more than build houses – to engage more wholeheartedly with the sustainable communities agenda and generate economic gains through housing investment – left too many tasks for one organisation. The case for restructuring and reorganising grew as much from the successes of the Corporation as from its failures. The proposals that emerged in this context are discussed in the following chapter.

9

The future

Introduction

The Housing Corporation operating in 2008 bore little relation to that of 1964. It was different in scale, ambition, experience and expertise. It can reasonably be argued that throughout its history its continuing operation was never guaranteed but, ironically, the unprecedented development of private finance after 1988 increased its usefulness for government and the importance of its regulatory role. Continuing private finance was essential for the national housing strategy and effective regulation was essential for the private finance sector. There was confidence in the existing institutional arrangements and advantages in continuity. The Housing Corporation and others had emphasised the value of co-locating registration and investment functions within the same body and this had been the conventional wisdom within government. If anything the Housing Corporation seemed more secure than at any stage; the more formal processes associated with periodic prior options and financial and managerial reviews, and the work of select committees, the Audit Commission and the National Audit Office had not called into question the continued role of the Corporation or indeed co-location.

However, uncertainties had arisen over time and the advent in 1997 of the Labour government had added to them. Best Value had introduced a new and more professional approach to inspection within public services and the creation of the Housing Inspectorate for the local authority sector had demanded a different approach for housing associations if their tenants were to be entitled to the same standards. Perhaps the conventional wisdom within government was changing. The experience and confidence of the Audit Commission had resulted in a more strongly articulated case for both inspection and regulation being carried out by bodies which had no other interest or involvement in the activities of those they were regulating or inspecting. The Treasury was becoming increasingly persuaded of this view. The discomfort felt by some, including Baroness Dean, that the Corporation and housing associations were too comfortable together and too focused on investment, with insufficient regard for tenants or the services delivered to them, could also be seen as less likely to be challenged when there was co-location.

By the time that Norman Perry was appointed chief executive in 2000, some people expected him to be the last – and he openly confirmed this expectation. His successor, Jon Rouse, was also given the same impression. The position taken by the Corporation in relation to inspection was also consistent with a view that the days of co-location were numbered. As indicated in the previous chapter, it was no longer presented as the preferred option by key figures in the Corporation itself. The presumption that things would change was increased as the new priority given by the government to housing and to expanding the supply of housing, following the Barker review, included expansion of social housing. The emphasis on sustainable communities, regeneration and mixed-tenure development also implied a different approach to investment in which it was important to do more than deliver a number of dwelling units: the task of building sustainable communities still required the dwellings to be built, but as part of more ambitious strategies developed with local authorities and other partners to add to economic, social and environmental goals. The review carried out by Martin Cave in 2007 added to discussion of how regulation as well as investment should be developed to suit a changing situation and changing priorities.

In this environment the last year of the Housing Corporation's operation was dominated by legislative proposals to bring together activities from the Corporation, English Partnerships and the sponsoring department, Communities and Local Government. Two new agencies were to be set up, which would eventually be the Homes and Communities Agency and the Tenant Services Authority. This would mean a division of investment activities (to be carried out within the former) from registration and regulation activities (to be carried out by the latter). This chapter sets out the key elements of the debate about this reorganisation and its implications for the future.

Reviews

In 2006 the responsibility for housing and planning policy moved from the Office of the Deputy Prime Minister to the new Department for Communities and Local Government (and from John Prescott to Ruth Kelly as secretary of state). Housing was at the centre of the department's new focus, and particular emphasis was placed on creating mixed communities, environmental sustainability and the importance of housing for the economy. Kelly (2006: 1) emphasised the economic importance of housing and reasserted the priority attached to home ownership. As well as ensuring that the target of 30,000 additional social homes a year by 2007/8 was achieved, it was time to consider what role social housing could play in delivering the government's wider objectives. This was the context for asking Professor John Hills to carry out an independent assessment of social housing.

The Hills review, *Ends and Means: The Future Roles of Social Housing in England*, was published in February 2007 and was welcomed by Kelly as the starting point for a debate. Hills's analysis of the social rented sector focused upon rationing, rents and subsidy. It presented these elements as the crucial determinants for the way in which social housing operated. So the character of the sector was determined by the bureaucratic rationing of access to it; household decisions about mobility, both in housing and employment terms, were affected by non-market rents and the nature of the subsidy system. Problems of lack of social mix and of worklessness were associated with rationing, rents and subsidy.

While these features are important influences on the operation of the social rented sector, it is difficult to see them as the sole influences and Hills's analysis of them was at times superficial and even at best not exhaustive (see Murie et al. 2007). The Hills review was not a formula for a renaissance of social housing and the secretary of state's response to it is interesting in that context. Social housing was stated to be as important as ever and the government would continue to strive to make it respond better to people's individual lives. Unlike the aspiration for other public services, the Hills review and subsequent government statements lacked any expressed concern to make publicly assisted housing provision the equal of what is available in the market – let alone the equal of the best in the market. The government's real drive continued to be to enable social tenants to move to home ownership. New approaches to making home purchase more accessible and a continuing emphasis upon affordable solutions for first-time buyers sounded like more of the same rather than any radical shift in policy. The Hills review set out where social housing could fit within a system predominantly based upon market provision and asset appreciation. It offered an agenda to ensure that the quality of social housing was adequate for a minor tenure seen as providing a springboard to home ownership, rather than a viable and sustainable alternative in its own right.

The results of a separate review of social housing regulation, led by Martin Cave, were published in June 2007. The Cave review, *Every Tenant Matters*, had a focus on regulation and referred to a tightly defined set of issues. In setting up the review Kelly noted that it was some thirty years since the housing regulation system had been introduced. Although levels of satisfaction with social housing were relatively high compared with other public services, these levels were falling and public expectations were of a greater influence over services. The current regulatory system needed to be more flexible and transparent.

The Cave review embraced what is conventionally regarded as the social rented sector (local authority housing, arm's length management organisations (ALMOs) and housing associations) and unregistered bodies able to apply for social housing grant (SHG). This definition led to an important bringing together of the social housing providers, which had previously been subject to separate regulatory regimes, within a proposed new, unified system. Equally important, the regulation of the private rented sector and leasehold management was not considered. Although one of the key considerations behind regulation is the protection of public interest and expenditure, this did not lead private renting to be included. The private rented sector receives substantial funding through housing benefit and performs worse than any other tenure in meeting the Decent Homes standard. Consideration of the future regulation and taxation regime for this sector alongside other parts of the housing market catering for similar populations would have been appropriate and indeed was set up subsequently.

The review set out a clear purpose for regulation to protect tenants, the wider quality of life and taxpayer interest. Among other criticisms it referred to the burdens of overprotective regulation and the unrestricted use of regulation for policy passporting. The criticism of using regulation to promote and develop wider government policies in addition to core housing activity was that there was insufficient regard for the costs involved. The Cave review formulated the requirements for a new system to ensure continued provision of high-quality social housing, to empower and protect tenants and to expand the choice of provider at all levels in the provision of social housing. It recommended the establishment of a new independent regulator, responsive to tenants and applying the principles of modern, risk-based regulation. Cave proposed that tenants should have a central role – and should be able to trigger intervention by the regulator when they identified systemic failings by their landlord. The aim was to establish a regulatory system focused on the needs of tenants rather than providers and important changes were proposed. It also, perhaps unavoidably, separated out the roles of developer, owner and manager. The consequence of this was that tenants' needs would be considered in relation to management and service delivery but not in relation to affordable rents. Given government capacity to alter policy in relation to subsidy and target rents as part of economic regulation, this could seriously undermine the ambition to empower and protect tenants. The second area effectively outside tenant influence was development and major regeneration. Decisions about regeneration are critical for choice and quality of living. The situation where the living conditions of tenants are unsatisfactory can sometimes only be changed through major investment and the new regulatory regime would not empower and protect tenants in this respect.

The review included important proposals related to a new independent social housing regulator, a single ombudsman for the sector and the provision of a national tenant voice. While there is no mention of markets and sub-markets or of regional housing strategies, local authorities' roles in place making are emphasised. This somewhat goes against the grain of recent policy urging cross-district market-based approaches but would be easy enough to reconcile. Nevertheless this, and the cautions expressed about the effects of mergers on tenants' interests, would present important challenges to larger housing associations with stock distributed widely across different districts. Taken in conjunction with the Hills review's support for buying and selling assets there was some reversion to a more community-based approach to social housing provision and this would seem necessary to make a reality of tenant empowerment and protection.

New legislation

By the time Gordon Brown became Prime Minister in 2007, housing policy had risen to the top of the agenda but it was still dominated by home ownership. Its direction was firmly set by the Barker review, carried out for Brown when he was Chancellor of the Exchequer. It is against this background that a new housing Green Paper, *Homes for the Future: More Affordable, More Sustainable*, and new legislation were prepared. The Housing and Regeneration Bill introduced into Parliament in November 2007 would help to deliver the commitments set out in the Green Paper earlier in the year.

The Green Paper highlighted the government's preoccupation with housing supply and affordability and reasserted the view that increasing supply would restrain house price growth and so address affordability problems.

While more social housing was part of the agenda it remained a small part. New approaches to planning and new growth areas and growth points were proposed to increase housing supply. In addition new policy vehicles and organisational arrangements were needed to deliver the new agenda and a new homes agency would play a key role in supporting local government in its place-shaping role. The plan was to set up a body, initially referred to as Communities England and later as the Homes and Communities Agency (HCA), that would bring together English Partnerships, the investment functions of the Housing Corporation and key delivery roles from CLG.

The Housing and Regeneration Bill introduced into Parliament in 2008 had three principal objectives: to improve the supply and quality of housing in England; to secure the regeneration or development of land and infrastructure in England; and to support in other ways the creation, regeneration or development of communities in England and their continuing wellbeing, with a view to meeting the needs of people living in England. As part of this, the Bill proposed the establishment of the HCA as set out in the Green Paper. Part 2 of the Bill suggested setting up a separate Office for Tenants and Social Landlords – later renamed the Tenant Services Authority (no doubt partly because of the speculation about what prefix would most commonly be attached to the abbreviation 'Oftenant'). This effectively would end the co-location of the investment and regulation activities previously combined within the Housing Corporation. While its investment functions would go to the Homes and Communities Agency, its registration functions would go to the new Tenant Services Authority (TSA).

Martin Cave's review appears to have finally enabled ministers to decide the future direction of the Housing Corporation. The government accepted the bulk of its recommendations, but published two consultation papers: *Delivering Housing and Regeneration: Communities England and the Future of Social Housing Regulation* and *Tenant Empowerment*. Two key questions were at the heart of the consultations: the location of the regulator, and whether local authority landlords should fall within the regulator's scope.

At this point something of a competition emerged for leadership of the new regulatory agenda. Although Cave had expressed the view that the Audit Commission lacked the support of all stakeholders, the government did not appear to be convinced. Consequently the Commission saw an opportunity to lead the new arrangement. Its chief executive, Michael O'Higgins, was pleased the government had taken 'a more even view' than the Cave report and suggested that the Commission was 'the logical place' for housing regulation.

He said that the Cave report, in focusing on housing regulation, did not give enough weight to the wider aspects of the agenda, such as place shaping and the broader agenda of having fewer regulators. He stated: 'Local authorities are not going to welcome another regulator on top of the Audit Commission.'

The alternative view was taken by the Housing Corporation and the National Federation of Housing Associations – the new organisation should be completely independent of other substantial functions although it could include staff from both the Commission and the Corporation. The Corporation's view was expressed by the acting chief executive, Steve Douglas, who was to be confirmed in that post at the start of July 2008: 'The Corporation supports the clear recommendations of the Cave review that the best option for tenants, housing providers, lenders and the government is a fully independent, stand-alone regulator ... However, as always with reviews of this kind, it is for ministers to decide.' He also stated that the Corporation had an experienced regulatory team that was praised by lenders, by the sector, the National Audit Office and others (see Hilditch 2007).

The Audit Commission's expressed response to the consultation was that there was an 'overwhelming case for locating the regulatory function for social housing' within it. A separate regulator for social housing 'would inevitably be a small body, without the clout and independence that the Commission provides', and it argued against a stand-alone regulator. Its detailed proposal was for an 'Office of Housing Standards' staffed by a mixture of Commission and Housing Corporation staff, plus a number of extra recruits. The Commission stated that it would be best placed to set up the proposed office, which would take on roles currently performed by the Commission and the Corporation. The body would be overseen by a board, which would include members of the Commission, housing providers, tenants and lenders, working alongside a separate tenant regulatory panel. The office would be in charge of the registration of new housing associations, financial regulation and inspection. It would have the autonomy to make its own decisions, but would work together with Audit Commission staff who regulate other public services. Roy Irwin, chief inspector of housing at the Commission, said that positioning the regulator within his organisation would ensure that it took account of the needs of areas in which landlords worked. Understanding why what worked in one place would not necessarily work elsewhere meant solving performance issues in relation to the particular localities in which a social landlord operated.

In contrast the Housing Corporation's submission favoured the establishment of a stand-alone regulator dedicated to the effective oversight of social housing 'unconstrained by other objectives and priorities'. 'While there are overlapping interests with the place-shaping role of local government, and its oversight by the Audit Commission ... the integrity of the function of social housing regulation would be best served by formal separation and independence from these distinct roles rather than by their co-location.'

Lenders' views on the matter, as expressed by the Council of Mortgage Lenders (CML), were unsupportive of the Commission, which they portrayed as 'confused' about the differences between inspection and regulation, the role currently carried out by the Housing Corporation. This confusion reflected the 'narrow focus' of the Commission's present role and there was concern that it 'exhibited less experience and understanding of regulation of finance and governance ... as opposed to [service] output-focused activities'. A strong regulatory regime was vital for lender confidence and a stand-alone independent regulatory body was preferred to the Audit Commission, which is part of government.

Faced with these alternatives and conflicting advice the government was persuaded particularly by the lenders, and so it decided to set up the Office for Tenants and Social Landlords. Yvette Cooper as minister for housing announced the decisions as follows:

> I am announcing that the regulator will be established as an independent, stand-alone body, called the Office for Tenants and Social Landlords. We intend to implement this through the forthcoming Housing and Regeneration Bill, which was included in the government's draft legislative programme ...
>
> The Office for Tenants and Social Landlords will take on the regulatory functions of the Housing Corporation. The investment functions of the Housing Corporation will pass to the Homes and Communities Agency.
>
> Unlike under the current regulatory framework, the new regulator will have the power to reduce red tape and regulation for registered social landlords that are performing well, and will also have stronger and more wide ranging powers to take action where tenants are not getting a good service. The new regulator will therefore put a much greater emphasis on service to tenants, with tenants' groups able to trigger inspections and interventions when problems arise. (Hansard 2007)

The Cave review recommended that the regulator's responsibilities should cover all social housing providers – registered social landlords, local authorities, ALMOs and others. The government was clear that tenants, regardless of who their social housing landlord was, should expect the same minimum standards of service and have similar opportunities for empowerment, to influence delivery and to seek redress. However, it also recognised that funding, governance and accountability arrangements varied significantly between providers, and it had made commitments in the local government White Paper to implement a new single performance framework for outcomes secured by local authorities working alone or in partnership. While the consultation on this indicated support for bringing local authority landlords into the scope of the regulator, it also highlighted the different governance and finance arrangements between the different sectors and the need to make arrangements which were consistent with the single performance framework for local authorities. The outcome of this was the establishment of an independently chaired advisory panel to provide support on handling these issues and the stated intention that cross-domain regulation should be in place within two years of the regulator coming into operation.

With regard to the location of the regulator, Cooper said:

> The Cave review recommended that there should be a separation of investment and regulation functions—both currently carried out by the Housing Corporation. He said that the new regulator could be established as part of the Audit Commission, but that he would prefer a new stand-alone regulator.
>
> Our consultation document recognised that locating the regulatory functions in the Audit Commission would build on its existing strengths and consumer focus, and it could be implemented quickly. However, we also recognised that a stand-alone regulator may be better at this stage at commanding the confidence of those who provide private finance for social housing. We consulted openly on this issue.
>
> In responding to the consultation document, registered social landlords, tenant representative bodies and lenders all favoured a stand-alone regulator because of the greater clarity of purpose of an independent regulator, and because of the importance of the regulator maintaining expertise in private finance issues. As it is vital that the new regulatory arrangements command the confidence of lenders in order to support increasing new social housing, I therefore propose to establish the new regulator as a stand-alone body. (Hansard 2007)

Because the separate regulation would continue – even if only for two years – it was inevitable that the Housing Corporation would make a greater impression on the new regulator than the Audit Commission. Within the Corporation the decision about the future of the regulator was regarded as a significant 'victory' over the Commission. The latter had waged a very public battle in 2007 to gain ownership of housing regulation – including public speeches by their chair at the conference of the Chartered Institute of Housing at Harrogate and interviews and articles in the trade press by Irwin. The absorption of the regulation function into the Commission would effectively have extinguished the Corporation's long regulatory role and delivered a very different sort of regulation. Although many assumed that the Commission had won the battle, the Corporation fought hard behind the scenes to secure a free-standing 'independent' regulator, supported largely by the CML (which expressed concerns about the Commission's ability to work effectively with the increasingly important private finance sector). This victory was significant – whilst the TSA will be a new regulator, with new powers, its backbone will be one inherited in staffing and leadership from the Corporation. The appointment of Anthony Mayer (a previous chief executive of the Housing Corporation) as the first chairman of the TSA and Peter Marsh (from the post of deputy chief executive within the Corporation) as the first chief executive appeared to confirm this view.

Alongside the decisions related to the regulator the government announced increased expenditure to achieve a larger affordable housing programme. The priority was to increase the supply of housing – building 70,000 social homes a year by 2010. Allocations totalling £8.4 billion would be shared across the regions over the next three years with every single region getting at least a 5 per cent increase every year during that time. Almost £2 billion from the regional housing pot would fund improvements to local authority-owned and private sector stock.

The role of the HCA, reporting to ministers, was set out in January 2008:

- Regeneration programmes from English Partnerships, including remediation of brownfield land, facilitating the provision of homes for key workers, implementing the National Coalfields Programme and developing its Strategic Sites Programme to facilitate the delivery of increasing numbers of new homes.
- Provision of new affordable housing, currently provided through SHG from the Housing Corporation.
- Delivery responsibilities for the Decent Homes programmes for the social housing sector from CLG, including ALMOs, Large-Scale Voluntary Transfer, the housing Private Finance Initiative (PFI) and a PFI for new supply. This would enable the agency to work closely with local authorities to join up delivery of decent homes with the wider

regeneration of communities. Ministers would continue to make final decisions on stock transfers and the establishment of ALMOs.

- Transferring programme management responsibility from CLG on housing market renewal, which would facilitate joining up with other agency programmes and allow the HCA to work with local authorities to develop multifaceted regeneration programmes that helped to renew communities as well as the housing market.

- Taking on the housing and regeneration delivery functions of CLG in support of the main existing growth areas, including Milton Keynes–South Midlands, London–Stansted–Cambridge–Peterborough and Ashford.

- Similarly, taking on housing and regeneration delivery functions from CLG in the Thames Gateway, including driving forward the implementation of the Thames Gateway Delivery Plan. The HCA's role would include the management of CLG's £500 million Thames Gateway programme for 2009–11.

- Fulfilling its objective of becoming the best delivery partner for local authorities. It would also work with local authorities to develop support for new and emerging growth points and become the government's main source of advice on the delivery of housing growth. Responsibility for selecting and assessing growth areas would remain with CLG and with ministers.

- Receiving the transfer of the ASC.

- Delivery responsibilities for the following programmes, currently undertaken by CLG: the Mixed Communities Initiative, the Hostels Capital Improvement Programme and specialist supported housing, and the National Land-Use Database of Previously Developed Land.

This would help provide a holistic approach to housing and regeneration and enable CLG to focus on the provision of strategic policy advice and managing cross-Whitehall relationships (Hansard 2008).

Establishing the HCA would bring existing regeneration and housing delivery programmes together under the auspices of a single delivery-focused agency. It would give local authorities a clear strategic partner to work with on housing and regeneration, and would enable better and more effective use of a range of assets, resources and funding streams to respond to the particular housing and regeneration problems in different communities. It would also play a key role advising ministers on achieving their ambition to deliver three million new homes by 2020.

The HCA's remit included promoting new social and affordable housing in sustainable mixed-tenure estates. The agency would work with local authorities to deliver investment for new housing and regeneration and would help to build capacity in local government to support the Sustainable Communities Act. It would also help the delivery of growth areas, and the 'streamlined delivery chain' created by combining English Partnerships and the Housing Corporation was intended to make the best use of private investment, public subsidy, land, assets and skills.

Over time, the evolution of the government's programmes and the addition of new initiatives resulted in fragmentation, reducing the scope for effective co-ordination of investment and achieving best value for money. Typically, investment in a locality or project involved several housing and regeneration funding sources (from the sponsoring department as well as through English Partnerships and the Housing Corporation). Key players came to projects at different points in time, facing different assessment criteria for decisions over funding, with no one responsible for offering local government rounded advice on the opportunities to improve a 'place', or to assess the minimum public intervention needed to 'tip' a project into private sector viability.

The HCA would support local authorities in the following ways:

1. building local authority capacity and skills;
2. helping local authorities to assess and unlock their strategic land portfolios;
3. providing a 'staircase of support', depending on the needs of a local authority;
4. supporting and enabling sub-regional working aligned to housing/employment markets (especially in growth and Pathfinder areas);
5. reducing complexity and fragmentation, which leads to confusion, increased transaction costs and project delays;
6. better aligning existing objectives and funding to allow rounded approaches to a 'place', to better address market failures and to maximise the impact of investment;
7. capturing part of the value of uplift from public investment to recycle for future investment;
8. moving from a position where it can fund social housing directly to a more market-sensitive approach that asks what investment is needed to open up a site, increasing private sector leverage and driving down costs;
9. increased procurement efficiencies associated with better economies of scale and the agency's negotiating power as an important regional operator.

The new agency would be responsible for delivery and there were plans for it to be tasked with supporting the regional assemblies (although these were proposed for abolition from 2010) and regional development agencies in helping to develop and deliver more integrated and aligned strategies for economic development, land and housing. The HCA would assist in marshalling resources to deliver regional priorities, for example, by helping to unlock strategic sites for infrastructure or housing growth areas. In December 2007 the chief executive of Sheffield City Council, Sir Bob Kerslake, was named as chief executive designate of the HCA. Although his post would not be formalised until the agency was launched, Kerslake appointed a full-time set-up team to lead the delivery of the detailed work necessary to bring the agency into being. This team comprised staff drawn from the Housing Corporation, English Partnerships, the Academy of Sustainable Communities (ASC) and CLG.

Special devolved arrangements were proposed for London – once the agency was established, a sub-committee of the HCA board would be set up with specific responsibility for London. The sub-committee would be chaired by the mayor, and the vice-chairman would be the chief executive of the HCA. The London boroughs would also be actively engaged through participation on the sub-committee and involvement in the delivery of individual schemes on the ground.

The new agency would be, in Kerslake's words, the best regeneration partner for local authorities. It would be the key agency in achieving the government's objectives in relation to the increase in housing supply, but it would not be just a bricks-and-mortar agency; it would also act as a catalyst for community regeneration.

Part 2 of the Housing and Regeneration Bill proposed the establishment of a separate agency originally to be termed the Office for Tenants and Social Landlords (Oftenant). Later in the process this agency was renamed the Tenant Services Authority (TSA) and it is referred to as such throughout the rest of this book. In the process of this legislation the housing association movement, led in particular by the National Housing Federation (NHF), expressed serious concerns about the regulatory arrangements that were being proposed. The Bill was produced without consultation. It is argued that this was because it had not been drafted in a final form, even by the time it received its first reading. The department may also have been nervous about leaks, but it seems reasonable to assume that it had not got far enough in its thinking to involve other organisations in discussions. In retrospect, this may have created a considerable amount of unnecessary tension between the housing association sector and the government. Many of the comments of the housing association sector were, in practice, accepted by the government and incorporated in amendments to the legislation; had these discussions been carried out behind closed doors, prior to the Bill being presented to Parliament, there would probably not have been such a visible breakdown of communications.

In the Bill as it was originally presented, the secretary of state was to have power to direct the regulator to set standards and this formulation emerged as a significant threat to the independence of housing associations. The old arrangements associated with the Housing Corporation involved a power to direct the Corporation in guidance, but the new formulation involved a much more direct line of control, relating to day-to-day activities and potentially incompatible with the diversity of the housing association movement.

A second key part of the Bill involved a mismanagement or misconduct test for regulatory intervention. In effect, under the Housing Corporation the secretary of state or the regulator would not intervene unless there was evidence of mismanagement or misconduct. Under the new formulation it would be possible for intervention to be triggered by a failure to implement part of government policy that was set as a standard – in other words the regulator would not just set a framework within which housing associations should operate, but would actually require housing associations to adopt certain practices.

The third matter of some concern was the proposal that the regulatory power should relate to non-housing matters. Rather than focusing purely upon rents allocation, management, finance and governance, regulation would relate to everything that housing associations did to their neighbourhood and to community responses. Again, the concern was that this would inhibit housing associations from developing approaches in response to the communities they were working with and from developing and promoting ideas coming through their governance systems; instead they would simply do what the government required through the regulator. In practice this regulatory regime would be very difficult to impose. How would the regulator act in relation to these non-housing activities? But the concern was that by the very fact that it had a regulatory competence in this area, it would inhibit actions. The alternative view, which the NHF preferred, was that the regulator should be able to take into account any non-housing activities the housing association was involved in. This would allow it to make a judgement about whether the association's distinctive policies were appropriate, rather than whether its distinctive policies were different from the standards being set by the regulator.

The government responded to all three of these issues, and the revisions to the Bill in the course of its progress through Parliament meant a relaxation of the original regulatory regime, a movement away from setting standards towards a more general regulation of housing associations that would preserve their autonomy and would operate much more like the previous regime adopted through the Housing Corporation.

In two other areas the government did not give way so quickly or at all. The first of these was the way in which it proposed to regulate the private sector. The theory in establishing a separate regulatory agency was that it would be involved in domain-based regulation, regulation of the product rather than who provides it. Given that private developers would be entitled to receive SHG or to provide affordable housing, a level playing field would require that private developers involved in low-cost home ownership and in delivering the government's affordable housing programme should be regulated in the same way as housing associations. If not they would effectively have a competitive advantage and the level playing field would not exist.

The second issue related to fees. The Housing Corporation as regulator had been funded through grant in aid directly by the government through the appropriate department (latterly CLG). However, the Housing and Regeneration Bill proposed that fees would be paid by the regulated to the regulator. Some £20 million would be involved. This was a reversion to the situation in the very early years of the Housing Corporation, when a charge was attached to projects. There was also a precedent for this in that other regulators, including those operating in the rail sector and communications, charged those they regulated for their activities. There may be some logic in arguing that the TSA should be organised in the same way and have the same kind of relationship with those it regulated as these other regulators. However, there are three fundamental issues at stake. Firstly, housing associations are non-profit agencies. Secondly, if they used their resources to invest in housing rather than pay a regulator, it would generate investment in excess of the proposed £20 million fee and would lever in other money. If, on the other hand, the government continued to pay through grant in aid, it would reduce the housing programme by only £20 million.

The third issue relates to the classification of housing associations as public bodies. The risk in developing a stronger regulatory regime and in changing the relationship between the government, the regulator and the housing associations is that they would not be regarded as private sector agencies, but rather as public bodies. The expert advice provided to the NHF and shared with ministers suggested there was a risk that if the Bill went through as originally proposed, the classification as non-public bodies could be put at risk. It is also important to recognise that under the original proposals the TSA would have greater regulatory powers than other regulators.

The NHF drew attention to other arguments underpinning the importance of government recognition and support of the sector's independence to determine and manage its own affairs. David Orr, the chief executive of the NHF, stated that the Bill posed a very real threat to the delivery of new social homes and the survival of a range of locally driven neighbourhood services. While parts of the Bill were necessary to create the right conditions for millions of new homes to be delivered in sustainable communities, it contained a number of major threats to the vital work of housing associations. It set out a substantial increase in the level of government control of associations, potentially ending their independence. It gave the communities secretary unprecedented power to compel associations to implement government policy, unrelated to housing, through a new regulator. The Bill also gave ministers the power to impose regulation on community services provided by housing associations themselves, paid out of their own money. While value for money must be assured, the proposed degree of central control represented a very real threat that housing associations, currently part of the voluntary and community sector, could officially be reclassified as public bodies by the Office for National Statistics when it compiled the government's accounts. This would mean that they would no longer be able to lever in billions of pounds of private money to match public subsidy, as the borrowing would show up on the public debt. In turn this would badly damage the government's programme to build three million homes by 2020 as it would halve the amount of money housing associations could use to fund the building of these homes. Subsequently, the Government stated in Parliament that the advice received from HM Treasury and the Office of National Statistics was that there was no risk of reclassification as public bodies and this meant that the NHF's concerns were unfounded.

During the past two decades housing associations had raised more than £35 billion of private finance to spend on new and existing homes, in addition to the £30 billion that ministers had invested in the sector. That made the housing association funding model the most successful public–private partnership ever, but this was now under threat. Because the Bill gave ministers a right to regulate associations' neighbourhood work it also threatened much vital community work being done by housing associations. Innovative local schemes, such as support programmes for women at risk of going into prostitution and young men at risk of offending, would be scrapped as associations felt compelled to work on what the government said were priorities. Ultimately it would mean that neighbourhood work would be driven by Westminster direction, not local need.

Key passages in the Bill could allow the new regulator, under direction from the secretary of state, to crack down on housing associations if they failed to follow central standards set by ministers, even if this meant that an association would have to break its legal commitments to its lenders or use up a dangerous amount of its financial reserves. For the first time the government would be regulating community services which had been funded by the housing associations themselves rather than the state. The NHF also argued that the government had breached Clause 9.6 of the compact agreement as it did not talk to the sector about the new measures in the Bill prior to its publication. The relevant clause states that the government undertakes to consult the sector on issues that are likely to affect it, particularly where the government is proposing new roles and responsibilities for the sector, for example in the delivery of statutory services.

Elsewhere, the Charity Commission expressed concern that the independence of charitable housing associations was being undermined through the Bill; a number of other organisations, including the Council of Mortgage Lenders, had expressed similar concerns.

The first briefing on the Bill provided by CLG was on the day of the first reading, so the only way that the NHF could engage with the legislative process was through public exchanges related to it. Civil servants and ministers were not responding to the representations made to them and because of this the NHF felt an obligation to enter into an explicit debate. Over time ministers and civil servants became more responsive, but there was a tendency for them to urge the NHF to trust the government that it would use its powers in a responsible way. While this might have been acceptable as long as existing ministers were in position, the weakness is that legislation provides powers to subsequent ministers, who would not necessarily have undertaken to act in the same way or might not feel under the same obligations.

The government, in the process of the debate in Parliament, accepted amendments to restrict the secretary of state, to direct only on the objectives of the regulator rather than to set standards. The power to direct was also restricted to rents, quality of service and tenant involvement, rather than housing associations' wider activities, and the tone of the debate did change significantly. The concern was to protect the interest of tenants while ensuring the independence of housing associations. One view is that the TSA was relieved at this change of heart, for its role as initially set out would have destroyed its independence as a regulator. At the same time the general interpretation is that the government, while unwilling and unable to commit more resources and more funding, wished housing to become more important and wished to achieve a greater housing programme through sweating the assets of housing associations; it was caught in the trap of having less resource but wanting more control and using the regulatory process to achieve the latter. The risk, not only to the independence of housing associations but to the housing programme, was that government inability to understand the needs of local communities would mean that greater control with less resource would be a fatally flawed way forward.

The Cave review was making the government aware of non-housing issues and it saw the advantage of housing associations acting in this field, but rather than leaving them to be the best judges of what should be put forward, it wished to take the power to direct these non-housing issues within its own embrace and so set standards for them. The government was confusing regulation as an enabling and standard-setting process with regulation as a control mechanism.

Before the Bill's final approval in the House of Lords amendments were accepted that removed the power of the regulator to force a housing association, after an inquiry, to amalgamate or transfer management or land or suspend officers merely on the basis that it had breached a regulatory standard. Ministerial consent would be required before it could use these powers. The HCA was also required to consult the regulator when drawing up contracts with private sector providers of low-cost home ownership in any bid, to ensure that as far as possible associations would not be at a competitive disadvantage. Other amendments would allow associations to dispose of land for non-social housing use without having to get permission from the regulator. These amendments meant that there were only three areas in which the minister could direct the regulator: rent, quality of accommodation and tenant involvement. The regulator's intervention powers were also more circumscribed in recognition of the desirability of providers being free to choose how to provide services and conduct business. Its power to appoint members to association boards was also restricted to a minority of the board, and associations could change their rules and constitutions (except in key strategic areas) without needing to get the permission of the regulator. Finally the regulation of profit-making and non-profit providers was equalised in a number of areas including the duty to supply information and insolvency powers.

The NHF's view was that this was a much improved Bill which ensured a brighter future for housing associations and residents. The key outstanding concern related to the new power of the TSA to regulate the self-funded and locally driven community work of housing associations.

The Cave review was making the government aware of non-housing issues and it saw the advantage of housing associations acting in this field, but rather than leaving them to be the best judges of what should be put forward, it wished to take the power to direct these non-housing issues within its own embrace and so set standards for them. The government was confusing regulation as an enabling and standard-setting process with regulation as a control mechanism.

Housing associations continued to be diverse in size and geography, but they now also showed diversity in their priorities in relation to community investment. Different associations were choosing different ways forward in terms of whether they went wholly for affordable housing numbers, the balance between new building for rented housing and for home ownership, and the way in which they addressed community and tenant involvement and sustainability in neighbourhood agendas. The regulator operating in this field, if it became too interventionist, would effectively operate as a straitjacket, rather than protecting the independence and choice that different housing associations had. Regulation of the wider social role and the absence of a level playing field between housing associations and the private sector would create a very unsatisfactory situation.

Some of the background to the whole of this debate is about the articulation of local government's role in place shaping and the role of housing associations as a key partner of local government in achieving this. At one level it is argued that local authorities were late in coming to a place-shaping agenda, their tradition having been principally one of narrow department- and profession-based service delivery rather than integrated community or neighbourhood policy development. Housing associations, perhaps unconvincingly, had adopted the slogan 'In Business for Neighbourhoods' and although this may not have been the way that they actually operated (more like 'in neighbourhoods for business') it is arguable that they are a key agency in any place-shaping agenda.

The HCA would be able to include the activities that English Partnerships was associated with in spending on land preparation, for example, although it is noticeable that in earlier periods the Housing Corporation had carried out that role. The detailed planning for the HCA was being carried out by the Corporation, CLG and English Partnerships; the NHF, the Local Government Association, the National House Builders Confederation and others were not being directly involved in the creation of the agency.

Conclusions

A new agency backed with an enormous three-year budget, and established with considerable cross-party support in the middle of a government's period of office, starts from a strong base. The new Homes and Communities Agency starts from a very different position than the Housing Corporation in 1964. It also has the benefit of the skills and experience of transferring staff and the wider policy and delivery experience gained within the different agencies that came together to form it. Finally it has ambitions to do more than build dwellings: to achieve wider social, economic and environmental goals and to be the key partner for local authorities and others in regeneration and a 'whole life, whole place' sustainable communities agenda. While the agenda for the new Tenant Services Authority may not sound so challenging, effective regulation will remain critical for lenders and the HCA as well as for tenants. The ways in which both agencies start and continue to work will be strongly influenced by the experience of the Housing Corporation but also by English Partnerships, CLG and local government. The largest group of staff for the new agencies are likely initially to come from the Corporation and both the new chief executive (Peter Marsh) and the chairman (Anthony Mayer) of the TSA spent formative years with the Corporation. The final chapters of this book set out some of the key considerations arising from looking back over the experience of the Housing Corporation and looking forwards to the challenges likely to face the new agencies and the HCA in particular.

10

Symbiosis? The relationship with government and others

Introduction

The Housing Corporation over its lifetime acted as promoter and regulator of housing associations and as the channel for investment and government housing policy. There is no dispute that the Corporation was the agent of government but there were and are different accounts and expectations about how this relationship worked. This chapter particularly draws on the interviews carried out for this study with key players – ministers, senior civil servants, chairmen and chief executives of the Corporation – to highlight key elements in the relationship and take stock of the lessons emerging. While reference is made to the longer history of the Corporation, the balance of discussion in this chapter relates to the last twenty years.

Independence

The central function of the Housing Corporation was as a link between different organisations that governments came to rely upon in order to deliver housing policy. In the inter-war years and the early post-war years the government operated with essentially a single partner, local authorities. It relied upon them not just to deliver housing policy but to exercise judgements about what policy was appropriate in different parts of the country. By the 1960s this model was under strain and a more prominent role for housing associations developed, both because of changes in the housing situation and because of shortcomings in the approach being developed in some places. The key decision about how to link housing associations into the policy system and use their energy and capacity was taken in 1974, when, rather than the government continuing to rely on local authorities, the Housing Corporation took on this link role. In effect housing associations could by-pass local authorities, and they did so more and more as funding from the Corporation increased and that from local authorities diminished.

Central government itself did not have the knowledge or other resources to link directly with housing associations and in any case such a direct relationship would often have been seen as unacceptable to independent housing associations. The Housing Corporation then met the requirements of various parties, including central government and the financial institutions that came to see the Corporation's regulatory role as essential if they were to invest in the sector. It was treated with more suspicion by local government, which resented the loss of control and the diversion of resources; and it was also treated with some suspicion by housing associations, which distrusted a central bureaucracy with dubious origins. While the housing association movement became less antagonistic over time, the local authority sector retained its resentments and continued to seek to establish the old order.

Lying behind the attitudes of other stakeholders and central to any assessment of the Housing Corporation are questions about how it has used its position within the policy community. Various terms are used to express different extremes along a government agency–independent subsidiary continuum. Perhaps the extremes are best expressed by chairmen and chief executives of the Housing Corporation. For some chairmen, with private sector experience, the innocent expectation was that they were being asked to take the chair of what was in effect the subsidiary and board of a holding company that was given terms of reference and an overall budget and left to get on with it. The reality was very different: the Treasury appeared regularly and counted every paperclip. There was absolutely no financial discretion whatsoever on the broad picture. There was responsibility for carving up the cake but no say in the size of the cake itself – even though the housing movement at least partly blamed the Corporation when the cake wasn't large enough. This situation may well have suited ministers and the sponsoring department, as it meant that some criticism of them was deflected. However, it also seems likely that the department always wanted tighter control. It had the fiscal control but would have liked to do other things that would have controlled the Corporation's funding regime more directly. This was even though it never had the ability to do those things because it lacked the people to do them.

The accounts of these processes stress the feeling of exclusion from policy debate at some stages. In the 1990s there were periods when the Corporation was actively excluded from groups set up to develop policy on matters that it was closely involved in. The feeling was that the department regarded the agency role as meaning 'you're at arm's length, you're not part of the policy community' and any involvement in policy discussion must be informal. There may have been old-fashioned status issues here related to civil service grades and seniority across the organisations, but whatever the reason, one response was for the Corporation, usually through the chairman, to seek influence through political lobbying – albeit probably with limited effect. In this context it is also widely emphasised that the Corporation had a very small public relations budget and did not seek to use its resources to exert policy influence locally or nationally through this. Some contrast is drawn with English Partnerships, which pursued a much more active and extravagant strategy to publicise what it was doing and could do.

The same issue applied in the regional offices: some Corporation staff did get involved with the government offices in the regions but this seems to have depended on personal relationships. There was nothing institutional which required staff responsible for housing in government offices to work with Corporation staff in their region.

As the Corporation's role expanded, so there was perceived a mismatch between the expertise within it and within the sponsoring department. Some detected a perverse pride that the Department of the Environment civil servants in the 1970s and 1980s knew very little about local government; their frame of reference was what was going on in Lambeth or Southwark councils, because that's where they all lived; and the situation had not changed subsequently and was equally true of the Treasury.

Within this general framework there are some examples of where the department appears to have directly frustrated innovation and change in the Housing Corporation. In the late 1990s the Corporation sought to set up a policy directorate. As the key housing organisation in the country it could have set one up without needing more funding from the sponsoring department. However, the department was able to block this because overall government policy at that time dictated no new recruits at senior management level. As the Corporation was a non-departmental government body the government embargo on recruitment applied even though it had identified the need for a policy directorate to advise it in order to carry out its role effectively and had also identified the money for it within its existing budget. While the Corporation had reduced overall staff numbers, had found the money internally to pay for the directorate and asserted the need for it because of changes in the sector and the need for people to develop policy to inform board discussions, it was not allowed to proceed. This affected the structure of the Corporation, as has been referred to by many observers: a lack of experienced senior staff and a big gap at senior level between the chief executive, deputy chief executive, director of regulation and director of investment, and the bulk of staff working on operational matters and running the organisation and its function.

Similar issues arose when the Corporation created an IT budget in the 1990s. In previous requests for grant in aid this had never been separately identified. But the reaction from the sponsoring department was essentially that it did not understand what online bidding systems and other aspects were. Issues also arose over detailed managerial matters, including proposals for new posts and for grading of posts: the department queried the grading levels and there was an excessive degree of invasive annoyance that provided much more aggravation for the Corporation than anything to do with housing.

Other examples exist where major restructuring of the Corporation was scrutinised but approved and the more general discourse is about successful innovation and developing approaches independently, which the department then accepted. It appears that these positive examples were more common in periods of confidence and expansion and when strong individual relationships existed. Throughout the history of the Corporation there were regular meetings and other contacts between chairmen and ministers and between senior civil servants and Corporation senior staff, and there was great care to inform continuously. Within this framework there was little detailed day-to-day supervision and the Corporation was left to 'get on with things'. In the appointment of successive chief executives, the department did give approval after careful examination but it did not have major influence. The reluctance of the DoE and the Treasury to accept the Corporation's thinking about private finance is a case in point where the Corporation's persistence and its success in convincing key ministers meant that a critically important policy did originate within the Corporation.

It is important not to overstate these examples – there was little interference in relation to the central activities of regulation and investment. Some chairmen appear to have welcomed observers from the sponsoring department while others expressly objected as they felt it would affect the dynamics of their meetings. Again this is a case where it appears that if the chairman expressed a strong view the department gave way. What emerges is a relationship between unequal partners but where the senior partner recognised the value of the agency it worked with and wanted a constructive relationship. To achieve this it engaged in regular meetings and exchanges and listened – more in some situations than in others. Both parties colluded in a process that recognised the sanctions the other had but sought not to bring them into play. In other words, the fact that the minister knew that there was always a resignation letter in the top right-hand drawer of the desk set some framework for a more equal relationship than suggested by the images of lap-dogs, poodles, organ grinder and monkey, or even master and servant. The relationship with ministers and the sponsoring department was important and the key to the independence that existed. It had to be cultivated and meant that representations were made about matters of concern but the final option was to resign rather than to go on a campaign.

It was important to get to know how to approach the department. It was always open to discussion as long as it was within the established protocols. Sometimes the department couldn't understand what was being proposed but if you persisted and maintained the dialogue, the penny would drop at some point. Chairmen were usually already familiar with this culture, having been involved with the government on other bodies. In some cases they recognised that Whitehall did not understand how property companies worked and how, after things had been built, partnerships worked. While there had been a culture change for local authorities, which had been introduced to Whitehall, Whitehall's understanding was not as strong as it could be. And even the Treasury was struggling to understand commercial risk and took longer than it should to evaluate it.

There were other ideas put to ministers and the department that clearly came to nothing. Some were too difficult for the people in the ministries and perhaps for some housing associations as well. Examples include early ideas to enable satisfactory tenants to build equity stakes and proposals to review periodically whether tenants still required their tenancy. It may be that neither of these was a good idea that should have been progressed but neither was formally pursued and discarded. Rather the culture was to refer to them as all being very difficult or to respond with a wall of silence, not really engaging in an argument, for or against. If such things were mentioned in meetings with civil servants the minister would be briefed about the Corporation's view but there was no certainty that there would be any other action and the department was adept at burying what was in its view unsuitable or untimely. In such exchanges the Corporation would keep going, but it got absolutely nowhere on some key issues about social housing. The department felt no obligation to go away and consider such matters and come back with a memorandum explaining its view or to respond in any formal way. The conventional response would come from the civil servants, not from the minister, and would stress difficulties, or that it would be difficult for tenants to take on board.

The crunch issue in the relationship between the Corporation and the department was finance and budgets. This was a persistent source of critical comment in annual reports and meetings and while chief executives may have accepted this as part of the agency relationship, it strained chairmen's views of what was acceptable. Again the reality of the agency relationship was about managing it and failures to do so effectively were as much a source of tension as any other – and indeed led to the one occasion on which a chairman resigned. Sir Brian Pearse as a banker had expectations of the role that were closer to a private sector subsidiary model and was unhappy with successive and disproportionate reductions in expenditure. The process of advising the Corporation of its budget had traditionally been to give the chairman and the chief executive the figures at about twelve o'clock at the ministry on the day of the Budget. They would then consider the implications. On this occasion, in 1997, Pearse was outraged partly because Scotland did not have the same draconian cut as England, whose budget that year was barely more than Scotland's. Pearse regarded this as scandalous and devastating to the staff, and the housing associations as well were up in arms. Pearse's view that it was not possible to stay under those terms is testament that the agency relationship only functioned effectively when the Corporation felt that it was more than a eunuch and was having an impact, albeit as an agency.

Throughout this it is quite clear that the Housing Corporation was an agent of government. It periodically struggled to escape from that role and tried to create independence but essentially this was to avoid being a passive agent. This was not an option as a passive agent had no credibility. It was important that the regulator acted as a champion for associations and to achieve this it had to fight its corner. The position for the Corporation was to take opportunities and make use of them. It could persuade and argue and the department would listen when that was done. It is also true that the department had different listening modes and part of the relationship involved an acceptance of 'polite listening' and 'but nothing came of it' as long as that was not always the stance.

One important perspective on this came from the Environment Select Committee in 1993. The account by the committee chair is instructive:

We began by considering the relationship between the corporation and its sponsoring department – the Department of the Environment. The Housing Corporation is a quango and is therefore quasi-autonomous, whatever that means. Some people told us that the Corporation was a creature – usually a poodle – of government. No one told us that it was too autonomous.

The committee's view is that under the outgoing chairman, Sir Christopher Benson, to whom I pay tribute, the corporation behaved in a correct but unpoodle-like manner. The committee was given a copy of the Corporation's top secret corporate plan. Frankly, we were surprised at its tone. Sir Christopher and his colleagues did not shrink from giving strong advice, whether it was welcome or not. The committee felt that the relationship between the Corporation and the department was about right. The Corporation spends a lot of public money and is rightly closely supervised in that. As a non-governmental organisation, however, it must remain free to express its views on policy matters – but only in private.

When people first learn that the Housing Corporation's corporate plan is not published they are surprised, given the huge sums of public money involved. The frank advice to which I referred is partly the reason why it remains a private document. The committee felt strongly that the plan should be published, as a contribution to the continuing public debate on social housing. The government did not feel able to accept the committee's recommendations, for reasons that I understand, but the Corporation has at least been able to produce its first three-year statement of plans and priorities.

Openness is also required in the appointment of the Corporation's board, which, in the committee's view, did not fully reflect the breadth of experience desirable in such an organisation. I therefore welcome the recent appointment of new members with experience of housing – in one case, a local authority housing manager and in another, a housing association tenant. The fresh perspectives that those new board members will bring will be of great value to the Corporation and to the government. (Hansard 1994)

The quango made its own luck rather than simply being passive. If it did not do something about an issue then it would not be a successful organisation. People who respect each other can argue against the departmental bureaucratic view; the set of rules were not inflexible and could be changed by persuasion, and it was evident that when they saw the logic, officials would come into line. In this sense one key test for independence relates to successful innovation. Throughout this book reference has been made to how the Corporation shaped both regulation and investment. The policy set by the government tended to be broad brush and it was for the Corporation to fill in the detail that in effect is a key part of the way policy is delivered and works in practice. In addition to this translation of the broad intent of government into detail, this book contains examples of more direct innovation. The examples given, as we have seen, are the development of private finance, shared ownership, the development of longer-term funding deals with housing associations following the comprehensive spending review, the development of black housing associations, regional and national programmes in Scotland and Merseyside, the federations of housing associations that built capacity in Leeds and other cities, and, ultimately, managing to maintain the diversity of the housing association sector.

Ministers and mandarins

These perspectives highlight the extent to which the successful operation of a non-departmental government body is dependent not simply on what it does but also on the strengths and weaknesses of key partners, especially the sponsoring department. People actively involved on either side of this relationship level criticisms at the sponsoring department. For housing professionals with a detailed working knowledge of practice and an institutional memory, expertise was lacking in the department at least at some stages. There was some feeling that there was nobody in the department who understood how housing worked either in construction terms or adminis-tratively: high flyers who had Oxbridge firsts but had never got their feet wet were completely devoid of any knowledge; and they did not like it when somebody who had got their feet wet went in and told them that they were moving in the wrong direction. Their view was that they would dictate the policy and leave it to the fools out there to operate it. Although they were seeking to dictate policy they could not be sure that that policy was workable.

In another criticism related to investment, it is argued that the department could not have interfered even if it had had the inclination to – because it lacked a coherent understanding or strategy. The 1980s saw ministers in denial of the conventional planning framework for housing and rejecting projection techniques; this was followed by an overreliance on the Housing Needs Index and a failure to develop any real understanding of the changing dynamics of different housing markets in different parts of the country. There was no housing policy or national projection and demand figures that would provide a robust basis for an investment policy. Especially with the sensitivity towards immigration trends no one within the government was willing to say what was actually needed in various regions and the Corporation developed its funding allocations on the basis of what it thought was needed. In this environment big policy initiatives would be inserted, including the whole sustainable communities plan – in which the Housing Corporation was not involved until relatively late on and then only in the paragraphs that mentioned it. The Corporation's investment plans and forward plans were then found to be out of synchronisation and only at that point began to be brought together – much later than would have been possible with greater sharing of ideas and understanding of processes. The early concerns expressed about low and changing demand, and the need to rethink strategies in different regions, were resisted by the department and the subsequent adoption of neighbourhood renewal strategies and then the Housing Market Renewal Pathfinders are testament to the failure of intelligence and forward thinking in the department, and in the latter case to the Corporation's ability to commission and support research that came to inform policy initiatives.

It is also striking that the department does not appear to have sought to learn from the experience of chairmen and board members through exit interviews or debriefing. Over the life of the Housing Corporation the sponsoring department went through its own periodic transformations and also lost a lot of specialist housing experience. The policy memory within the department rested in a smaller, but very knowledgeable and experienced, residual group, while it expanded within the Corporation over time and as its remit grew. It is possible to suggest that the relative expertise within department and agency crossed at some stage in the 1990s, and in a wide area of key policy debate what was formally the junior partner (the Corporation) had more understanding and policy expertise than its master, creating an uncomfortable tension that was sometimes used effectively but sometimes not. Although there was regular, almost daily, contact there was a lack of real communication. There were missed opportunities to exchange senior personnel to break down barriers, even though when a civil servant did come to work with the Corporation it increased awareness of why particular practices were adopted and broke down the view that the Corporation did things for no good reason.

Relationships with ministers were important: Sir Hugh Cubitt's relationship with John Stanley and Baroness Dean's with John Prescott are both examples of strong friendly relationships which engendered confidence and a willingness not to interfere. Chairmen met with ministers frequently and this applied to

Scottish and Welsh ministers as well as English up to 1988. Some ministers had been involved with housing associations in some way before they went into government (Sir George Young and Nick Raynsford are good examples); some were already or became strong housing specialists. Changes of ministers presented problems and in some periods were too frequent to build strong relationships or to allow the minister to develop a strong understanding. There is a view that when there was a high turnover of ministers of housing even the department itself struggled to brief effectively and the process of government was affected. In this sense the relationship worked best when a housing minister (who could be expected to develop a closer understanding than a secretary of state with much wider responsibilities) was in post for a long time or, as in Raynsford's case, came to the job with expertise from the beginning.

Although the Housing Corporation operated with good access to ministers, most issues would at least be raised during regular meetings with civil servants. The accounts of the way the Corporation was managed in these meetings suggest a tendency to caution – to refer to legal or other difficulties. In at least some cases this instinct was challenged and taken to the minister and when this was done the minister tended to be less cautious. Examples of this in recent years include the issuing of press releases about housing associations in supervision and remuneration packages for senior executives of housing associations. And the lesson learned from these experiences was again to always make sure that the minister was briefed. The word of the day and the culture developed was 'no surprises'. The Corporation was appointed by the government, it was accountable, it took taxpayers' money through the government and it would be a very foolish chairman who just ploughed his or her own furrow without consulting or informing the department.

The Corporation's own chief executive was a key player throughout and arguably its most powerful figure. Effective chief executives were seen to be proactive and to develop strong partnerships within the Corporation (with staff, board and chairman) and outside (with the sponsoring department and the National Federation of Housing Associations/National Housing Federation).

Lobbyists and deliverers

The way the Housing Corporation managed its relationships with government in order to retain its integrity and independence meant that it would not always act as the champion of the housing association movement and certainly would not campaign for it. This in turn affected its relationship with the trade association – the National Federation of Housing Associations (subsequently the National Housing Federation). Nevertheless the federation was extremely effective in feeding its views to the department at important times and generally had a good relationship with the Corporation.

When the government proposed to change the framework for rent setting in 2001 the housing association sector wanted the Corporation to be its lobbying body, but the Corporation saw that as the role of the federation – its own role was to assess the situation and independently advise ministers of its opinion. One view of this is that the minister could listen more easily than where there was a more public debate. Perhaps the strength of the position was that both routes could be pursued.

There was also some division of labour, with the federation as the trade association, seeing it as its job to lead in the area of corporate governance. It felt that it was its job to issue and update guidelines and develop training. The regulatory activities of the Corporation related increasingly to governance but it developed its approach in the knowledge of what the federation was doing. In a similar way it worked closely with the housing ombudsman on matters relating to tenants.

Just as the sponsoring department needed the Housing Corporation, so the Corporation needed housing associations. It had to build and maintain trust and effective relationships to deliver what the government wanted. To this extent there was a symbiotic relationship between government, its agency and the independent housing associations. Through the history of the Corporation this relationship changed. It grew from one of distrust and even distaste to one of partnership but did not always remain on an even keel. The continuity of staffing on both sides broke down some barriers and the recruitment by the Corporation of people with credibility within the housing movement, because they had worked with or within it, was also important. In some cases it was felt that too relaxed a relationship developed especially between longer-established male chief executives of large associations and key Corporation staff.

Criticisms were levelled at the Corporation both for being too lax in its supervision and for being too intrusive. The failures in relation to the co-ownership sector have already been referred to but it is appropriate to note the verdict of the Council of Co-ownership Housing Societies: 'The promotion and development of co-ownership housing societies contained many improprieties for which individual co-owners ultimately have to pay.' This was partly because of the Corporation's 'ingenuous approach to the activities of professionals and … failure to ensure effective supervision' (DoE 1975: 58, quoted in Birchall 1991: 12–13).

Some of the strains that continued and came to the surface related to the jealous regard that housing associations have for their independence. The advent of registration and regulation was not welcomed by all and generated considerable work for small organisations, which could see little or no advantage resulting from it. Members of Parliament received letters from almshouse residents who were fearful of the Corporation's bureaucracy and heavy-handedness in regard to well-established almshouses (e.g. Hansard 1989). It is salutary to remember the verdict of one commentator who stood up at the back of the room at an annual meeting of the National Association of Almshouses following the speech by the then chairman of the Corporation and said: 'I would just like it to be known that in the 1,000 years of existence of my almshouse charity the two greatest disasters to have befallen this charity were the Black Death and the advent of the Housing Corporation, not necessarily in that order.'

There was a shift in the type of regulation from social to economic regulation or from a substantially subjective activity that was affected by the personality of the regulator towards a more formal performance measurement system more focused on management of assets, finance and risks and with clearer protocols and criteria for regulation. The new regulatory code was designed to be closer to a public utilities model of regulation. It needed more internal expertise, and more financially literate people were recruited to the regulatory side.

The volume of paperwork and the incremental creep of regulation towards a technical measurement exercise were a matter of concern. Few statistics mean anything without interpretation and context but those submitting annual returns were not confident that the regulator had the capacity for sensitive interpretation. While regulation was recognised as the key to maintaining reputation with tenants, funders and others, the systems adopted tended to be seen as insufficiently geared to the needs of the associations.

Elsewhere caution was expressed about the implications of the professionalisation and management efficiency agendas pursued by the Corporation. While early resistance to steps designed to improve probity and accountability was not widespread and now seems very unenlightened, the later cautions about mergers and pressures to modernise may have more justification. They were clearly not accepted by the whole of the housing association movement.

This discussion immediately opens up a central question related to the evolution of the housing association sector. It was, and is, diverse. However, stock transfer introduced a group of new, large associations with different origins and governance arrangements and different types of stock. In addition the development of group structures and mergers among existing associations increased the number of large cross-regional associations. The differences between different types of association became greater and this posed problems for the federation in seeking to represent them and for the Corporation in developing appropriate ways of working with them.

The way in which the expansion agenda for housing associations progressed may also have generated an uncertainty that damaged relationships. Although the Corporation was widely seen as encouraging mergers, it was not transparent about its attitude. It never expressed any official views on whether mergers were good or bad. Associations that wanted to merge had to justify the merger to the Corporation; if the Corporation thought it was in the public interest, it was approved. Few mergers were forbidden but they did not get an easy ride, because the registration committee was rigorous. At the same time the implication of the investment policy was of increasing scale and the whole strategic partners concept was driven by efficiency considerations, which were welcomed by the Treasury. Channelling investment funds to a smaller number of organisations was administratively easier for the Corporation than dishing out money to hundreds of associations every year. It was easier to apply proper controls and the strategic partners approach was a reaction to the stresses on the organisation as well as a wish to achieve greater efficiency, although the inspection results did not show that big meant better as far as efficiency in repairs or tenants' services were concerned.

Co-location and regulation

The Housing Corporation's responsibility for both investment and regulation was seen as a strength for many years but the desire to separate the two ultimately led to its demise. Throughout the account in this book there have been references to a range of factors associated with co-location and why it came to be seen as undesirable. Some of these are to do with changing orthodoxies and the professionalisation of inspection and regulation. Others are to do with the increasing size of the housing association sector, the scale of the investment programme and ambitions that investment should produce sustainable communities and not just dwellings. In the context of this chapter it is appropriate to refer more fully to the changing nature of regulation and the shifting relationship between regulator and regulated.

In the early years of the Housing Corporation there was no requirement that it should act as a regulator. It registered housing societies that wished to be able to access loans. As the Corporation's role expanded it chose to register any housing associations that sought registration for whatever reason – usually to access government finance. Its registration grew into annual monitoring and subsequently into regulation.

It is apparent that in this early period many housing associations resented the Corporation and regarded it as an obstacle. They did not respect its expertise and did not feel that it shared their ambitions for housing – and this was true in the reluctance of the Corporation to provide, at different times, accommodation for students or fair rent housing for lower-income house-holds, or to engage with older inner city housing. There was a gap between the aspirations of the Corporation, interpreting its brief from 1964, and the ambitions especially of newer inner city associations. In comparison with later periods this early phase of primitive regulation was one of regulatory deficit – deficit in the sense of either a lack of regulation or a lack of sufficient awareness of what happened on the ground to develop regulation that had meaning for housing associations. This situation began to change in 1974 with a transition to what has been referred to as regulatory capture.

Mullins and Riseborough (2000) present regulatory capture as part of a process of incorporation of housing associations by the state through the public subsidy of new development after 1974. In this period dependency on public funding from the Housing Corporation and local authorities meant a different attitude to regulation. While many associations would still have preferred to be without it, it was worth putting up with. The regulatory mechanisms had the effect of strengthening sector identity and networks. Regulation involved a regime that housing associations were expected to conform to and this played an important part in promoting a particular set of relationships between associations. Mullins and Riseborough emphasise, however, that housing associations themselves influenced and benefited from this regime – for example through the reinforcement of sectoral norms relating to meeting housing needs and equal opportunities, and by involving users and excluding potential profit-distributing competitors. The term 'regulatory capture' provides a good description of the ways in which housing associations actively used policy networks such as trade associations to shape this regulatory regime. Expressed in another way, regulatory capture meant a real shift from the distanced disrespect prior to 1974 to a closer and more comfortable working relationship after it.

Mullins and Riseborough then argue that the reprivatisation of housing associations with new private financing complementing public subsidy after 1988 involved a redrawing of the boundaries between public and other sectors. Housing associations became the chosen vehicle for decentralisation of state housing through the transfer of development activity and assets from local government. In the subsequent period growth was very rapid but the terms on which housing associations expanded were also very different. Private finance introduced powerful new stakeholders in the form of banks and building societies, increased risk and involved the adoption of business techniques. Those involved got used to growth, which itself became a major rationale for some organisations.

Mullins (2000) states that the last years of the Conservative government were a period of sustained conflict between local authorities and the Corporation over local investment priorities for housing associations, and he identifies this as one of the developments which impelled the paradigm shift from social democracy to liberalism. The increasing emphasis on private funding of housing associations and the ability of some associations to draw on accumulated surpluses appeared to indicate their growing independence from the state and their emergence as a third sector consistent with the liberal model rather than as a sponsored state-dependent sector in the social democratic model.

The notion of a shift from the social democratic to the liberal model appears consistent with political changes observed with the transition from state housing to non-profit housing and it is in this context that there is increasing discussion of housing associations and the Housing Corporation as quangos or as elements of the quango state with the replacement of democratically accountable bodies by unelected or appointed bodies. This transformation has also been described as a move to competition, with conflicting objectives for voluntary organisations arising from the increased emphasis on competitiveness. Less importance was placed on the voluntary label, many associations preferring to be seen as social entrepreneurial bodies approaching social purposes in a businesslike way. Mullins and Riseborough (2000) identify challenges associated with the reduced supply of public funding after 1993 and challenges to the legitimacy of housing associations as local spending bodies. Housing associations began to reposition themselves in relation to central government and local authorities and many were involved in possible mergers or in diversification to other activities including regeneration and care.

While there was a shift to competition, the Corporation maintained its cosy or corporatist relationship with housing associations and they continued to influence how it operated regulation. This worked effectively while there was no prospect of any other arrangement – but the advent of the Audit Commission, Labour's new Best Value regime and a new view of the dangers of co-location were to upset the relationship. The reasons why the Housing Corporation failed to be selected as the housing inspectorate grew directly out of regulatory capture. Its relationship was too comfortable and it missed the opportunity to demonstrate a capacity to be a robust inspector. It was too aligned with housing associations as producers and investors and had invested too little in tenants or in inspecting service delivery. And once the Corporation had lost inspection, the housing associations lost the capacity to shape how inspection was done.

Following the transfer of the inspectorate regime to the Audit Commission the Housing Corporation overhauled its own regulatory regime. This had to integrate effectively with that of the Audit Commission but it was the latter that made the running. The era of regulatory capture was over and regulated competition was an increasingly apt description of the relationship. In the final phase, with the new Tenant Services Authority, regulated competition is likely to remain. The close relationship between the housing associations and their regulator associated with earlier periods is unlikely to re-emerge. However, three lessons from the past remain.

Firstly, the government and the Housing Corporation gave too little attention to consumers' interests and services delivered for tenants. The government was too preoccupied with turning tenants into home owners and the Corporation (and associations) was so concerned with spending the budget that it neglected other matters. In the future the politics of housing tenure are likely to mean that pathways to home ownership remain important but they should not result in a neglect of those who remain as tenants. Secondly, while the cosy relationship between housing associations and the Housing Corporation may have had dangers, a distrustful and disrespectful relationship will not generate the best outcomes. There needs to be a strong dialogue between regulator and regulated and a proper regulatory stance does not rule out strong consultative and collaborative processes. Thirdly, Anthony Mayer's earlier concerns about the need for an exchange between regulator and investor will apply when these activities are held by two separate agencies as much as they did when there was co-location. Perhaps this is one area where the continuity of personnel will help to avoid having to learn old lessons over again.

Lessons

The story of a large non-departmental government body acting as the agency for government in Britain and working in a politically sensitive policy area involves dynamic or changing relationships. An effective agency–department relationship does not emerge simply out of formal and legislative arrangements but is also about how people in the respective organisations interact. It involves building strong links and respecting the resources and expertise that each has. As Anthony Mayer said in 1998:

> The focus for the ongoing working relationship between the Corporation and the DETR is the sponsoring directorate ... If a problem arises it is almost invariably [the head of the directorate] who is the first port of call. In terms of exercising the external accountability function this is the key relationship. Most of the time it is conducted in co-operative and cordial terms. But in the final analysis we exist to do jobs for government; if we fail to do so, or if there is a risk of our failing, then an element of censure on a direction from DETR is inevitable. This is perfectly proper given the relationship. (Mayer 1998: 113)

While the agency has ultimately to defer to the sponsoring department it is likely to be effective and a resource for government only if it is given space to build and use its expertise. In effect the sponsoring department needs to grant the agency significant independence and achieve a balance that enhances the whole policy area. In many ways the Housing Corporation appears to have been managed with opportunities to lead and innovate, and its relationships with both the department and other partners were mostly effective and constructive. The questions raised are about intrusions into detailed managerial matters on the one hand and the lack of policy expertise and confidence within the department on the other. It also appears that as the agency matured it outgrew its parent in size and the scope of its involvement in the policy area. This meant that the management of its relationship with its partners changed.

The central lesson of this history relates to the achievement of symbiosis, whereby a group of organisations regard it as desirable that their partners flourish and consequently forgo some of their negative capacity in order to promote positives. It involves operating with give and take rather than working to a formal rule book and it involves sharing information, being receptive to suggestions and learning from one another. The process is close to the exchange of resources referred to in the relationship between central and local government and underpins ideas of governance as distinct from government. In an era of governance, the government generates more value from an agency by granting it room to manoeuvre and space to innovate – by giving it some independence in practice even if it has none in theory. Without this it would not attract and sustain contributions from some individuals and the process of government would become more sterile. In practice the management of this relationship is likely to be uneven and pass through different phases – helped or hindered by different working relationships.

Regarding the experience of the Housing Corporation, there are a number of deeper underlying factors that created the environment in which the symbiotic relationship flourished. An expanding budget and a positive economic and public expenditure environment make it easier to bend and respond, while adverse economic environments limit the scope for invention and innovation. Beyond these there are also individual and organisational factors that increase the likelihood of effective partnership working. Three elements that are particularly referred to concern internal staffing (the chief executive and his or her relationship with other staff within the Corporation); the relationship between the chairman and the board; and the confidence of the sponsoring department.

One view is that, over time, the Corporation developed its own civil service. Its staff came to be imbued with a strong public service ethic, creating an organisation that actually cared about standards. The weakness here could be in an opposition to change and the lack of experience of other situations – local government, housing associations or working with tenants.

The board also changed over time. There were no guidelines about what sort of people and disciplines it would involve and there were shifts over the years with a greater emphasis on private finance and property background in the 1970s and 1980s and more on direct housing experience and tenant representation later. Although it is difficult to point to where the board was effective, there was of course debate and controversy and particular individuals brought particular issues and expertise. Chairmen often knew very little about the Corporation at the beginning but quickly became enthusiasts and devoted considerable time to the task – as did other board members, who often had regional remits. Initially the board operated in an informal way typical of the times. The rules about conflicts of interest were loose and it was common for board members to be also involved with individual associations as well as to have other interests. Following the Housing Act 1974, which amended the 1964 Act, members of the Corporation were required to declare any interest that was likely to affect prejudicially the exercise of their functions as members. It was agreed to set up a register in which members' interests in other relevant organisations might be recorded and to make the information available to those members of the Corporation's staff who might be concerned.

Perhaps most fundamentally the sponsoring department needed to be committed and to have confidence and belief that the non-departmental government body would work. The department had to be satisfied that there were people capable of doing it and in response the organisation had to prove that it was capable and maintain the confidence and trust of the central departments. The lowest points in the Corporation's history appear to be those when confidence and trust were weakest, related either to problems with performance and delivery or differences of individual approach and style. In this context, however, the sponsoring department's view was increasingly insufficient and the Treasury became increasingly important. There was a view that the Treasury was not best pleased with the Corporation, had never felt it was a wonderful organisation and considered it a bit of a sleepy backwater.

Conclusions

This chapter has offered a more discursive account of key aspects of the working of the Housing Corporation and has identified important elements that are likely to continue to be important in the future. However, it is also necessary to attempt to capture differences in emphasis that arise in discussion with different participants in the process and that have carried more or less weight over time. This is best expressed in terms of different models of the government–agency relationship or the operation of a non-departmental government body. For this discussion the term 'quango' is used.

Initially, and to be consistent with the rest of this chapter, we can say that none of the models presented here is a one-dimensional, unidirectional, linear model where all of the power rests with the department, which makes all of the decisions and where the Housing Corporation is a powerless operational agency. Having disposed of this, we can identify five models that have applied through the history of the Housing Corporation. These are set out briefly in turn.

- A technical agency model: the quango as a centre for the development of techniques and technical responses to policy problems including the legal and technical complexities of regulation and the management of investment to achieve value for money.

- A political management model: the quango as an alternative agency to manage the politics of policy – to explain and promote the government's policy agenda and even take some of the direct pressure related to difficult decisions away from ministers.
- A pluralist governance model: the quango as an acceptable body to assemble and co-ordinate the resources available in different organisations. In this case the emphasis is upon the capacity to bring diverse bodies together in a way that would not be feasible for a government department directly.
- A private sector subsidiary board model: the quango as the equivalent of a subsidiary of a private company. In this the subsidiary is subject to a superior board but is given a budget, told to live within it but left alone with powers to operate. It is able to decide what it does to achieve targets – it would not have a moratorium imposed or suddenly have its budget cut.
- A wholly autonomous model: the quango as financially and legally independent but working within the spirit of government policy and operating collaboratively with regional and local government.

Throughout the history of the Housing Corporation there were tensions about which of these models was being adopted. These were tensions within the Corporation and between it and its partners, including the sponsoring department. In general the dominant assumptions were about hybrid versions of these models. Over time there was movement from the technical agency model, which was most evident in the early years, towards a more political management model associated with Lord Goodman, who was very happy to be the foil of the government, and Sir Lou Sherman; following this was the search for independence associated with Sir Hugh Cubitt, Sir Christopher Benson and Sir Brian Pearse – all of whom came from the private sector and tended to use it as their frame of reference; finally there was a swing back to political management and then to a pluralistic governance model. But this perspective is stronger if some individuals, chairmen in particular, are referred to. Chief executives (with exceptions), Corporation staff and civil servants in the sponsoring department and the Treasury were more inclined to the 'less independent' models. For housing associations the pluralistic governance model or even more autonomous models were assumed. It is not evident that the shifting assumptions and lack of shared assumptions about the role of the Housing Corporation were enormously damaging. Indeed they may have generated some creative tension, meaning that, especially where there was a desire to assert greater independence, the Housing Corporation contributed more.

11

The direction of housing: quangos and governance

Introduction

Housing policy and the system of housing provision in Britain changed significantly over the years in which the Housing Corporation was in existence. Its successor agencies will no doubt also operate in a changing environment. They will themselves contribute to change but will also be affected by ongoing trends and unanticipated events. This chapter returns to some of the key themes set out at the beginning of the book and draws some initial conclusions related to the governance of housing. It focuses on two key debates about government and public policy in Britain, related to the role of quangos and then to wider changes in government, the hollowing out of the state. In both of these debates the key question considered is how the evidence related to housing and the Housing Corporation fits with dominant views. Finally the chapter sets out a perspective on the governance of housing in England. These different elements are presented as a lead in to the final conclusions presented in the next chapter.

The Housing Corporation as quango

The previous chapter of this book discussed features of the relationship between the Housing Corporation and its sponsoring department and other partners. It considered the agency role but emphasised the negotiated and changing nature of this role. A different way of presenting this is to look at the Housing Corporation as a quango. Some definitions of quangos would exclude non-departmental government bodies but in practice the Housing Corporation was widely referred to as a quango, its future was considered in this context in the early 1980s, and it is appropriate to discuss it in these terms. The development of quangos has been presented as a fundamental change in the governance of Britain (Skelcher 1998). The change involved the transfer of power from directly elected and relatively transparent central and local government to the closed world of quasi-government, to appointed boards or quangos. Skelcher focuses particularly on quangos with executive power – weighing values, making decisions and allocating resources for public purposes. These executive quangos, unlike their advisory and quasi-judicial counterparts, perform an essential governmental role. Skelcher identifies them as a class of organisations having considerable public significance yet remaining largely outside democratic, political activity. They are appointed rather than elected and have responsibility for shaping, purchasing, delivering and adjudicating across the arenas of public policy. They play key roles in almost every area of public policy and service delivery, including health, education, agriculture and science, and have become an integral part of the British state. The explosion of new quangos was associated in particular with the NHS and education and the replacement of large public bureaucracies by a multiplicity of smaller bodies in contractual and market-type relationships with one another. Alongside this the role of elected politicians has been translated into strategic policy makers (Skelcher 1998: 2).

Skelcher refers to the quango's status as a new genus of agency observed on the American scene and also to the origin of the term. Quangos were private sector bodies created as a result of legislation or executive action to fulfil public purposes and dependent on public funding for their existence. Their programmes were influenced by political priorities set by the government, and accountability was assured through auditing and other regulatory devices such as contracts (Skelcher 1998: 5). The acronym QUANGO, by which these organisations became known in the UK, was coined by Professor Anthony Barker and subsequently interpreted as either 'quasi-autonomous non-governmental organisation' or 'quasi-autonomous national governmental organisation' depending on the author in question. Barker and his colleagues saw quangos as a fourth sector set against government itself, the market and the public corporations responsible for nationalised industries. This involved a broader definition than in America and created something of a catch-all within which to locate the various bodies created for public purpose that did not sit comfortably within any of the other three categories.

The spirit of this definition has remained ever since, especially in the way that quangos are sometimes defined by what they are not (not elected, not accountable and so on) rather than what they are. Skelcher argues that, although it is not a clearly defined concept, the term 'quango' has the virtue of providing a broad umbrella under which a wide array of organisations can cluster and be examined. Other abbreviations have emerged, including EGO (Extra-governmental organisation), QUALGO (Quasi-autonomous local government organisation) and NDPB (Non-departmental public body). The Housing Corporation is strictly speaking one of these last, but also falls within the broader embrace of the term 'quango' as it is generally used. Non-departmental public bodies are public bodies that are not organisational parts of a government ministry. As such they differ from, for example, National Health Service bodies, such as health authorities and trusts, which are regarded as departmental public bodies since they operate within a hierarchical structure. Health ministers exercise authority through the NHS Executive in its regional outposts to influence the structure and commissioning and purchasing activities for health authorities in their contracting with NHS trusts and other providers. This is a distinctive position compared with the Housing Corporation and housing associations. A further distinction is usually applied to the nationalised industries, which are referred to as public corporations, although they can also be seen as part of the system of quangos because of the nature of appointment to their boards. As the privatisation programme in the 1980s and 1990s removed many of these bodies they are less significant than they were in the past.

The government recognises three types of NDPB: advisory bodies, tribunals and executive bodies. The Housing Corporation was an executive body. In general executive bodies have direct responsibility for the execution of a particular function or activity and their own budget and staff. Their powers may be defined in statute or be created by administrative action. Some operate nationally and some in specific localities (e.g. the six housing action trusts, each of which undertakes regeneration in small areas of public housing).

Housing associations strictly fall outside the normal definition of 'quango' because it relates to a formal relationship with government. They are non-recognised bodies that are highly significant in numerical and constitutional terms and have a central role in spending public money to secure the provision of social housing whatever their philanthropic and charitable origins. Housing associations also tend to be either registered charities or companies registered under the Industrial and Provident Societies Act. They have a different legal basis from housing action trusts or NHS trusts, which are set up under statute and are governed by different regulations.

There has been a strong critique of quangos as they have developed within the British system of government and the following paragraphs seek to set out the main elements of this critique. Two key hesitations apply when this material is considered, and are returned to in this chapter – whether the critiques of local quangos are wholly relevant to the Housing Corporation (or to housing associations that operate at a local level) and whether the practices that have developed partly in response to these critiques are effective.

Much of the literature on quangos is preoccupied with their growth in the 1980s and 1990s and concerned with the loss of local government power to non-elected bodies. In the UK as a whole at the end of the 1990s there were about 2½ times as many members of local appointed executive bodies as local councillors (Skelcher 1998: 15). Davis (1996) focuses wholly upon local government and refers to a major transformation in the way that local communities are governed and a growth of government by appointment.

Skelcher and Davis (1996) refer to a 'new magistracy', boards of individuals who in most cases were appointed by a central government minister, other agencies or the existing board members themselves; there is undoubtedly an important debate to be had about the processes through which these bodies are appointed and how they operate. However, the references to housing in terms of the new magistracy are to housing action trusts, set up by the Conservative government from 1991 onwards. Skelcher and Davis also refer to other organisations, including urban development corporations, but not directly to housing associations or the Housing Corporation.

On one level housing associations are subject to exactly the same series of criticisms as the new quangos, established to carry out activities that otherwise would have been carried out by local authorities: and indeed the transfer of resources from local authorities to housing associations means that they have been used in this way. However, these organisations, in most cases, already existed. They are not, in that sense, a new magistracy but a continuing old one. This is not true of the associations set up to take the transfer of local authority stock through policies including Large-Scale Voluntary Transfer and the Estate Renewal Challenge Fund. Nevertheless it is problematic to represent housing associations in the same terms as the new quangos or the new magistracy. Indeed it could be argued that the functioning of housing associations alongside local authorities, prior to the attacks on local government associated with the new quangos, was a source of strength. Housing associations provided some alternatives to the monopolistic local authority landlord; they provided some alternative centres of power and organisation with resources which in particular circumstances helped in the management of local areas; and they were valued by local authorities because they could do different things in different timescales and had a different relationship with the public.

It is true that some local authorities were antagonistic towards housing associations in this period; however, the relationship was more commonly constructive. For example, local authorities valued the contribution that housing associations could make within an urban renewal environment or in setting up co-operatives and alternative forms of tenure. They also valued their role in providing specialist housing services or providing activities that went beyond the narrow confines of housing to include training and other activities.

In this sense there was a governance structure in the housing sector before the era in which academics began to see a shift from government to governance. It is a structure where local authorities worked with a variety of other housing bodies in a constructive way. Perhaps the shift is from a position where governance was a chosen strategy for local government to one that it had no alternative but to adopt because of the withdrawal of resources, powers and responsibilities. In that sense housing associations straddle different eras of government from laissez-faire to one in which local authorities valued the options they were given by working with housing associations and then to one in which they have no choice but to work with housing associations.

The other major argument advanced by Davis and Skelcher relates to the fragmentation of local governance. This connects with debates about the hollowing out of the state and, more importantly, about the way in which a plethora of different agencies work together and their relationships between one another and with the public. It is argued that this plethora of agencies ultimately affects the performance of different services and, crucially, works to some extent against the contemporary concern about integration of services. Davis and Skelcher (1997: 24) comment that 'quangoisation has led to increased vertical integration with performance targets for services intended to increase efficiency'. But this vertical integration has largely been in functional 'chimneys', unable to respond easily across the organisational divide. For example, in bodies such as health authorities and health service trusts the vertical linkages to the NHS Executive and the Department of Health may take precedence over the necessary horizontal linkages.

These issues are particularly important in relation to housing. The multiplicity of housing associations may be seen as a strength in terms of providing choice and alternative routes into adequate housing for citizens. It does not, however, lend itself to a better-co-ordinated and integrated policy. Perhaps this is most evident where the ownership of properties by housing associations is scattered. Where the agenda for particular neighbourhoods requires a more coherent and integrated strategy, the existence of a large number of associations with small numbers of properties and limited resources to contribute to the development of coherent local policy responses may be a barrier to the development of effective service delivery and the regeneration of these neighbourhoods. In this way the strength of housing associations (their diversity and their ability to provide tenants with some choice) may also be their weakness. This issue has been addressed in debates about the rationalisation of stock ownership and, for example, arguments about lead associations, followers and associations that should exit from areas. The cynical view, however, is that few associations choose to exit, but remain as passive, non-contributing rent collectors that make no positive contribution to regeneration in areas with significant problems.

Much of the discussion so far relates to local democracy and while this links, but does not wholly fit, with discussion of housing associations, it does not fit with the Housing Corporation as a national-level NDPB. In this context it helps initially to consider the published views set out by Anthony Mayer (1998) when he was chief executive. He referred quite explicitly to the Corporation as a quango set up by statute, proposed by the secretary of state for environment, transport and the regions and approved by the House of Commons. Mayer suggested that many arguments about the lack of accountability of NDPBs were ill informed and he set out the formal accountabilities of the Corporation firstly with respect to the DETR. He commented: 'The Housing Corporation has no independent right of existence. If the secretary of state decided we should cease to exist then, subject to the approval of the House of Commons, statute could so secure.'

The Corporation operates under a management statement and a financial memorandum agreed with the department and these published documents set out what it can and cannot do, its degrees of freedom and its stewardship reporting requirements. Mayer stated:

> Every year ministers give us output and value-for-money targets for our funding of new social housing which we are required to meet. Our annual report is laid before Parliament and we are also required to produce annual stewardship reports for each area of work, in addition to formal in-year reporting arrangements.

Every five years ministers commission a wide-ranging review of our work known as the finance management and policy review [FMPR]. This makes recommendations on our operating practices which we are required to implement. The FMPR is preceded by a prior options study under which we are required to justify our existence. (Mayer 1998: 112–13)

Mayer noted that the last prior options study had identified the Corporation as the most appropriate vehicle to regulate and fund registered social landlords. Other mechanisms of accountability of the Corporation to government involved the requirements of government accounting boards and government codes of practice. These included a code of best practice for board members and access to Corporation information, staff rules and procedures for handling complaints.

Mayer went on to outline accountabilities to the National Audit Office and its power to review any or all of the Corporation's activities or decisions and access all working papers as part of its annual programme of inspection work and value-for-money studies. The Public Accounts Committee (PAC) received these reports and was entitled to summon and cross-examine both the Corporation's chief executive and the department's accounting officer, censure performance and publish recommendations for remedial action. Mayer stated that the existence of even the possibility of a PAC hearing clearly needed a strong discipline. Preparations for a hearing could take up most of the time of the senior executives involved for up to a month.

In addition Mayer referred to other external scrutiny:

- The Environment, Transport and Regional Affairs Committee and MPs: 'In a typical year I signed around 100 letters to members of Parliament about constituency cases.'
- The courts: 'All of our funding and regulatory decisions are subject to judicial review. Section 6 of the Housing Act 1996 has made it explicit that the body agreed that our failure either to register them as a social landlord or to deregister them may appeal to the High Court.'
- The parliamentary commissioners for administration: 'Individual members of the public can complain to the ombudsman through his or her MP.'
- External auditors appointed by the secretary of state to report to him or her annually on the propriety, effectiveness and efficiency of the Corporation's activities and structures.

Internal accountabilities were also involved. Board members were appointed by the secretary of state. The appointment process entailed preparation by DETR officials of a shortlist of candidates with the required skills and expertise across the social housing spectrum. The minister chose from this shortlist. There were no fast track ministerial nominees and no political appointments, and the process conformed to the government code of practice for appointments. All board appointments were advertised. Mayer argued that the existing lines of accountability did not mean that there was no case to do things differently. However, the case for doing things differently should not be based on an overstated assertion of a lack of accountability.

Mayer concluded with a plea for a better-informed debate about quangos. Perhaps we have now moved on from the situation where there is a debate about whether quangos are a good thing to one which accepts that quangos are likely to be a continuing feature of British politics and any debate has to be more differentiated, referring to different types of quango operating in different contexts and to the forms of accountability that are appropriate for them. In some contexts it might be concluded that quangos are undesirable but the overarching denunciation of quangocracy is likely to be a thing of the past. Davis and Skelcher (1997) refer to issues about appointments and patronage: patronage and political bias, the characteristics of appointees, standards of conduct. All of these things have been strongly examined and the Nolan committee and others have suggested actions which would raise the standards of conduct. In these respects the operation of quangos has improved enormously and the worst practices that were associated with some of them at an early stage are less likely to apply today. This of course does not alter the main argument that services should be provided through directly elected bodies, but it does mean that the argument becomes much more one of principle rather than one related to the practices within quangos that are unacceptable.

A separate strand of the debate about quangos emphasises their tendency to make policy issues technical (Skelcher 1998: 99). The Housing Corporation adopted this approach fully in service specification contracts, performance measurement and priority setting, all of which reinforced the technical overlay on what in reality were some deeply political questions. The addition of an inspectorate and deference to technical audit functions can be seen as part of the same tendency. Appointed members were introduced into a technical world and were expected to grapple with these technical questions. This may be seen as a way of enabling appointed board members to see themselves as independent and not engaging in party politics or indeed in political decisions. Skelcher comments that research on members of local appointed bodies reveals a high level of agreement with the view that they are politically independent together with a lack of willingness to change this situation. This is a position to which, according to best-practice advice, members of housing association boards are expected to adhere. It is a requirement that boards operate in a non-political way and that members of the boards do likewise. Ultimately the debate about the desirability of quangos is weighted in terms of attitudes towards democracy. The advocates of control by elected politicians have periodically suggested ways in which the reform of quangos could mean a return to greater direct control through electoral processes. For example the Association of Metropolitan Authorities in 1995 recommended that the Housing Corporation be abolished and that its functions should be divided between government offices for the regions and local authorities, with regulatory functions transferred to the Audit Commission. This would increase local accountability for public expenditure on local housing needs. In practice this route has not been followed (see Skelcher 1998: 168–9). However, the way in which quangos operate has been subject to much stronger attempts to open it up. In the case of the Housing Corporation there was a major change from the situation where the board of the Corporation was appointed by the secretary of state with no advertising or transparent process of selection and appointment. Members were not required to divest themselves of other appointments which might conflict and, as mentioned above, it was common in the early years of the Corporation for board members to also be leading members of individual housing associations.

As the years passed these practices changed. It became unacceptable for Corporation board members to be on the boards of housing associations, nor was it acceptable that they should immediately return to housing association boards once they left the Corporation board. At the same time vacancies for appointment to the Corporation board were advertised and there was a more transparent process for selection and appointment. Rates of payment were published in the annual report of the Housing Corporation. In relation to housing associations there were similar processes to strengthen their governance, with a greater emphasis upon the operation and effectiveness of boards, their membership and skills, the processes to be adopted and the appraisal of performance. Reference was also made to codes of conduct, regulation of conflict of interest, more formalised arrangements for audit and risk management and greater scrutiny of the operation of boards.

Restricting the discussion to the Housing Corporation itself, it is possible to construct some arguments around its merits in terms of a quango. This is a slightly artificial argument because the Corporation did not acquire local government roles but rather adopted some of the roles that otherwise would be the responsibility of central government. But it drew funding and therefore decision making down from local authorities and to this extent any simple evaluation of the Housing Corporation as a quango would identify it as adding to the democratic deficit.

However, in terms of this debate (see Skelcher 1998: 179), it can be argued that the existence of a separate Housing Corporation brought particular expertise into government and enabled key stakeholders to be incorporated into public policy processes. It enabled some explicit balance of social, economic and gender differences to be reflected on the board. It enabled a single-purpose board to develop with a focus on housing while the central department had a wider remit. It enabled judgements on application and the interpretation of public policy to be made by individuals who had some degree of independence from government and it meant a delegation of authority that reduced the executive decision making of ministers and their immediate mandarins. Finally, the implementation of public policy may well have been enhanced because it was undertaken, at board and executive level, by individuals who were committed to the delivery of the housing service and who brought considerable energy and imagination to it.

The critiques of quangos, having led to strengthened approaches to their accountability, have been eroded to some extent. At the same time the failures of central government departments make the alternative to quangos such as the Housing Corporation less savoury. Their direct control through central government departments would exacerbate the apparent inability of those departments to cope with the volume and variety of business that they have without making serious errors. This has become a feature of much of the debate about the operation of government in Britain, the best example being the Home Office, which was described by an incoming home secretary as 'not fit for purpose' in the early 2000s. This does not provide a good foundation for arguments that quangos should be drawn back into the bosom of central government and Westminster.

There is a separate argument about the proliferation of different agencies where the public is not clear of what their roles are. In the housing sector there was one single NDPB operating as the agency of government in relation to housing, and in the future there will be two. This is a relatively simple and straightforward arrangement. The Housing Corporation's regional offices did not have independence from the parent. There is a proliferation of housing associations, but most of them are long-established and well founded bodies;

the regulatory process itself was centred on the Housing Corporation and will rest in future with the Tenant Services Authority. The argument about whether we should have a plethora of housing associations is not the same as the argument that applies in some other areas of governance, simply because they are long-established independent organisations with a diversity of functions and with organisational and professional capacities of different types. Indeed some of the argument in recent years has been more about concern that the growth in the size of housing associations and the tendency for mergers between them may have reduced their diversity and attractiveness.

This is almost turning the argument on its head and recognising that the question needs to be approached in a different way in 2008 than it would have been in 1974 or 1984. The strength of the governance of housing in 2008 is in the variety of different organisations with different cultures, skills and resources. Of course this can be overstated and too many small organisations may be ineffective, but the debate starts on the other foot. It is a debate about the benefits of having alternative suppliers of rented housing with different strengths rather than a single local alternative in the local authority or even a single alternative to the local authority in one large housing association.

Changes in governance

Discussions of government and policy in Britain in the past tended to focus on central government and its relationship with local government. Government was done by the state centrally and locally. It was an uncomplicated and self-evident reality that generated studies focused on Parliament, legislation, the civil service, the administration of government and, latterly, accounts referring to local politics and policy. Discussions of government and policy in Britain today are very different, emphasising the range of organisations involved in policy and capturing the difference by referring to governance rather than government.

The policy changes of the 1980s, associated with the governments of Margaret Thatcher, have been referred to in a variety of ways in the academic literature. It is generally argued that the Conservatives embarked upon a programme of change to public policy designed to roll back the state. The traditional role of the government in welfare provision was changed, in addition to privatisation, through the creation of new private, quasi-public and voluntary bodies with tasks in delivering welfare services. This is part of the shift from government to governance, from government directed by the state to governance through a wide range of partners working with the state. In this new governance there is debate about whether the government is still steering or has a less critical role in a partnership enterprise.

Some commentators have also referred to the hollowing out of the post-Keynesian welfare sate. This implies that the state has experienced a loss of control over the policy arena and effective management of the public sector precisely because it reduced its role in directly delivering services. Much of the debate about the reorganisation of government relates to the extent to which the state has expanded and centralised its activities or withdrawn and shared its activities with others. This hollowing out of the state refers in particular to the extent to which activities that used to be provided directly by the state are now still the subject of public policy but are no longer directly provided by the state. These activities are provided through national agencies or at a local level by a variety of different bodies, including some that have been set up specifically for that purpose by the government (such as urban development corporations, housing action trusts and others), that represent a reorganisation of government activity with conscious outsourcing and the development of competitive tendering.

It is not the purpose of this book to review these arguments in any general sense but rather to comment on where the accounts of the Housing Corporation or of the development of housing policy connect with them. At one superficial level the involvement of a large number of housing associations and of an arm's length public agency, the Corporation, would appear to fit with a model of the hollowing out of the state. Rather than direct public provision, perhaps through local authorities' council housing, the state has moved to provide its housing services and to carry out its housing policy through a large number of independent or semi-independent organisations, so emasculating the local state but also losing direct control over what happens. However, in the housing field there are some contradictions in this position.

The debate about the hollowing out of the state is connected with the neo-liberal agenda promoted in the 1980s and is presented in contrast to the Keynesian management of the economy in the early years of the post-war welfare state, which sought to redistribute economic activity, and the benefits of economic activity, regionally. In this Keynesian era the government sought to manage the whole economy and to introduce a planned hierarchy of places. In contrast the neo-liberal agenda set up different places as competitors with one another and the state withdrew from attempts to redistribute or equalise in favour of competitiveness at a regional and urban level.

Mark Goodwin (2004) argues that the policies pursued by Clement Attlee's government in the immediate post-war period involved evening out spatial differentials in terms of employment, housing, transport and other civic amenities. Uneven geographical development was linked to uneven social development and the aim was to reduce both by using all of the land in the best interests of the whole. Moreover, this was to be achieved through a comprehensive programme of policies aimed at reducing spatial disparity. Goodwin refers to a series of policies which underpinned this but emphasises planning and regional policies. He refers to the development of positive planning associated with the control of land use White Paper of 1944 and followed by the employment policy White Paper of 1945. He refers also to the Distribution of Industry Act, the New Towns Act, the Town and Country Planning Act and the National Parks and Access to the Countryside Act. The combination of these was seen as an effective and detailed attempt to deliver a redistributive agenda backed by the power of the national state in relation to interest rates and fiscal policy. Goodwin concludes that the result was a set of integrated policies which had a definite vision of the urban at the core. This was a vision which saw the city as an integrated whole, although made up of distinct communities and neighbourhoods, in turn being integrated into its wider regional setting. It was a vision which was based on a particular understanding of the nature of the urban problem and hence solutions to it. The problems for cities were socially and politically constructed and essentially physical in nature: overcrowding, sprawl, poor housing and derelict land. The responses were also physical: urban containment, new and overspill towns, inner urban redevelopment and regional balance.

While this is a compelling argument the weakness is in the detail. There is a danger of constructing an image of a much more comprehensive and coherent public policy framework than existed in practice. There is some inconsistency between the image of a highly integrated and co-ordinated attempt to restructure urban areas and the reality of the way housing policy was organised. The assumption of comprehensive micro-management does not fit with the way housing was provided in the early post-war period.

MacKenzie and Grove (1957) provide an account of the organisation of the Ministry of Housing and Local Government at that time. They state that the ministry was one of those which in the post-war period greatly extended its organisation in the regions so that in effect it had nine geographically organised branches, each physically located in its area and acting as first filter for much of the business from that area. In 1954, by which time there had already been some contraction in staff from the post-war period, there were still regional offices of substantial size although these too were to be reduced in 1955 and 1956. The weakening of the regional organisation had occurred at an earlier stage (MacKenzie and Grove 1957: 409). But it is also apparent that when it came to housing central government's approach was laissez-faire throughout. While it determined the thrust of housing policy and the scale of the national programme and introduced new legislation, it was local authorities that were the leaders of the housing drive in the post-war period. And it was left to local authorities to decide how much they did and of what type. Dame Evelyn Sharpe, writing as a former permanent secretary in the MHLG, said:

> Except in relation to the number of houses they may build local authorities probably enjoy in relation to housing greater independence of Whitehall and more freedom to develop their own policies than in any other major service. In tenant selection, rent fixing and general management they have complete discretion. Ministers are frequently pressed to intervene in this subject but are usually glad enough to disclaim responsibility. General advice is given to authorities from time to time but they are free to go their own way and do. These are indeed matters which must be settled locally but the degree of local independence does not make it any easier when it comes to trying to meet housing needs which often have no relationship to local boundaries. Similarly the sale of subsidised council houses to tenants, although requiring a minister's consent, has until recently been left to local discretion by means of a general consent. (Sharp 1969: 74)

Central government did not exercise detailed control over what happened in housing. In housing there was already a hollowed-out state with a greater dependence on local authorities and a willingness at the centre for them to be energetic or lethargic, and the role of the private sector was significant throughout. Even when the public sector housing programme was at its height and building licensing operated, some new building was provided for the private sector and private builders were involved in completing contracts for the state. In addition the majority of older housing was still privately owned. The managed system in housing involved management with, and of, the private sector.

This mixed economy of housing still represented policy that was directly orchestrated by the state. However, it is a very different position than the representation of a highly concerted and co-ordinated Keynesian agenda. Similarly, when we come to look at the changes in this arrangement they do not quite fit with the hollowing out of the state model in other respects. There were already housing associations involved in providing housing at an early stage and even more so following the explosion of new housing associations in the 1960s. As has been stated already this means that the new third-arm alternatives to direct state provision were not creatures of the state or the direct products of new legislation and new policy. Housing associations and the Housing Corporation grew and strengthened in the environment of the neo-liberal hollowed-out state but they were not simply the products of it. Their route to playing a major role in housing is a slightly different one.

Rather than being an account of hollowing out the state or losing centralised control to a wider governance agenda, the housing story is one in which the early years were marked by a relatively relaxed agenda from the central state and an acceptance of enormous local variation that was hardly compatible with a systematic and integrated urban planning approach. This was followed by a period of centralisation of policy from the 1970s, where the variation in activity by local authorities was seen as a source of difficulty and the desire to reduce expenditure and restrict municipal enterprise resulted in a reduction in resources to local government and a concentration of power in the nationalisation of policy at a central level (Murie 1985). At this stage some money was leaking out to housing associations but their real growth came slightly later on, after the emasculation of council housing with privatisation through the right to buy and the beginning of Large-Scale Voluntary Transfer. Only then was the sharing of resources among a wide range of non-governmental bodies, the housing associations, through the Housing Corporation, achieved. Arguably this, combined with the growing importance of regional housing strategies, represents a stronger urban planning and regeneration agenda than had existed in the 1980s and 1990s.

None of this means that the arguments about the hollowing out of the state are incorrect, it merely suggests that the housing service does not always fit with generalised theoretical propositions about the way that government and governance have changed in Britain. A closer examination of housing suggests either that it follows a distinctive course or that the grand models of changes in governance need some adjustment before they are completely effective. Hollowing out is virtually synonymous with a loss in governmental control, due primarily to the emergence of a plethora of agencies and organisations now involved in policy making and implementation. However, in the case of housing generally it could be argued that more recently, in spite of the plethora of agencies and organisations, there has been greater governmental control than there was in the early post-war years. Aulakh (2004) argues that the way the housing service developed in the period of supposed hollowing out is more complex than this theory suggests. The traditional provision of housing was replaced by new areas of activity, most notably around holistic provision, integrating housing with a range of other social and economic activities. This is an explicit attempt to reposition housing as a focal point from which to create cohesive communities and address problems of social exclusion. In this way the role of the housing department in housing management has become broader, not more limited.

While the local authority shares its activities with increasingly powerful housing associations, it is not clear that it is fundamentally less powerful, because it has changed its relative role; and central government has become more powerful with a stronger articulation of its demands through government offices, the regional development agencies and the regional assemblies. The role of these regional actors through regional housing strategies and in influencing the allocation of resources is much more fully developed than in the past. The synergy between a regional spatial strategy joining up with local planning strategies and a housing and economic strategy has begun to mean a much greater orchestration of what is happening locally by the agencies of central government. This hardly fits with a view of hollowing out. Perhaps what it involves is a continuing loosening of control over end-point delivery in the implementation of policy but a much more co-ordinated and powerful control over strategic decisions related to the levels of investment in different places. Local government is weaker in relation to central government but government remains a dominant player in the local arena. As Aulakh argues, it is time to shift the paradigm of the alleged weakness of state control to one that is more sensitive to its domination and centrality in the policy-making and implementation process.

A different perspective on this is provided by Hadley and Hatch (1981), who argued that the increased expenditure on social policies in the 1960s and 1970s did not yield the results that were expected. In response to this failure of the state, the government embarked on a series of inquiries and reforms, particularly large-scale reforms in the management of local government, the personal social services and the NHS. Hadley and Hatch argued that there was very little to suggest that the public, as users of the institutions concerned, were an important source of pressure for change. Such evidence as exists of general public attitudes implies either satisfaction, particularly with the health service, or indifference, especially as regards local government (Hadley and

Hatch 1981: 58). However, at least some of the professionals and administrators running the services favoured radical changes.

The reforms that followed in these three areas of government are generally grouped together as representing centralisation. The most ill-starred major reorganisation was that of the health service (Hadley and Hatch 1981: 77). In 1974 the tripartite organisation created when the NHS had been set up (in 1948), consisting of hospitals, local authority health services and family practitioner services, was replaced by a national pyramid in which all of the separate services were unified. At the base were district management teams, over them area health authorities and at the pinnacle the secretary of state. The reorganisation was a massive and costly operation which subsequently came in for devastating criticism. It may be argued that subsequent attempts to remedy the defects of this reform have generated increasing levels of dissatisfaction with bureaucracy, administrative costs, accountability and systems of control and have brought the health service into general disrepute.

These developments are referred to in the context of the Housing Corporation for two reasons. Firstly, housing escaped this particular form of reorganisation and centralisation much as it had escaped the reorganisations associated with the immediate post-war period. While Malpass and others have tended to see the failure to reorganise in the 1940s as symptomatic of a lack of real commitment to a continuing housing programme, it seems possible that the escape from the reorganisation fashionable in the 1970s was a more fortunate one. Privatisation and other developments mean that centralisation certainly applied to housing but there was no hierarchical restructuring of the type described for the NHS. Indeed Hadley and Hatch, in referring to alternative ways of organising the highly centralised social services that are the focus of their study, draw attention to the different experience of housing. They comment that, although the voluntary work component in housing provision is very small compared with, say, personal social services, the government made a deliberate decision to develop a more plural pattern of provision. Instead of relying almost exclusively on local authorities to provide rented accommodation, substantial resources were directed through the Housing Corporation to housing associations. While most of the accommodation provided by housing associations conformed closely to the standard set for local authorities and was managed in a conventional way, the significance was in the variety of providers and the inclusion of different types of landlord, including specialist associations and housing co-operatives. Housing escaped the reorganising tendency of the

1970s and Hadley and Hatch argued (1981: 159) that in so far as a national superstructure is required it should take on the character more of the kind presented by the Corporation.

It is not the purpose of this book to pursue the argument that the Housing Corporation is a model for organising other services. Indeed the specificity and distinctiveness of housing services makes it very difficult to transfer experience to areas which involve very different kinds of relationship with consumers and delivery of very different services. However, it can be concluded that the existence of the Corporation and housing associations may have protected the housing sector from some of the experiments in centralisation that would otherwise have existed. Rather than representing this as a grand plan, it is more likely that the pragmatism of government planning meant that, by the time the grand-design reorganisations of the 1960s and 1970s came onto the agenda, the housing sector had a sufficiently complex and well-functioning pluralistic structure as to look like an unattractive arena for experiment.

When the Housing Corporation was set up in 1964 it was not seen as a mechanism to promote pluralism and see off centralising tendencies. Nor has it in fact seen off all centralising tendencies, but it has channelled any such tendencies in particular directions. By the 1980s and later the organisational strength of the Corporation and housing associations proved one of the best protections against technologically or ideologically driven reorganisation. The diversity and plurality of the system became a source of strength in itself. Perhaps it is also worth considering the extent to which this Housing Corporation-managed system achieved high levels of efficiency and avoided the major crises that were associated with some elements of the centralised services adopted in other areas of policy. In recent years NHS trusts, which accumulated enormous deficits, or had to lay off staff, or cease to carry out serious operations, have been regarded as demonstrations of mismanagement and the failure of forecasting and effective working. By comparison housing has managed its realm extremely effectively.

Hadley and Hatch conclude their discussion of the tendency for centralisation by suggesting that there are seven important assumptions which dominated government circles in the 1960s and early 1970s:

- The feasibility and desirability of the standard solution.
- Major changes in the organisation of the service should be planned and introduced by central government.
- Larger organisations are likely to be more efficient than smaller organisations.

- Management of public services will be most efficient if designed on scientific, rational principles.
- Users' role in the management of social services and local government should be marginal.
- Efficiency is more important than democracy.
- Major changes in organisation can be successfully designed and introduced without prior testing on a smaller scale.

It is this conventional wisdom that housing substantially escaped. It may be argued that not all of these axioms are still generally accepted in government circles. However, some of them are and some of them have continued to dominate the approach to the management of public services. Some of those which would be denied in the rhetoric of government may still effectively continue to operate, in particular those related to user engagement and democracy.

The housing service, emerging from decades of management through a governance system involving different central government departments, the Housing Corporation and local authorities as well as a diverse range of housing associations, is much less easy to typify in terms of this kind of dominant agenda. While the promotion of efficiency and economies of scale may be seen as indicating an underlying tendency to move in this direction, the complexity and diversity of the housing sector means that at the same time there are examples of blossoming smaller organisations which capture the headlines because they do a very good job and bear effective comparison with the organisations that are deemed to have the benefits of economies of scale and management efficiency.

Conclusions

This chapter has suggested that the Housing Corporation as the key housing quango and housing associations as local quangos have some distinctive characteristics in terms of their role and origins and that these affect how well the existing critiques of (largely local) non-elected bodies apply to them. These differences in origin and the complex arrangements to improve accountability do not mean that they are in any way superior to bodies that have developed in other areas of government. However, it is important to recognise that while they may not be superior they are different and have their own strengths and capacities; they are diverse, have their own histories and traditions which continue to influence the way they operate and (with the exception of the Housing Corporation) have boards that are not directly appointed by government – although in some cases boards may be appointed by methods that equally lack transparency, as when they appoint their own successors.

Again this does not mean that housing associations are not associated with the problem of the democratic deficit – the absence of both an electoral process and other mechanisms through which the public can influence the body and hold it to account. Board accountability in housing associations is not through ministers to Parliament and accountability locally is not always transparent. The models of governance that have been promoted may be too technical and deferential and too much based on a hierarchical private sector boardroom model – and insufficiently informed by the experience of more inclusive traditions of working-class, membership and mutual organisations. These latter may be more effective if the real involvement of tenants and residents at board level is desired. Leaving this aside, it is inaccurate to represent housing associations as always beyond the influence of local communities. Housing associations have been subject to regulation through the Housing Corporation and are open to the inspectorate of the Audit Commission and the operation of the housing association ombudsman. All of these elements provide significant opportunities for the citizen or the tenant to seek remedy for grievances, which may be felt just as strongly as those felt by many in relation to the activities of services run by elected local and certainly central government.

While the development of quangos in other areas of public policy is relevant to what has happened in housing, a different timescale has been involved. The housing service included non-elected organisations, housing associations, well before the development of the modern welfare state. And the new housing associations that came into operation, for example in the 1960s, were not generated by legislation or the demands of central government; indeed they rather emerged because of the failures of legislation and of government policy in relation to inner city and older housing. The Housing Corporation was set up not in this environment of appointed administrations replacing elected bodies, but in a period in which local government had an increasing role and increasing budgets to provide housing services. The Corporation's role was complementary rather than one of replacement.

Over time the Corporation and the housing associations were no doubt used to achieve demunicipalisation within the housing sector. This involved reducing the role of local government in the direct provision of housing through the transfer of stock to housing associations and through the channelling of the new-build programme towards housing associations rather than local government. But even then the government made use of a set of organisations that had grown up in a different environment. It did not construct a new set that bore no relation to local communities. The Housing Corporation itself was dependent on the capacity of the housing association sector. This sector's variety means that the Corporation itself supported diversity rather than a single type of preferred local agency. One major risk for the future is that this tradition may come under threat.

12

Conclusions: changing direction – governance with competition

Introduction

The aim of the final chapter of this book is to consider the implications of the history of the Housing Corporation for the future of housing policy and the governance of housing. Initially it reflects upon the changing role of the Housing Corporation and its partners and against this background considers its achievements. This is followed by a commentary on the changing environment for housing policy and the revival of interest in housing by government. The final section offers some conclusions arising from these various elements.

The changing role of the Housing Corporation and its partners

This book has described the emergence of a distinctive set of arrangements governing housing policy and delivery in England – with the broad pattern, although not the detail, applying elsewhere in the UK. These distinctive arrangements did not emerge as part of a radical plan in the early post-war reconstruction period, or as part of the critique of the failure of the state in the 1960s and 1970s and the associated reorganisations applying new public sector management fashions to different areas of service. They emerged following the choice by central government to leave housing to local government. The central department adopted a laissez-faire approach: it emphasised building targets and identified priorities within the housing agenda rather than a detailed strategy related to the various dimensions of housing provision. So central government would focus on promoting slum clearance, new high-rise building or low-cost home ownership but did not have the inclination or capacity to address the rest of the agenda. It had traditionally left this to local authorities, which developed their own distinctive approaches and left different legacies that reflected that.

Different towns and cities are variously associated with legacies from a strong planning tradition; an innovative approach to private sector house improvement; strong links with housing associations providing for homeless households; or effective housing provision for households with special needs. Locally accountable elected local authorities used their powers and interpreted their duties differently. Not all were energetic builders or inspectors and enforcers of standards in the private sector. While the discussion of how best to address the housing problems in the 1960s defended the role of local authorities and emphasised the need for more resources, the shortcomings of local authority stewardship of housing were also apparent – especially in the failures related to slum clearance policies and strategies to address homelessness.

The expansion of housing associations at this stage was a response to policy failure. The establishment of the Housing Corporation at approximately the same time was aimed neither at addressing the same problem nor at replacing the local authority role. It has been argued that the Corporation's initial direction, with a narrow focus on cost rent and co-ownership housing provision, was inappropriate and that it was its transformation into an agency with a wider role in housing in 1974 that really established it as a key part of the policy system.

The earlier chapters of this book have outlined the Corporation's changing activities. While it has always been an agency of government and involved in working with housing associations, its investment role has changed:

- starting with a distinctive role promoting new forms of tenure and attracting private finance, but well away from the main agendas dominating housing at the time;
- moving to the mainstream of policy with a dependence on public expenditure in improving of older property and supporting fair rent accommodation and special-needs housing;
- supporting a greater mix of housing interventions, including affordable home ownership and rented housing but still principally involving public expenditure;
- developing and promoting a new mixed public/private funded programme including affordable home ownership as well as statutory rented housing, where rents were regulated under statute and by policy but no longer subject to statutory control;

- alongside other activities, overseeing the transfer at a positive value (or, if at a negative value, with direct public funding to write off debt and fund catch-up repairs) of a significant part of the council housing sector to housing associations working with mixed public/private funding.

The early contribution of the Housing Corporation, supporting the development of cost rent and co-ownership housing, lost momentum and the co-ownership legacy was obliterated through sales after 1980. Provision for co-ownership sales was included in the Housing Act 1980 and has been included in subsequent Housing Acts (latterly the Housing Act 1996, Section 8). As well as the 861 societies which have completed sales to members, a few societies have met their end by other means – including conversion to conventional co-operatives and transfer of engagements to another registered social landlord. In 2008 there were eleven registered co-ownerships on the Corporation's books (including one originally funded by the Public Works Loans Board), eight unregistered co-ownerships and six registered local authority co-ownerships. In addition six societies had completed sales (included in the 861 total) but had not yet completed the steps necessary to secure removal from the Corporation's register.

Of the nineteen societies still functioning as co-ownerships, one was due to complete sales in 2008, two were actively considering sales, two had restrictions on their head leases which prevented sales, thirteen had no interest in sales amongst their members, and one was not a viable option because it had experienced major structural and repair problems causing high levels of vacancy and necessitating significant further borrowing.

The Corporation's investment role moved to other activities, following government policy but also the energies and capacity of housing associations, but it is important to recognise that some of the prominent housing associations operating in 2008 trace their origins back to the cost rent and co-ownership era (Malpass 2000: 139).

Through its life the Corporation's regulatory role became wider and deeper. It moved from a policy of registering cost rent and co-ownership societies to a more comprehensive coverage of housing associations and to a more thorough statutory approach to regulation, performance management and promotion of risk-based management. In this process it developed different relationships with housing associations – from a distant position representing the enemy for many associations, there was a process of regulatory capture involving closer relationships at least for some. This gave way in turn to a more formal regulated competition.

Large numbers of agencies were involved in housing throughout this period. This applies centrally (with, at the very least, the department responsible for housing, the Treasury, the department responsible for housing benefit as well as the Housing Corporation itself) and locally (with adjacent local authorities and large numbers of housing associations with shared territories); it applies within the housing sector (with public and private agencies and professions all specialising in different aspects of service delivery) and to its near neighbours (including planning and all those whose services shape neighbourhoods and affect whether dwellings are attractive to live in). There are different ways of typifying this situation. In one sense it is flexible and responsive. In another it represents a fragmented structure, unco-ordinated and competitive. It lacks the command-and-control characteristics that characterised the public sector-led procurement associated with earlier periods.

The dominating influence of local authority housing procurement that was apparent in 1964 was no longer visible in 2008. While local authorities in many cases still have substantial housing stocks, they have declined with the right to buy, and in many cases local authorities have transferred their stock completely to housing associations. Those local authorities which still own housing are preoccupied with meeting the Decent Homes standard, investing in the refurbishment of existing housing and better managing of that housing, either directly or through arm's length management organisations. Although there had been a very small increase in the amount of new council housing building, it remained of minimal importance in 2008. The power of local authority housing departments, their architects and engineers and indeed of the local authority as a whole, associated with its procurement of council housing, had shrunk dramatically or even disappeared. The local authority roles related to housing construction that have grown in importance are those of planning and economic development associated with the disposal of local authority-owned sites and wider development planning.

In considering questions about quangos, agency relationships and governance, there is a temptation to seek formulas that apply to all services, irrespective of local context, at all times – a search for universal rules. In practice, and drawing disproportionately on experience related to housing, such universal rules do not exist. The discussion of policy options in 1964 was vastly different than in 2008. Society and the economy have changed and the housing market with them. Housing services continue to be shaped principally by the legacies from the past and new investment only incrementally reshapes what is available – perhaps 1 per cent of the housing stock each year is new

Table 12.1: Housing association global accounts: balance sheet, £ million

		1999/2000	2005/6
	Fixed assets		
	Housing properties at cost or valuation	46,512	74,033
less	Capital grants	-24,193	-30,856
less	Depreciation	-219	-1,378
	Net book value of housing properties	22,100	41,799
plus	Other fixed assets	1,466	1,927
	Total fixed assets (A)	23,566	43,726
	Current assets		
	Cash & short-term investments	1,633	1,357
plus	Non-liquid current assets	127	1,097
plus	Other current assets	820	2,158
	Total current assets (B)	2,580	4,612
	Current liabilities		
	Short-term loans	259	569
plus	Bank overdrafts	39	47
plus	Other current liabilities	1,472	2,713
	Total current liabilities (C)	1,770	3,329
	Total assets less current liabilities (A + B - C)	24,376	44,890
	Long-term creditors and provisions		
	Long-term loans	15,169	28,924
plus	Other long-term creditors	297	1,623
plus	Provisions	37	787
	Total long-term creditors and provisions (D)	15,503	31,334
	Reserves		
	Total reserves (E)	8,873	13,556
	Total loans, provisions and reserves (D + E)	24,376	44,890

Individual figures have been rounded to the nearest million. Totals are derived from unrounded numbers and may not equal the sum of the rounded numbers.

Source: Wilcox (annual).

Table 12.2: Housing association global accounts: income and expenditure
1999/2000–2005/6, £ million

	1999/2000	2005/6
Income from social housing lettings		
Rents receivable, net of voids	3,742	6,588
Service charges	452	561
Charges for support services	0	220
Grants from local authorities and others	265	388
Housing Corporation revenue grants	117	12
Housing Corporation major repairs grants	9	16
Total income from social housing lettings	4,585	7,785
Net income from other activities	–38	21
Surplus on disposal of fixed assets	109	536
Total income (A)	4,656	8,342
Operating expenditure		
Management costs	916	1,601
Maintenance costs	849	1,806
Major repairs expenditure	449	1,041
Service costs	751	914
Care/support services	14	264
Other costs	376	824
Total operating expenditure (B)	3,355	6,450
Interest and other income and expenditure		
Interest payable and other similar charges	1,150	1,671
less Interest receivable and other income	–175	–147
Net interest payable (C)	975	1,524
Other charges (D)	53	48
Total expenditure including net interest charges (E) (B + C + D)	4,383	8,022
Surplus for year before tax (F) (A – E)	273	320
Tax payable (net of grants) (G)	13	10
Surplus for year after tax (F – G)	260	310

Source: Wilcox (annual).

dwellings. Housing also is a fixed, immobile asset and each dwelling strictly has a unique location. To that extent, unlike cars or washing machines, no two dwellings are the same. Even if this pure definition is relaxed, it is clear that differences in estate, neighbourhood or broad location affect the desirability and value of dwellings. In some services these things are less important. For social security it may be argued that place is unimportant and uniform benefits can be offered anywhere and be altered overnight. The problems of managing and delivering an effective medical care system are more affected by less flexible elements to do with the construction of hospitals or the availability of qualified staff, but it is still arguable that treatment is not transformed by where it is delivered to the extent that applies in housing.

Table 12.3: Dwellings below the Decent Homes standard in England: percentages of all dwellings by tenure

Tenure	1996	2001	2003	2004	2005
Social sector					
Local authority	53.9	41.7	39.6	34.9	33.7
Housing association	47.6	33.1	28.8	26.2	23.8
All social sector	52.6	38.9	35.3	31.3	29.2
Private sector					
Owner-occupied	39.7	29.2	27.7	26.6	24.9
Private rented	62.4	50.7	47.5	42.6	40.7
All private sector	42.6	31.9	30.2	28.7	27.1
All tenures	44.7	33.3	31.2	29.2	27.5

Source: Wilcox, from English House Condition Survey 2005.

Any evaluation of the performance of the Housing Corporation is made more complex by this. Key issues relate to how far it, together with its partners, was able to be flexible and innovative and to take account of different market contexts and the requirements of different communities. At this level evaluation would need to be at a fine-grained level, referring to particular cities, towns and neighbourhoods. Such an evaluation is beyond the scope of this study. Nevertheless it is possible to refer to important dimensions of performance.

At the close of the Corporation's operations the value of the fixed assets of housing associations was in excess of £43 billion (see Table 12.1). Housing associations together presented a very healthy balance sheet. The Corporation's income and expenditure account was equally healthy (see Table 12.2), while the condition of its dwelling stock was also better than in the past and better than in other parts of the rented sector (see Table 12.3). The regulatory code requires housing associations to meet the Decent Homes standard by 2010 and they are expected to pay for this from within their own resources. It is evident that housing associations and local authorities are in a better position and making more progress in meeting this standard than is the private rented sector.

Achievements and failures

Throughout its life the Corporation worked with a large and diverse set of organisations, principally with the sponsoring department, which changed its name and key contact personnel repeatedly, and with housing associations. It was initially involved in Scotland and Wales as well as England and reference has been made to its success in supporting the emergence of a distinctive approach in Scotland. In this context Walker et al. (2003) contrast the experience of tenants once they are housed. In England and Wales the Corporation promoted consumerist approaches that involved providing tenants with information about their landlord and opportunities for involvement and decision making. In Scotland, by contrast, tenant governance and a community-based housing association model was seen as the norm. Although only 24 of the 196 registered associations in Scotland were actually community based, managing 18 per cent of the association stock, their influence was much greater and 82 per cent of Scottish associations had tenants on their management committees. In practice many associations which were not technically community-based housing associations shared their local focus and limited ambitions for expansion. Walker et al. (2003) suggest that historically the Housing Corporation in England found this model of involvement more problematic and had greater difficulties in accommodating tenant-controlled organisations and co-operatives.

There are examples of the relaxation of the centralising tendency in England and reference has been made, for instance, to developments in Liverpool, the promotion of black and minority ethnic (BME) associations and actions to grow associations through federal structures, such as in Leeds. The development of joint commissioning and encouragement of closer working with local authorities and through regional housing strategies has also been apparent. The investment in research to evidence the case for housing market renewal and the support given to the development of proposals in this area also demonstrate that there was some capacity to break away from a 'one size fits all' approach. But they are not examples of building capacity that would support sustained distinctive approaches comparable with the Housing Corporation in Scotland. And none of them has the tenant at its heart. Baroness Dean's concern that the Corporation was not very tenant oriented in the past is difficult to dispute.

The actions taken by the Corporation in relation to black-led housing organisations provide important lessons that connect with agendas about sustainable communities and regeneration. The Housing Corporation had success in its strategy to respond to the lack of attention paid to BME communities by many mainstream housing associations by promoting the formation of black-led organisations. But this does not appear to have impacted on the ways that other associations worked and was not sufficiently resourced either through investment funds or capacity building to create a large group of associations that could be sustained independently. Race equality issues have not gone away and the shift to emphasise that all housing associations must be more aware and have proper policies and strategies and practices has not strengthened the position of black-led organisations. The black-led associations themselves went through changes as key individuals who were experienced in terms of managing moved on. Although the Corporation still supported them and continued to meet with the Federation of Black Housing Organisations, without ring-fenced funding the support was not manifested in terms of money, which is what black-led associations wanted in order to increase their stock of housing. Government policy also began to move against race-specific projects and the emphasis shifted to community cohesion, sustainable communities and shared values. Where black-led associations merged with larger associations they were no longer so visible and the black housing voice was reduced.

Initiatives to respond to the demands or needs of particular groups or mixed communities living in particular areas are not easy to promote or deliver but they may be even harder to sustain once the difficult tasks seem to have been done, as key personnel leave and policy priorities change. Agendas about efficiency and economy can too easily become formulas that are applied irrespective of the distinctiveness of communities and places.

Within the housing association movement there were organisations (especially the larger ones and those based in London) that built closer links with the Corporation and those that were more distant. The dialogue with the National Federation of Housing Associations/National Housing Federation was an important one throughout. Beyond this inner circle of partners there was a wider policy community including other government departments, private sector financial institutions, local authorities, regional partners and, latterly, English Partnerships. As the activities of the Corporation and of housing associations changed so the key stakeholders changed. For example, liaison with lenders was a major activity between 1964 and 1974 and again after 1988 but was less prominent in the period of public subsidy dependency; and the nature of regional stakeholder involvement changed with the development of regional housing statements and then strategies.

Against this picture of changing roles and relationships with other agencies it is possible to outline achievements and lessons related to the operation of the Housing Corporation over its life cycle. Initially it is important to emphasise the extent to which the outputs and outcomes and even processes associated with the Corporation are the result of co-production with its partners. As has been discussed earlier, the Corporation needed its partners to deliver what was planned; and in turn its partners needed it. There are two cases where this general argument breaks down. The first is where housing associations had no ambition to invest and the rigours of registration and regulation were seen as an unnecessary or undesirable burden. This is not to deny that investing housing associations would have preferred a less rigorous or burdensome regime – but that these associations saw that they gained from working with the Corporation. Consistent with this view is the one that the Corporation was only as good as its partners and vice versa. The second case where the general argument set out above breaks down is where the financial relationship between central government and the Housing Corporation was dysfunctional. This relates to insufficient lead times in announcing financial allocations, unexpected cuts in allocations leading to inefficient programming and in some cases drastic curtailment of activity, and the annual basis of allocations and performance assessment. The Corporation had a remarkable record of almost always spending almost all of its allocation within the financial year – matching its spend to its allocation much more closely than either central or local government departments. However, some of the devices used may have meant that best value for money was not always achieved or the level of subsidy was not transparent (e.g. where social housing grant was given on schemes negotiated with builders under the planning legislation and including affordable housing as a condition of planning consent). The move to three-year financial allocations was a very important step, enabling the Corporation to manage this dilemma (whether to underspend or to spend less efficiently).

There have been assessments of the Housing Corporation in the past and the periodic departmental reviews gave positive verdicts on its performance. They also continued to support the co-location of regulation and investment activity. Lewis and Harden commented (1982: 126–7):

In the 1960s ... the largely middle-class preserve of co-ownership schemes temporarily occupied a central position in the work of the Corporation. Its priorities, its powers and its working context within the wider housing field were all to change, more than once. Even a seasoned bureaucracy with a clear professional self-image would have needed a steady hand to negotiate these changes with any success. New goals for new clienteles among the public were to be sought by new policies and working routines. No ready supply of experienced people existed outside the Corporation: on the contrary, the movement looked to the Corporation. In this most challenging situation the tendency to recruit a certain number of returning colonial expatriates lacking either the organisational or the housing experience required in this body compounded the problems of growth and policy uncertainty.

Lewis and Harden went on to suggest that the big success of the Housing Corporation was in delivering, and being able to respond to, the government's increasing demands for output – especially in later years in the numbers of new dwellings. Their biggest reservation was that

within the total supervisory scheme of the DoE plus the Corporation, short-term financial considerations have tended to predominate. If allowed to continue this could lead to the spread of unlettable flats and the creation of new categories of housing difficulty, to say nothing of the damage to general community cohesion. (Lewis and Harden 1982: 136)

In the Corporation's subsequent development the work and staff changed out of all recognition but the issues related to financial timescales continued to be of concern. The ability to deal with regulatory matters and to ensure that there were no disasters, and to do this in house without interventions from ministers and civil servants, was also consistently referred to in any commentary on the Corporation. Its role was more than simply a negative agency role, for it brought new things to the table or added to the things that were being passed down to it.

Table 12.4 sets out a long list of achievements associated with the Corporation and includes a brief reference to any specific dimensions. In many cases these achievements are double edged – they may be expressed in a less positive way – and the table identifies any such alternative perspective. In some cases the negative perspective may have a stronger provenance than the positive one. Such cases are included at the end of the table.

The table highlights the contested nature of many claims about the Corporation. In many cases what is being claimed may appear to be second best. The list of achievements should not be taken as a list of things that the Housing Corporation and housing associations are intrinsically better equipped to deliver than, say, local authorities. Whether, under different circumstances, local authorities could have matched these achievements is not at issue here. In an ideal world local authority housing would have been better funded and the necessity for the Corporation or housing associations to be involved would have been less: the level and certainty of investment would have been higher and consideration of stock transfer would have taken place in a more balanced financial and political environment – where the pressures from central government and the financial advantages were less skewed towards transfer. But in the reality of the political, economic and public expenditure context of the time these ideal alternatives did not exist. In this way achievements can be assessed only against the background of what was possible at the time. Table 12.4 does not refer to the Corporation's operation of a system of delegations that it was not empowered to operate, as discussed in Chapter 8. There are different views of this failure – it may be seen as a failure of legislation rather than of the Corporation. It may also be considered that decisions to acknowledge and address the problem represent an achievement.

Table 12.4: Achievements and failures of the Housing Corporation

Achievements		Reservations
Building organisational and financial capacity in the not-for-profit sector	The Corporation directly fostered the formation (especially through co-owner-ship and stock transfer policies) and growth of important housing associations and built strong relationships with housing associations and. By 2008 it had experienced, competent, professional staff and the organisational and financial attributes that enabled them to play an active part in leading new development and regeneration activity	In some cases this has been at the expense of the local authority sector and so the net gain is less than it appears

Operating successfully within the agency framework	The Corporation maintained a good working relationship with ministers and civil servants and was able to exploit opportunities for innovation in relation to processes and products as well as in the detail of policy administration	It was too constrained by the agency relationship
Successfully meeting spending targets	In only a few years (especially 1989/90) was this not achieved	Some value for money issues remain
Successfully resolving problems with poorly managed associations	No housing association tenants lost their homes because of association business failure and the Corporation managed merger or other processes to deal with any problems	Against the undoubted benefits, the costs of this practice to the public purse, individual organisations and the recipient remained unclear
Maintaining the confidence of lenders	The Corporation achieved this even in the light of periodic problems experienced by individual associations and through the delegations crisis of 2006	
Developing an effective regulation system	The Corporation developed a system that had the confidence of lenders and others	Some questions about regulatory burden and costs
Developing effective rules and procedures for investment	The Corporation enabled investment to be managed and monitored effectively	Some specific failures and questions about value for money
Being an effective promoter of delivery of policy	The Corporation translated inadequately specified policies into fully specified and workable investment and regulation activity, generating direct benefits for households in need	Having less impact on policy formulation

Enabling an active improvement of the older housing stock	The Corporation enabled the shift from slum clearance and the house improvements after the legislation of 1969 and 1974 to take off	Some mini-HAG developments were to very low standard and the older stock improved to what was to be a thirty-year life standard is prominent in the low-demand problems thirty years later
Developing high-quality housing for letting at low or affordable rents	The Corporation developed new build for rent from 1974 subject to different policies on rents. In order to meet the needs of households at all stages in the life cycle it incorporated the Lifetime Homes standard in later years	A limited attention to design quality and size in earlier years and tendency to favour smaller units rather than larger dwellings more in tune with aspirations and suitable for bigger families
Developing models for mixed public and private finance that enabled further growth in the provision of rented housing	Without this the willingness of government to invest in housing would have been reduced and private finance would not have been so significant	This involved higher rents and created the mechanism for privatisation
Maintaining and enhancing a diverse housing association sector and through this potentially providing choice within the rented sector	Particular innovations were related to co-ownership societies, community-based associations, BME associations and new stock transfer associations with different governance arrangements	Some of the associations promoted proved short lived and later pressures for mergers worked in the opposite direction, reproducing the monopoly landlord associated with local authority control and in some cases even larger and more distant landlords
Maintaining and enhancing a strong special needs and supported housing activity	Specialist housing and housing associations	Slow integration of specialist services into provision by general needs housing associations including stock transfer associations
Responding to the needs of homeless households and the badly housed	Nominations and allocations policies	In some cases this has contributed to problems associated with concentrations of households in a similar position

Mitigating the risks associated with demunicipalisation	The Corporation enabled demunicipalisation to be achieved without losses to the rented sector and with proper guarantees of standards of landlord behaviour. The alternative was transfer to profit-making landlords who were poorly regulated through recourse to the courts	Accountability issues have not been successfully addressed and may have become more problematic where more 'private sector' business models have been adopted
Promoting a variety of low cost home ownership products and enabling wider access to home ownership	IFS, shared ownership, DIY shared ownership, HomeBuy, right to buy, right to acquire	Most of these products achieved limited uptake and were costly to promote and deliver
Maintaining investment in affordable and social housing in an often unfavourable environment	Consistency of meeting spending and other targets	
Being able to respond to opportunities to increase the programme	Year-on-year increases as well as extraordinary opportunities such as the Housing Market Package of 1993 were managed effectively	The Housing Market Package also generated tensions and problems for the housing association sector
Enabling effective contributions by housing associations to regeneration and wider neighbourhood initiatives	Housing Plus, Estate Renewal Challenge Fund and other examples	Some elements of operation (e.g. conversions and disposals of properties) have made regeneration more difficult

Failures *Mitigation*

Failing to anticipate or act effectively to avoid an increasingly residual role for housing	The Corporation disregarded the evidence related to this	The drivers of residualisation were beyond the control of the Corporation
Facilitating a centralisation of housing policy	The Corporation created the opportunity for policy passporting with significant (often unidentified) costs in some cases	Policy passporting is beneficial to tenants at least in some cases

Failing to develop an effective co-operative sector	This was a prominent aspiration from 1964 and especially in the later 1970s	Co-operatives lack a strong (British) tradition that can be built upon, have to be supported at ground level and cannot be imposed
Failing to develop a strong regional capacity that would anticipate changing demand and the distinctive housing situations associated with different regions and sub-regions	Regional offices existed throughout but only developed a distinctive approach in Scotland	There were periods when there were more serious attempts to build regional strength
Contributing to the fragmentation of local governance and of local ownership of property by housing associations	Patterns of disposal and investment often have little spatial logic and make effective neighbourhood management more difficult	Some stock rationalisation has taken place recently

The revival of housing policy

Housing policy now has a long pedigree in Britain. In more than 100 years it has passed through different phases and attracted different levels of priority and support. At various stages governments have been unwise enough to declare the housing problem largely solved or reduced to particular local problems and pockets. The 1980s and 1990s were associated with deregulation, demunicipalisation, privatisation and an assumption that the government's role would change but also diminish as it became an enabler (at local and central levels) rather than a provider. It would provide the framework within which the market would be able to deliver the housing that was needed. Housing had already dropped down the list of policy priorities and, with the government limited to its new enabling role, was not likely to climb back up. In practice this has not proved true.

As has been outlined previously, in the early years following the election of the New Labour government in 1997 there were very limited changes to housing policy. However, housing policy subsequently stepped up a gear with a Green Paper, the Sustainable Communities Plan, and responses to a series of reviews by Kate Barker and others. The policy priority remained very clearly with home ownership and enabling but there were concerns that new supply was not coming forward as a sufficient response to the demand for housing. This was exacerbating affordability problems, which in turn were damaging for economic performance and international competitiveness. The Barker reviews identified the planning system in particular as contributing to this situation and in effect recommended changes to the framework within which builders and developers could respond. In practice two different versions have emerged of what the housing problem is. One is couched in terms of sustainability, and includes issues of mixed communities, segregation, concentrations of deprivation and neighbourhoods that are dysfunctional in certain ways. The other solely emphasises the supply of housing and an apparent link between supply and price, between price and the ability of first-time buyers to enter owner occupation and between high housing costs and the performance of the UK economy.

As housing has moved up the political agenda again, it is not clear that the majority of people see it as a problem. Those who are satisfactorily housed may not recognise the housing problems faced by others and indeed, in many cases, have a vested interest in a continuing appreciation of house prices. In many cases they also are reluctant to see the housing crisis solved by new building near to them. The 'not in my back yard' view means that you cannot leave the housing crisis to local government. But central government, because it lacks the knowledge and understanding of what is happening at the local level, is unable to develop the most appropriate responses. The strength and diversity of organisations committed to resolving the conflicts that exist around housing are constantly being tested in this environment.

By 2007, with a new government led by Gordon Brown, housing policy had risen towards the top of the agenda. For the first time in many years, the housing minister, although still not a Cabinet member, attended Cabinet. The Barker review remained the touchstone for policy. While it noted the failure of the private sector to fill the gap left by the reduction in public housing construction and articulated the case for a limited revival in the building of social rented housing, its main message was the need to increase overall housing supply. There was a stronger case for investment in social rented housing, but not at anything like the level that had existed before 1980. The reviews carried by John Hills and Martin Cave did not suggest a renaissance of social rented housing or ambitious programmes for new building and regeneration, and the view that the planning system was the obstacle to solving the affordability crisis continued to dominate. Housing was much higher up the political agenda but the policy being pursued was essentially the same: it was still dominated by home ownership and would continue to reinforce the trend that had created not only greater differences between tenures but, more importantly for future policy, greater inequalities within the home ownership sector. By 2007 the right to buy had almost run out of steam. Changes to discount rates, the declining numbers of stock transfer tenants with a preserved right to buy and the rise in property values meant that the numbers of properties being sold under the right to buy had diminished very considerably. The government was introducing new HomeBuy schemes to provide shared ownership options for council tenants and others who were unable to access mainstream home ownership (ODPM 2005) but sales under Social HomeBuy were very low (Murie and Rowlands 2008). In 2007, for the first time since 1979, new building in the social rented sector exceeded sales of social rented dwellings to owner-occupiers. It is against this background that a new housing Green Paper and new legislation were prepared (see Chapter 9).

Market strengths and weaknesses

Although this book has noted the increased importance accorded to housing over the last decade of the Corporation's life, the most important driver of the housing market in that period was not housing policy. Economic growth and a long period of high employment, rising incomes, and stable and low interest rates and inflation were more important and fuelled a long house price boom. In a period of low direct taxation, households on high incomes experienced a considerable growth in income and saw housing as the best hedge against uncertainties, inflation and old age.

After a downturn in the early 1990s, rapid house price inflation and an 'affordability crisis' characterised the period through to 2007, when relatively small increases in interest rates and, more importantly, the international credit crisis emanating from the USA brought them to a halt. Up to this point, low interest rates, the experience of the appreciation of property values and the favourable record of investment in housing compared with investment in pensions or stocks and shares fuelled overconsumption. Inelastic housing supply meant that the increased willingness to invest in housing largely generated a growth in prices and this growth was uneven. It was highest in the more buoyant economic areas and in areas where dwellings were of better quality or higher status, or could be relied upon to command higher rates of appreciation and to be good investments.

Essentially, the consequence of the government's new housing policy (and its continuing emphasis on market provision), operating against the background of deregulation of financial institutions, much greater income inequality and differential ability to borrow and to spend, was house price inflation and increased social and spatial inequality. A larger, more differentiated home ownership sector became a characteristic of the society: rather than an aberration, it was a predictable consequence of a succession of policies operating in an economy based on unequal reward systems.

It is important to note three other responses in this situation. Firstly, the house-building industry responded to the pressures from government to build more (and to measures to secure affordable housing through the planning system) by shifting to build apartments and smaller properties. The new politics of urban housing involved central and local government, developers, planners and the architectural establishment in support for high-density, brownfield and inner urban housing that took pressure off greenfield sites and avoided the political opposition to such development (Murie and Rowlands 2008). There was considerable growth in apartments, which had not previously been a significant part of the built environment in England except in London. The balance between houses and flats in new residential construction in England shifted from 79:21 in 1991/2 to 60:40 in 2004/5.

A second effect linked to change in the building industry and the increased investment capacity of affluent households was the growth of the buy-to-let market. Deregulation of the private rented sector in the late 1980s was expected to lead to a revival of private renting. Because tenants had fewer rights and there was no control over the rents that were charged, landlords were no longer deterred from investing in property to let. However, in the initial decade (up to 1997) following deregulation, there was little sign of significant growth or the development of a new private rented market. The new market that began to emerge in the second decade was less explained by deregulation itself than by new practices among developers, lenders and investors. There has been a considerable increase in the buy-to-let market especially through the purchase of apartments and the growth of second-home ownership. The growth of the buy-to-let market could again be seen as a natural accompaniment of a buoyant home ownership market and the view that investment in land and property was the safest and the most likely to bring the best rate of return. The practice of developers in selling apartments off plan has also been identified as favourable to the investment purchaser (see Murie and Rowlands 2008).

Thirdly, it is important to recognise the different ways in which the individual consumer has reacted to the affordability crisis. There is some confusion in the housing research literature in England. There are contributions which emphasise the impossibility of ordinary households meeting the thresholds required to buy properties. And yet these thresholds only exist because people actually do buy the properties. The year 2007 saw record net lending at a time when affordability problems affected first-time buyers. How do we explain rising house prices if nobody can afford them? Perhaps the research community is looking in the wrong direction? It is looking at first-time buyers and people on average incomes and seeing them as unable to pay large prices when it should be looking at more affluent groups with higher incomes and dual incomes and with an ability to pay more for housing or even to purchase more than one property. It is this group that is able to buy properties at inflated prices and exacerbate the affordability crisis for others. In between these two groups, there are those who adopt all sorts of mechanisms which enable them to bridge the gap. They borrow much more than the multiples of incomes that government and researchers suggest are appropriate. This may not always present a problem, because they use mortgage products that have lower interest repayments in the initial period or they rely upon the fact that their incomes rise rapidly in the occupations that they work in and the proportion of their income represented by mortgage payments declines rapidly as their income rises – down to a level that is much more acceptable to the researchers' instincts. We also know that people borrow from friends and family, are helped by other family members, make use of savings and inheritances, purchase on a joint basis, make use of credit card and other borrowing to manage budgets that are stretched by mortgage payments and so on. Of course, this leaves a larger number of people at risk if interest rates rise or if they lose jobs or their relationships break down.

The long boom in house price increases came to a sudden and unpredicted end in 2008 as the housing market entered an unprecedented crisis. Patterns of lending for house purchase in the USA had changed for various reasons, including government minority home ownership programmes, and there was a growth in sub-prime lending to lower-income groups using low-start and variable interest loans. While interest rates were low these loans were affordable and there was a boom in borrowing, some of which was financed by British and other international banks. When interest rates rose and sub-prime borrowers were unable to meet mortgage repayments (especially once the initial rates had given way to full rate payments) there was a crisis both in the US housing market and for the lenders exposed in that market – including British lenders. The 'credit crunch' that began in the USA impacted severely on British banks, which were faced with a crisis in financing their existing mortgage portfolios – and were unable to take on significant new business. Banks which borrowed internationally to finance the loans they made were unable to find such finance, or else its costs were much too high. In this environment lenders in Britain had to revert to rationing mortgages, largely withdrew from the buy-to-let market and sub-prime lending and became much more conservative in lending generally. First-time buyers, who had previously been able to borrow more than the value of the property they wanted to buy, would be offered less than the value (75 per cent was often referred to) and had to find the balance elsewhere. With first-time buyers and buy-to-let purchases dramatically reduced, builders found they could not sell what they had already built, so sale prices fell and builders stopped building more. The numbers of transactions in the market overall halved and the government's targets shifted from increasing building to maintaining building activity at a lower level. It is not yet clear how these market patterns and the long-term behaviour of builders, consumers or lenders in Britain will be affected by the credit crunch but the expectation in 2008 was that the effects of the crunch would be severe for a further two years.

The credit crunch was brought dramatically to life with the collapse and subsequent nationalisation of the Northern Rock bank. This collapse was not directly attributable to its involvement in international (North American) borrowing but arose because of its reliance on borrowing from other financial institutions to finance its loans. When this market collapsed, not only was it unable to finance new loans but it could not refinance its existing loan portfolio satisfactorily. Hit by the collapse of the US market, Northern Rock was faced with significant losses; a run on the bank followed, which drew the central bank (the Bank of England) and government in. Following this, and with continuing problems in obtaining funds to finance loan portfolios at competitive rates, lenders generally have become more prudent. As a consequence the costs of funds increased sharply and savings rates were increased to attract funds, borrowing became more expensive and borrowers became more circumspect. Lenders will no longer lend on demand or lend sums that represent such high proportions of property value. House price inflation has given way to decline, builders have found it more difficult to sell, especially where they were overdependent on speculative and buy-to-let pur-chases. One consequence is that, against the intention of policy, new housing supply through new construction seems likely to decline. Rather than moving towards the Barker-based targets of 240,000 completions a year by 2016 (a 30 per cent increase from 2006) completions in 2008 will show a decline and are expected to be nearer 120,000 and may be even lower in 2009. The weakness of the Barker-based perspective on housing and the overselling of the market-led, supply-driven solution is evident from this.

While affordability has been presented as a crisis, it is endemic when incomes are unequal and this inequality impacts on house prices. Prices that are driven by higher incomes, not surprisingly, move beyond the reach of those on lower incomes. In practice this was a manageable crisis for government and for many householders. The increased supply of credit also helped to mask the underlying problem. It presented an opportunity for those who could buy and whose properties appreciated in value and it was certainly much less of a crisis than a lack of demand or a lack of house price inflation, which begins to generate a reluctance to buy and sell, negative equity and the problems associated with the late 1980s. It is this prospect that faces some households following the credit crunch. The affordability crisis also generated fewer concerns about repossession and mortgage arrears than the situation following the credit crunch.

The credit crunch presents a new challenge for housing policy. The market before the crunch was making the major contribution to meeting housing need and demand – but was not doing enough. Consequently the government had begun to be drawn in to a more active policy to increase supply. Deregulation and privatisation had not enabled the government to disengage and relax as the market responded in its new environment. But with the credit crunch the prospect was of a significant reduction in activity – just at the point that the government was seeking an increase. If the government's housing targets were to be met it now looked as if it would need an even more interventionist strategy and would need to use its agencies to achieve this. The most obvious impact of the credit crunch on the Housing Corporation in its closing phase was the announcement by the Prime Minister in May 2008 of a £200 million package to buy up homes from builders and developers. Although this amount falls short of the 1993 Housing Market Package, especially in real terms, it demonstrates again the value of the agency to the government. As the problems within the house-building sector increased, the possibility that a larger rescue package would be needed was also apparent. Concern that the private housing market would not recover quickly and that this would affect the volume of transactions and new construction also led to suggestions for new interventions by the government to guarantee mortgage finance and so enable lenders to finance their mortgage portfolios through wholesale lending. The larger cross-government package of new measures to meet housing market challenges announced in September 2008 focused on home ownership and support for the house-building industry. It included a £400 million boost in spending power for social housing providers by bringing forward funding from 2010/11 to 2008–10.

Taking stock

The housing market in England after an era of privatisation and deregulation involves a much smaller state sector than in the past and higher levels of home ownership. However there are some elements that merit further comment:

- The social rented sector remains large by European standards. The organisational and financial strength of social landlords in England as well as their share of the market leaves a strong interventionist tradition and capacity closer to Dutch or Scandinavian systems than to neo-liberal, wholly market-based, systems.
- The growth of home ownership has been moderated by transfers from owner occupation to renting and by the growth of investment in private rented housing; these have reshaped the market in ways that were not anticipated by policy makers. At the same time the tenure has become 'stretched', with greater distance between the top and bottom of the market. Those at the bottom are often in a position more comparable with social rented tenants than with home owners in the high-status, high-price market.
- New private housing construction has not increased to fill the gap left by reduced public investment and this problem has been exacerbated by the credit crunch. There is both an overall shortfall in rates of new building relative to demographic growth and a disproportionate invest-ment in smaller high-density apartments.
- The expectation that deregulation and privatisation would mean that the state withdrew from housing has proved false. In the short term problems emanating from the credit crunch frustrate this expectation but in the long term it is only achievable with a dramatic reduction in local planning powers that would put the interests of builders and developers into direct confrontation with those of existing residents.

- There has been a divergence in neighbourhood trajectories related to the growth of private renting and the stretching of the home ownership market. While some areas remain almost exclusively home ownership enclaves there are few that are solely social rented. The least attractive and aspirational areas have seen the lowest growth of home ownership and the greatest transfer from home ownership to private renting. These areas have low-income households but weaker neighbourhood management as the ownership of rented housing has become more fragmented.

- Privatisation has not simply transformed neighbourhoods into mixed home ownership and social rented areas but has achieved varied outcomes with some areas of more fragmented rented ownership. These trends may become more marked in the future as resales of properties sold under the right to buy increase with the ageing of original purchasers.

- The diversity of housing associations has increased and the transfer of council housing to the housing association sector through Large-Scale Voluntary Transfer has enormously increased the importance of the non-municipal part of the social rented sector. But this, as well as different development strategies, leaves associations with very different resource levels and desires to engage in regeneration, address neighbourhood problems and management or increase tenant and resident involvement in these activities. In some cases the legacy from the past activity of housing associations (as with other housing providers) may need to be modified.

- The focus of government thirty or more years ago was still upon meeting housing needs as part of the traditional approach associated with the post-war welfare state, providing housing where there was a demand for labour or creating the conditions for social harmony. Government interest in housing appeared to decline in the 1980s and 1990s but has increased subsequently. There has been increasing concern about economic competitiveness and the impact of housing on it, the economic consequences of housing market development, affordability problems and the failure of the deregulated system to deliver the quantity of housing needed. In the recent phase of housing policy, council housing continues to be a declining, residual sector and the wider social rented sector has also declined in proportionate terms. Market processes dominate the housing sector more than at any time since 1939. England is a nation of home owners although the continuing growth of home ownership is no longer assured. The polarisation between the social rented sector and home ownership has reached a plateau or perhaps has bottomed out. Because the population remaining within the social rented sector as a whole is so predominantly a low-income population, there is no room for it to become more residual: indeed the profile of tenants is likely to change. At the same time the ageing of the population in owner occupation introduces relative residualisation into that tenure by increasing the number of low-income households. In addition the emphasis upon regeneration and the competitiveness of cities has begun to change the nature of the social rented sector in other ways. Considerable expenditures are involved in modernising estates and the concern is to create mixed-tenure older or newer estates. A different policy philosophy associated with the competitiveness of cities sees a stigmatised, ghettoised social housing sector as undesirable and seeks to redress that by restructuring the social rented sector rather than simply leaving it to decline. But intervening effectively, going beyond expressing such a philosophy and actually delivering, is an outstanding challenge.

At the same time the owner-occupied market is changing dramatically. It is becoming increasingly differentiated and there are clear divisions of home ownership related to differences in the types of property that are owned, the rights and responsibilities associated with ownership (leaseholders and freeholders), the value of the property, its location and the extent to which it provides access to a range of other services including schools. Affordability problems have also become commonplace. The significance of housing is no longer simply as a source of shelter but relates to access to other services and to the accumulation of wealth.

If we are to understand what is happening to housing policy in England we need to set the debate up to recognise the centrality of home ownership, not just to housing policy but to the government's approach to welfare provision and a wide range of services. Owner occupation, not social housing, is at the centre of housing policy and indeed of the new welfare state (see Groves et al. 2007; Murie 2008). We have moved away from a welfare state that emphasises citizens' rights, away from a preoccupation with universal benefits, uniformity of benefit and equality of treatment. We have moved towards a welfare system which seeks to encourage individuals to make provision for themselves, especially through savings and the acquisition of assets. The government is concerned to encourage home ownership as part of that asset-based welfare system and recognises that inequality is an inevitable dimension of such a system. The asset-based welfare state is essentially one that has abandoned equality of provision, although it may seek to encourage everybody to save and to own.

If inequality and affordability are endemic then policy responses are unlikely to eliminate these issues. Affordability problems will be a continuing feature of the housing provision system in England. If they ever went away they would be replaced by an even bigger crisis of housing market collapse and negative equity. Except in these situations it will be the norm to have prices rising at rates which suit some but not others. The challenges for policy will be how to maintain that buoyant market, which gives confidence to the mass of the population and retains their political and electoral support, and at the same time give some hope to those falling off the ascending escalator and those not on it at all. Rather than chase housing supply in the hope that this will dampen affordability problems, it may be better to recognise that affordability problems are endemic (except in periods where there is an equally damaging crisis) and address the needs of households unable to compete in this environment. The agenda then switches back to building more affordable housing targeted at this group. Within this framework it is still possible to promote pathways to home ownership but it may be best to first of all enable people to access housing and address their subsequent route through the system afterwards.

It is reasonable to argue that the Housing Corporation in its old guise was insufficiently equipped to operate effectively in this new environment. The wider remit of the Homes and Communities Agency (HCA) reflects the concern to do more than build dwellings – to have a planned economic impact, to participate in and help shape the creation of sustainable communities, whether they are newly built, are flourishing older communities or involve renewal and regeneration activity. The era of policy marked by new organisational arrangements including the creation of the HCA in 2008 may prove a watershed. It is not a reversion to the period of domination of housing by public sector procurement associated with investment in council housing between 1919 and 1979. But nor does it represent a system in which local authorities and government essentially bowed out and left housing to the market. While they have an enabling rather than direct provision role, the enabling role is far from being the passive long-stop anticipated by some following deregulation and privatisation. Indeed the legacy of the period in which housing had low priority in public policy and was being left to the market is one in which the shortcomings of that approach are evident. The backlog of disrepair associated with underinvestment in social rented housing has begun to be addressed through

Decent Homes and other investment policies. But there are still problems of homelessness and bad housing (with sub-standard homes again being more associated with the private sector), overcrowding has increased, there is greater insecurity of tenure, projected household growth is in excess of the rate of new building, housing shortages are increasing and there is a now deeply entrenched crisis of affordability affecting the options of lower-income households in particular. The reduction in public sector housing investment in the period from the mid-1970s onwards did not release the market as anticipated. The experiment with withdrawal from an active housing policy left a legacy of problems and failed to deliver the continuous improvement in living standards that might be expected to be associated with a stronger economy and greater wealth. At the same time the unsatisfactory nature of important parts of all tenures demonstrates that the proposition that housing problems are solved by promoting council housing or home ownership, or indeed any tenure, is false. Changing the balance of tenures does not address the problems that exist within them.

Housing in 2008 has, against the expectations of many, risen even further up the political agenda. This is partly because of the flawed legacy from the previous era but also because of the increased importance attached to housing wealth within the modern welfare state and to housing choice in economic performance. In the past there has been a somewhat instrumental view of the role of housing in the economy. The conventional wisdom was that it had little significance except in ensuring that there was a labour force that was healthy enough to play its role in production. Changes in the structure of employment and the economy, in participation in employment and in transport and commuting have altered the perception of the importance of housing. In the new knowledge-based economy, enterprises are less locationally constrained by where labour or raw materials are plentiful. Rather than being a necessary requirement in places where employment has been generated through exploitation of other assets, housing is one of the assets that helps to drive the economy. The emphasis then shifts from minimum standards for the health of the labour force to neighbourhoods of high-quality homes that are diverse enough to attract and retain people with different lifestyles, aspirations and choices and be a key building block for economic growth.

These kinds of consideration highlight the need for housing providers to recognise that, as well as processes of physical obsolescence that render properties unsuitable for use, there are processes of social obsolescence and of choice that affect the demand for housing. Just as a dwelling that was once highly desirable may deteriorate physically over time and become much less desirable, so there are dwellings that may remain physically sound but no longer meet the aspirations of households seeking housing. Some dwellings (and particularly houses) can often be extended and adapted sufficiently to reposition them in the market but others are not so easily recycled. The challenge for a new agency focused primarily on the social rented sector or on providing affordable housing is made no simpler by these developments. It will too easily be open to the criticisms that have at various stages been levelled at council estates – that they house people who do not need such housing because they could afford to buy; and that they are ghettos for the poor and damage life chances. The escape from these opposites is presented as the mixed-tenure estate – the implication being that mixed tenure will enable the social rented housing to be targeted on those with lower incomes and in need, while the presence of other tenures will prevent the development of the ghetto. But this is an untested hypothesis and goes against at least some evidence. Older mixed-tenure areas in English inner cities as well as council estates which now have mixed tenure because of the right to buy continue to have high concentrations of deprivation. Where the housing and the estate are unattractive because of dwelling type and mix, estate design and layout, location or poor local facilities, including schools and other factors, mixing tenures will not attract many middle-income households in. Where new estates are involved, such middle income households will move in and buy only if the quality of the development is high. Sustainable developments are likely to be mixed tenure but must also be high-quality attractive developments and that has implications for costs. It also emphasises the need for effective and close working between different stakeholders – at regional, local and neighbourhood level.

The role of the successor bodies and housing associations in the future will be to add to the supply of housing but also to address the problems associated with the least attractive parts of the rented sector, to engage with neighbourhood management and regeneration and to connect with environmental issues. There will be a need for greater ambition in developing regeneration and remodelling options for the worst estates. It will also be necessary to address the limitations of the Decent Homes agenda (and the problems of estates and dwellings that remain unattractive even after the Decent Homes standard has been achieved), problems associated with segregation and overall affordability.

In rethinking the role of social housing and the wider contribution that can be made through its development and management, there are a number of other important opportunities that could be taken advantage of for lower-income households. The explicit attachment of the social rented sector to energy efficiency would reduce heating bills and benefit those least able to afford high energy costs as well as making an important contribution to environmental strategies. Higher subsidies to achieve this kind of objective need not be reflected in higher rents especially if account is taken of the disadvantage that tenants have in relation to asset appreciation. The social rented sector should be seen as a mechanism for achieving regeneration, improving social cohesion and strengthening civic renewal and local democracy. The key agencies can be catalysts for change and landlords are part of the capacity and continuity to achieve better management in urban and rural areas. In this sense the agenda is more than about housing, it is about estates and social regeneration agencies, community equity trusts, better neighbourhoods and wider management of space. In this context the merits of smaller and more patch-based social landlords or new forms of co-operative embracing greater tenant control should be explored.

Lessons and issues

The new agencies taking over responsibility from the Housing Corporation and others will be operating against the policy background outlined above and can also draw upon the knowledge of the achievements and failures of the Corporation. While none of the issues faced may strictly be new ones, they will come in different forms and present different challenges. Among the wide range of issues that could be considered, some relate to the ending of co-location while others relate to the opportunities associated with a new start.

Table 12.5 refers back to the matters previously identified as achievements and failures and briefly outlines the lessons that flow from these. Essentially they are how to build on achievements and avoid the repetition of failures. While these are tasks that need to be shared between government and other agencies, an indication of which of the new agencies being set up in 2008 has the key role is provided.

Some of the issues referred to above require some further explanation and this is provided under eight headings.

Sponsors and agents
Much of the discussion of the experience and success of the Housing Corporation has referred to the agency relationship between the Corporation and its sponsor

Table 12.5: Learning from the achievements and failures of the Housing Corporation

	Implications	Responsibility
Achievements		
Building organisational and financial capacity in the not-for-profit sector	Recognise the importance of organisational and financial capacity used in conjunction with other local and regional bodies	Both TSA and HCA
Operating successfully within the agency framework	Both the sponsoring department and agencies must develop a shared view of the most effective way to work together (see below)	Both TSA and HCA
Successfully meeting spending targets	Maintain focus on meeting targets and on value for money	Mainly, but not exclusively, HCA
Successfully resolving problems with poorly managed associations	Capture previous experience to do this effectively	Mainly, but not exclusively, TSA
Maintaining the confidence of lenders	Maintain dialogue with lenders	Mainly, but not exclusively, TSA
Developing an effective regulation system	Periodically assess relationships and regulatory capture	TSA
Developing effective rules and procedures for investment	Capture previous experience relating to investment and value for money	HCA
Effectively promoting delivery of policy	Develop regional and sub-regional capacity and understanding of markets (see evidence base below)	Both TSA and HCA
Enabling active improvement of older housing stock	Maintain asset management approaches	Both TSA and HCA
Developing a model for mixed public and private finance that	Maintain the model but with a continuing scrutiny of costs in	HCA

enabled further growth in the provision of rented housing | provision and use (including rents, service charges and energy costs) and with a concern to build high-quality dwellings |

Maintaining and enhancing a diverse housing association sector and through this potentially providing choice within the rented sector | Adopt a strategy that recognises and tracks the different types of provider including bodies providing specialist housing | Both TSA and HCA

Responding to the needs of homeless households and the badly housed | Maintain strong relationships with local authorities and monitor new lettings but also address issues of segregation and concentration | HCA

Mitigating the accountability risks associated with demunicipalisation | Maintain strong regulation but also develop new ways of addressing accountability issues | TSA

Promoting a variety of low-cost home ownership products and enabling wider access to home ownership | Review and rationalise in the light of realistic identification of costs of provision and costs for the (often marginal) owner-occupiers | HCA

Maintaining investment in affordable and social housing in an often unfavourable environment | Maintain planning horizon of three years or more; fund acquisition of strategic sites; maintain commitment to regeneration projects over a longer timescale (e.g. Estate Renewal Challenge Fund, New Deal for Communities, market renewal areas, growth areas and equivalents that follow these) | HCA

Being able to respond to opportunities to increase the programme | Ensure that there is capacity to respond to short-term changes in the market and, in some cases, building the market | HCA

Enabling effective contributions by housing associations to regeneration and wider neighbourhood initiatives	Develop long-term funding arrangements	HCA

Failures

Failing to anticipate or act effectively to avoid an increasingly residual role for housing	Make social rented housing (and the neighbourhoods they are in) attractive; promote quality and mix of properties; develop estate- and area-based regeneration initiatives with strong socio-economic as well as housing elements; develop effective neighbourhood management	HCA
Facilitating a centralisation of housing policy	Develop strong regional capacity and local engagement	Both TSA and HCA
Failing to develop an effective co-operative sector	Evaluate the potential of new forms of organisational governance and funding in a new environment	Both TSA and HCA
Failing to develop a strong regional capacity	Develop strong regional capacity and local engagement; develop robust regional evidence base	HCA
Contributing to the fragmentation of local governance and of local ownership of property by housing associations	Develop incentives to encourage and achieve rationalisation; ensure investment patterns do not increase fragmentation	HCA

department in government. In Chapter 10 it was argued that this generally operated in an effective way, enabling the Corporation to develop procedures and practices that rendered the broad policy agreed with the department more effective in practice. Nevertheless there were episodes and inclinations towards more detailed scrutiny — sometimes of matters such as staffing and salaries — that were regarded as unnecessary, diversionary or misconceived. The HCA will have wider investment-related responsibilities and a larger investment budget than its predecessor. It will accumulate more knowledge and expertise than its sponsoring department, especially if it works effectively with local authorities and builds real expertise within regions. Logically this would mean redrawing the boundaries between agent and sponsor – perhaps more along the lines of a subsidiary operating in the private sector. Continuing liaison and dialogue will be essential, and in relation to policy may need to be enhanced, but it will be necessary for the sponsoring department to withdraw from detailed operational monitoring. The Tenant Services Authority (TSA) will also have a separate and new set of relationships, with both Communities and Local Government and the Department for Business, Enterprise and Regulatory Reform.

The distinctiveness of the housing market in London should be mentioned. It has a completely different structure, with a much larger privately rented sector and a smaller owner-occupied sector. Its house prices are dramatically higher than those in other cities and affordability problems and maintenance and repair problems are very different as a consequence. The London case highlights the need for a differentiated approach to policy – just as the Scottish experience is testament to the effectiveness of such a differentiated approach in the past. And it is important to recognise that many of the regions of England have populations that are larger than that of Scotland. Evidence-based policy in relation to housing is likely to suggest the need to develop different policy frameworks for different market situations. It may also be that the greater involvement of the regional development agencies (RDAs) provides a framework which could support further devolution of decision-making. Implementation of the government's *Review of Sub-national Economic Development and Regeneration*, published in 2007, anticipates a change in the structure and delegation of strategies. The question will be whether ministers and civil servants located at the national level enable their high-level framework to be implemented flexibly and responsively at regional and sub-regional levels. The dominant instincts of the civil service in relation to notions of precedent and fairness lead it to favour a national approach but if evidence-based consideration points in a different direction these instincts may have to be suppressed. The cynical view would be that the evidence-base for policies will not cut much ice, or there will be an attempt to generate evidence which either supports the policy preference or mystifies the picture.

Evidence-based policy
The changing nature of housing markets and issues of competitiveness suggest the need for the next phase of housing policy to be more based on evidence

than hitherto. Peter Malpass has argued that the rise of housing associations in the past should be seen as incremental and opportunistic (Malpass 2008). More generally housing policy in England includes major departures and experiments based on hunches and simplistic theoretical assertions, without any examination of evidence to suggest that they would be successful. Rent decontrol in the 1950s, slum clearance, encouragement of high-rise building and the right to buy were all flagship policies pursued without evidence-based preparation. There was an active denial either that residualisation of council and social rented housing was taking place, or that it mattered, and the failure to properly plan for and anticipate the low and changing demand that became the key to Housing Market Renewal and housing interventions in large parts of the Midlands and north of England is testimony to the lack of investment in research and development activities commensurate with the importance of the policy area. Where research is completed it is not clear that it has any influence on policy. Other than recurrent surveys, the research commissioned by the department has been sporadic and not comprehensive, predicated on a national picture and rarely robust enough to be useful at a regional let alone local level. There are strongly held views that it fits with the preferences of some civil servants for policy-based evidence rather than the collection of evidence from which to develop policy.

In many cases the evidence that does exist is contested or unclear or can be interpreted in different ways. It consistently suggests that there are wider impacts of policies or there are consequences which need to be addressed elsewhere in the policy framework. Much of the evidence related to housing highlights the different contexts and environments in which housing policy operates and calls into question the appropriateness of trying to introduce the same policies in very different markets and environments. The ways in which the HCA translates research into practice and the development and use of research in the sub-national review context will be critical. But there are anxieties: the RDAs and regional observatories have tended to give very little attention to housing and lack specialist expertise; and the Housing Corporation's Centre for Market Research and Intelligence is to be located within TSA.

In the next phase of housing delivery this record has to be improved. While some national data collection may be best left with the central department it is more appropriate to develop capacity at the regional level, closer to the users and most informed interpreters. Scotland could be seen as providing one model for the English regions. In Northern Ireland the Northern Ireland Housing Executive has been responsible for house condition and continuous household surveys as well as a wide-ranging research programme and this may be a useful model. The much larger English regions could emulate this performance and work with other regional actors, within the context of integrated regional strategies, to build evidence at a regional and sub-regional level both to inform and to evaluate policy. The principal customers for any regional and sub-regional evidence base will include RDAs, the regional housing bodies and the HCA at a regional level. Evidence-based approaches to policy in housing seem most likely to work where they are strongly supported and championed by influential organisations and where the evidence is available at the time that decisions are being considered – in the absence of evidence some other, perhaps reactive, basis for policy development is used.

Regions and markets

The new agencies are to be national agencies and a key issue is how far they apply a common formula to an increasingly uneven housing market where there is a need for very different interventions. In future a single integrated regional strategy will embrace regional housing, economic and spatial strategies and will provide the framework for housing policy experiment and delivery. This can stimulate best practice and exchange of experience in a way that can increase the value for money and effectiveness of spending within any region. But for this to happen the HCA centrally must have the same confidence and provide the same support as was forthcoming in the Scottish case. Just as the central department must recognise when its scrutiny and control moves from prudent and constructive to disabling and destructive, so the HCA centrally will have to exercise the same type of restraint in relation to the regions. Strong well-staffed regional offices with capacity to build and challenge evidence and to innovate are essential if the opportunities associated with housing investment, regeneration and neighbourhood management are to play a full part in future regional and sub-regional strategies.

Rents and housing costs

Tenants lack control over rents and because of the importance of rents not only for household budgets but for benefit expenditure, this is an area where decisions are to be made in the future by ministers. However, again there will be important issues of liaison and this should not prevent different regional strategies related to rents. A single national formula does not take account of the different markets operating in different parts of the country. In addition there are issues related to service charges, council tax and energy costs that need to be considered along with rents. In a period of high energy costs energy-efficient dwellings will have a profound effect on the budgets of lower-income households as well as being consistent with wider sustainability agendas. But higher investment to facilitate this efficiency may only be achievable if grant levels are allowed to bear some of the cost and if the pressure to reduce construction costs are moderated by such considerations. These will be issues for both the HCA and the TSA.

Divisions of responsibility

Whatever view is taken of the reasons for splitting regulation and investment functions, it is important to recognise the challenge that the division will present. In this context it is interesting to note Anthony Mayer's response to the argument that in order to minimise any potential conflict of interest, regulatory and funding responsibilities should be split. He said:

> There is an argument of principle here. How can I properly be accountable to the secretary of state and to Parliament for £20 billion of taxpayer funds invested in registered social landlords unless I can ensure that their stewardship lies in safe hands? There is also argument of practice: our funding and regulatory roles reinforce each other. We can turn off the funding tap if the performance of a registered social landlord is unacceptable. And our regulatory roles enable us to ensure that registered social landlords who receive public funding are suitable recipients of it. (Mayer 1998: 117)

Those who had been involved with the Housing Corporation in the past tended to share this view. Splitting regulation from the actual operations of the business was seen as highly dangerous and difficult to achieve in practice. To be a regulator there is no particular need to be deeply involved in the management of the sector – so the Financial Services Agency (FSA) does not need to be desperately involved with the Bank of England – but the reverse is not true. For the Bank of England to do its job, it needs to be absolutely au fait with what are the ten biggest worries in the mind of the FSA. The implication of this view is that not only does there have to be a strong dialogue between regulator and investor but the investor can only do the job effectively on the understanding that there is attendance at occasional key committees of the regulator. Without this the investor lacks the intelligence required to make the right decisions. In addition the chief of the funding agency and the chief of the regulatory agency have to get on together and be constantly in communication to ensure that they have a shared understanding of key issues. There is a need for a relationship in which both parties check with each other if they are alerted to a potential problem. In the atmosphere of 2008, in the aftermath of the Northern Rock crisis and the wider credit crunch, this view was strengthened by the perceived failure of people at the top of organisations to recognise the real risks across the board and to get involved with the totality of the business. Without knowing what the regulatory body is becoming concerned about, the investor is unable to do the job and manage risk properly. The investor also needs to be convinced that the regulators are good at their job.

Regeneration and renewal

In the next phase of housing policy housing interventions will not be undertaken in isolation. New developments will connect with agendas for growth areas, regeneration and 'preventative' action to maintain sustainable communities. In each case they will form part of actions to shape places that also involve investments by other stakeholders. The practice moves beyond mixed funding and public/private sector joint ventures towards more ambitious holistic and integrated renewal. The previous experience of English Partnerships is highly relevant to this, but in order to achieve development that transforms neighbourhoods and benefits existing residents as well as others, it is important that investment enables long-term projects and that housing providers and local authorities as well as other partners are able to contribute effectively throughout. The problems associated with neighbourhoods with the greatest concentrations of unattractive housing and, because of this, concentrations of lower-income and vulnerable households are likely to feature more prominently in housing and planning agendas over the next decade. Effective engagement with these requires different partnerships and approaches than have been adopted by most housing associations in development in recent years.

Patch and accountability

Some of the most trenchant criticisms of housing associations, and the most adverse comparisons with local authorities, relate to property holdings that are geographically scattered and lack of effective accountability. Members of Parliament have referred to low levels of tenant participation in housing associations; for example, in 2006 the Tory MP Greg Hands said:

Tenants' associations are packed with placemen who agree with the political direction of the borough in question, or are filled with people deemed politically acceptable to the individuals in charge. We need to strengthen tenants' rights and their participation in housing associations. Housing association tenants are the poor cousins when it comes to tenant power, and that must change. (Hansard 2006c)

These issues are most strongly voiced in relation to associations with stocks of dwellings scattered across one or more regions and are least expressed where there are geographically concentrated or patch-based ownerships. There has been a tension between arguments about efficiency, economies of scale and mergers and about local responsiveness and tenant involvement. Neither the government nor its agencies have satisfactorily explained the relationship between imperatives related to efficiency and those concerned with tenant empowerment and protection. Following the Cave review and in view of the importance of regeneration, it may be that no single model will come to dominate but that there will be a need to encourage patch-based organisation.

In the context of regeneration it is also important to acknowledge that continuing management costs are strongly related to the location and type of stock (flats and high density). Landlords operating in less deprived non-metropolitan districts with fewer flats and a stock size smaller than average for the sector are more likely to achieve better measured performance but the significance of this reflects the limitations of the measures used. The management task faced by landlords is also fundamentally different in different locations. Although the task is labelled as 'housing management', it is in all cases a mixture of managing people, properties and places, and different landlords construct the task in different ways. There are different costs and challenges in managing a residual housing stock rather than a stock for which there is a high demand, or in operating in dense urban environments rather than rural areas. In some cases local authority or housing association landlords are operating alongside a very large privately rented sector while in others they provide the majority of rented housing and are the alternative to home ownership in a relatively high-priced market.

It is also clear that tenants often do not distinguish between housing management functions and broader service provision, even when they are tenants of housing associations. Thus expressing dissatisfaction with housing management may refer to issues that actually fall within the remit of other departments or organisations, such as refuse collection, traffic management, policing or education. Yet divorcing housing management from these other issues may be increasingly artificial. The impact of mainstream spending by local authorities on a range of other services is important for successful housing management. In this context the agenda for housing organisations is often to work more effectively with other service providers to ensure that the package of services delivered locally meets with the requirements of tenants. Given that the increasing differences between neighbourhoods have had a disproportionate impact on the housing service, a pre-condition for improving the performance of housing management is an effective framework of neighbourhood renewal and management. The Neighbourhood Management pilots and other examples point towards approaches that increase the responsibility taken, by local authorities and others, for sustainable community strategies and sustainable places.

Managing assets
Since the 1970s, within the general picture of a decline in opportunities to rent, the expansion of the housing association sector has been the exception. From its all-party acceptance as the 'third arm' in housing the housing association sector operates within a new financial regime and with new assured tenancies. Because the government does not regard borrowing on the private financial market as public expenditure, it sees housing associations as able to generate more housing investment for any given sum of public expenditure than local authorities can. With a continuing need for subsidised housing has come the gradual emergence of registered housing associations as the only alternative landlords who could deliver a guaranteed package for tenants. The stock of housing built up by housing associations represents an enormous asset. Facing this is the risk that a government might seek some short-term electoral and financial gain by legislating for the sale of assets which have been built up with the aid of public funds – reopening the issue it was defeated on in 1980. The long-term value of a stock of properties in good condition and with declining borrowing set against it is not best used by selling it, especially if deep discounts are involved. A long-term strategy would recognise the advantages of retaining the stock and managing the asset effectively – borrowing against it as its value matures and investing in ways that reflect emerging housing needs. This is the approach built in to the later years of operation of the Housing Corporation and it remains a robust approach. There is nevertheless a risk that the government, if it does not support selling the asset, seeks to sweat it too much – to encourage a level of borrowing against values that would not be regarded as prudent in other contexts.

Conclusions

The Housing Corporation survived through a changing political, economic and housing market environment. Some practices appear stranger today than they did in the past and there are cautions about judgements that take too little account of context. It is reasonable to argue that the first test of the value and success of the Corporation was that it survived for so long. It is equally reasonable to suggest that a second test is that its successor organisations have been able to carry forward the expertise and capacity generated by the activities of the Corporation and its partners and not start again and learn the same lessons. There is good reason to believe that the tasks for a more vigorous and economically and socially engaged housing policy need new agencies – but they should benefit from the activities of their predecessors. Stability and continuity of funding are crucial for any effective agencies and the periodic short-term crises and cuts in budgets were not the best environment for the Corporation in its early years. The move to three-year budgets and longer indicative planning timescales marked an important step forward.

By 2008 the credit crunch and the collapse of the housing market introduced a new break in continuity. It seems unlikely that this will prove a short-lived 'blip' and that the market will revert back to its earlier pattern. It is more likely that there will be long-term caution over lending to support buy-to-let and the building of high-density apartments and that lenders will generally revert to a more cautious approach. After decades of privatisation and withdrawal of the state from housing, the government has been drawn into a more interventionist role. A more deregulated system has not enabled the state to leave housing to the market.

Although there was an increased emphasis on regulation it is easy to see in retrospect that the Housing Corporation's relationship with the government and with housing associations was dominated by its concern to deliver investment. It was a regulator on behalf of producers, ensuring that the government received good value for money and that the lenders would be confident in providing finance for the production of housing. It is argued that the Corporation developed a rather comfortable or even cosy relationship with housing associations, what has been called regulatory capture. Both parties wanted to see effective investment taking place and each needed the other if they were to achieve what they were tasked to do. The collusive relationship that emerged from this situation placed very little emphasis on service delivery or on governance and a major critique of housing associations grew out of this. While it had always been argued that housing associations were less accountable than local authorities they were often run by self-perpetuating boards of the great and good with very little direct representation by tenants and relatively little attention being given to the quality of service delivered. The contrast that had been painted between the large, bureaucratic monopoly local authority landlords and more responsive housing associations was built in to early approaches to stock transfer, with the break-up of monopoly provision seen as an objective. But this agenda began to give way to an argument for economies of scale and efficiency that lent support to larger housing associations, group structures, mergers and preferred partners. The outcome, affected by stock transfer and new investment activity, was the re-emergence of very large landlord organisations, which raised questions about accessibility and knowledge of the places they were operating in. While they did not always have a monopoly in one place, comparable with local authority housing in the past, they were often more absent, with properties widely distributed within and even between the regions of England, and their capacity to give tenants a voice or use their resources to respond to wider community and neighbourhood agendas was sometimes compromised.

The view that both the Housing Corporation and housing associations had given insufficient attention to service delivery and to their tenants began to change the approach of the Corporation and of government. By the mid-1990s the concerns about unaccountable public bodies and standards in public life were also raising questions about housing associations, the Corporation and other bodies. The relationship between the Corporation and housing associations, or even between the government, the Corporation and funders, rather than being seen as efficient and effective ways of developing the housing programme, were seen as demonstrating an insufficient concern for tenants and local communities. The greater the shift towards service delivery, tenants' interests and improved governance, the more the cosy relationships began to break down. The development of the Housing Inspectorate (and its location within the Audit Commission) and an ombudsman service began to put different pressures on housing associations and the Corporation.

The last ten years of the Housing Corporation's operation can be seen as ones in which the external pressures and a changing conventional wisdom about the appropriate ways of managing public services destabilised the way in which it operated. The co-location of investment and regulation had in the past been identified as a source of strength. It had been argued that it was because there was co-location that the Corporation could ensure that public money was well used and that private money would not be put at risk. However, the new conventional wisdom began to suggest that co-location was actually a source of weakness and there was a need to separate the regulatory from the investment activity. The new Homes and Communities Agency will operate with a much stronger housing association sector with real organisational and financial capacity. It will be able to develop better understandings of the kinds of intervention that will work in different cities and regions. And it will be able to respond to changes in the economy and the housing market. The new Tenant Services Agency will equally be able to build on the experience of regulation of housing associations and to strengthen the governance and service delivery dimensions. It will be interesting to see the extent to which these two arms are able to work effectively together; while co-location may be inappropriate, a constructive working relationship is necessary, for if the TSA is unaware of the difficulties associated with investment it may begin to operate in ways that are counter-productive. It will be important for the TSA to recognise that the quality of housing is still the fundamental determinant of satisfaction and that better management, governance and participation are not substitutes for good-quality housing. At the same time it is very important that the HCA recognises that good housing producers and investors are not necessarily good landlords and the issues around accessibility to managers, pepper-potting of stock and patch-based development will remain crucially important. Both agencies will be faced with the legacy of fifty years of housing policy in which the social rented sector has declined from being a tenure of choice to something much closer to a tenure of last resort. The task for both will be to begin to reverse that process. Unless there is action to regenerate the worst housing in the social rented sector and to make the social rented sector sufficiently attractive so that some people who could move away choose to stay in it, the prognosis for the sector is not good.

The abolition of the Housing Corporation means the end of an important phase in housing policy and the end of an organisation which had grown from very different and very modest beginnings to become a key player in housing policy in England. While its demise may have been predictable and reflects changing views about how public services should be delivered as well as the changing scale and nature of the programme, it should not be seen as a measure of the failure of the organisation. Indeed it may even be that it is the Corporation's success that has led to the need to reorganise it. As the government and others were persuaded that housing associations were the key agencies to develop the housing programme, so the need for some reorganisation and rationalisation of structure became apparent – and for some separation and specialisation between regulation and investment, developing a much stronger regional capacity, not just a capacity to allocate funds but to make a constructive and creative contribution to the development of policies and strategies and through these to regional economies.

The prospect for housing in the aftermath of the credit crunch is of a severe shortfall in residential building for at least two or three years and many commentators think it unlikely that eventual 'normalisation' will involve rates of building any higher than had been achieved in 2006 and 2007 – much lower than the targets set by government and related to demographic change. Altering the planning system will not relieve this problem. At the same time, for the foreseeable future (and perhaps for five or ten years at least) the market will operate with greater caution towards lending, and lower-income households will experience problems of access to mortgages as well as difficulties in affording to buy. This will have particular effects on specific parts of the market and zones of towns and cities. There will be further market stretching with prices in some parts of the market continuing to be inflated by high demand, especially from higher-income groups, and other parts of the market falling further behind with purchases by lower-income households accessing various sources of finance and by private investors. This market stretching will itself present problems of social cohesion and sustainable communities, and the different dynamics in different parts of the market may generate some of the problems previously associated with low-demand areas. High turnover and neglect of management and maintenance by landlords further damage neighbourhoods and undermine demand and stability.

In this scenario the task for the new Homes and Community Agency and the Tenants Services Authority will be even more central to policy than envisaged when they were first thought of. The government's policy objectives as related to supply will be realised only through a larger social rented programme and new partnerships between housing associations, local authorities and the private sector, which will enable a greater expansion of house building than would happen otherwise. As part of this, attention will also need to be given to the risks associated with the sale of property and agreements that give greater confidence to both builders and purchasers. It may mean some greater institutional support on a continuing basis for mortgage rescue or mortgage allowances and alternative sources of mortgage funding and flexible tenure arrangements that enable households to reduce as well as increase their equity stake in different circumstances – rather than falling into arrears or having to move. A larger social rented or affordable housing programme implies breaking the view that social rented housing will be a residual tenure; it also implies building high-quality housing that could be part of any tenure, form the cornerstone for developing new communities or act as a key ingredient in regenerating and modernising neighbourhoods. Finally this scenario is likely to raise questions once more about the regulation of the private rented sector. Where this sector caters for similar households and the same part of the market as the social rented sector, its failure to meet reasonable standards and deliver to tenants what is required of the social rented sector will prove problematic. It will be appropriate to extend scrutiny, regulation and sanctions to this tenure if there is to be inclusive and continuous improvement in the housing situation of different groups in society.

In 2008 the new HCA and TSA inherit some very strong traditions. They will also have to negotiate sensible arrangements with government departments and housing associations and others — learning from the past. At the same time they are immediately faced by a crisis associated with the credit crunch, highlighting the uncertainty and unpredictability that affected the operation of their predecessors. While effective systems and structures will remain important, the new organisations will also still need imagination and innovation and a willingness to trust the expertise held at local and regional levels in different organisations, including themselves.

References

Ashworth, W. (1954), *The Genesis of Modern British Town Planning: A Study in Economic and Social History of the Nineteenth and Twentieth Centuries* (London: Routledge & Kegan Paul).

Aulakh, S. (2004), 'The Transformation of the UK State: Rolling Back or Rolling Out', in E. Bohme, F. Bonser and K. Spencer (eds), *Transatlantic Perspectives on Liberalization and Democratic Governance* (Münster: Lit).

Bentham, G. (1986), 'Socio-tenurial Polarization in the United Kingdom 1953–83: The Income Evidence', *Urban Studies*, vol. 23, pp. 157–62.

Birchall, J. (1991), *The Hidden History of Co-operative Housing in Britain* (Uxbridge: Department of Government, Brunel University).

Birchall, J. (1992), *Housing Co-operatives in Britain* (Uxbridge: Department of Government, Brunel University).

BMRB (British Market Research Bureau) (1986), *Housing and Savings* (London: Building Societies Association).

Bowley, M. (1945), *Housing and the State 1919–1944* (London: George Allen & Unwin).

BSA (Building Societies Association) (1983), *Housing Tenure* (London: Building Societies Association).

Burney, E. M. (1967), *Housing on Trial: A Study of Immigrants and Local Government* (London: Oxford University Press).

Campbell, H. (1970), 'Housing Co-operatives in Britain', *Annals of Public and Co-operative Economics*, vol. 41, pp. 325–37.

Campbell-Smith, D. (2008), *Follow the Money: The Audit Commission, Public Money and the Management of Public Services 1983–2008* (London: Allen Lane).

Carbery, T. (1969) *Consumers in Politics: A History and General Review of the Co-operative Party* (Manchester: Manchester University Press).

CHAC (Central Housing Advisory Committee) (1969), *Council Housing: Purposes, Procedures and Priorities* (London: HMSO).

CHAC (Central Housing Advisory Committee) (1971), *Housing Associations* (London: HMSO).

Clapham, D. and K. Kintrea (1987), 'Importing Housing Policy: Housing Co-operatives in Britain and Scandinavia', *Housing Studies*, vol. 2, pp. 157–169.

Clapham, D. and K. Kintrea (1992), *Housing Co-operatives in Britain: Achievements and Prospects* (Harlow: Longman).

Cochrane, A. and J. Clarke (1993), *Comparing Welfare States: Britain in International Context* (London: Sage).

Conservative Party (1987), *The Next Moves Forward* (London: Conservative Central Office).

Cullingworth, J. B. (1966), *Housing and Local Government in England and Wales* (London: George Allen & Unwin).

CURS (Centre for Urban and Regional Studies) (1970), *Report of the Surveys of Housing Associations and Local Authorities on the Work of Voluntary Housing Bodies* (Birmingham: Centre for Urban and Regional Studies, University of Birmingham).

Davis, H. (ed.) (1996), *Quangos and Local Government: A Changing World* (London: Frank Cass).

Davis, H. and C. Skelcher (1997), 'Reviewing QUANGOs: A Research Synthesis', in R. Hambleton (ed.), *New Perspectives in Local Governance: Reviewing the Research Evidence* (York: Joseph Rowntree Foundation).

DETR (Department of the Environment, Transport and the Regions) and DSS (Department of Social Security) (2000), *Quality and Choice: A Decent Home for All – The Housing Green Paper* (London: Department of the Environment, Transport and the Regions).

DoE (Department of the Environment) (1975), *Final Report of the Working Party on Housing Co-operatives* (London: HMSO).

DoE (Department of the Environment) (1977), *Housing Policy: A Consultative Document*, Cmnd 6851.

DoE (Department of the Environment) (1987), *Housing: the Government's Proposals*, Cm 214.

Doling, J. (1997), *Comparative Housing Policy: Government and Housing in Advanced Industrialized Countries* (London: Macmillan).

Donnison, D. (1967), *The Government of Housing* (Harmondsworth: Pelican).

Dunleavy, P. (1981), *The Politics of Mass Housing in Britain 1947–1975: A Study of Corporate Power and Professional Influence in the Welfare State* (Oxford: Clarendon Press).

Emsley, I. (1986), *The Development of Housing Associations: With Special Reference to London and Including a Case Study of the London Borough of Hammersmith* (London: Garland).

Englander, D. (1983), *Landlord and Tenant in Urban Britain 1838–1918* (Oxford: Clarendon Press).

Esping-Andersen, G. (1990), *The Three Worlds of Welfare Capitalism* (Cambridge: Polity).

Feinstein, L., R. Lupton, C. Hammond, T. Mujtaba, E. Salter and A. Sorhaindo (2008), *The Public Value of Social Housing: A Longitudinal Analysis of the Relationship between Housing and Life Chances* (London: Smith Institute).

Forrest, R. and A. Murie (1983), 'Residualisation and Council Housing: Aspects of the Changing Social Relations of Housing Tenure', *Journal of Social Policy*, vol. 12, pp. 453–68.

Forrest, R. and A. Murie (1989), 'Differential Accumulation: Wealth Inheritance and Housing Policy Reconsidered', *Policy and Politics*, vol. 17, pp. 25–39.

Forrest, R. and A. Murie (1990), *Selling the Welfare State: The Privatisation of Public Housing*, 2nd ed. (London: Routledge).

Forrest, R., A. Murie and P. Williams (1990), *Home Ownership: Differentiation and Fragmentation* (London: Unwin Hyman).

Gallup (1988), *Council Tenants 30 March–12 April 1988: Research on Behalf of NCC* (London: Social Surveys (Gallup)).

Garside, P. (2000), *The Conduct of Philanthropy: The William Sutton Trust 1900–2000* (London, Athlone Press).

Gauldie, E. (1974), *Cruel Habitations; A History of Working-Class Housing 1780–1918* (London: Allen & Unwin).

Gilbert, B. B. (1970), *British Social Policy 1914–1939* (London: B. T. Batsford).

Gittus, E. (1976), *Flats, Families and the Under-Fives* (London: Routledge & Kegan Paul).

Goodwin, M. (2004), 'The Scaling of "Urban" Policy: Neighbourhood, City or Region?', in C. Johnstone and M. Whitehead (eds), *New Horizons in British Urban Policy: Perspectives on New Labour's Urban Renaissance* (Aldershot: Ashgate).

Greve, J. (1964), *London's Homeless* (Welwyn: Codicote Press).

Griffith, J. A. G. (1966), *Central Departments and Local Authorities* (London: George Allen & Unwin).

Groves, R. (1971), 'Voluntary Housing in Denmark and Britain', unpublished thesis.

Groves, R., A. Murie and C. Watson (2007), *Housing and the New Welfare State: Perspectives from East Asia and Europe* (Aldershot: Ashgate).

Gulliver, K. (2000), *Social Concern and Social Enterprise: The Origins and History of Focus Housing* (Studley: Brewin).

Hadley, R. and S. Hatch (1981), *Social Welfare and the Failure of the State: Centralised Social Services and Participatory Alternatives* (London: Allen & Unwin).

Hamnett, C. (1984), 'Housing the Two Nations: Socio-tenurial Polarization in England and Wales 1961–81', *Urban Studies*, vol. 21, pp. 389–405.

Hamnett, C. (1999), *Winners and Losers: Home Ownership in Modern Britain* (London: UCL Press).

Hamnett, C., M. Harmer and P. Williams (1991), *Safe as Houses: Housing Inheritance in Britain* (London: Paul Chapman).

Hansard (1979), HC Deb, 15 May, vol. 967, cols 79–80.

Hansard (1986), HC Deb, 4 February, vol. 91, cols 153–4.

Hansard (1988), HC Written Answers, 14 December, vol. 143, cols 631W–632W.

Hansard (1989), HC Deb, 26 July, vol. 157, col. 1014.

Hansard (1990a), HC Deb, 24 May, vol. 173, cols 397–405.

Hansard (1990b), HC Deb, 3 July, vol. 175, col. 937.

Hansard (1994), HC Deb, 14 March, vol. 239, col. 630.

Hansard (1995), HC Written Answers, 28 June, vol. 262, col. 656W.

Hansard (1996), HC Written Answers, 31 October, vol. 294, cols 192W–193W.

Hansard (1997a), HC Written Answers, 10 February, vol. 290, col. 84W.

Hansard (1997b), HC Written Answers, 11 February, vol. 290, col. 101W.

Hansard (2000), HC Written Answers, 6 June, vol. 351, col. 213W.

Hansard (2003), HC Ministerial Statements, 16 September, vol. 410, col. 45WS.

Hansard (2006a), HC Ministerial Statements, 14 February, vol. 442, col. 78WS.

Hansard (2006b), HC Deb, 25 April, vol. 445, col. 504.

Hansard (2006c), HC Deb, 25 April, vol. 445, col. 528.

Hansard (2006d), HC Deb, 11 May, vol. 446, col. 545.

Hansard (2006e), HC Deb, 11 May, vol. 446, col. 554.

Hansard (2007), HC Ministerial Statements, 15 October, vol. 464, cols 47WS–48WS.

Harden, I. and N. Lewis (1988), *The Noble Lie: The British Constitution and the Rule of Law* (London: Routledge).

Harloe, M. (1995), *The People's Home?: Social Rented Housing in Europe and America* (Oxford: Blackwell).

Harloe, M., R. Issacharoff and R. Minns (1974), *The Organisation of Housing: Public and Private Enterprise in London* (London: Heinemann).

Henderson, J. and V. Karn (1987), *Race, Class and State Housing: Inequality and the Allocation of Public Housing in Britain* (Aldershot: Gower).

Hilditch, M. (2007), 'New turf war begins', *Inside Housing*, 22 June.

Hill, S., M. Lupton, G. Moody and S. Regan (2002), *A Stake Worth Having? The Potential and Options for Tenant Equity Stakes* (Coventry: Chartered Institute of Housing / London: Institute for Public Policy Research).

Hills, J. (2007) *Ends and Means: The Future Roles of Social Housing in England* (London: Centre for Analysis of Social Exclusion, London School of Economics and Political Science).

Holland, P. (1981), *The Governance of Quangos* (London: Adam Smith Institute).

Holmans, A. E. (1987), *Housing Policy in Britain: A History* (London: Croom Helm).

House of Commons Environment Committee (1993), *The Housing Corporation*, second report, Session 1992/93, HC 466-1 (London: HMSO).

John, C. (1965), 'The Housing Corporation: Its Aims and Programme', *Housing Review*, vol. 14, pp.110–12.

Jones, C. and A. Murie (2006), *The Right to Buy: Analysis and Evaluation of a Housing Policy* (Oxford: Blackwell).

Kelly, R. (2006), 'Housing, Community and Opportunity', speech to Chartered Institute of Housing conference, 20 June.

Kemeny, J. (1995), *From Public Housing to the Social Market: Rental Policy Strategies in Comparative Perspective* (London: Routledge).

Kemeny, J. (2005), '"The Really Big Trade-Off" between Home Ownership and Welfare: Castles' Evaluation of the 1980 Thesis, and a Reformulation 25 Years On', *Housing, Theory and Society*, vol. 22, pp. 59–75.

Lambert, J., C. Paris and B. Blackaby (1978), *Housing Policy and the State: Allocation, Access and Control* (London: Macmillan).

Lewis, N. and I. Harden (1982), 'The Housing Corporation and "Voluntary Housing"', in A. Barker (ed.), *Quangos in Britain: Government and the Networks of Public Policy-Making* (London : Macmillan).

Lowe, S. (1986), *Urban Social Movements: The City after Castells* (Basingstoke: Macmillan).

Lowe, S. (2004), *Housing Policy Analysis: British Housing in Cultural and Comparative Context* (Basingstoke: Palgrave).

McCafferty, P. and D. Riley (1989), *A Study of Co-operative Housing* (London: HMSO).

Mackenzie, W. J. M. and J. W. Grove (1957), *Central Administration in Britain* (London: Longmans, Green).

Malpass, P. (1990), *Reshaping Housing Policy: Subsidies, Rents and Residualisation* (London: Routledge).

Malpass, P. (1998), *Housing, Philanthropy and the State: A History of the Guinness Trust* (Bristol: University of the West of England).

Malpass, P. (2000), *Housing Associations and Housing Policy: A Historical Perspective* (Basingstoke: Macmillan).

Malpass, P. (2001), 'The Uneven Development of "Social Rented Housing": Explaining the Historically Marginal Position of Housing Associations in Britain', *Housing Studies*, vol. 16, pp. 225–42.

Malpass, P. (2004), 'Fifty Years of British Housing Policy: Leaving or Leading the Welfare State?', *European Journal of Housing Policy*, vol. 4, pp. 209–27.

Malpass, P. (2008), 'Housing and the New Welfare State: Wobbly Pillar or Cornerstone?', *Housing Studies*, vol. 23, pp. 1–20.

Malpass, P. and D. Mullins (2002), 'Local Authority Housing Stock Transfer in the UK: From Local Initiative to National Policy', *Housing Studies*, vol. 17, pp. 673–86.

Malpass, P. and A. Murie (1987), *Housing Policy and Practice*, 2nd ed. (Basingstoke: Macmillan).

Malpass, P. and A. Murie (1999), *Housing Policy and Practice*, 5th ed. (Basingstoke: Macmillan).

Mayer, A. (1998), 'The Housing Corporation: Multiple Lines of Accountability', in M. Flinders and M. Smith, *Quangos, Accountability and Reform: The Politics of Quasi-Government* (Basingstoke: Macmillan), pp. 111–19.

Merrett, S. (1979), *State Housing in Britain* (London: Routledge & Kegan Paul).

Merrett, S. (1982), *Owner-Occupation in Britain* (London: Routledge & Kegan Paul).

MHLG (Ministry of Housing and Local Government) (1965), *The Housing Programme 1965 to 1970*, Cmnd 2838.

Ministry of Health (1933), *Report of the Departmental Committee on Housing*, Cmd. 4397.

Mullins, D. (1999), 'Managing Ambiguity: Merger Activity in the Nonprofit Housing Sector', *International Journal of Nonprofit and Voluntary Sector Marketing*, vol. 4, pp. 349–64.

Mullins, D. (2000), 'Social Origins and Transformations: The Changing Role of English Housing Associations', *Voluntas: International Journal of Voluntary and Nonprofit Organisations*, vol. 11, pp. 255–75.

Mullins, D. (2002), 'Redefining "Competition" as "Competitiveness": The Best Value Activities of Registered Social Landlords', *Public Money and Management*, vol. 22, no. 2, pp. 25–30.

Mullins, D. and A. Murie (2006), *Housing Policy in the UK* (Basingstoke: Palgrave Macmillan).

Mullins, D. and M. Riseborough (2000), 'Non-Profit Housing Agencies: "Reading" and Shaping the Policy Agenda', in M. Harris and C. Rochester (eds), *Voluntary Organisations and Social Policy in Britain: Perspectives on Change and Choice* (Basingstoke: Palgrave), pp. 154–70.

Mullins, D., P. Niner and M. Riseborough (1993), 'Large-Scale Voluntary Transfers', in P. Malpass and R. Means, *Implementing Housing Policy* (Buckingham: Open University Press), pp. 169–84.

Murie, A. (1985), 'Housing', in M. Loughlin, D. Gelfand and K. Young (eds), *Half a Century of Municipal Decline 1935–1985* (London: Allen & Unwin).

Murie, A. (2006), 'Moving with the Times: Changing Frameworks for Housing Research and Policy', in P. Malpass and L. Cairncross (eds), *Building on the Past: Visions of Housing Futures* (Bristol: Policy Press), pp. 15–50.

Murie, A. (2007), 'Housing Policy, Housing Tenure and the Housing Market', in K. Clarke, T. Maltby and P. Kennett (eds), *Social Policy Review 19: Analysis and Debate in Social Policy 2007* (Bristol: Policy Press), pp. 49–66.

Murie, A. and R. Forrest (1980), 'Wealth, Inheritance and Housing Policy', *Policy and Politics*, vol. 8, pp. 1–20.

Murie, A. and R. Rowlands (2008), 'The New Politics of Urban Housing', *Environment and Planning C: Government and Policy*, vol. 26, pp. 644–59.

Murie, A., P. Niner and C. Watson (1976), *Housing Policy and the Housing System* (London: Allen & Unwin).

Murie, A., R. Pocock and K. Gulliver (2007), *Hills, Cave and After: Renewing Social Housing* (Birmingham: Human City Institute).

Nevin, B., P. Lee, L. Goodson, A. Murie and J. Phillimore (2001a), *Changing Housing Markets and Urban Regeneration in the M62 Corridor* (Birmingham: Centre for Urban and Regional Studies, University of Birmingham).

Nevin, B., P. Lee, A. Murie, L. Goodson and J. Phillimore (2001b), *The West Midlands Housing Markets: Changing Demand, Decentralisation and Urban Regeneration* (Birmingham: Centre for Urban and Regional Studies, University of Birmingham).

ODPM (Office of the Deputy Prime Minister) (2005) *HomeBuy: Expanding the Opportunity to Own*. (Wetherby: Office of the Deputy Prime Minister).

Parker, R. A. (1967), *The Rents of Council Houses* (London: George Bell).

Pooley, C. (ed.) (1992), *Housing Strategies in Europe 1880–1930* (Leicester: Leicester University Press).

Prime Minister's Office (1980), *Report on Non-Departmental Public Bodies*, Cmnd 7797.

Rex, J. and R. Moore (1967), *Race, Community and Conflict: A Study of Sparkbrook* (London: Oxford University Press).

Ridley, N. (1987), news release, Department of the Environment, 29 September.

Rodger, P. (1992), 'Scotland', in C. Pooley (ed.), *Housing Strategies in Europe 1800–1930* (Leicester: Leicester University Press).

Royal Commission on the Distribution of Income and Wealth (1977), *Third Report on the Standing Reference*, Cmnd 6999.

Saunders, P. (1990), *A Nation of Home Owners* (London: Unwin Hyman).

Scottish Development Department (1987), *Housing: The Government's Proposals for Scotland*, Cm 242.

Sharp, E. (1969), *The Ministry of Housing and Local Government* (London: George Allen & Unwin).

Skelcher, C. (1998), *The Appointed State: Quasi-Governmental Organizations and Democracy* (Buckingham: Open University Press).

Skelcher, C. and H. Davis (1996), 'Understanding the New Magistracy: A Study of Characteristics and Attitudes', in H. Davis (ed.), *Quangos and Local Government: A Changing World* (London: Frank Cass).

Titmuss, R. M. (1950), *Problems of Social Policy* (London: HMSO).

Usher, D. (1987), *Housing Privatisation: The Sale of Council Estates* (Bristol: School for Advanced Urban Studies, University of Bristol).

Usher, D. (1988), *Council Estate Sales: Studies of Local Experiences and Future Prospects* (Bristol: School for Advanced Urban Studies, University of Bristol).

Waddilove, L. (1962), *Housing Associations* (London: Political and Economic Planning).

Waldegrave, W. (1987), 'Some Reflections on Housing Policy', Conservative Party News Service, 28 August.

Walker, R., D. Mullins and H. Pawson (2003), 'Devolution and Housing Associations in Great Britain: Enhancing Organisational Accountability?', *Housing Studies*, vol. 18, pp. 177–99.

Wicks, M. (1970), 'Labour and the Private Landlord', *Social and Economic Administration*, vol. 4, pp. 97–107.

Wilcox, S. (ed.) (annual), *UK Housing Review* (Coventry: Chartered Institute of Housing / London: Building Societies Association).

Wilding, P. (1972), 'Towards Exchequer Subsidies for Housing 1906–1914', *Social and Economic Administration*, vol. 6, pp 3–18.

Further reading

Archbishop of Canterbury's Commission on Urban Priority Areas (1985), *Faith in the City: A Call for Action By Church and Nation – The Report of the Archbishop of Canterbury's Commission on Urban Priority Areas* (London: Church House).

Barker, K. (2003), *Review of Housing Supply: Securing Our Future Housing Needs – Interim Report* (Norwich: HMSO).

Barker, K. (2004), *Review of Housing Supply: Delivering Stability: Securing Our Future Housing Needs – Final Report* (Norwich: HMSO).

Barker, K. (2006), *Barker Review of Land Use Planning: Final Report* (Norwich: HMSO).

Cave, M. (2007), *Every Tenant Matters: A Review of Social Housing Regulation* (Wetherby: Communities and Local Government).

Central Housing Advisory Committee (1944), *Design of Dwellings* (London: HMSO).

Committee on Standards in Public Life (1996), *Second Report*, Cm 3270.

Communities and Local Government (2007), *Delivering Housing and Regeneration: Communities England and the Future of Social Housing Regulation* (Wetherby: Communities and Local Government).

Communities and Local Government (2007), *Homes for the Future: More Affordable, More Sustainable*, Cm 7191.

Cullingworth, J. B. (1965), *English Housing Trends: A Report on the Rowntree Trust Housing Study* (London: George Bell).

Department of Health and Social Security (1974), *Report of the Committee on One-Parent Families*, Cmnd 5629.

Department of the Environment (1971), *Fair Deal for Housing*, Cmnd 4728.

Department of the Environment (1973), *Better Homes: The Next Priorities*, Cmnd 5339.

Department of the Environment (1988), *Tenants' Choice* (London: Department of the Environment).

Department of the Environment and Welsh Office (1987), *Tenants' Choice: The Government's Proposals for Legislation* (London: Department of the Environment).

Housing Corporation (2008), *Report of the Ujima Inquiry* (London: Housing Corporation).

Local Government Association (1997), *A New Financial Framework for Local Authority Housing* (London: Local Government Association).

Ministry of Housing and Local Government (1961), *Homes for Today and Tomorrow* (London: HMSO).

Ministry of Housing and Local Government (1965), *Report of the Committee on Housing in Greater London*, Cmd 2605.

Murie, A. (1999), 'The Acquisition and Sale of Properties by Social Landlords: Justifications and Consequences', *Netherlands Journal of Housing and the Built Environment*, vol. 14, pp. 293–308.

National Federation of Housing Associations (1985), *Inquiry into British Housing: Report* (London: National Federation of Housing Associations).

Office of the Deputy Prime Minister (2003), *Sustainable Communities: Building for the Future* (Wetherby: Office of the Deputy Prime Minister).

Appendices

The Housing Corporation: chairmen of the board

Herbert Ashworth 1968–73
Lord Goodman 1973–7
Sir Caspar John 1964–8
Sir Lou Sherman 1977–80
Sir Hugh Cubitt 1980–90
Sir Christopher Benson 1990–94

Sir Brian Pearse 1994–7
Peter Cooke 1997
Baroness Dean of Thornton-le-
  Fylde 1997–2003
Peter Dixon 2003–8

The Housing Corporation: members of the board

H. Ashworth 1964–73
D. H. D. Alexander 1964–80
Sir Caspar John 1964–9
W. S. Jones 1964–74
A. Meikle 1964–72
Sir Edward Norman 1964–70
M. Schofield 1964–8
Sir W. M. Younger 1964–8
H. Campbell 1968–74
E. Clark 1968–73
P. Crabbe 1968–75
L. E. Waddilove 1969–82
Sir Stanley Morton 1972–5
K. Ryden 1973–6
Father P. Byrne 1974–8
J. R. Coward 1974–80
Lord Goodman 1974–7
Lord Greenwood of Rossendale
  1974–8
J. Kegie 1974–82
D. W. Llewellyn 1974–8

D. Mumford 1974–80
W. L. Taylor 1974–80
B. Cooper 1976–9
L. Williams 1976–82
A. Alexander 1978–81
G. Henderson 1978–80
H. G. Ashton 1979–85
H. B. Sneddon 1979–82
N. H. Burdett 1980–86
Sir Hugh Cubitt 1980–90
A. Fletcher 1980–83
W. G. Muir 1980–81
C. S. Shepherd 1980–86
C. Thornton 1980–86
M. J. Benson 1982–8
J. D. Richards 1982–9
J. H. V. Sutcliffe 1982–8
D. G. Cochrane 1983–95
I. J. A. Dyer 1983–9
H. Lloyd Williams 1983–9
H. R. Walden 1985–8

D. H. L. Hopkinson 1986–8
W. I. McIndoe 1986–90
Rt Rev. W. Wood 1986–95
Lady Montgomery 1987–97
J. Allen 1988–9
M. Boleat 1988–93
S. Clarke 1988–95
W. P. Cooke 1988–97
R. Holt 1989–92
R. Thompson 1989–98
Sir Christopher Benson 1990–94
R. Burgess 1990–92
D. Gleeson 1990–95
D. Kleeman 1990–98
Sir Norman Wakefield 1990–93
J. Unwin 1992–2002
R. Council 1994–6
G. Cracknell 1994–2002
Sir Brian Pearse 1994–7
D. Waddington 1994–2002
S. Denman 1995–2002
K. Griffin 1995–2002
P. Williams 1995–2002

J. Foster 1996–2002
E. Armitage 1997–2003
S. Button 1997–2006
Baroness Dean of Thornton-le-
 Fylde 1997–2003
Y. Hutchinson 1998–2005
A. Winckler 1998–2005
I. Monckton 1999–2005
R. Arthur 2000–2004
Sir Duncan Michael 2000–2008
G. Huka 2001–4
J. Fawcett 2002–8
S. Moledina 2002–8
S. O'Neill 2002–8
S. Drew Smith 2002–8
P. Dixon 2003–8
C. Holmes 2004–8
K. Lavery 2004–8
P. Rogers 2004–8
C. Atherton 2005–8
K. Barker 2005–8
D. Hoodless 2005–8

The chief executive was a member of the board from 1974 onwards. English Partnerships was also represented on the board from 2002 onwards by its chief executive. Sir Bob Kerslake also joined the board as the first chief executive of the Homes and Communities Agency, and began in post on 31 March 2008.

The Housing Corporation: chief executives
Roger Lloyd Thomas (general manager) 1964–73
Richard Madge 1973–84
David Edmonds 1984–91
Anthony Mayer 1991–2000
Norman Perry 2000–2004
Jonathan Rouse 2004–7
Steve Douglas 2008

Simon Dow was acting chief executive in 2000 and Steve Douglas was acting chief executive in 2007 before being confirmed in the post of chief executive.

Index